Protecting Your Pension For Dummies®

Cheat Sheet

Collecting Important Information before You Retire

As we explain in Chapter 8, the following documents and information tell you what you can expect to receive from your plan benefits and can help you determine whether your benefits have been correctly calculated. Collect this information throughout your working life, and file it in a safe place so you aren't scrambling to retrieve it all when you reach retirement. Of course, you should look everything over before filing it away.

Pension plan papers

- The complete plan document
- All summary plan descriptions
- All revised summary plan descriptions or summaries of material modifications
- All plan amendments
- Summary annual reports (before December 31, 2007)
- Annual funding notices (after December 31, 2007)
- Individual benefit statements
- Other documents under which your plan operates, such as collective bargaining agreements
- All disclosure notices if your plan is underfunded

Personal information

- Your birth certificate
- Your spouse's birth certificate
- Documents reflecting your original date of hire with all your employers and any subsequent dates of hire with the same employer
- Documents reflecting all termination dates with all your employers
- Confirmation that you worked at least 1,000 hours each year, such as year-end pay stubs
- Memos or letters from your company, union, or bank that relate to your pension plan

Other useful information

- The name of your pension plan
- The plan's Employer Identification Number (EIN)
- The plan's Plan Number (PN)
- The name of the plan administrator
- How you can contact the plan administrator
- The date you'll be vested in the plan
- The date you're entitled to take early retirement under the plan
- The normal retirement age at which you can retire with full benefits
- The date you'll reach normal retirement age
- Whether your plan allows you to receive your benefits in a lump sum or as an annuity in monthly installments for life

D0911794

For Dummies: Bestselling Book Series for Beginners

Protecting Your Pension For Dummies®

Cheat Sheet

Hiring a Pension Attorney

If your claim for benefits was denied and you've lost your appeal, it's time to shop for legal representation. The following is a quick rundown of what you need to do to hire a pension attorney; see Chapter 19 for more information.

1. **Identify the type of attorney you need, based on the type of pension plan you have.**

   Most likely, you need an attorney who has worked with private pension plans and has practiced in federal court. If your fellow retirees are in the same boat as you, look for an attorney who's handled pension class action litigation (representing an individual on behalf of a group of people).

2. **Find a few good candidates with the help of personal recommendations, organizations that provide pension counseling services, bar associations, and general online resources.**

3. **Call to set up an interview with the attorney who comes most highly recommended.**

   Explain the nature of your concerns about your pension and what you've already done to address those concerns. If it sounds like the attorney can handle your complaint, schedule an appointment to meet and ask what you should bring with you. And don't forget to ask if you'll be charged for the appointment!

4. **Prepare for the interview by writing down your questions and gathering the important documents requested by the attorney.**

5. **During the interview, ask questions about potential conflicts of interest, his or her pension litigation experience, his or her working process, and payment options.**

6. **If you feel comfortable with the first attorney you interview, trust your instincts and hire him or her.**

   If you have any doubts, however, repeat the process with a few other candidates, and then make your decision.

For Dummies: Bestselling Book Series for Beginners

legally blind
20/800

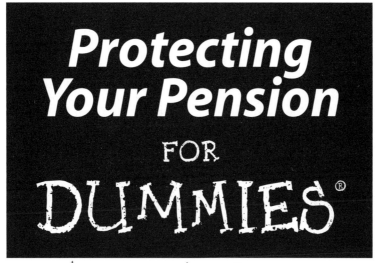

Protecting Your Pension

FOR DUMMIES®

maybe central vision but
no peripheal or vice versa

by Robert D. Gary and Jori Bloom Naegele

BICENTENNIAL
1807
WILEY
2007
BICENTENNIAL

Wiley Publishing, Inc.

About the Authors

Robert D. Gary and **Jori Bloom Naegele** first began representing pensioners in 1986. Since that time, they and their law firm, Gary, Naegele & Theado, LLC, located in Lorain, Ohio, have represented more than ten thousand pensioners. Most of these claims were handled through class action lawsuits where pensioners across the country sought recovery from their respective pension plans for underpayments of their pension benefits. These cases have returned tens of millions of dollars that the retirees should have received when they first retired. Their pension class actions have resulted in decisions establishing important legal precedents benefiting pensioners nationwide.

Bob has a JD from Case Western Reserve University School of Law and an LLM from New York University School of Law. He has been in private practice for the last 25-plus years. He started his legal career in the United States Department of Justice in the Organized Crime and Racketeering Section, where he got his first taste of how vulnerable pensions can be to manipulation. He was a Special Assistant to the Governor of Ohio as well as an Assistant County Prosecutor. He has been recognized throughout the years, having received a United States Department of Justice Special Achievement Award for sustained superior performance, a personal commendation from the Director of the FBI for trial performance, a proclamation from the Ohio Office of the Governor recognizing him as an outstanding citizen of Ohio, and special recognition from the Ohio General Assembly for a unique class action settlement that resulted in the distribution of free food to a million needy families in Northern Ohio. He has lectured and published articles in legal publications on class action–related topics.

Jori received her JD from Case Western Reserve University School of Law in 1979, and she's been an advocate of retirement issues for most of her legal career. In addition to representing pensioners, she's also advocated on behalf of all employees, helping to secure not only retirement benefits but safer and hostile-free workplace environments. She has donated her time and skill to helping seniors and others through her pro bono work and has been actively involved in her professional community as well. She has served as the president of her local bar association, as a mediator for the Equal Employment Opportunity Commission (EEOC) and state and federal court, and has published articles and lectured on a variety of legal topics. She was appointed by a former Ohio Attorney General to its office's Ethics and Professional Responsibility Advisory Counsel and was recognized for her service on the Ohio Supreme Court's Task Force on Gender Fairness.

Over the years, Bob and Jori's experience has shown them repeatedly that there is a wide gap between the knowledge of those who administer pension plans and those who depend on them for their financial security. Attempting to close that gap was the inspiration for this book. They realized that if ever there was a time for a book on planning for and protecting retirement benefits, it is now because the Pension Protection Act of 2006 has turned the gap of information into a chasm. It's their hope that with this book pensioners will be better equipped to deal with the rules regarding their own pensions and be able to ask the right questions of the professionals, whether they be attorneys, accountants, or financial advisors.

Bob and Jori have practiced law together for almost 25 years. They invite you to visit their firm's Web site at www.gntlaw.com or e-mail them at office@gntlaw.com. Gary, Naegele & Theado, LLC is located at 446 Broadway, Lorain, Ohio 44052, and the phone number is 440-244-4809.

Dedication

Bob: I was laboring over some ERISA rules when my nine-year-old grandson Asher sat down next to me and read what I was writing. In Asher's best dead-pan, he said, "I have to get this book." This book is dedicated to a special group of future pensioners who have yet to enter the workforce — my grand-children, Asher, Andrew, and Olivia Belle — with the expectation that at some time they will read some future edition of this book.

Jori: This book is dedicated to my children, Michael and Sydney, with the hope that they'll one day soon be a part of the working world, that they'll love their work, and that they'll be armed with the right balance of knowledge, information, and compassion to make the right choices in life.

Authors' Acknowledgments

Our thanks goes to all those at Wiley Publishing, Inc., who allowed us to share our vision of this book and who helped make this project a reality. First of all, we'd like to thank our friend Roy Kaufman, one of Wiley's talented attorneys, whose advice and direction helped give birth to the proposal of this *For Dummies* book. Special thanks to Acquisitions Editor Lindsay Lefevere, whose ideas, suggestions, and guidance were always helpful and insightful, and to Project Editor Georgette Beatty, who shepherded us through the writing process and always kept us on task. Thanks also to Copy Editors Jessica Smith and Vicki Adang for their fine editing and to University of Alabama School of Law profes-sor Norman Stein, our technical reviewer. Our sincere thanks to Composition Services and to everyone at Wiley for their roles in getting this book to press.

In addition to the folks at Wiley, we'd also like to extend thanks to Aileen Fonda, our secretary at Gary, Naegele & Theado, LLC, for all her help with this book and to the rest of our office as well, for making sure our office con-tinued to function during our occasional and not-so-occasional absences. To our family and friends, thanks for your support throughout this project. We know you're as excited as we are to see this book come to fruition.

We'd especially like to thank Jori's husband, attorney Richard Naegele, a Fellow of the American College of Employee Benefits Counsel and pension-guru extraor-dinaire, for spending countless hours with us reviewing text, sharing his wisdom, and debating the finer points of pension law. Dick's pension expertise, including teaching hundreds of pension seminars, drafting of plan documents, and author-ing numerous articles for pension and tax journals, enabled him to help us zero in on the really important stuff, and we are grateful for all his assistance. It also made for some interesting and lively conversations at the dinner table, and Jori is truly appreciative of Dick's patience and support for going above and beyond. Bob extends his gratitude and appreciation to his wife, Karen, whose gentle prodding and encouragement kept him on schedule and anchored.

Publisher's Acknowledgments

We're proud of this book; please send us your comments through our Dummies online registration form located at www.dummies.com/register/.

Some of the people who helped bring this book to market include the following:

Acquisitions, Editorial, and Media Development

Project Editor: Georgette Beatty

Acquisitions Editor: Lindsay Lefevere

Copy Editor: Jessica Smith

Technical Editor: Norman Stein

Editorial Manager: Michelle Hacker

Editorial Assistants: Erin Calligan Mooney, Joe Niesen, Leeann Harney

Cartoons: Rich Tennant (www.the5thwave.com)

Composition Services

Project Coordinator: Lynsey Osborn

Layout and Graphics: Brooke Graczyk, Denny Hager, Stephanie D. Jumper, Barbara Moore, Laura Pence, Heather Ryan, Alicia B. South, Christine Williams

Anniversary Logo Design: Richard Pacifico

Proofreaders: Aptara, Dwight Ramsey

Indexer: Aptara

Special Help
Victoria M. Adang

Publishing and Editorial for Consumer Dummies

Diane Graves Steele, Vice President and Publisher, Consumer Dummies

Joyce Pepple, Acquisitions Director, Consumer Dummies

Kristin A. Cocks, Product Development Director, Consumer Dummies

Michael Spring, Vice President and Publisher, Travel

Kelly Regan, Editorial Director, Travel

Publishing for Technology Dummies

Andy Cummings, Vice President and Publisher, Dummies Technology/General User

Composition Services

Gerry Fahey, Vice President of Production Services

Debbie Stailey, Director of Composition Services

Contents at a Glance

Table of Contents

· ·

Introduction

• •

*T*here are no pension superheroes or TV shows featuring exciting pension stories. And people don't go around telling lots of rip-roaring pension jokes or pithy anecdotes. Yet pensions may be the single most important and least understood subject in the country. You're reading these words at a time when pensioners face a critical turning point for the future of pensions as they have traditionally existed in this country. On August 17, 2006, the Pension Protection Act of 2006 became law. These more than 800 pages of legislation will leave no pension plan untouched.

You have chosen to come to grips with your retirement, and hopefully you understand that knowing the rules of the game is the only way to protect your pension. This book is a partnership; you have done your part by picking it up. As far as our part is concerned, we hope that we can help unravel the tangle of rules that control your pensions. Time and time again as we completed this book, critics told us that no one wants to read about pensions. You've already proved that theory wrong.

The reason to read this book is the same reason that we wrote it. Our goals and your goals are one and the same. We both want to close the knowledge gap that exists between those who control pensions and those who receive them. Without the basic framework to understand what your plan can and can't do, it's impossible to know whether to laugh or to cry. We give you the basic tools to understand your rights, know what questions to ask (and when to ask them), and where to find the answers. And if your employer hands you a bag of lemons instead of the pension you were expecting, we explain how to fight back and turn your lemons into lemonade.

About This Book

You've worked hard to earn your pension benefits, and we want to help you keep them. We cover it all, from start to finish, in this one book. We explain the basics about different types of retirement plans, the rules that apply to them, and how to request essential plan documents so you can ensure that you truly get the pension you deserve. We discuss the different workplace situations that can potentially put your plan in jeopardy or affect your ultimate payout. These situations include events such as when your employer merges with another company or sells its business or when you terminate employment. We also explain the personal issues, such as divorce and bankruptcy, that you need to look out for when trying to protect your pension.

This book also tells you what to do and how to do it when you don't get the pension amount that was promised to you. For example, we take you through the administrative appeal process so that you know what you need to do to continue to protect your benefits. If you lose at this point, we walk you through the litigation process and even give you some pointers on how to select the right attorney to protect your interests.

As valuable a resource as this book may be, it only skims the surface of an extremely technical topic. Everyone's circumstances are different, so it's possible that your situation may result in a conclusion that's different from the one that we suggest in this book. In other words, don't assume that just because you read it here that we're telling you, personally, what to do. Pension law involves rules and regulations, statutes and court decisions, IRS determination letters, and decisions of plan administrators, and they're all subject to potentially different interpretations. So, we can't provide answers to your *specific* questions, but we can suggest ways to help you find out more about a particular topic. We provide resources when we can so that when you need to seek expert advice (which we all do from time to time), you can do so in a more educated way. What's most important, however, is that you can identify the issues that are essential to successfully protecting your pension.

Feel free to use this book as a reference when you want to find out more about a particular topic, but if you prefer, you can sit down and read the book cover to cover.

Conventions Used in This Book

We include a few conventions to help you navigate this book with ease:

- ✔ **Boldfaced** words highlight the key words in bulleted lists and numbered steps.
- ✔ *Italics* emphasize key words and important terms.
- ✔ `Monofont` indicates Web addresses.

When this book was printed, some Web addresses may have needed to break across two lines of text. If that happened, rest assured that we haven't put in any extra characters (such as hyphens) to indicate the break. So, when using one of these Web addresses, just type in exactly what you see in this book, pretending as though the line break doesn't exist.

What You're Not to Read

Feel free to skip anything marked with the Technical Stuff icon; those gems are interesting but not crucial to your understanding of pensions. The same goes for sidebars (the shaded gray boxes throughout the book).

Foolish Assumptions

When writing this book, we kept a few assumptions in mind about you, dear reader:

- ✔ You're nearing retirement or have already retired.
- ✔ You may be an employer, a human resources professional, or a plan administrator.
- ✔ You may be a pension attorney looking for more information to provide to your clients.
- ✔ You may be a small business owner who can appreciate these issues from the perspective of employer *and* employee.
- ✔ You may be a financial advisor interested in understanding today's pension issues from the perspective of the retiree.

How This Book Is Organized

This book is organized into seven parts, starting with the big picture and then honing in on different subject areas as they relate to retirement plan protection.

Part I: Focusing on Pension Fundamentals

This part provides an overview of the various types of pension plans and the rules and regulations that govern them. We tell you about the protections that are ensured by the law known as the Employee Retirement Income Security Act (ERISA) that started the trend toward pension protection in 1974. The new and important changes to the pension laws that came about through the Pension Protection Act of 2006 are covered in this part as well.

Part II: Making Sure That You Receive the Pension You Earned

In this part, we explain what it takes to qualify for a pension, and we go over the rules for accrual and vesting. We tell you what documents to assemble for retirement, and we explain why you need them and how to get them. Finally, we give you a heads-up on distribution issues. (That's right; we talk about you finally getting your money!)

Part III: Guarding Your Pension from Your Employer

In this day and age, nothing is certain except change. So, in this part, we address the possible changes that your employer can undergo, and we explain their possible impact on your pension. Whether your employer merges with another company, sells to another company, or decides to amend or terminate its plan, all of these scenarios can have a significant impact on your retirement benefits. In these circumstances, you need to know how to move quickly to ensure that your pension benefits are still there and how to protect them until you're entitled to receive them. In this part, you also find out what your employer and the plan's paid advisors (called fiduciaries) can and can't do, and we tell you what you can do to protect your pension from their actions, inactions, or transgressions.

Part IV: Shielding Your Pension from Life's Ups and Downs

Financial problems, divorce, and premature death are potential life problems for just about everyone. And when these unfortunate events occur, they undoubtedly affect your pension. So, this part tells you the rules about borrowing from your pension. It also explains how and when your pension assets need protection from your creditors, what to expect in a divorce, and how to extend your pension to your beneficiaries if you die before them.

Part V: Taking Action When Bad Things Happen to Good Pensioners

It's more common than you'd like to think: Plans often fail to pay the full amount that pensioners are entitled to receive. This failure to pay the right amount can happen for any number of reasons, and in this part we point out some of the most obvious. We also explain what you need to do to enforce your rights, starting with an appeal to the plan, and if that isn't successful, ending with the final resort of filing a lawsuit in federal court.

Part VI: The Part of Tens

The chapters in this part address ten important issues that may arise for three different categories of people: employees who are still working, retirees or those getting ready to retire, and small business owners. Any one of these 30 items may turn out to be the important issue for you.

Part VII: Appendixes

We provide a glossary in Appendix A of the fancy terms and the alphabet soup of abbreviations that are so loved by those who write pension laws. This glossary allows you to quickly look up the definitions of any words that you come across in your dealings with your pension plan. Appendix B contains the charts and tables that we discuss throughout the book. These items can help you compare the different kinds of plans and can graphically explain some of the more technical concepts that we discuss.

Icons Used in This Book

See those pictures in the margins throughout this book? They're icons that point out specific information. Here's what they mean.

This icon points out new information that results from changes in the pension laws that occurred following the passage of the Pension Protection Act on August 17, 2006.

This icon means just what it says. It highlights points that you should keep in mind as you're reading.

This icon gives you the skinny on the technical issues that may befuddle even rocket scientists. These technical tidbits aren't necessary to the discussion at hand, so if you'd rather skip them, feel free to do so.

If we've marked something with this icon, know that it's helpful information that we think can make a task easier.

This icon puts you on red alert. Ignore this critical advice at your own financial, or even legal, peril.

Where to Go from Here

Even though we'd love for you to read this entire book from cover to cover, we understand that not all of you will. The book is laid out in a modular format that provides you with easy access to all the general information that you need. If you have a specific subject that you want to know more about, feel free to go immediately to that part to find out more. The table of contents and the index are helpful for getting you to the right page quickly. However, if you know little to nothing about pension plans and have no idea of even the first question to ask, we recommend that you browse through the table of contents for an overview of the topics we cover. Or you can start with Chapter 1, which gives you the basics on pensions. If you have the luxury of time, we encourage you to read as much as possible, even if you choose to skip around chapter by chapter. Finally, if you think your family, friends, or co-workers can benefit from this book, please share it with them.

Part I
Focusing on Pension Fundamentals

The 5th Wave   By Rich Tennant

"The pay's not great, but where else can you get a retirement plan that will last for eternity?"

In this part . . .

Saving for your retirement is one of the most important things you can do for yourself and your family. So when your employer offers a retirement plan as part of its benefits package, consider this a fabulous opportunity. After all, can you really expect to sock away all the money you need for retirement without a retirement plan? To take full advantage of this opportunity, however, you must know the fundamentals of the type of plan being offered and the rules and responsibilities attached to that plan. In this part, we introduce the act that lays down those rules: the Employee Retirement Income Security Act of 1974, known as ERISA.

These days, when it comes down to who's paying for your pension, the times are changing. In this part, we give you a heads-up on the ongoing shift from the traditional employer-funded defined benefit plans, which provide lifetime monthly benefits (similar to Social Security), to the ever more prevalent employee-funded defined contribution plans, including 401(k) plans. We also explain the benefits of Individual Retirement Accounts (IRAs), a popular way to supplement your employer's retirement plan, and we show you the ins and outs of monitoring your plan's investments.

Chapter 1

Navigating the Ins and Outs of Pensions

. . . .

. . . .

You've worked hard for years, and you're looking forward to your well-deserved retirement. But are you truly ready? With this book, you'll be on your way. We want to help you prepare for this exciting time in your life, but we don't want to bog you down with legal details. We'll let the pension experts argue the fine points of pension law. Instead, in this book, we give you just the information that you need to understand your pension so you can protect it effectively.

For instance, we explain the differences between a defined benefit plan and a defined contribution plan. Already know that? Well, we go on from there to tell you about accrued benefits and vesting, how to take a loan from your plan (if you need one), and what happens to your pension in a divorce. You can also find out what happens when your plan goes broke or your company is sold. Finally, we give you information about fighting back when the plan takes advantage of you.

We introduce all these topics (and more) in this chapter; all of this information can help you grab hold of the pension that you worked so hard to earn.

Checking Out Pension Rules

The basic idea behind pension plan rules is to hold companies accountable for the promises they make to their employees regarding retirements. In exchange for following the rules, Congress provides pension plans special tax benefits. The pension plans that are given these special tax benefits are called *tax-qualified pension plans* (see the next section for more info).

The federal law that regulates pensions is called the Employee Retirement Income Security Act, but it's also known by its nickname, ERISA. ERISA has been around since 1974, and despite its amendments and the other retirement plan legislation enacted since then, the act was in need of a face-lift. After several years of wrangling, on August 17, 2006, the Pension Protection Act, known to friends and foes as the PPA, was enacted to update ERISA. The PPA is the most comprehensive pension legislation since ERISA. Both pieces of legislation, however, are alive and well. These federal laws apply to private pension plans — from your dentist's small plan to the billion-dollar plans of our country's biggest corporations.

Government employees, public school teachers, police officers, and firefighters participate in state pension plans that are created and regulated by state law, not federal law. This book doesn't cover these types of plans; we focus primarily on private plans that are governed by ERISA.

Pension plans covered under ERISA must do the following:

- ✔ Disclose certain plan information
- ✔ Set minimum standards for eligibility, accrual, and vesting
- ✔ Spell out fiduciary obligations
- ✔ Provide the right to file suit

For more about ERISA and the basics of pension rules, see Chapter 2.

Getting a Grip on Tax-Qualified Plans

For the most part, tax-qualified pension plans for private companies boil down to two basic varieties that are known as *defined contribution plans* and *defined benefit plans*. More and more companies are replacing their defined benefit plans with defined contribution plans. In Chapter 3, we explore the various types of plans that are included within these two groups.

Building your pension with defined contribution plans

A defined contribution plan is set up by your employer. Once it's set up, the plan provides you with an individual account until the money is distributed upon retirement. With this type of plan, you make tax-free contributions while you're still working. Your company may or may not match those contributions and make additional contributions, tax-free, to your plan. The benefit you receive at retirement is based on the amounts contributed to your account and the investment gains and losses it experiences. When you retire, your account balance is the amount that you have available — and when it's gone, that's all there is.

Here are some of the varieties of defined contribution plans that we cover in Chapter 3:

- ✔ Profit-sharing plans
- ✔ 401(k) plans
- ✔ Money purchase plans
- ✔ Employee stock ownership plans (ESOPs)
- ✔ Target benefit pension plans

Receiving cash for life with defined benefit plans

The defined benefit plan is more like traditional Social Security — after retirement it provides you with a fixed amount each month for as long as you or your designated beneficiary live. It doesn't matter whether your pension fund makes a bundle with its investments or loses a bundle; you're always entitled to the same monthly benefit or annuity. Here are the three types of defined benefit plans that we discuss in more detail in Chapter 3:

- ✔ The traditional defined benefit plan
- ✔ The cash balance (or hybrid) plan
- ✔ The 412(i) plan

Moving Forward with 401(k) Plans

Because the PPA now requires that defined benefit plans be fully funded and because defined benefit plans provide less flexibility to employers and are flat-out expensive to administer, many companies have been making a big shift in their pension plans to *401(k) plans*. These plans are an increasingly popular type of defined contribution plan. As we point out in Chapter 4, the following different types of 401(k) plans exist:

- Traditional 401(k) plans
- Safe Harbor 401(k) plans
- SIMPLE 401(k) plans
- Individual (or solo) 401(k) plans
- Roth 401(k) plans

401(k)s are popular with both employers and employees. Employees like them because their elective deferrals to the plan and the investment gains aren't subject to taxes until they're distributed from the plan. Also helpful is the fact that employee deferrals are always 100 percent vested. Employers enjoy 401(k) plans because contributions are deductible on their federal income tax returns. It's a win-win situation for everybody. The type of 401(k) plan that your employer may offer usually depends on its size and financial situation.

Funding Your Retirement with the Help of IRAs

An *individual retirement account,* or IRA, is a plan that allows employees (under age 70½), self-employed individuals, and certain other individuals to put money into personal retirement accounts. You may be able to deduct some or all of your contributions to a traditional IRA depending on whether you, your spouse, or both of you are covered by a qualified retirement plan. If you and/or your spouse are covered, the amount of your tax deduction may be reduced depending on your adjusted gross income at the time you file your taxes. Generally, the amount in your traditional IRA, including earnings, isn't taxed until it's distributed to you.

An IRA is especially beneficial if you aren't already participating in an employer-sponsored retirement plan because it provides you with a way to save for your retirement on a tax-advantaged basis.

Varieties of IRAs include the following:

✔ Traditional IRAs

✔ Roth IRAs

✔ SIMPLE IRAs

✔ Simplified Employee Pension (SEP) Plans

Chapter 5 covers the different types of IRAs, including the rules about contributions, penalties, and distributions.

Tracking Pension Investments

When it comes to investing the money contributed to your pension, one of two things can happen: Either the plan officials direct the investments or you're permitted to direct the investments yourself. Naturally, the latter type of investment is called a *self-directed investment.*

When plan officials direct the investments in your pension plan, it's important that you do the following:

✔ Check on exactly who's investing your money.

✔ Examine your plan's selected investments.

✔ Track the performance of your plan's investments.

✔ Watch out for signs that the plan isn't following investment rules (and take action if something's amiss).

If you have the option of self-directing your investments, follow these guidelines:

✔ Find help in selecting your investments (for example, consult your plan's financial advisor, if there is one, or get a second opinion from your own financial advisor).

✔ Check your investments regularly (and change them if they aren't working for you).

Head to Chapter 6 for the scoop on investments in pension plans.

Ensuring That You Get Your Pension

To make sure that you get the pension that you deserve, you need to know the rules about a few important issues: eligibility, accrual, vesting, and distributions. You also need to use the right tools to plan for your retirement. We explain what you need to know in the following sections.

Getting the skinny on eligibility, accrual, and vesting

You can't participate in your employer's pension plan until you become eligible. And only after you become eligible do you begin to accrue benefits. (*Accrual* is the growth you earn in your account as you work.) At some point, your accrued benefits *vest,* meaning that they can't be taken away from you. Simple enough, right? Of course, the devil is in the details: How do you become eligible? What determines how you accrue benefits? When do these accrued benefits vest? Here are the basics (see Chapter 7 for more details):

✔ **Eligibility:** Your retirement plan can set age and service requirements before you can be part of its pension plan. But these requirements, by law, can't be unreasonable.

✔ **Accrual:** Your plan has a formula it uses to calculate how your benefits accrue. This formula is contained in your *summary plan description* (SPD), which is a plan document that must be made available to you upon your request. Your plan can't reduce the rate of the accrual of the benefits that you've already accrued, but it may do so for future benefits.

✔ **Vesting:** It's up to your company to determine when your benefits become vested, and this information must be specified in your SPD. Don't worry, though; your company must comply with minimum vesting schedules. Your company can vest your benefits in the following two ways:

  • With *cliff vesting,* which is an all-or-nothing approach where you become totally vested after a passage of time

  • With *graded vesting,* which is a method where you vest a percentage of your accrued benefit each year that you work

Your own contributions to a defined contribution plan are yours no matter how long you've been working and how young or old you are.

Making retirement planning a priority

Quite obviously, it's best to plan for retirement while you're still working. This means, first off, that you have to know your *net worth.* Add up your assets (for example, your savings accounts, your investments, and the equity in your home) and then subtract your debts (expenses such as credit card debt, home mortgage, car loans, and so on). Hopefully your assets are greater than your debts; those assets that are left add up to be the value of your net worth.

After you calculate your net worth, you need to consider the type of retirement that you want to have (frugal, extravagant, or something in between). Then you have to figure out how much you need to save along with your pension. Again, the time to set up a budget and begin figuring out how much you need to save is while you're still working and actually have money to budget.

Your pension plan documents are instrumental in helping you understand how your pension benefits are calculated, so it's important to assemble your pension documents and keep them safe. But also be sure to go a step further — get in the habit of checking the accuracy of the personal information that your plan maintains for you. Review the pension SPD, plan amendments, and other items you have in your possession.

Chapter 8 has all the info that you need to help you plan your retirement, including painting a complete picture of your retirement and finding financial help.

Receiving your pension distribution

When it comes to your pension, the bottom line goal is to actually receive your benefits. The first step, then, is to follow your plan's requirements for applying for a pension benefit. Keep in mind the following considerations:

- ✔ If you take your distribution before you're 59½ years old, you may be socked with a penalty tax for taking it too soon.
- ✔ You may be forced to take a distribution in some instances.
- ✔ If you wait until you become 70½, you may be socked with a penalty for taking your distribution too late.
- ✔ Special rules apply if the distribution is made after your death.

Also, if your plan offers the option to take your benefits in a lump sum or as an annuity (in which you receive monthly payments for the rest of your life), you need to decide which option is best for you.

One more thing: You need to decide whether you want to roll over your pension money from one tax-qualified plan into another tax-qualified plan or into an IRA. If so, you must be aware of the restrictions regarding what can be rolled over and what it can be rolled over into.

For example, only eligible rollover distributions can be rolled over. These distributions include lump-sum distributions (not annuity payments) that aren't minimum required distributions (that are required at age 70½) and that aren't due to hardships. Your plan administrator will provide you with notice about this prior to your distribution, and you'll have 60 days to roll over part or all of your benefits currently in a tax-qualified plan. If you don't roll over your eligible distribution into an IRA or other tax-qualified plan within 60 days, it will be considered a taxable distribution.

If you fail to roll over your eligible distribution *directly* from the qualified plan to an IRA or other tax-qualified plan, 20 percent of the distribution will be withheld for federal income tax (and 80 percent will be distributed to you). You can still roll over an amount equal to 100 percent of the distribution within 60 days, but because you're receiving only 80 percent, you'll have to come up with the other 20 percent from somewhere else, like your savings account.

You can find many of the answers to your rollover and distribution questions in Chapter 9.

Keeping Your Pension Safe from Your Employer

Sometimes the major pension issue that you face is keeping an eye on the fox that was hired by the farmer (your company) to guard the henhouse (your pension). In other words, your company, like our proverbial farmer, hired a financial advisor called a fiduciary, whose job it is to look after your interests and see that your plan money is invested wisely. This assignment is full of temptations for the fiduciary, who truly can be like a fox in a henhouse. The fiduciary, for example, must resist the temptation to recommend investments that have high fees or that are sold by a broker who might provide a referral fee for the business. In the following sections, we introduce you to the employer issues that can significantly affect your pension.

Watching your fiduciary

A *fiduciary* is someone who offers investment advice to a plan or who has control over plan assets. Your plan fiduciaries may include plan trustees, the plan administrator, pension consultants, and other investment professionals. To remain ethically sound and unbiased, fiduciaries must

- ✔ Do what's in the best interests of plan members
- ✔ Act with skill, prudence, and diligence
- ✔ Follow the plan documents
- ✔ Diversify plan assets and minimize expenses

Fiduciaries must not

- ✔ Invest the plan's money for their own benefit
- ✔ Involve themselves in transactions that aren't in the plan's best interest
- ✔ Get money for themselves in exchange for giving another person business

As a member of a pension plan, you need to know who your fiduciaries are. Ask questions. And be curious if your fiduciaries are abusing their power. The fastest way to end a negative practice is to expose it. See Chapter 10 for more information about fiduciaries.

Understanding the impact of acquisitions, mergers, and other major job changes

Your company is in the business of making money; that task is its first priority. So, to a large extent, it makes decisions based on the expected returns. And, well, some business decisions are great for the company but bad for your retirement. It's inevitable that you'll sooner or later come across sales, mergers, bankruptcies, job switches, and other changes that are neither anticipated nor expected. It's quite possible that these activities will affect your pension, so we suggest that you sit up and take notice. The list of possible changes in the case of such events may include the following:

- ✔ The termination of your existing pension plan and replacement by a new plan
- ✔ The merger of your plan into the plan of a successor company
- ✔ A transfer of all the records relating to your pension from one location to another (just think what happens to your luggage when you fly from one location to another)
- ✔ The conversion of your defined benefit plan to a defined contribution plan or a cash balance plan
- ✔ A reduction or an increase in how your future pension is calculated

The list of changes goes on and on. What's most important, however, is that you're proactive when it comes to protecting your pension. Therefore, when your company goes through big changes, be sure to do the following:

- ✔ Find out as soon as you can what changes your company will make and what impact they'll have on your pension.
- ✔ Determine the key people who administer the plan and, if appropriate, get to know them.

✔ Double-check that all of your pension documents have landed in the proper location.

✔ Make sure that you've received credit for the time that you worked at the previous company and that the rest of your file has the right information.

Head to Chapter 11 for more information on dealing with acquisitions, mergers, job changes, and employer bankruptcies.

Knowing what happens if your plan is changed or terminated

It's true that your pension plan can be amended. But if your plan wants to make changes, it must follow the rules; some options available under the plan are protected from amendments, but others aren't. The plan can ask the Internal Revenue Service (IRS) to issue a determination letter stating that the IRS believes the plan amendment conforms to IRS rules. However, no matter what, if the plan intends to make a significant change, it must provide you with a notice called a *summary of material modifications* (SMM). This document provides a summary of the changes.

Your employer also has the right to terminate its defined benefit plan or defined contribution plan. However, when a qualified plan is terminated, each affected participant becomes 100 percent vested in his or her accrued benefits as of the date the plan terminated. Depending on what kind of plan it is and why the plan is terminated, different rules apply.

A defined benefit plan can be terminated in the following three ways:

✔ **A standard termination:** Your employer can end the plan in a *standard termination* only after showing the Pension Benefit Guarantee Corporation, or PBGC (the federal agency that insures defined benefit pension plans), that the plan has enough money to pay all benefits owed to its participants. The plan must either purchase an annuity from an insurance company or, if the plan allows, issue a lump sum payment that covers your entire benefit.

✔ **A distress determination:** If the plan isn't fully funded and your company is in financial distress, your employer may apply for a *distress termination* from the PBGC. However, the application won't be granted unless the employer proves to the PBGC or a bankruptcy court that it can't continue in business unless the plan is terminated. If the PBGC grants the application, it usually takes over as trustee of the plan and pays the plan benefits, up to the legal limits, using the plan's assets and funds guaranteed by the PBGC.

✔ **An involuntary termination for lack of funds:** Sometimes the PBGC takes action on its own to end a pension plan. An *involuntary termination* usually occurs when the PBGC determines that plan termination is needed to protect the interests of plan participants (for example, if a plan won't be able to pay benefits when due) or of the PBGC insurance program itself.

When a defined contribution plan is terminated, the money in your plan account is yours; it can't be taken away from you for any reason. The PBGC doesn't provide any protection for defined contribution plans because the contributions made to your account are in your own individual account (meaning that whatever's in that account is yours). Interested in finding out more? Check out Chapter 12 for full details on plan amendments and terminations.

Safeguarding Your Pension from Life's Trials

Practically no one gets through life without some trauma, and that trauma may affect your pension:

✔ You may unexpectedly run short of money, and you may find that the only place to come up with ready cash is to borrow it from your pension plan.

✔ You may go through a divorce, and your ex-spouse may have rights to your pension that are governed by special provisions.

✔ You may have to file for bankruptcy. In this case, it's important to know whether your pension will be protected from your creditors.

Even more certain is the fact that everyone alive will someday wind up dead (sorry to be blunt!). In anticipation of that day, it's necessary to consider pension survivorship benefits for your loved ones.

In the following sections, we explain how to keep your pension safe through life's ups and downs.

Getting a loan from yourself

Imagine that you need some money to pay for an unexpected medical bill and that your pension plan is sitting there flush with cash. Your plan, in this case, may appear to be a big, fat available target. However, do remember that strict rules control loans from your pension plan, and real consequences will cost you real money if you break those rules.

A loan from your pension plan is like a loan from the bank. Consider these similarities:

✓ It must be in writing and must have a reasonable rate of interest.

✓ A repayment schedule must be prepared and the loan must be secured.

Also, your plan documents must specifically provide that loans are permitted. These documents must set out the procedure for applying for the loan and must establish the basis on which a loan will be approved or denied.

If you fail to pay back the loan on time (in other words, if you *defaulted* on the loan), it's treated as though the plan made a taxable distribution to you (referred to as a *deemed distribution*). This means that you must pay taxes on the outstanding balance of the loan at the time of the default. If this deemed distribution occurs before you're age 59½, you'll have to pay an additional 10 percent tax on the outstanding balance as well. Keep in mind that if the plan offers an annuity form of payment, you also need spousal consent for the loan.

All in all, if possible, try to avoid borrowing from your plan. When you take money out — for whatever reason — that money is no longer working to provide you a sound retirement.

But if taking out a loan from your plan is your only option, it's definitely one worth considering. For the scoop on taking out a loan from your pension plan, see Chapter 13.

Protecting your family

What happens to your pension benefits when you die? In many instances, you can provide for survivorship benefits to a spouse or other designated beneficiary. The extent of those benefits, however, depends on whether you die before or after retirement. The two means of providing survivorship benefits are the *qualified preretirement survivor annuity* (QPSA) and the *qualified joint and survivor annuity* (QJSA). The QPSA typically kicks in if you die *before* you retire while the QJSA kicks in if you die *after* you retire.

Not all plans offer survivorship benefits, however. The rule is that all defined benefit plans must offer survivorship benefits as well as defined contribution plans that provide for a life annuity (which provides a series of regular payments over your lifetime).We cover survivorship benefits in greater detail in Chapter 14.

Watching out for your ex

Divorce is a fact of modern American life. If you're facing a divorce, the judge who's hearing your case has the authority to make provisions from your pension plan for your soon-to-be ex. The judge makes this provision by issuing an order called a *domestic relations order,* which the plan administrator must approve. After approval, the order becomes final and is referred to as a *qualified domestic relations order,* or QDRO for short. The QDRO can allocate pension benefits to provide marital and child support and it can divide marital assets. Your pension benefits may be one of the most valuable assets accumulated during your marriage, and the QDRO is the legal mechanism used to split up those benefits, just as other marital assets are divided between you and your spouse.

The QDRO, however, can't (among other things)

✔ Provide for benefits that aren't available under your plan

✔ Provide for benefits for your ex's new spouse

The rules regarding QDROs are complicated, so take a look at Chapter 15 for more details.

Staying safe from creditors and personal bankruptcy

As a general rule, your pension benefits are protected from creditors if you have to file for bankruptcy. In fact, your typical defined benefit or defined contribution pension plan is protected from creditors whether or not you have filed for bankruptcy. This protection is one of the big benefits of a tax-qualified pension plan.

If you do file for bankruptcy, protection from creditors extends also to:

✔ Traditional and Roth IRAs, which are protected up to $1 million

✔ SEPs or SIMPLE IRAs

✔ Section 403(b) plans (tax-sheltered annuity plans) and Section 457 plans (plans for employees of state and federal government)

In some situations you get no protection from creditors. For instance, your pension distributions aren't protected. If you anticipate that creditors may come after you because of financial woes (or, worse, if you have to file bankruptcy), proper planning must be done to make sure that you have no assets available for your creditors. This is an area where the advice of a good bankruptcy or pension attorney is a must to ensure that your retirement savings are in the proper type of plan to receive sufficient protection from your creditors. Don't try to muddle through these issues on your own. For more information, head to Chapter 16.

Taking Action When Necessary

There may come a time when you and the plan have a parting of the ways over what pension amount you're entitled to receive. Fortunately, when this happens, you can assert your rights. As you find out in the following sections, you don't have to like it or lump it. The company may have the big bucks, but a good lawyer on your side can quickly even the playing field. You must take certain measures to protect your rights, starting with filing an appeal to the plan if you're shortchanged and following the plan's appeal process until you've exhausted it. If you still aren't successful, you can bring a lawsuit in federal court.

Eyeing potential distribution problems

Your pension plan has attorneys, accountants, and pension actuaries to help it with its pension issues. At first glance, you would think that a lone pensioner has no chance against such a formidable opponent. Not true. If the plan makes a systemwide error, such as the use of the wrong interest rate, it impacts all retirees the same way. In that instance, it isn't just you against the plan — lots of pensioners who are in the same boat probably have the same claim.

Sometimes your plan may not be aware of its errors, so you should be on the lookout for problems. A few common errors include the following:

- ✔ Your wages or years of service haven't been properly reported.
- ✔ Your plan ignored new vesting requirements or increases in pension benefits.
- ✔ Cuts in benefits have been applied to you retroactively.

What you should *not* do is nothing. Be proactive and intercept small problems before they become big ones. Head to Chapter 17 for full details on potential distribution problems.

Filing your claim and appealing a denial

The first step in actually receiving your pension benefits is filing a claim with your plan. Plans have set procedures in their SPDs for how to file a claim. Make sure that you comply with the plan's rules for filing your claim. You can expect to hear back from your plan within a certain period of time after it receives your claim; if you don't file properly, you'll never know when your time starts to run or if the plan is even processing your claim.

After successfully filing, if your claim for benefits is denied in full or in part, you'll receive a denial letter. At this point, you must file an appeal to protect your rights. The plan and the denial letter tell you exactly how to file this appeal. If you fail to appeal the denial of your claim in a timely manner and you don't follow the plan's procedures as required, you may find yourself in the position of not being able to file a lawsuit down the road, if necessary. We cover the entire appeal process in Chapter 18.

If you lose the appeal, you must decide if you want to take the plan to court. If you decide that you do want to sue the plan, keep reading to find out what comes next.

Hiring a lawyer

There's really no magic in hiring the right lawyer. If you're involved in a pension case, hire a pension attorney. If your claim is going to be brought under ERISA, find an ERISA specialist who practices in federal court. You may also be able to find a lawyer who handles state-based pension cases. Whatever the case may be, the lawyer you choose should not only be familiar with the subject matter, but also should have some record of success in bringing these types of cases. Set up a meeting to interview the attorney under consideration to help determine if he or she is the right choice.

Before you see the attorney, gather the relevant documents and have a clear idea of what your concerns are. We explain exactly what you need to do to hire the best attorney for your needs in Chapter 19.

Litigating a pension claim

ERISA provides that you have a right to sue your plan. And you don't have to worry about backlash from your employer or plan because ERISA also forbids employers and plans from retaliating against a pension participant because of a claim that he or she brought against them. So if you need to file a claim, have at it.

Once a pension lawsuit is filed in court, it follows a predictable path. It starts with the filing of the complaint by the plan participant and the answer that's filed by the defendant (the plan). From there it moves to the discovery process by the parties to figure out the position of each side. Then it's time to file a motion with the court asking for a ruling in your favor. If you aren't fortunate enough to win this summary judgment motion, your case will most likely go to trial unless it's settled before that. We dissect the basics of pension litigation in Chapter 20.

Many pension cases are filed by one or two individuals on behalf of a group (called a *class action*), because the claims of the pensioners may be virtually identical. Court approval is necessary in order for the case to be considered a class action, but if it's granted, the court then monitors the class action to ensure that the rights of the group are protected by the representative client and the attorneys who file the case. Tens of thousands of pensioners have recovered large amounts of money through pension class actions. Obviously it's preferable to get the correct pension benefit right off the bat, but even years after your initial distribution it may not be too late to right a wrong.

Chapter 2

Acquainting Yourself with Pension Rules

In This Chapter
▶ Reviewing the basic framework that governs pension plans
▶ Surveying pension plan requirements under ERISA

*P*eople work for many reasons, but at the top of the list is the desire to support themselves and their families. And they don't want to stop supporting their families after they stop working either. That means employee benefits offered by employers, in the form of pension plans that provide income after retirement, are critical.

Your employer isn't required to provide a pension plan for you and your fellow employees, but if it does, you (as well as the other participants) and the employer have rights and responsibilities. These rights and responsibilities are set forth specifically in the law known as the Employee Retirement Income Security Act of 1974 (ERISA). The ultimate goal of ERISA is to make sure that the contributions made to your plan while you're working are still there when you retire.

In this chapter, we go over the basic terms that you need to understand ERISA and the requirements set by ERISA for pension plans. If you're familiar with the rules that your plan must follow, you'll be better equipped to understand the documents that your plan provides you. Also, if you understand what's required for plan participation, you can make sure that you're doing everything to qualify for the benefits that you'll rely on for your retirement. And finally, understanding these rules can help you determine if your employer is following the rules as well.

ERISA primarily applies to private retirement plans, which are typically defined benefit or defined contribution plans that are sponsored by employers and unions. Almost all employee benefit plans, however, are subject to some provisions of the act. ERISA doesn't generally apply to state and local government plans, church plans, or those covering only self-employed persons. Instead, these plans are subject to various rules under the Internal Revenue Code.

Before You Begin: Basic Information for Understanding ERISA

ERISA came about after years of concerns about the mismanagement and abuse of private pension plans. Throughout the 1900s, many pieces of legislation were proposed in an attempt to address these concerns. Ultimately, in 1974, ERISA was signed into law by President Gerald Ford.

The goal of ERISA is to protect the interests of participants and their beneficiaries in employee benefit funds. ERISA provides requirements for the disclosure of important information to better protect plan participants. ERISA also imposes certain requirements that all pension plans must meet, such as rules about how long an employer can require you to work before you earn your pension benefits. Similarly, ERISA includes rules to ensure that those who manage pension plans do so responsibly by meeting certain standards of conduct. (To familiarize yourself with these standards, check out Chapter 10.) If plans don't comply with the imposed restrictions, the plan managers may be subject to certain penalties. And the plans themselves risk being disqualified and losing their tax benefits and/or incurring other penalties.

As a general rule, your employer can deduct the contributions it makes to the plan on behalf of its employees as long as it complies with certain requirements of the Internal Revenue Code and ERISA. It's a win-win situation for everyone.

In the following sections, we provide some basic information that you need to know in order to fully understand ERISA, including a few important terms and brief descriptions of the plans that ERISA covers.

Simple (yet important) definitions

It's difficult to avoid certain pension terminology because the laws involving pension plans are filled with these words and phrases. We include a glossary in Appendix A that serves as a quick and easy reference for all the pension jargon that you're likely to see. But for now, here are some of the most common words and phrases that appear frequently throughout ERISA and this book:

✔ **Retirement plan/pension plan:** Throughout this book, these terms are used interchangeably. The term *pension plan* basically refers to any type of retirement plan. A *retirement plan* (or simply *plan*) is an arrangement that provides people with an income or pension during retirement, when they're no longer earning a steady income from employment. Plans may be set up by employers, insurance companies, the government, unions, or other institutions (such as employer associations or trade unions), and they're typically classified as defined benefit plans or defined contribution plans, depending on how the benefits are determined. (See the later section "An overview of pension plans covered by ERISA" for more about both types of plans.)

✔ **Pension fund:** A *pension fund,* which is often referred to as simply "a fund," is the fund that maintains the employer's and employee's contributions to the pension plan, along with the earnings on the investments. This fund must be kept separate and apart from the employer's assets.

✔ **Plan participant:** The *plan participant* is the individual who's participating in a pension plan by virtue of his or her employment (or former employment) with an employer that's offering the benefit. This person receives pension benefits subject to the terms of the plan.

✔ **Plan beneficiary:** A *plan beneficiary* is an individual designated by a plan participant (or in some cases by the plan) to receive benefits from the plan if the participant dies.

✔ **Plan administrator:** The *plan administrator* runs your plan and maintains the pension records. The administrator also hires and fires the plan's employees and/or consultants with approval of the plan's board. But most importantly, the administrator performs some functions that directly impact your pension. For example, the administrator does the following:

- Determines eligibility for plan participation and for accrual and vesting of benefits (see Chapter 7 for details on these topics)

- Decides whether to accept your claim for benefits

- Distributes your benefits to you (see Chapter 9 for general distribution info)

- Advises you of your various retirement options as well as your rights under the plan

✔ **Fiduciary:** A *fiduciary* is anyone who exercises any discretionary authority, responsibility, or control over a plan, anyone who handles the plan's assets, or anyone who's compensated in some manner to render investment advice regarding a plan's assets (or who has authority or responsibility to do so). See the later section "Spelling out fiduciary obligations" for more details.

Generally speaking, though, your employer and the plan administrator are both fiduciaries. Other people or entities may also be fiduciaries depending on what they do for the plan.

✔ **Plan year:** A *plan year* is any consecutive 12-month period during which you work or are paid for at least 1,000 hours. A plan year may be either a calendar year (for example, January through December) or a different 12-month period (for example, July through June), and it usually coincides with the fiscal year of the plan.

✔ **Years of service:** This term refers to the number of years that you've worked for your employer. For most plans, 1,000 hours in a plan year constitutes a year of service for purposes of qualifying to receive retirement benefits from the plan.

✔ **Accrued benefit:** The term *accrued benefit* refers to the amount of your normal retirement benefit that you've earned at any given point in your career. The term *total accrued benefit* refers to the total amount of your accrued benefits earned as of a particular date.

The meaning of "tax-qualified plan"

ERISA sets the framework that governs all tax-qualified retirement plans. If a plan fulfills all the specified requirements set out in ERISA and the Internal Revenue Code, it's qualified to receive favorable tax treatment by the IRS — and then it's considered a tax-qualified plan (see the section "Gotta Do It: ERISA's Requirements for Pension Plans" later in this chapter for more details on the requirements). Qualified retirement plans serve two major functions: They provide employee benefits and they defer taxes. Some of the benefits of tax-qualified plans include the following:

✔ **Employers can take a tax deduction for their plan contributions.** As a general rule, employer contributions to the plan are deductible in the year made as long as they're made before the due date for the corporate tax return (including extensions).

✔ **Employees don't have to pay taxes on plan assets until they receive the money.** In other words, pension plans are *tax-exempt,* meaning that they don't pay taxes on the pension fund. The contributions continue to earn interest, tax-free, until the money is distributed. A participant's obligation to pay taxes is deferred until he or she receives payments from the plan.

✔ **Both participants and employers generally get tax breaks when involved in retirement plans.** Income tax brackets are generally lower at the time benefits are received following the participant's retirement or death. This means that the government will be able to take less of your money.

Also, Social Security taxes are paid neither on employer contributions to tax-qualified retirement plans nor on distributions to participants from such plans.

✔ **Qualified plans provide a means of forced savings.** It's difficult for most people to save money outside of a retirement plan, so having one forces you to save, thereby cushioning your retirement.

Qualified plans provide protection of assets from creditors' claims. Because the goal of ERISA is to provide and secure your retirement benefits, it provides protection for these assets from creditors who think you should use your retirement fund to pay them. See Chapter 16 for more information on what protections are provided for the different types of plans and how you can better plan to keep your assets safe from your creditors before your financial situation worsens.

An overview of pension plans covered by ERISA

Tax-qualified ERISA pension plans usually come in two varieties: *defined benefit plans* and *defined contribution plans.* Even though we discuss these plans in detail in Chapter 3, it's important to understand the basics now so that you can identify the type of plan you have. After you know what type of plan you have, you can examine the rules that govern the different plans and determine how to make sure you get the benefits that you deserve. Your employer may have one of these types of plans, both, or none at all:

✔ **Defined benefit plans:** Under a traditional defined benefit plan, the level of benefits you receive at retirement is fixed. However, the employer's contributions in any given year are *not* fixed. All of the employer's contributions are placed in a single account (not in an individual account for just you). The promised benefit that a participant is to receive is calculated based on factors such as age, salary, and years of service.

When the employer provides the money to fund the plan, it's considered an *employer funded* plan. The management of a defined benefit plan and the investment of the plan's assets are within the employer's control. Defined benefit plans are insured by the federal government's insurance company, the Pension Benefit Guaranty Corporation (PBGC). So if a plan fails, most participants will be paid most of their benefits, up to $49,500 per year.

Examples of defined benefit plans include cash balance plans and 412(i) plans (which are also known as fully insured plans).

✔ **Defined contribution plans:** These types of plans don't promise a specific benefit amount that you receive at retirement. Instead, they're funded during your employment by you, your employer, or both of you. The final payout depends on how much you and your employer contribute and how well your investments perform.

Examples of defined contribution plans include 401(k) plans, Employee Stock Ownership Plans (ESOPs), money purchase plans, and profit-sharing plans.

Gotta Do It: ERISA's Requirements for Pension Plans

 At a bare minimum, ERISA requires that certain standards be met in order for private pension plans to be considered tax-qualified (and therefore receive favorable tax treatment and other benefits). Employers don't have to establish retirement plans, but those that do must comply with the following requirements:

- ✔ Regularly and automatically provide participants with important information about the plan

- ✔ Set minimum standards for employee participation in the plan and for employer funding

- ✔ Impose fiduciary duties on those who administer a plan (in other words, set the standards of conduct, responsibilities, and obligations that must be followed by those in charge of the plan)

- ✔ Provide participants the right to sue for the recovery of benefits and breaches of fiduciary duties

- ✔ Guarantee the payment of certain benefits through the PBGC, which is the federal agency that insures the pensions of employees covered by private defined benefit pension plans

We discuss all these requirements in the following sections.

Disclosing certain plan information

Plan administrators are required by ERISA to give you (in writing) the most important facts about your retirement plan's features and funding. Some of these facts must be provided to you automatically, and other facts are available to you upon your written request. Some are free of charge and others require you to pay a copying fee.

By reviewing the information provided, you become an informed participant. Only after understanding what your plan requires of you and how you become eligible for benefits can you take the steps necessary to protect your rights to your earned benefits. The list of information that you're entitled to receive includes the following:

- ✔ **The summary plan description:** One of the most important documents that you're entitled to receive is called the *summary plan description,* or SPD. This document gives you a summary of what the plan provides and how it operates. Your plan administrator is legally obligated to give you a copy of the SPD when you become a participant of an ERISA-covered plan or when you start receiving benefits under the plan. You must be provided with a copy of the SPD within 30 days of your written request to your employer.

If the plan is ever changed substantially, you must be informed through a document called the *summary of material modifications,* which must be given to you free of charge. Plans are also required to provide updated versions of the SPD from time to time.

✔ **Documents and instructions under which the plan operates:** This group of documents and instructions includes the plan document (the complete document upon which the summary plan description is based), the collective bargaining agreement, and the trust agreement. Upon your written request, this information is available to you free of charge for your inspection. Or for a reasonable copying fee, you can request in writing that a copy of the information be mailed to you.

✔ **The summary annual report:** You're entitled to automatically receive the summary annual report (SAR) yearly and free of charge. This document is a summary of the annual financial report that most retirement plans must file with the Department of Labor on a document called the Form 5500. (You can see a sample Form 5500 at `www.irs.gov/forms pubs;` just search for it by name.)

Effective for plan years beginning after December 31, 2007, the Pension Protection Act of 2006 (PPA) has repealed the requirement that defined benefit plans provide a SAR. Instead, under the PPA, participants must be provided with an annual funding notice (for each plan year) that includes more specific information than previously required in the SAR.

To find out more about your plan's assets and other financial matters concerning the plan, you may also want to ask your plan administrator for a copy of its full annual report.

✔ **Notice to plan participants who are in underfunded plans:** A defined benefit plan that's less than 90 percent funded must give notice to its participants by reporting the funding level of the plan. This notice must be provided free of charge and automatically within two months after the due date for filing the annual report.

Federal law requires all multiemployer defined benefit plans to provide an annual notice to participants, beneficiaries, and other interested parties (including the PBGC) about the plans' funding status.

The PPA increased the levels at which notice is required, and effective for plan years beginning after December 31, 2007, you must be notified within 30 days after benefit restrictions have been imposed on your defined benefit plan as a result of its not reaching certain target percentage limits for funding. In 2008, for example, a plan that's not within 92 percent of its target will be subject to restrictions; this percentage increases each year until 2011, when you'll be notified if your plan isn't 100 percent funded.

- **Individual benefit statement:** Prior to the PPA, you were entitled to receive this statement, which describes your *total accrued benefits* (total benefits earned to date) and total nonforfeitable benefits (total of those benefits that can't be taken away from you), upon written request once every 12 months, at no charge to you.

For plan years starting after December 31, 2006, defined contribution plans must provide benefit statements to participants automatically, on a quarterly basis if you self-direct your investments and on a yearly basis if you don't. (See Chapter 6 for more about self-directed investments.) In the case of defined benefit plans, the plan must either provide a statement every three years or provide an annual notice informing participants of their right to request such a statement in any given year. These statements are provided at no charge to you.

The PPA has made significant changes to what these statements must provide, and although the model benefit statements that may be used by plan administrators aren't expected to be out before August 17, 2007, it's anticipated that the statements will contain more detailed benefit information.

See Chapter 8 for more details about each of these documents and how to request information in writing.

Setting minimum standards for participation, accrual, and vesting

Vesting refers to the amount of time that you must work before you earn the right to your accrued benefits. When you're *fully vested,* this means that your accrued benefits belong to you, even if you leave the company before retirement age. It's important to know the rules and when you can expect to be fully vested. Otherwise you may find yourself working forever (because you won't know when to stop) or not working long enough to get all the benefits that you've earned.

Prior to ERISA, pension plan benefits were insecure because employees were often required to work many years before they became vested in their retirement plans. Because of ERISA, minimum standards for counting years of service for vesting purposes exist, which means that plan benefits are more stable. Plans may provide more generous vesting rules, but ERISA sets the minimum standards that we describe in the following sections. (Check out Chapter 7 for more information about eligibility, accrual, and vesting.)

Age and length of service

You must be permitted to participate in a pension plan if you've reached the age of 21 and have completed one year of service. Plans other than 401(k)s can require two years of service before you're eligible to participate. However, if the plan requires two years of service for eligibility, your benefits under the plan must be 100 percent vested (not forfeitable) at all times. And if at the time you're hired, you're an older worker who's closer to retirement, your employer can't exclude you from plan participation on the grounds of age.

The protection of your benefits from reduction or elimination

Your pension plan provides you with a number of different rights and options, and some of these rights are *protected.* Generally speaking, protected rights can't be reduced or eliminated; nor can they be granted or denied based on the whim of your employer on any given day. Your protected rights include the following:

- ✔ **Early retirement benefits:** If your employer offers the option to retire earlier than the normal retirement age, the employer can't amend the plan in order to eliminate the right to take such early retirement as it relates to benefits that you accrued before the amendment. But your employer can amend the plan to take this right away for benefits that you accrue after the date of the amendment.

- ✔ **Retirement-type subsidies:** These are subsidies paid under the plan that are above and beyond the benefit paid under the plan's basic benefit formula. Your employer can't retroactively eliminate these types of subsidies for employees who ultimately meet the conditions for the benefit. But the employer can eliminate the benefit for service in future years.

   In addition, the employer can tell employees that if they want to take the retirement-type subsidy, they won't receive any further growth in their benefit for service after the amendment eliminating the subsidy. This is known as *benefit wear-away.*

- ✔ **Accrued benefits:** Even though ERISA doesn't prohibit your employer from amending its plan to reduce the rates that benefits will accrue in the future, your employer must give you written notice of a significant reduction in the rate of benefits before the plan amendment goes into effect. In some cases, the amendment will not be effective if the notice isn't given.

Spelling out fiduciary obligations

ERISA sets forth fiduciary obligations to protect your plan from mismanagement and misuse of assets. These obligations apply to anyone who has certain responsibilities to the plan or exercises authority or control over the plan, such as administering it, managing it, or disposing of the plan's assets. The primary responsibility of a fiduciary is to run the plan solely in the interest of participants and beneficiaries. (In other words, he or she works on behalf of your interests, not the company's.) A fiduciary must exercise care, skill, and prudence and also must diversify plan investments to minimize the risk of large losses. He or she must follow the terms of the plan documents unless, of course, the documents are inconsistent with ERISA. In that case, ERISA should be followed.

In addition to these fiduciary duties, ERISA prohibits fiduciaries from getting involved in a *conflict of interest.* A conflict of interest in this case could be, among other things, dealing with plan assets in the fiduciary's own interest, acting in a manner that's adverse to the interests of the plan or its participants, or receiving any consideration (dollars or other means of compensation) for the fiduciary's own personal account.

No consent is necessary for a person to be considered a fiduciary. If a person has authority or exercises authority or control as explained earlier in the section, he or she can be considered a fiduciary. For example, the following individuals are considered to be plan fiduciaries:

- Plan trustees
- Plan administrators
- Members of a plan's investment or administrative committee
- Investment managers
- Any person who selects or appoints any of the previously mentioned people

Chapter 10 has what you need to know about keeping an eye on your pension plan's fiduciaries.

Providing the right to file suit

Under ERISA you have a responsibility to file a claim for the benefits that you're due under your plan. And even more importantly, your plan is required to set forth a reasonable procedure for processing your benefits claim and for appealing if your claim is denied. Review your SPD to see how your plan's claim procedure works (see the earlier section "Disclosing certain plan information" for more about the SPD).

If your plan fails to set up a claims procedure, the law requires you to present your claim to the plan administrator, an officer of your employer, or the unit that usually handles claims procedures. Other than notifying the plan administrator or the other folks we mention, your hands are pretty much tied because suing won't get you very far (a procedure will likely be specified, but you won't be paid any damages for your troubles).

In the following sections, we explain the general procedure set forth by ERISA for appealing a denied claim and filing suit.

Appealing a denial

Your claim for benefits may be *denied in whole* if you haven't yet worked for your employer for the minimum number of years, if you aren't the required age, or if you're otherwise not eligible for benefits. Or it may be *denied in part* (meaning you don't get all the benefits you think you have coming) if you weren't properly credited for the time you worked for this employer, if the benefits were computed with the wrong interest rate, or if the plan simply wants you to submit additional information.

If your claim for benefits is denied in whole or in part, the plan is obligated to notify you of this in writing. This notification must be given within 90 days of the plan's receipt of your claim for benefits, and it must state the reasons for the denial and the special plan provisions upon which the denial is based. The written notice of the denial must also explain how to file an appeal.

The plan must provide you with at least 60 days to appeal any denial, and typically the plan then has 60 days within which to issue its ruling. If the plan notifies you in writing that it must hold a hearing, it may take an additional 60 days to issue its ruling.

Exhausting your administrative remedies

Ultimately, the plan must notify you of its final decision regarding your appeal. It must also include the reasons that support its decision and any references to the relevant plan documents. If the plan rules against you and you disagree with this final ruling, your ship is not yet sunk. As long as you've followed and completed (in timely manner) all the steps available to you as spelled out in your plan's claim procedure, you've *exhausted your administrative remedies* (yes, that's a technical term). If you've made it this far, courts will permit you to file a lawsuit seeking your benefits under ERISA.

If you don't exhaust your administrative remedies, you could lose the right to sue in court. Courts may excuse a failure to exhaust if exhaustion is impossible for some reason or if it would be a completely futile exercise, but if at all possible, we recommend that you exhaust.

See Chapter 18 for full details about undergoing the appeal process.

Filing a civil action under ERISA

As long as you've exhausted your administrative remedies as outlined in your plan's claim procedure, you're entitled to file a civil action in a federal district court in order to do any of the following:

- ✓ Recover the benefits due to you and to enforce your rights under the plan
- ✓ Obtain access to the plan documents that you're entitled to receive and that you requested in writing (and that were never given to you)
- ✓ Clarify your right to future benefits

✔ Stop any act that violates the terms of your plan

✔ Stop any act that violates the fiduciary obligations of ERISA, such as the plan's failure to act for the exclusive benefit of the participants or using the assets of the plan for interested parties

✔ Stop the plan from improperly valuing plan assets

✔ Enforce your right to be provided a statement of your vested benefits after you've terminated employment

✔ Obtain review of any action of the PBGC that affects you adversely

We explain how to find and hire a pension attorney in Chapter 19 and how to prepare for pension litigation in Chapter 20.

Knowing that your employer can't retaliate

Luckily, ERISA prohibits employers from retaliating against its employees in order to avoid paying a benefit. In other words, it's unlawful for an employer to discharge, fine, suspend, expel, discipline, or discriminate against any employee or his or her beneficiary for the purpose of interfering with their rights under the plan or the law.

If you're worried about how the actions you take to enforce your legal rights may affect your job or your work environment, stop right there and remember this: Your employer can't take any of these actions if you exercise any of your rights or prospective rights under a plan or under ERISA (or if you give information or testimony in a proceeding that's related to ERISA). It goes without saying that the use of force or violence to coerce or intimidate you for the purpose of interfering with your rights or prospective rights isn't permitted and is punishable by a fine of up to $10,000 and/or up to one year in prison.

You should note, though, that some employers still do illegal things. If your employer does retaliate against you, it sometimes can be a long and expensive process to have the statute enforced.

Federally enforcing pension rights

ERISA was enacted to protect your rights in qualified private retirement plans by setting the minimum standards we discuss in the previous sections and by providing remedies for you in case all doesn't go as planned. The Department of Labor and the Internal Revenue Service are in charge of interpreting and enforcing your rights under ERISA. If you have a defined benefit plan, it's most likely protected and insured by the PBGC.

The Department of Labor

The Department of Labor (DOL) has the authority to enforce Title I of ERISA, which sets forth participant rights and certain employer and fiduciary duties. The DOL is also responsible for making sure that pension plans operate properly and that their assets are managed prudently.

The DOL's Employee Benefits Security Administration (EBSA) is the agency that enforces the rules governing the conduct of plan managers, the investment of plan assets, the reporting and disclosure of plan information, and the enforcement of the fiduciary provisions of ERISA.

Any of the plan documents we identify earlier in the chapter can be obtained directly from the DOL for a nominal copying charge, which they'll bill you for. You can find out more information about getting these documents from the DOL by going to www.dol.gov/ebsa/publications/how_to_obtain_docs.html.

If you don't have Internet access (or you just like traditional communication), here's the mailing address and the phone number of the DOL:

U.S. Department of Labor
Employee Benefits Security Administration
EBSA Public Disclosure Room
200 Constitution Avenue, NW, Room N-1513
Washington, DC 20210
Phone: 202-693-8673

The Internal Revenue Service

The U.S. Treasury Department's Internal Revenue Service (IRS) is responsible for ensuring compliance with the Internal Revenue Code and its rules for operating a tax-qualified pension plan, including pension plan funding and vesting requirements.

The IRS Web site (www.irs.gov) contains forms and documents that you can easily download. It also provides information about a variety of tax topics, including IRAs and other retirement plans. Finally, if you want to, you can download publications dealing with tax changes and new legislation.

The Pension Benefit Guaranty Corporation

ERISA established the Pension Benefit Guaranty Corporation (PBGC), which is an agency of the federal government that guarantees and insures defined benefit plans by administering the plan termination insurance program. For example, if you're in a defined benefit pension plan that doesn't have enough money to pay you all the benefits that you've been promised, the PBGC may terminate your plan, take it over, and pay out benefits up to the current limits set by law. (In 2007, the maximum amount guaranteed for retirees age 65 is $49,500 per year. The max amount is a bit higher or lower depending on whether you're over or under age 65.)

How is the PBGC able to do this? The sponsors of the defined benefit plans pay insurance premiums established by Congress, just like insurance premiums you pay for things like auto or homeowner's insurance. In addition to the insurance premiums, the PBGC's operations are financed by investment income.

To find out more about the PBGC and to see whether it insures your pension, go to www.pbgc.gov. You can also reach the PBGC by e-mail (through a link on the Web site) or by mail or phone at:

PBGC
P.O. Box 151750
Alexandria, VA 22315-1750
Phone: 800-400-7242

When contacting the PBGC, it's helpful if you provide your Social Security number and the plan's name or number, which is located in the upper left corner of correspondence to you from the PBGC. You can also find this information on the plan documents.

Chapter 3

Exploring the World of Tax-Qualified Plans

*T*he government supports employment-based retirement benefits that are voluntarily provided by businesses. It shows its support by granting employers favorable tax treatment as long as their retirement plans meet certain requirements set out by the Internal Revenue Code and the Employee Retirement Income Security Act of 1974 (ERISA). If a retirement plan satisfies such requirements, it is considered *tax-qualified.* As we discuss in Chapter 2, the perks of tax-qualified plans are a big deal for everyone: Employers can take a tax deduction for their plan contributions, employees don't pay taxes on plan assets until they receive the money, and earnings on qualified plans are tax-deferred.

In this chapter, we hit the highlights of qualified plans and discuss why some plans are a better fit than others. See Appendix B for charts that compare the major types of tax-qualified plans and list the limitations on contributions and benefits.

You Get What You Give: Defined Contribution Plans

Defined contribution plans are those in which you, your employer, or both of you contribute money to an investment account whose purpose is to accrue money for your retirement. In a defined contribution plan:

✔ An individual account is provided for each employee, into which the employee or the employer (or both) contributes. The contributions can be at a set rate or be based on a percentage of the employee's compensation. The contributions are then invested on the employee's behalf. Employer contributions may be either mandatory or discretionary, depending on the type of plan.

✔ An employee has no way of knowing how much the plan will ultimately provide upon retirement. The final payout is based on the amount of yearly contributions made before retirement and how well the investments perform (see Chapter 6 for more about the investing of plan assets).

✔ There are restrictions as to when and how the funds can be withdrawn without being socked with penalties.

We discuss these important basics of defined contribution plans and the many different types of plans in the following sections.

Beginning with basics on benefits, contributions, and limitations

Employers that are considering whether to sponsor a defined contribution plan have several options. All the options take into consideration the benefits that the employer hopes to offer employees, the contributions the employer is able to make or wants to commit to making, and the maximum contribution limits that change year to year in order to keep up with inflation.

What factors affect your ultimate retirement benefit?

Defined contribution plans are referred to as *individual account plans*. Each participant's ultimate benefit under the plan is dependent on the amount that has accumulated in the participant's plan account at the time the employee begins receiving benefits. While the contributions are defined or determined each year, the ultimate retirement benefit is based on these factors:

✔ **Credits:** A participant's account under a defined contribution plan may be credited with the following:

• Employer and employee contributions

• Investment earnings or losses

In the case of profit-sharing plans, the participant's account is also credited with forfeitures from the accounts of other participants who terminate employment before being fully vested under the plan.

✔ **Deductions:** Plan administrative expenses may be charged against the account.

What's the maximum contribution?

The maximum contribution to an individual's account under a defined contribution plan for a given year is the lesser of 100 percent of the individual's compensation or a specific dollar limit. For example, in 2007, the dollar limit for employer and employee contributions and any forfeitures is $45,000. These maximum contribution amounts by the employer and employee are called the *limitations on annual additions.* Investment earnings aren't part of the annual additions.

Although the dollar limit is $45,000 in 2007, this amount is adjusted annually due to inflation. The Internal Revenue Service (IRS) typically issues a notice in October or November of each year to unveil the limits for the following year. Go to www.irs.gov to get this updated information.

Employee contributions to 401(k) plans (which we discuss later in this chapter and also in Chapter 4) fall under their own set of limitations. In this type of plan, an employee can elect to have the employer contribute, on a pretax basis, a portion of his or her wages. These wages, which are deferred from the employee on a salary reduction basis, are contributed directly to the 401(k) plan. These deferred wages are called *elective deferrals.*

The maximum elective deferral that an individual can defer into a 401(k) plan for a given year is limited to the lesser of 100 percent of compensation or a specific dollar amount set by the IRS, which is adjusted each year for inflation. (The dollar amount for 2007 is $15,500.) Remember that the elective deferrals are included in the maximum amount that can be contributed yearly to a defined contribution plan. In other words, the $15,500 is part of the $45,000 basic limit (for 2007).

Individuals age 50 or older are permitted to defer up to an additional $5,000 to a defined contribution plan each year. These additional contributions are called *catch-up contributions* because they're designed to help older employees who haven't yet saved enough to "catch up." These contributions are in addition to both the normal elective deferral limits and the annual addition limitations. So for 2007, an individual age 50 or older can defer a total of $20,500 ($15,500 + $5,000) and receive total contributions to the plan of $50,000 ($45,000 + $5,000).

How and when can you make withdrawals?

Withdrawals from defined contribution plans are subject to strict rules. As a general rule, distributions aren't allowed before you terminate employment with the employer that's sponsoring the plan. However, under certain circumstances, distributions can be made prior to termination. These distributions, which are referred to as *in-service distributions,* are usually restricted to the occurrence of certain events, such as when you reach a certain age (59½, for example) or when hardships occur (maybe you need money for medical expenses or to prevent eviction or foreclosure). In Chapter 9, we discuss distributions in more detail.

In order for withdrawals or in-service distributions to even be considered, they must be provided for in your plan document. Make sure you have a copy of your summary plan description (SPD) early on to see what benefits your plan provides in the event that you experience a hardship and need a little help. (Check out Chapter 2 for more on the SPD.)

Surveying different defined contribution plans

These days more companies are offering defined contribution plans rather than defined benefit plans. Part of the reason is because these plans provide more options to employers in terms of when and how they choose to contribute, or whether they contribute at all. Employees share the responsibility of contributing to their defined contribution retirement plans with their employers, thereby lessening the burden on those employers who choose to contribute to their employees' retirement accounts. Defined contribution plans also are inexpensive to set up and administer compared to defined benefit plans. This is because defined benefit plans involve extra expenses, such as hiring an actuary to determine the proper funding levels for future defined benefits.

Depending on the employer's size, how much it's financially able to contribute, and how much it's willing to contribute, there are a variety of defined contribution plans to choose from. We explain them in the following sections.

You'll find two of the charts in Appendix B particularly helpful for comparing these types of plans: the Comparison of Types of Tax-Qualified Retirement Plans chart and the Retirement Plan Dollar and Percentage Limits chart.

Profit-sharing plans

Profit-sharing plans are the most flexible of all qualified plans and are used for sharing profits from the business with employees, whether or not the business has profits in a given year. If it has been a good year, the employer may be more inclined to make a generous contribution, but that's its choice. The employer isn't obligated to make contributions to the plan every year, but each year that it does, it may contribute any amount between 0 percent and 25 percent (or 15 percent for plan years commencing prior to 2002) of the annual compensation of the covered employees. Because employer contributions aren't mandatory, the contributions that employers make are called *discretionary contributions*. Employees don't contribute to these plans.

Profit-sharing plans are a great choice for employers that aren't sure how much they can contribute each year. Because these plans aren't actually tied to profits and because the contributions are totally discretionary on a year-to-year basis, what's not for the employer to like?

It's also easy to see why profit-sharing plans are so popular among employees. To employees, these plans mean that an additional chunk of money is being put away for their retirement. And even though it's discretionary whether they'll receive a profit-sharing contribution each year, when they do, it's a bonus, because employees receive it without contributing anything (unless you count the time and energy that they contribute to the company each day).

401(k) plans

A *401(k) plan* is a retirement plan sponsored by the employer that allows the employees to elect to defer a portion of their compensation into the plan. These deferrals, which are called *elective deferrals,* are typically made on a pretax basis, meaning that the money is contributed with pretax dollars. Taxes are deferred until the money is taken out.

It's up to the employer whether it wants to have a 401(k) plan to which only the employees contribute or whether the employer itself will also contribute in some way, such as matching its employees' contributions or making profit-sharing contributions (which are referred to as *employer nonelective contributions*). A 401(k) plan is a good choice for employers that want their employees to help with the funding of their retirement benefits.

With a 401(k) plan, not only are you provided with a retirement plan into which you can (and should) defer wages, tax-free, but if your employer offers to match your contribution or provide profit-sharing contributions, this is like free money to you. Simply put, you'll receive retirement contributions that you wouldn't otherwise get if you didn't defer on your own. You'd be crazy not to take full advantage of any match that's offered.

Because of the recent popularity of 401(k) plans, which allow both employers and employees to make pretax retirement contributions, we devote Chapter 4 to these plans.

Cross-tested profit-sharing plans

A *cross-tested profit-sharing plan* is a profit-sharing plan that allows employers to provide different levels of contributions to different classifications of employees. In other words, this plan allows employers to have a contribution percentage formula for one category of participants that's greater than the contribution percentage formula for other categories of participants. These plans are *cross-tested,* meaning that special tests (called *nondiscrimination tests*) are applied to make sure the plan doesn't discriminate in favor of the highly compensated employees (HCEs). As with other profit-sharing plans, the amount of the contribution is discretionary and employees don't contribute.

Because cross-tested plans can be designed to provide higher levels of contributions to some classes of employees and not others, employers can provide older or more highly compensated employees (including the owners) with larger retirement plan contributions than are provided to other employees. HCEs often prefer increased retirement plan contributions over increased compensation because they understand and appreciate the tax benefits of qualified plans. The only downside to this type of plan is that it's more complicated for the employer to administer than an ordinary profit-sharing plan. However, this disadvantage may be outweighed by the benefits.

As a general rule, the contributions under a cross-tested plan on behalf of HCEs can't be more than three times the percentage of compensation contributed on behalf of non–highly compensated employees (NHCEs). For example, if HCEs receive a contribution of 9 percent of compensation, NHCEs must receive at least 3 percent of compensation.

Money purchase pension plans

A *money purchase pension plan* is funded by the employer, which may contribute up to 25 percent of the compensation of all eligible employees. The employer's contributions to the plan are fixed without regard to the employer's profits. Instead, they're usually based on a fixed percentage of each participant's compensation. Employees don't contribute to this type of plan.

The money purchase plan may be appropriate for employers that can determine profit trends and don't mind being required to make yearly contributions to the plan. The obligation on the part of the employer to fund a money purchase pension plan makes this type of plan different from most profit-sharing plans. As we explain earlier in this chapter, it's okay if employers choose not to contribute to profit-sharing plans because their contributions are discretionary. But with a money purchase pension plan, the company's contributions are mandatory. If the company fails to make a contribution, it can incur a penalty tax. So if the company has a bad year financially and can't afford to make the contribution it said it would, it's too bad, so sad for the company. These days, employers are frequently choosing not to adopt money purchase pension plans (or they're rethinking the continuation of them). This is because profit-sharing plans now provide companies tax-deductible advantages, with flexibility and discretion to boot.

From your point of view as an employee, this is a great deal. Your employer has committed to making annual contributions on your behalf. Essentially, you're being rewarded for your loyalty. Do remember that money purchase plans require that the plan provide survivor benefits for spouses (unless the employee and spouse agree to forego such benefits).

Plans that are collectively bargained by unions are often money purchase pension plans because the collective bargaining agreements require mandatory employer contributions to the plans.

Target benefit pension plans

A *target benefit pension plan* is a type of defined contribution plan under which contributions are weighted in favor of older employees. For example, a 55-year-old employee may receive a contribution equal to 20 percent of compensation, while a 35-year-old employee may receive 8 percent in the same plan. For the most part, target benefit plans have been replaced by cross-tested profit-sharing plans, which provide greater flexibility in terms of both contributions and plan design than target benefit plans.

Employee stock ownership plans

An *employee stock ownership plan* (ESOP) is a tax-qualified defined contribution plan that allows employees to become owners of their employer's stock. In fact, stock ownership is the whole purpose of ESOPs — they're put into place to encourage employees to participate in corporate ownership. An ESOP is the only employee benefit plan that's required by law to invest primarily in the stock of the sponsoring employer.

ESOPs may be used by corporations to raise capital for the corporation or, in the case of a privately held company, to purchase stock from a shareholder. Tax advantages of the ESOP make the borrowing of funds less expensive through the ESOP than if the corporation borrowed the funds directly from a bank.

One potential danger of an ESOP for plan participants is the lack of diversification of the investments, because at least 50 percent of the plan's assets is required to be invested in stock of the sponsoring employer. It's never a good idea to have a majority of your assets in any particular investment, but it can be particularly devastating when that one particular investment is in the stock of your employer. In such a situation, the employer's failure can cost you not only your job but your retirement savings as well. Other downsides for the participants can include the following:

- ✔ Employee securities can be improperly valued.
- ✔ Employee stock can be improperly allocated to individual participant accounts.
- ✔ Voting rights may not be provided to plan participants.
- ✔ The employer's loans aren't primarily in the interests of plan participants.
- ✔ Fraud, embezzlement, theft, or other criminal actions can occur.

Benefits from the Boss: Defined Benefit Plans

Defined benefit plans are traditional retirement plans that promise a fixed monthly benefit for life when an employee retires (much like Social Security). The plan may state this promised benefit as an exact dollar amount, such as $100 per month at retirement. Or the employer may calculate a benefit through a plan formula typically based on the employee's age, years of service, and average compensation for a certain period of time. Defined benefit plans are generally funded entirely by the employer, meaning that employees don't contribute to these plans.

The employer's contribution in any given year isn't fixed, but it's determined actuarially. For example, the plan's actuary estimates how much the plan will ultimately have to pay in benefits and how much investment return the plan will earn. Using complex formulas, the actuary then tells the employer how much it should contribute in each year so that the plan will be able to keep its benefit promises. Because it's unlikely that the actuary's guesstimates about the future will be completely accurate, the actuary is constantly adjusting the amount that the employer will have to contribute in each future year. For example, if the actuary guesses that the plan will earn 8 percent on investments but the plan actually makes 10 percent, the plan will then have more assets than the actuary predicted, which means that the employer may be able to reduce future contributions for a period of time.

Despite the large selection of defined contribution plans (which we discuss earlier in this chapter), there are only three types of defined benefit plans: the traditional defined benefit plan, the cash balance (or hybrid) plan, and the 412(i) plan. We discuss these plans, as well as basics about the benefits, contributions, and limitations to defined benefit plans, in the following sections.

A few terms may be new to you as you read more about defined benefit plans. Understanding these terms will help you better understand the plans themselves (we go into more detail about these terms in Chapter 9):

- ✔ An *accrued benefit* is the portion of your normal retirement benefit that you have earned at a given point in your career. For example, under a traditional defined benefit plan, the accrued benefit is the amount that you would receive monthly for life starting at the plan's normal retirement age (generally, age 62 to 65).

- ✔ An *annuity* is a series of equal payments to a person at evenly spaced intervals, usually for life.

 ✔ A *lump sum* is exactly what it sounds like: You receive all your benefits at once. However, if you want your benefits distributed in one fell swoop rather than over a period of time, the lump-sum distribution must be the present value of the accrued benefit. *Present value* simply means the value, in today's dollars, of promised future payments. Most traditional defined benefit plans don't permit lump-sum distributions.

Looking at benefits, contributions, and limitations

Unlike limitations to defined contribution plans that are based on annual contributions *to* the plan, the limitations on defined benefit plans are based on the benefits that can be distributed *from* the plan. The maximum annual benefit under a defined benefit plan is the lesser of 100 percent of average annual compensation or a specific dollar amount, which is adjusted each year for inflation. (The dollar amount for 2007 is $180,000.) The annual benefit limit is based on benefits commencing at age 62. So, the limit is reduced for benefit payments commencing prior to age 62 and increased for benefit payments commencing after age 65.

The IRS adjusts the dollar amounts each year based on the preceding 12-month period rates of inflation. The updated dollar limits are usually announced after September 30 each year, usually sometime in October. Go to www.irs.gov for the updated dollar limits.

Benefits for participants with fewer than 10 years of participation under the plan must be proportionately reduced. For example, a retiring participant with five years of participation in a defined benefit plan would have a maximum annual benefit of 50 percent of compensation.

Checking out different defined benefit plans

The different types of defined benefit plans provide different advantages and disadvantages. For example, traditional defined benefit plans are best for older employees who have spent all or most of their careers with a single employer. Younger employees who may change jobs several times during their careers may benefit more from cash balance plans. We explain the details in the following sections.

Traditional defined benefit plans

Under a *traditional defined benefit plan,* the level of benefits you'll receive at retirement is fixed by the plan's formula. However, the employer's contribution in any given year varies according to the plan's actuarial assumptions, methods, and experience. The plan is based on three factors: your age, your salary, and the number of years you've generously given of yourself to your employer's workforce. Because of this, your pension benefit grows slowly at first but takes off as you get older, your salary increases, and you've put more years of service into the pot.

There can be an endless set of variations for the employer to choose from in selecting a formula that designates how you receive a defined benefit plan's benefits. Your plan must state the selected formula in the SPD. Some examples of plan formulas include the following:

- ✔ **Flat benefit plan:** The benefit under the plan is a flat dollar amount after a specified number of years. For example, a participant who has at least 10 years of service may receive a benefit of $500 per month at age 65.

- ✔ **Fixed benefit plan:** The benefit under the plan is a fixed percentage of compensation — such as 10 percent of your average monthly compensation starting at age 65.

- ✔ **Unit benefit plan:** The benefit under the plan is based on either a specified unit dollar amount multiplied by years of service or a percentage of compensation multiplied by years of service.

Contributions by the employer to a defined benefit plan are mandatory. ERISA sets minimum funding rules to ensure that sufficient money is available to pay promised future benefits to you when you retire. These funding rules have been amended by the Pension Protection Act of 2006. The employer is now allowed to contribute larger amounts than projected to ensure proper funding for the future defined benefit. However, if the plan investments fall below what's projected, the employer is required to make additional contributions to make up for the shortfall. Any employer that fails to comply with the minimum funding requirements is subject to severe sanctions provided by ERISA for its failure to meet the funding obligations.

Some of the advantages of traditional defined benefit plans include the following:

- ✔ Guaranteed retirement income security for employees

- ✔ No investment risk to participants

- ✔ Is funded entirely by the employer

- ✔ Rewards an employee's longevity and age with higher benefits

Ask Janet about cash balance plans?

How did my defined benefit plan become underfunded?

Today, some defined benefit plans are under-funded, which means that they don't have enough assets to pay all of the benefits that have already been earned. How does this happen? There are five major reasons:

✔ The plan may have suffered poor invest-ment performance.

✔ The employer may not have been contribut-ing enough to the plan, even though the employer may have been complying with ERISA's minimum funding standards.

✔ Interest rates may have fallen, therefore increasing the expense of paying benefits.

✔ Some employers increased benefit levels a few years back and haven't yet fully funded those benefit increases.

✔ Some plans allow employees to choose among different forms of benefits (for example, an employee may be allowed to choose a lump-sum distribution instead of an annuity), and sometimes one benefit turns out to be especially valuable and is selected by larger-than-expected numbers of employees.

Due to the uncertainty of the funding require-ments, many employers have been terminating their traditional defined benefit plans in recent years and replacing them with 401(k) plans or cash balance plans.

Employers like the idea of providing their employees with a guaranteed level of retirement benefits with the traditional defined benefit plan. But that's about it for the plus side; defined benefit plans are more expensive for employers to administer than defined contribution plans. And they're somewhat inflexible due to the mandatory funding obligations.

Today, many traditional defined benefit plans are in trouble because the cash that's available to meet these promised future benefits is dependent on the fluctuations of the plan's investment portfolio. In other words, the employer contributes to the pension plan, and the plan managers then invest the con-tributions in order to earn interest and increase the fund balance. Because a defined benefit plan funds a benefit to be paid in the future, the employer bears the risk that the fund won't be sufficiently funded at the time that retirement distributions need to be paid out. When the stock market is stag-nant or when the economy is poor, the fund's investments may grow too slowly. Over 70 percent of the companies in the S&P 500 have defined benefit plans, and the deficits in these plans amount to more than $182 billion! In the event that the plan isn't sufficiently funded, the employer must increase its contributions to the plan.

Cash balance or hybrid plans

A recent trend, especially among large employers, has been to convert traditional defined benefit plans to *hybrid pension plans,* which are also known as *cash balance plans.* These plans are defined benefit plans that are designed to mimic the benefits of defined contribution plans.

Even though cash balance plans are designed to mimic defined contribution plans, they contain many of the most important advantages of defined benefit plans. For example, benefits don't depend on how much an employee is willing or able to contribute, as in a 401(k) plan, and the employer bears the investment risk (not the employee). And like the traditional defined benefit plan, the cash balance plan offers payment of an employee's benefit in the form of a series of payments for life. Almost all cash balance plans, however, also offer a lump sum payment option, which is the form of benefit that most cash balance participants elect.

The retirement benefits in a cash balance plan are described differently than in a traditional defined benefit plan, in which benefits are expressed as a retirement annuity. In a cash balance plan the benefit is expressed as an account balance, a dollar amount, that grows over time. The account is credited annually with the following two amounts:

- ✔ A pay credit, which is simply a percentage of the employee's compensation for the year
- ✔ An interest credit on the balance of the account

At retirement, the account balance is converted to an annuity benefit under a formula in the plan.

The way the benefit grows in a cash balance plan looks very much like a defined contribution plan, but it's different in a fundamental way: There aren't really accounts. These "accounts" are often referred to as *hypothetical accounts* because they don't reflect actual contributions to an account or actual gains and losses of the account.

One major difference between a traditional defined benefit plan and a cash balance plan is that older workers in a traditional defined benefit plan earn more valuable benefits each year than younger workers. In cash balance plans, however, the value of a year's benefit accrual can be identical for older and younger workers with the same salary.

Cash balance plans also often permit *vested participants* (those who have worked enough years to have their benefits under the plan be *vested,* or not forfeitable) to choose to receive their benefits in a lump sum if they terminate their employment (whether they quit or are fired) prior to retirement age. If a participant has a spouse, this election must be accompanied by the spouse's consent. (See Chapter 9 for more information about lump-sum distributions.)

Younger employees find cash balance plans particularly attractive because their benefits are generally accrued at the same level as the benefits of older employees. Cash balance plans are also advantageous for those who don't spend entire careers with one employer but instead work for several different ones. This is because benefits in cash balance plans, like benefits in defined contribution plans (but unlike most traditional defined benefit plans), tend to be portable. In other words, the benefits are generally payable in a lump sum to the employee upon termination of employment and can be rolled over to an individual retirement account (IRA) or to the retirement plan of a subsequent employer.

Older employees, on the other hand, may not prefer cash balance plans. If an employer switches from a traditional defined benefit plan to a cash balance plan, older employees who've worked for the same employer for many years can see their pension benefits drastically reduced. This reduction happens because employees generally accrue the largest portion of their retirement benefits after age 50 in traditional defined benefit plans. Benefit accruals for older employees under cash balance plans are often much lower than the benefit accruals under traditional defined benefit plans. It's no wonder that older employees see themselves at a disadvantage.

Employers may prefer cash balance plans because the level of contributions tends to be more predictable.

412(i) plans

A *412(i) plan* is a tax-qualified, employer-sponsored defined benefit plan that promises employees that, upon retirement, they will receive a specific benefit amount annually (or more frequently) based on a formula that considers compensation, years of service, or both. Employers contribute to 412(i) plans just as they do to other defined benefit plans. These plans are fully insured and funded exclusively by a combination of life insurance and annuity investment contracts, or annuity investment contracts alone. Investments are guaranteed by the insurance company, so employees face no risk with regard to the investment aspect of the plan. Because the benefits are guaranteed and paid by an insurance company, section 412(i) plans are often called *fully insured plans.*

Don't be confused by the term *annuity investment contract*. When we talk about annuities earlier in this chapter, we mean a form of payment that's spread out over a person's life. Here we discuss insurance and annuity contracts as investment vehicles purchased from an insurance company.

These plans receive special treatment under Internal Revenue Code Section 412(i), which is why they're called 412(i) plans.

A 412(i) plan may appear to be desirable to an employer that owns a highly profitable small business or professional practice that has no more than five to ten employees and that produces a steady stream of cash flow to meet the annual or more frequent contributions required to be made to the plan. This special type of defined benefit plan allows for maximizing tax-deductible contributions, and it generates the maximum deduction allowed by any type of plan on a fully guaranteed basis.

With 412(i) plans, however, the interest rates guaranteed by the insurance company are often quite low, and the plans can be subject to high fees and other charges. Additionally, these plans have been subject to special scrutiny by the IRS due to perceived abuses with such plans. These abuses are largely related to providing excessive benefits to the owners of the businesses that are sponsoring the plans.

Section 412(i) plans may appear to be attractive to employees because an insurance company guarantees a rate of return on the investment of the plan's assets and because these plans may provide greater contributions in early years than other types of defined benefit plans. However, the guaranteed return is usually at a very low rate so that more of the benefits under the plan will be based on the employer's contributions to the plan and less will be based on the plan's investment performance. So, the employer may have larger contributions in a 412(i) plan to produce the same level of benefits provided in a traditional defined benefit plan.

Something Special: Other Retirement Plans

In addition to defined contribution and defined benefit plans, there are two special types of tax-qualified pension plans for certain employers. These plans include the following:

- **Section 403(b) plans,** which provide benefits for certain tax-exempt employers and employees of public schools

- **Section 457 plans,** which provide retirement benefits for employees of state and local governments

Section 403 (b) plans

A *Section 403(b) plan* is also known as a *tax-sheltered annuity plan,* or TSA. The plan is referred to as a 403(b) plan because it is established pursuant to Section 403(b) of the Internal Revenue Code. It's also covered under ERISA.

Any *eligible employee* can participate in a 403(b) plan. An eligible employee includes the following people:

- ✔ Employees of tax-exempt organizations established under Section 501(c)(3) of the Internal Revenue Code
- ✔ Employees of public school systems who are involved in the day-to-day operations of a school
- ✔ Employees of cooperative hospital service organizations
- ✔ Certain ministers

Section 403(b) plans permit employees to elect to defer compensation in the same manner as 401(k) plans, which we discuss earlier in this chapter. Similar to 401(k) plans, 403(b) plans can also provide for employer matching contributions and other employer nonelective contributions. The pros and cons of these plans are the same as those of 401(k) plans.

Section 457 plans

Section 457 plans are retirement plans sponsored by state and local governments to provide retirement benefits for their employees. The tax treatment of such plans is governed under Section 457 of the Internal Revenue Code. Unlike other plans, however, such plans are governed by state law. The design of the plans and the level of benefits for state and local government employees are governed by the legislature of the particular state and by state boards, such as a public employee retirement system governing board.

These plans frequently are based on a combination of employee and employer (the employer being the state or local government) contributions and benefits and are often restricted to annuity-type payouts providing monthly benefits to the employee and the employee's surviving spouse.

Each state's plan is unique, so if you're a state or local government employee who wants to know more about Section 457 plans, contact the particular board in your state.

Chapter 4

Using 401(k) Plans to Your Advantage

*I*n Chapter 3, you become familiar with the basics of defined contribution plans; both you and your employer make contributions to such a plan. In this chapter, we focus on a special, extremely popular type of defined contribution plan: the 401(k). With this type of plan, you may voluntarily contribute a portion of your salary, pretax, to an account, and your employer may match some or all of your contribution. Your contributions are *deferred* (paid directly) into your account. So, you save money for retirement before you see it, and in this way, you don't really feel like you're parting with it. Your funds grow, tax free, until they're withdrawn.

There is a wide variety of 401(k)s out there, and we give you an overview in this chapter. Be sure to check out *401(k)s For Dummies* by Ted Benna and Brenda Watson Newmann (Wiley) for full details on these plans.

Chances are that your employer first tells you about the type of retirement plan it offers when you're either interviewing for a job or hired. Many workplaces these days have employee handbooks or personnel manuals that contain information about working for the company, including a section on retirement benefits offered, such as a 401(k). For more information about the kind of 401(k) your company offers and whether it makes any contributions, you can also request a copy of the plan's summary plan description (SPD). When it's time to sign up for the 401(k), your employer will give you a form known as an *elective deferral form* and provide you more specific information.

Understanding the Benefits of 401(k) Plans

If you're an employee and you're given the option to participate in a 401(k), especially where your employer will match your contributions, you'd be a fool not to take advantage of the opportunity. Basically, with this plan, you're getting free money just for saving a portion of your own salary. It doesn't get better than that!

Here are some additional reasons why you should love the 401(k):

✓ **You get to decide whether you want to contribute to your account, and you also get to decide how much you want to set aside.** And to top it off, these contributions are all done on a *pretax* basis (in other words, you contribute money from your salary before taxes are taken out). If your employer offers matching contributions, the more you contribute, the larger the match and the quicker your retirement fund will grow. (We discuss your contributions and your employer's later in this chapter.)

✓ **Participants age 50 and older are allowed to make additional "catch-up" contributions to their accounts.** These contributions allow folks who are closer to retirement age to save more money for retirement. You can find out more about catch-up contributions later in this chapter.

✓ **You're immediately 100 percent vested when it comes to your own contributions.** In other words, your contributions can't be taken away from you, no matter what. Your money is yours!

Employer matching contributions may not vest until a certain number of years have passed. For example, if you leave your job with a company before you're 100 percent vested, the nonvested portion of your benefits (those from your employer) will be forfeited. (We give you the scoop on vesting later in this chapter.)

✓ **The more you contribute pretax to your 401(k), the lower your taxes will be.** And who doesn't want lower taxes?

✓ **When you leave the company, you may be able to take your benefits with you.** Unlike many pension plans, with 401(k)s, generally all your contributions can be moved from one company's plan to the next company's plan or to an IRA if you change jobs (see Chapter 5 for more about IRAs). This ability to move your contributions is referred to in the tax world as *portability*.

✓ **The money that you and your employer contribute has the potential to grow and multiply (like rabbits!).** This growth may happen through investments in stocks, mutual funds, money market funds, savings accounts, and other investment vehicles. (Chapter 6 has more information about investments in pension plans.)

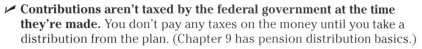

- ✔ **Contributions aren't taxed by the federal government at the time they're made.** You don't pay any taxes on the money until you take a distribution from the plan. (Chapter 9 has pension distribution basics.)

- ✔ **You can withdraw money without a penalty if you terminate employment with your employer after your 55th birthday.** Although your withdrawal before age 59½ may be subject to a 10 percent penalty, if you terminate employment with your employer after you turn 55, you aren't subject to that penalty.

- ✔ **401(k) plans can permit loans and hardship withdrawals.** If you run into financial hard times, your plan may allow you to take a withdrawal to pay certain specified hardships you've run into. We discuss these perks later in the chapter.

- ✔ **Your 401(k) is protected by the Employee Retirement Income Security Act of 1974 (ERISA).** It's protected because it's a personal investment program for your retirement (Chapter 2 has more on ERISA).

Looking at the Traditional 401(k) Plan

A company of any type and size (whether it's a start-up or an established big business) that's interested in allowing its employees to make a higher level of salary deferral than they can in other retirement plans is likely to offer a traditional 401(k). Does that description fit your employer? If so, it's essential to understand the basics of the traditional 401(k) plan.

The rules governing the traditional 401(k)

A 401(k) plan is considered *tax-qualified* under Section 401(a) of the Internal Revenue Code and enjoys *tax-deferred benefits* if it satisfies the general qualification requirements for defined contribution plans that we discuss in Chapter 2. What sets the 401(k) apart from other retirement plans is that it must contain provisions regarding the following:

- ✔ Employees may elect to have a portion of their salary deferred to the qualified retirement plan (sometimes called a *trust*).

- ✔ The amounts that an employee contributes to a plan may be distributed only upon retirement, death, or termination of employment. Under certain situations, distributions may be made while the employee is still working (these are called *in-service distributions*), but they're usually restricted to the occurrence of specific events, such as reaching age 59½, suffering a disability or hardship, or the termination of the plan.

- ✔ The amounts that employees contribute must at all times be fully vested.

Keeping the pieces of the pie equal with nondiscrimination tests

A *nondiscrimination test* doesn't test for discrimination based on race, sex, or religion. Instead, it looks for discrimination based on compensation. For instance, in the field of pension law, a company can't discriminate between *highly compensated employees* (HCEs) and *non–highly compensated employees* (NHCEs). Antidiscrimination rules are intended to prevent HCEs and owners from unfairly benefiting from a 401(k) plan. A company can discriminate between different groups of HCEs and between different groups of NHCEs, but it can't discriminate in favor of HCEs over NHCEs. Simply put, if a company offers a benefit to HCEs, the same benefit must be offered to NHCEs.

So who, exactly, qualifies as a HCE? In a nutshell, any employee who's paid well for doing his or her job is considered a HCE. The important thing to remember is that whether you're highly compensated in any given year is based on your compensation from the employer for the prior year. For example, if you receive compensation of $100,000 or more in 2007, you're considered to be highly compensated in 2008. (The IRS set this limit, similar to the other dollar limits it sets, and the limit is adjusted yearly for inflation to keep up with the cost of living.) Also, you're considered to be highly compensated if you own 5 or more percent of the company — even if your compensation is less than $100,000. The spouse, parents, and children of employees who own 5 percent are also considered to be HCEs.

If your plan provides that if more than 20 percent of an employer's employees are paid more than $100,000, the employer may elect to limit the HCEs to the top 20 percent of employees in order of pay.

We know that you'll groan if we introduce even more rules regarding 401(k) plans, but we must (you don't want to lose out on any money, do you?). So, remember that 401(k)s are also subject to the following special qualification rules:

✔ The eligibility requirement for joining a 401(k) can't be more than one year of service. (We discuss eligibility for pensions in Chapter 7.)

✔ Elective contributions must meet a nondiscrimination test — the *Actual Deferral Percentage (ADP) test* — demonstrating that plans don't discriminate in favor of highly compensated employees. (See the nearby sidebar for more about nondiscrimination tests.) The ADP test compares the deferral rates of highly compensated versus non–highly compensated employees to make sure that companies extend their 401(k) plans to the rank-and-file employees, not just the higher-ups.

✔ Employer matching contributions and employee after-tax contributions must meet a nondiscrimination test called the *Actual Contribution Percentage (ACP) test.* This test is virtually identical to the ADP test except that it doesn't measure employee deferrals; instead, it measures employer matching contributions and/or employee after-tax contributions.

✔ No individual participant can make an elective contribution that's greater than the annual dollar limitation set by the Internal Revenue Service (IRS). The dollar amount, which is the lesser of 100 percent of compensation or $15,500 for 2007, plus a $5,000 catch-up if you're over 50, is adjusted each year for inflation. (Flip to Chapter 3 for more on these and other contribution limitations.)

This dollar limit is a yearly amount that applies to *all* employee contributions, so if you work for more than one employer, you don't get to double it.

The features of the traditional 401 (k)

A 401(k) is a powerful tool in helping to promote financial security in retirement. And of all of the 401(k) plans, the traditional 401(k) offers the most flexibility (we describe the others later in this chapter). In the following sections, we explain some important features of the traditional plan.

Knowing how much you can contribute

The great thing about 401(k)s is that you can decide how much to defer into a traditional 401(k) each year. Your contributions are made on a pretax basis from your salary and are referred to as *elective deferrals.* Typically, you're permitted to change the level of your deferrals as often as your plan provides. Contact your human resources department or your plan administrator to find out how to change the level of your deferral.

Even though you can decide how much salary to defer each year, do remember that you can't go over the set dollar limit (set by the IRS). In 2007, for instance, the dollar limit is $15,500, and it increases yearly in $500 increments based on cost-of-living adjustments. Your elective deferrals are also limited to 100 percent of your compensation. So in other words, your maximum elective deferral is the lesser of these two numbers: the yearly dollar limit or 100 percent of your compensation. For example, if your compensation is $7,000 in 2007, you can contribute only up to $7,000. However, if your compensation in 2007 is $15,500 or more, you can contribute up to $15,500.

If you're highly compensated, your employer must advise you of any limits that may apply to you.

If you contribute (accidentally or otherwise) more than the maximum pretax limit to your 401(k), the excess amount must be withdrawn by April 15 of the following year. The excess contribution, in addition to the earnings on the excess, is considered *nonqualified* and can't remain in your 401(k). As a result of this violation, you may have to pay taxes and penalties on the excess.

Because employee contributions are discretionary, there's no minimum amount that you're required to defer. However, if your employer offers to match your contribution and you don't contribute anything, there's nothing to match. It's your loss. We always opt for deferring as much income as you can and saving wisely for your retirement; if your employer offers a match, contribute the most you can. Otherwise, you're losing out on a great opportunity for essentially free money.

Catching up at age 50

Imagine for a moment that you didn't defer quite as much money into your 401(k) during your early years, and now that you're 50, you've realized what kind of shape you'll be in during retirement. Sounds pretty scary, huh? The truth is that most of us never defer quite as much as we like or save as much as we hope. Well, as long as you're over 50 (or turn 50 within the *plan year,* which is any consecutive 12-month period of time under which the plan operates) and your plan permits it, you can make an additional elective contribution, called a *catch-up contribution,* over and above the regular 401(k) contribution limits that we discuss in the previous section. Catch-up contributions are a little perk for older employees who have fewer years ahead of them to sock money away for retirement.

The dollar limit for the catch-up contribution is $5,000 for 2007. (This limit increases in $500 increments each year.) Therefore, the maximum elective deferral for someone who's 50 or older is $20,500 for 2007 (the regular $15,500 elective deferral limit plus the $5,000 catch-up).

Even if your salary is below the $15,500 elective deferral limit, you can defer 100 percent of your compensation up to $15,500 *plus* an extra $5,000 as a catch-up contribution. So if you're 50 or older and earn only $7,000 in 2007, you may defer an additional $5,000 for your catch-up contribution.

Keep in mind that your employer isn't required to allow catch-up contributions, but there's not much reason for it not to because your contribution dollars are at work. In addition, even if your employer agrees to match your elective deferrals, it doesn't match a catch-up contribution. Check with your plan administrator or your employer's human resources department to find out whether your plan permits catch-up contributions. Whatever the case may be, it's our recommendation that you maximize whatever contributions you can because it's the best investment you'll ever make!

Making a match with your employer

Employers have a number of options in terms of how they choose to contribute to their employees' accounts. The most popular method of contributing to an employee's plan is for your employer to match your contribution. Two types of matches exist:

✔ **Discretionary match:** In this type of match, your employer may choose to kick in money for every dollar that you contribute, usually within limits set by the plan or by law. Your employer sets the formula depending on how much it wants to contribute, and it has the discretion to choose make a contribution on a year-to-year basis.

✔ **Mandatory match:** In this type of match, the plan requires the employer to make a matching contribution according to a certain formula. The employer may choose to fully match contributions, dollar for dollar, or it can partially match contributions.

For example, your employer can offer a matching contribution of 50 percent up to 6 percent of your pay. Very simply, this means that for every dollar you contribute to your plan, up to a limit of 6 percent of your pay, your employer contributes 50 cents. If your elective deferrals are 6 percent of your compensation or greater, your employer will contribute an amount equal to 3 percent of your compensation. In other words, if you defer 7 percent of your compensation, your employer contributes only 3 percent.

Your employer's contributions, plus your own contributions, can't exceed the yearly overall IRS limits; for 2007, the limit is the lesser of 100 percent of your compensation or $45,000 (plus $5,000 for a catch-up contribution, for a total of $50,000, if you're at least 50).

For example, if you're over 50 and earn more than $15,500 in 2007, you can make the maximum employee contribution of $20,500 ($15,500 plus a $5,000 catch-up contribution). Because the overall IRS contribution is $50,000 for someone who's at least 50, your employer can contribute up to $29,500 (the $50,000 maximum limit minus your $20,500 maximum deferral).

Determining when you're vested

Vesting is a term that's related to how much of your 401(k) is actually yours. With 401(k) plans, your contributions are 100 percent vested at all times. For example, if you defer money to your 401(k) and then decide to leave your job, you're entitled to 100 percent of the contributions that you've made to your plan. (These contributions are also called *nonforfeitable contributions.*)

But you have to remember that the same isn't true with your employer's contributions. These contributions vest over a number of years according to a *vesting schedule* (this is your employer's way of trying to get you to stay at your job as long as possible). So, if your employer made contributions to your plan, but you haven't worked at the company long enough to be vested, you won't be able to take all the employer's contributions when you leave the company.

Although the money *you've* contributed is 100 percent vested, the value of the principal may either grow or shrink depending on how it's been invested and what's going on in the marketplace. So keep in mind that $1,000 deferred doesn't automatically equal $1,000 withdrawn! Find out more about investments in Chapter 6.

Effective January 1, 2007, employer contributions made to defined contribution plans, including 401(k) plans, must be vested no less rapidly than under a *three-year cliff schedule* or a *six-year graded vesting schedule,* as shown in Table 4-1. This is faster than in the past.

Table 4-1	Vesting Schedule for 401(k) Plans	
Year	3-Year Cliff	6-Year Graded
1	0%	0%
2	0%	20%
3	100%	40%
4		60%
5		80%
6		100%

For full details on vesting, including cliff and graded schedules, head to Chapter 7.

Checking out investment options

You can select a variety of investment options when dealing with your 401(k). As an employee participating in the plan, either you'll be permitted to direct the investment of your accounts or a trustee selected by your employer will manage the fund on your behalf. (Chapter 6 has more on investing.)

Your account balance determines the amount of retirement income you'll receive from the plan. While contributions to your account and the earnings on your investments will increase your account balance, fees and expenses paid by your plan will reduce the growth.

Helping yourself to a hardship distribution

Under certain circumstances, you may be allowed to access funds in your 401(k) plan before retirement, but you'll be hit with a penalty. For example, if you're an active employee and find yourself undergoing financial hardship, your plan may permit you to make a withdrawal from the principal portion of the funds that you contributed (you can't access the earnings on your contributions). Your plan may also permit a hardship withdrawal from your employer's contributions to your account.

You can receive distributions on account of hardship only if they're necessary due to your "immediate and heavy" financial need. Also, the distribution can't be greater than the amount needed to satisfy the hardship, and you must not have other resources to satisfy the hardship. The plan must set forth uniform standards as to what constitutes a hardship.

You should know what constitutes a hardship and how to request such a distribution; this information is contained in the summary plan description. See Chapter 8 to find out how to request this and other important plan documents from your plan administrator. The following situations automatically constitute an immediate and heavy financial need:

- ✔ You have unreimbursed medical expenses from healthcare for you, your spouse, or any of your dependents. (*Unreimbursed medical expenses* are those that you're responsible for and that aren't reimbursed by insurance.) Amounts for medical expenses may be obtained prior to actually incurring the expense if the plan has a specific procedure to permit such withdrawals.

- ✔ You're purchasing a principal residence.

- ✔ You need to make payments to prevent eviction from your principal residence or to prevent foreclosure on your mortgage.

- ✔ You have expenses for the repair of damage to your principal residence due to fire, storm, or other casualty.

- ✔ You need to make tuition payments for the next 12 months of postsecondary education for you, your spouse, or your dependents.

- ✔ You have burial or funeral expenses.

Your employer must determine that you've exhausted all your financial resources before you can get a hardship distribution. Your employer must rely on your good word that you were unable to gain funds from the following resources:

- ✔ Reimbursement or compensation by insurance

- ✔ The selling of your assets

- ✔ The elimination of your elective contributions under the plan

- ✔ A nontaxable loan distribution from any employer's plan

- ✔ A loan from a commercial source like a bank

Because your employer relies on your representation that you have no other resources available to you, including the stoppage of your elective contributions to the plan, participants who take a hardship withdrawal from their plan are prohibited from making elective deferrals for six months following the hardship distribution.

The Pension Protection Act of 2006 allows hardship distributions to any designated beneficiary, not just a spouse or dependent. In other words, since August 17, 2006, this category has been expanded to include anyone you designate as your beneficiary, such as a domestic partner of the same or opposite sex or simply a significant other or extended family member.

Getting a loan from your 401(k)

Yes, some employers' 401(k) plans permit loans, but as you may guess, a number of limitations and restrictions apply. To be sure that your loan isn't treated as a taxable distribution (called a *deemed distribution* from your plan), it must meet these requirements:

- You must repay the loan within five years.
- The loan repayment schedule must be made in substantially equal payments consisting of both principal and interest and in at least quarterly installments.
- The loan must be evidenced by an agreement that sets forth the terms of the loan (including the date of the loan, the specific amount of the loan, and the repayment schedule).

Flip to Chapter 13, where we cover loans from pension plans in greater detail.

Checking Out Other Varieties of 401(k) Plans

You may not work for a large company that offers the option of a traditional 401(k), but don't worry; it's entirely possible that your employer offers one of the alternative plans in the following sections. We also explain the plan that you may use if you're self-employed.

Finding Safe Harbor 401(k) plans

Any type of employer and any size company may choose a Safe Harbor plan, which is funded by mandatory employer contributions and optional employee contributions. This plan is used most often by employers that don't mind having mandatory funding obligations and that can afford to make the contributions.

A *Safe Harbor 401(k)* allows employees of all different salary levels to make the maximum salary deferral contributions, just as in a traditional 401(k) plan. (For 2007, this contribution is the lesser of 100 percent of your compensation or $15,500, plus an additional $5,000 catch-up contribution if you're 50 or older.) If you've worked 1,000 hours in the previous year and are at least 21 years old, you're eligible to participate in this type of plan.

One difference regarding the Safe Harbor 401(k) plan is that it doesn't require the discrimination testing that the traditional 401(k) requires (see the earlier section "The rules governing the traditional 401(k)" for more info). Employers are excused from this requirement because they agree to make mandatory matching contributions to their employees' salary deferrals or direct contributions to the accounts of all eligible employees.

The mandatory match is 100 percent of the employee elective deferrals up to the first 3 percent of employee compensation, plus 50 percent of the next 2 percent. For example, if you choose to defer 5 percent of your compensation, your employer contributes a match of 4 percent of your compensation.

> 3%   (100% match of the first 3%)
>
> + 1%   (50% match of the next 2%)
>
> 4%   match

Instead of making a matching contribution, your employer may choose to contribute an amount equal to at least 3 percent of compensation (called an *employer nonelective contribution*) on behalf of all eligible employees, regardless of whether those employees actually defer into the Safe Harbor plan.

Another difference between the Safe Harbor 401(k) and traditional 401(k) is that all eligible employees are 100 percent vested immediately in their contributions *and* in their employer's contributions (the 3 percent employer nonelective contribution or the mandatory match). If your employer also makes a discretionary contribution to the plan (see the earlier section "Making a match with your employer" for more about discretionary contributions), you aren't automatically vested in these contributions, which are subject to a vesting schedule as for other 401(k)s.

Easing into SIMPLE 401 (k) plans

An employer that employs no more than 100 employees earning at least $5,000 in compensation and that doesn't maintain another qualified plan may adopt a *SIMPLE (Savings Incentive Match Plan for Employees) 401(k)*.

Employees may elect to defer some of their compensation to a SIMPLE 401(k), but they aren't required to do so. The maximum annual elective deferral that may be made is $10,500 in 2007 and indexed for inflation in $500 increments. In addition, employees age 50 or older can make a maximum $2,500 catch-up contribution, also adjusted yearly for inflation in $500 increments.

In SIMPLE 401(k) plans, your employer can make either a dollar-for-dollar contribution matching your elective deferral up to 3 percent of your compensation for the year or a nonelective contribution of 2 percent of compensation for each eligible employee who earned at least $5,000 in compensation during the prior plan year. Your employer can't make any other contributions. You're 100 percent vested in both your contributions and employer contributions at all times.

Like the Safe Harbor 401(k), the SIMPLE 401(k) doesn't undergo nondiscrimination testing, and the plan may permit participant loans and hardship withdrawals.

The SIMPLE 401(k) is just that: a simpler version of the 401(k). The drawback to you and other employees is that the maximum elective deferral is smaller than with other 401(k)s, but the plan is easier for small employers to administer because of the easy-to-calculate benefit formula.

Going it alone with solo 401(k) plans

The *solo 401(k),* which may also be called the *individual 401(k)* or *uni (k),* is designed specifically to benefit owner-only small businesses, the self-employed, and independent contractors. To be eligible for this type of plan, the sole proprietor must have no additional employees other than a spouse or a business partner.

If they're two different people, a business partner and a spouse both can't participate in this type of 401(k). Only the owner and spouse (who's receiving income from the business) or the owner and a business partner are allowed to participate.

A business that employs part-time employees may still be eligible to participate in a solo 401(k) if the employees are

- Under age 21
- Employees with less than one year of service
- W-2 employees who work less than 1,000 hours per year
- Certain union employees
- Certain nonresident alien employees with no U.S. income

The contribution limit for a solo 401(k) is $45,000 in 2007 (the same limit for all defined contribution plans) plus the $5,000 catch-up contribution for those 50 and older. This limit makes it an ideal choice for the sole proprietor or self-employed individual who wants to max out on contributions and has only one other person's account to fund (a spouse's or business partner's).

Loans are permitted from your solo 401(k), up to 50 percent of the total 401(k) value with a $50,000 limit. See Chapter 13 for more information on loans from pension plans.

As far as funding is concerned, the solo 401(k) is completely discretionary and the owner (that's you) can change the contribution levels depending on whether it has been a good year.

To set up a solo 401(k), you should contact an attorney knowledgeable in retirement plan matters, especially one who has experience in the drafting of assorted retirement plan documents and who can explain the ins and outs of various plans to determine what's best for your particular circumstances. (We explain how to find a pension attorney in Chapter 19.)

Paying taxes up front with Roth 401 (k) plans

When you contribute to a traditional 401(k) or any of the other previously described 401(k) plans, you get a tax deduction on the contribution. Thanks to this deduction, money that would ordinarily be paid to the government remains in the account, tax deferred, until it's withdrawn.

From your point of view, you hope your account will grow and add to your retirement. From the government's point of view, it hopes that your account will grow, too, because when you retire and withdraw the money, that's when your tax deferral ends. At that point, the government hopes that there's lots of money to tax. So, the government gives you a tax break today to get more taxes from you in the future!

The *Roth 401(k),* however, works in reverse. The money that you earn today is taxed today. When you start your withdrawals, you receive them tax-free. Who wouldn't love to receive tax-free money during retirement? Certainly you would enjoy it, but the government likes the Roth system as well. The government likes this system because it's getting paid today instead of several years down the road. Wimpy knew when he said, "I'll gladly pay you next Tuesday for a hamburger today," that he was getting the better end of the bargain.

The Roth 401(k) plan is provided primarily by larger employers that can absorb the additional administrative costs and complexities that the plan presents. Unlike the *Roth IRA,* which has income limitations that restrict some individuals from participating (check out Chapter 5 for more on the Roth IRA), the Roth 401(k) has no such income limits.

A Roth 401(k) is never established as a completely separate plan. Rather, when it's offered, it's as an option as part of a traditional 401(k). In this case, you have the opportunity to contribute some or all of your elective deferrals to a Roth 401(k), a traditional 401(k), or a combination of the two. Just remember that if you choose to contribute to both, you don't get to contribute twice as much money — contribution limits remain the same regardless of whether you choose a traditional 401(k), a Roth 401(k), or both. The contribution limit for 2007 is $15,500 for people under age 50 and $20,500 when you add in the $5,000 catch-up contribution for those 50 and older. Employer contributions are identical for both traditional and Roth 401(k) plans.

The Roth tax treatment applies only to the employee's elective deferrals. Employer matching contributions or employer nonelective contributions continue to be treated as tax-deferred contributions and are taxable to you, the employee, when distributed from the plan.

As in a traditional 401(k), any deferrals that exceed the maximum limits must be removed no later than April 15 of the year following the year of the designated Roth contribution. Unlike the case with a traditional 401(k), however, if the excess deferrals aren't distributed by April 15, the contribution will be taxed both in the year of contribution and the year of distribution (in other words, it's subject to double taxation). Earnings attributable to the excess Roth deferral are taxed only in the year of distribution.

For the most part, distributions are subject to the same restrictions as traditional 401(k)s, but some differences do exist. The big one: Earnings are tax-free only if the employee is age 59½ or is disabled or deceased *and* the first Roth 401(k) contribution was deposited five or more tax years ago. If the plan allows rollovers (see Chapter 9 for rollover basics), the date to follow is the date that the first Roth 401(k) contribution was made to the prior plan. The plan administrator is responsible for tracking the five years and the basis on the contributions to determine the tax that may be due upon distribution. The five-year period is based on tax years, not the elapsed time from the first contribution. (A *tax year* is the year for which the contribution was made.)

For example, if your first Roth deferral is on December 15, 2008, the first year of the five-year period is 2008. However, if the initial Roth deferral is on January 5, 2009, 2009 would be the first year of the five-year period.

Chapter 5

Increasing Your Income with IRAs

*I*ndividual retirement accounts, or IRAs, are different from the defined bene-fit and defined contribution plans we discuss in Chapter 3 and from the 401(k) plans (a popular type of defined contribution plan) we discuss in Chapter 4. Unlike 401(k)s and other plans established by employers to fund retirement benefits for their employees, IRAs are tax-deferred personal retire-ment plans set up by individuals to help fund their own retirement benefits.

In 1974, the U.S. Congress first authorized IRAs. By authorizing these new plans, Congress hoped to give Americans a tax break on their hard-earned income and hoped that the IRA would be an incentive for people to save (saving is much more fun when you don't first have to pay taxes on it!). At just about the same time as IRAs were born, some companies decided that they would no longer provide pensions or retirement benefits to their employees. The IRA then became a great tool for employees to control their own retirement funding.

So if your employer doesn't offer a pension plan, you may find that an IRA is right for you. It's also a great option when you receive a distribution from an employer's retirement plan; you can set up either a traditional IRA or a Roth IRA to hold and invest your retirement plan distributions. Other IRAs out there, such as SIMPLE IRAs and Simplified Employee Pensions (SEPs), are offered only by employers. We cover all the bases in this chapter.

You can set up IRAs or get information on IRAs from many investment firms. For example, www.schwab.com and www.vanguard.com are two sites that contain information on IRAs. These sites also can assist you in setting up an IRA.

The Fundamentals of Traditional IRAs

The *traditional IRA* is the basis for all other types of IRAs. In the following sections, we explain the fundamentals of traditional IRAs, including eligibility, contributions, rollovers, investments, and distributions. (For a detailed look at both rollovers and distributions of IRAs and tax-qualified plans, head to Chapter 9.)

Beginning with the basic rules

Generally speaking, an IRA is a trust or custodial account (established with a financial or investment institution) set up for the exclusive benefit of you or your beneficiaries (like your spouse, domestic partner, and children). The account, which can be set up at any time, is created by a written document called a *trust agreement* or a *custodial agreement.* The agreement must state the following rules:

- The trustee or custodian must be a bank, a federally insured credit union, a savings and loan association, or an entity approved by the Internal Revenue Service (IRS) to act as trustee or custodian.

- The trustee or custodian generally can't accept contributions that exceed the maximum dollar limit effective for a taxable year.

- Contributions, except for rollover contributions, must be in cash.

- You must have a nonforfeitable right to the assets of the IRA at all times.

- Money in your account can't be used to buy a life insurance policy.

- Assets in your account can't be combined with other property, except in a common trust fund or common investment fund.

- You must start receiving distributions by April 1 of the year following the year in which you reach age 70½.

Although IRAs are among the easiest types of retirement accounts to establish and maintain, they still can be somewhat confusing, so talk to a financial professional to set one up.

Determining your eligibility

Unfortunately, not everyone is eligible to set up a traditional IRA. So before you proceed, you must determine your eligibility. You know that you can set up and make contributions to a traditional IRA if you meet the following requirements:

✔ You (or, if you file a joint return, your spouse) received taxable compensation during the year. According to the IRS, compensation is what you earn from working, including the following:

- Wages

- Salaries

- Tips

- Professional fees

- Bonuses

- Self-employment income

- Commissions

- Taxable alimony and separate maintenance payments that you receive from your divorce decree or a separate maintenance order for support

For the purpose of determining eligibility, the IRS treats as compensation any amount properly shown on your W-2 in Box 1.

✔ You didn't become 70½ years of age by the end of the year. (No minimum age exists for setting up an IRA. You can set up IRAs for your kids if they've earned income.)

In most cases, you can have a traditional IRA whether or not you're covered by any other retirement plan. However, if your *modified adjusted gross income* (MAGI) is above a certain dollar amount, you may not be able to deduct all or any of the contributions to your IRA if you (or your spouse) are covered by an employer retirement plan. (We cover MAGI and deductible contributions to IRAs in the later section "Types of contributions.")

If both you and your spouse have compensation and are under the age of 70½, you have to set up separate IRAs. In other words, you can't both participate in the same IRA. The later sidebar "Double your pleasure: Contribution limits when both you and your spouse have IRAs" has the nitty-gritty on the math behind contributing to separate IRAs.

Contributing to a traditional IRA

Several issues come into play when you begin talking about your IRA contributions, including what types of contributions you can make, what the limits are, whether catch-up contributions are permitted, and, of course, when you can actually make contributions. We explain what you need to know in the following sections.

No matter what, you can't contribute any money to your traditional IRA after you reach age 70½.

Types of contributions

IRA contributions only come in the following two flavors:

- **Deductible contributions:** These can be deducted for tax purposes.
- **Nondeductible contributions:** These can't be deducted. (Easy, huh?)

If you're covered by an employer retirement plan, you can deduct the full amount you contribute to your traditional IRA as long as your *modified adjusted gross income* (MAGI) is, for 2007, $50,000 or less (or $80,000 or less if you're married and filing jointly).

If your MAGI is more than $50,000 and less than $60,000 (if you're filing as a single individual or head of household) or more than $80,000 and less than $100,000 (if you're married, filing jointly, or a qualifying widow/widower), you're still in luck. In this case, you can generally deduct a proportional part of your contributions to your traditional IRA. But if your income is above these limits, sorry, you can't make a deductible contribution to your traditional IRA. However, you're still free to make a nondeductible contribution.

You should be aware that the compensation limits restrict your ability to make a deductible contribution to an IRA only if you're an active participant receiving contributions in an employer retirement plan.

Contribution limits

Like most retirement plans, IRAs are subject to contribution limits (the IRS can't possibly let you have too much of a good thing!). The most that can be contributed to your traditional IRA is the lesser of the following:

- Your taxable compensation for the year
- $4,000, which is the limit for 2007

For example, if you're 34 years old and single and you earn $25,000 in 2007, your IRA contributions for 2007 are limited to $4,000, which is the set maximum for that year. On the other hand, if you're a single college student who's working only part time and earning $3,500 in 2007, the maximum amount you can contribute to your IRA is $3,500, which is limited to the total amount of your compensation. Table 5-1 sets out the contribution limits for 2007 and beyond.

Table 5-1	Maximum Dollar Amounts for IRA Contributions
For Taxable Years Beginning	*Maximum Contribution Amount*
2005–2007	$4,000
2008 and after	$5,000

The previously mentioned limits are the most that can be contributed regardless of whether the contributions are to one or more traditional or Roth IRAs (we discuss Roth IRAs later in this chapter). In other words, if you have more than one IRA, the limit applies to the total contributions made on your behalf to all your traditional or Roth IRAs for that year. If you make more than the allowed contributions, they'll be subject to a 6 percent excise tax until they're corrected — either distributed from the plan or used toward a contribution in a subsequent year.

The maximum contribution limit will increase yearly due to inflation starting in 2009. However, the IRS will make adjustments only if the cost of living increases by $500 or more. If the increase meets that requirement, the adjustments will be made in multiples of $500, rounded down. For example, if the increase in the cost of living is $499, no adjustment will be made. And if there's an increase of $999, this will create an adjustment of $500.

See the nearby sidebar "Double your pleasure: Contribution limits when both you and your spouse have IRAs" for the math details on contributing to IRAs when you're married.

Catch-up contributions

Traditional IRAs, like 401(k)s and other retirement plans, allow *catch-up contributions* for people who are 50 or older. If you meet this age requirement, you can contribute an additional $1,000 annually to your IRA. These contributions apply on top of the maximum contribution limits. This means that if you're over 50 years old, you can make a total IRA contribution of $5,000 for 2007 (which consists of the $4,000 maximum limit plus the $1,000 catch-up).

Double your pleasure: Contribution limits when both you and your spouse have IRAs

If you and your spouse file a joint return and your taxable compensation is less than that of your spouse (even if your compensation is $0), the most that can be contributed for the year to your individual IRA is the smaller of the following two amounts:

✔ $4,000 for 2007 ($5,000 if you're age 50 or older).

✔ The total compensation that can be included in the gross income of both you and your spouse for the year. However, that total must be reduced by the following two amounts: your spouse's IRA contribution for the year to a traditional IRA and your spouse's contributions for the year to a Roth IRA (we discuss Roth IRAs later in this chapter).

What this means to you is that the total combined contributions that can be made for the year 2007 to your IRA and your spouse's IRA can be as much as $8,000 ($9,000 if only one of you is 50 or older or $10,000 if both of you are 50 or older) — even if one of you doesn't make much.

Consider, for example, the scenario of Tarzan and Jane. Jane, a full-time student in her 20s, with no income during the year, marries Tarzan, an older guy in his 30s who works at the local zoo. By working at the zoo, Tarzan has taxable compensation of $40,000. (Hard to believe Tarzan found such a good job!) He's a saver and wants to contribute $4,000 to a traditional IRA. If he and Jane file a joint tax return, each of them can contribute $4,000 to separate traditional IRAs. The couple can do this even though Jane has no compensation because Tarzan's compensation can be added to her zero compensation (after reducing Tarzan's compensation by his $4,000 contribution).

Look at it this way:

$40,000 (Tarzan's compensation) + $0 (Jane's compensation) = $40,000

$40,000 − $4,000 (Tarzan's contribution to his own IRA) = $36,000

The amount of $4,000 is less than $36,000 (which is Jane's "compensation" for the purposes of calculating her contribution limit), so Jane can contribute $4,000 to her own IRA (the maximum yearly limit).

The timing of contributions

As we mention in the section "Beginning with the basic rules" earlier in this chapter, all contributions (except for rollovers) must be in cash. Here's when you can make those cash contributions:

✔ **Yearly:** In this scenario, you write a check (money orders or cash both work, too) once a year to your IRA for the maximum contribution or for whatever amount you elect to contribute that year.

✔ **Many times throughout the year:** With this contribution method, you make small contributions to your IRA throughout the year.

You must make your contributions by April 15 of the year following a particular tax year. For example, you can wait until April 15, 2008, to make IRA contributions for the 2007 tax year. However, make sure that your IRA statement properly credits your contribution to the taxable year 2007 rather than 2008.

Picking your investments

An IRA isn't an investment itself, but rather it's an account into which you contribute your money. You have the option to invest your contribution in stocks, bonds, CDs, mutual funds, and other securities and investments, including real estate. Read Chapter 6 for more on different types of investments.

Because your money grows tax-deferred in a traditional IRA, don't invest in something that grows tax-free in a regular account, such as a municipal bond. Instead, choose investments that would be taxed if they were in a regular account, such as a stock mutual fund or a CD.

IRA funds aren't permitted to be invested in collectibles. If you do invest in these items, the amount you invest is considered distributed in the year invested, which means that you may have to pay an additional 10 percent tax on these early distributions (find out more about distributions later in this chapter). Collectibles include (among others) the following:

- Artwork
- Rugs
- Antiques
- Metals (except for certain kinds of bullion)
- Gems
- Stamps
- Coins (except certain coins minted by the U.S. Treasury Department)
- Alcoholic beverages
- Certain other tangible personal property

If you decide to go with a brokerage firm when you set up your IRA, you may be restricted to choosing investments from that firm's products, which may include fees for the services they provide. Make sure that you get all the necessary information regarding the investment of your IRA assets ahead of time, including service charge fees, so that you can make educated decisions and not be surprised down the road.

Rolling over to a traditional IRA

A *rollover* is when you move your money from one tax-deferred place to another without paying taxes. But to roll over successfully, your distribution must be eligible for direct transfer, thereby avoiding tax consequences. Rules also exist for who can roll over money into an IRA and when. For full details on rollovers to IRAs (and to tax-qualified pension plans), see Chapter 9.

Taking your distribution

After you reach the magical age of 59½, you can start withdrawing money from your IRA without penalty (whether or not you've actually retired). Upon withdrawal, your earnings will be subject to income tax (but remember that these earnings have been growing tax-deferred for as long as you have been saving!). Then, the April 1 after you reach the age of 70½, you're required to start taking a minimum withdrawal each year. If you fail to take distributions by that date, you'll be taxed at a 50 percent rate on the amount that should have been withdrawn.

So after you hit 70½, you have to calculate your *minimum required distribution* for a given tax year. To do so, divide the value of your account at the end of the previous year by the number of years in the Uniform Distribution Table in Appendix B (this table shows life expectancy factors based on the age of a pensioner). The table is based on a participant with a beneficiary 10 years younger than the participant. However, your IRA distributions are based on the Uniform Distribution Table even if your beneficiary isn't 10 years younger than you.

For example, imagine that you're 72 and your traditional IRA account is worth $100,000 on December 31, 2007. The minimum distribution period at age 72 is 25.6 years (based on the Uniform Distribution Table). That means you need to withdraw a minimum of $3,907 from your traditional IRA account in 2008. ($100,000 divided by the 25.6-year life expectancy equals $3,906.25; then you round up to the higher dollar figure.) Your minimum withdrawal will change every year based on the change in your account balance and in the life expectancy in the Uniform Distribution Table.

Any withdrawals taken prior to reaching age 59½ may not only be subject to income taxes (as all withdrawals are), but they may also be subject to a 10 percent penalty imposed by the IRS for early withdrawal. As with most rules, however, some exceptions apply to the early withdrawal rule. Here are the situations when an exception applies:

- ✓ You have unreimbursed medical expenses that are more than 7.5 percent of your adjusted gross income.

- ✓ The distributions are used to pay deductible medical expenses.

- ✔ You're disabled.

- ✔ You're the beneficiary of a deceased IRA owner.

- ✔ You're receiving distributions in the form of an annuity payment spread out over your life expectancy or the life expectancy of you and your beneficiary.

- ✔ The distributions are to be used for college expenses for yourself, your spouse, your child, or your grandchild.

- ✔ You use the distributions to buy, build, or rebuild a first home (limited to a lifetime limitation of $10,000).

For additional details on pension distributions, see Chapter 9.

You can't borrow funds from your IRA or use your IRA as security for a loan. If you do use your IRA for these purposes, all the funds in the IRA (not just the loan amount) will be considered distributed (and therefore taxable). Additionally, you can't use an IRA to invest in a business you own or to buy property from yourself.

The Nuts 'n' Bolts of Roth IRAs

A *Roth IRA,* for the most part, is subject to the rules that apply to a traditional IRA (which we cover earlier in this chapter). However, a Roth IRA has a few of its own unique characteristics, which we explain in the following sections. The Roth IRA is named for its chief legislative sponsor, the late U.S. Senator William V. Roth, Jr. Roth IRAs became effective in 1998.

In order for the Roth IRA rules to apply, the account must be designated as a Roth IRA when it's set up. If the account isn't initially set up as a Roth IRA, it won't receive Roth IRA treatment, so make sure that the application form clearly indicates what you want. Roth IRAs are set up with the same institutions and in the same manner as traditional IRAs (see the earlier section "Beginning with the basic rules" for more information).

Eligibility requirements

In order to participate in a Roth IRA, you must meet the following requirements:

- ✔ You must be 18 years of age or older.

- ✔ You must have a MAGI of less than $110,000 (single) or $160,000 (married and filing jointly). We discuss MAGI in the earlier section "Types of contributions."

And remember that individuals with 401(k)s or other retirement plans *are* eligible to participate in Roth IRAs.

Contribution rules

Unlike with a traditional IRA, you can't deduct contributions to a Roth IRA for tax purposes. Rather than deducting a contribution up front, as with a deductible traditional IRA, the tax benefits are *backloaded* (meaning that the funds are distributed tax-free). Qualified distributions from Roth IRAs are completely tax-free. So unlike deductible IRAs and tax-qualified plans that provide tax deferral, Roth IRAs provide true tax-free buildup of investment earnings. In addition, you can make contributions after you reach age 70½, and you can leave amounts in your Roth IRA as long as you live.

The contribution limits for a Roth IRA are the same as the limits for traditional IRAs and are limited to the lesser of $4,000 per year (not including rollovers) or 100 percent of your compensation. Limits will remain at this number until 2008 when they increase to $5,000.

The amount of your contribution depends on your income and on how you file your tax return:

- ✔ **Single filers:** If you're a single filer who earns up to a MAGI of $95,000, you qualify for a full contribution. To qualify for a partial contribution, you must earn $95,000–$110,000.

- ✔ **Joint filers:** If you and your spouse earn up to a combined MAGI of $150,000, you qualify for a full contribution. To be eligible for a partial contribution, together you must earn $150,000–$160,000.

Individuals can't contribute if they exceed these income limitations. In fact, excess contributions to a Roth IRA are subject to a 6 percent excise tax, and these contributions are assessed annually until the excess is corrected.

With Roth IRAs, catch-up contributions are permitted for individuals who are 50 or older — just as they're permitted with traditional IRAs. So if you're 50 years old or older, you can contribute $5,000 per year for 2007 and $6,000 per year in 2008. In the end, you're allowed to contribute an extra $1,000 to catch you up to where you want to be.

Contributions to a SEP or a SIMPLE IRA aren't taken into account for purposes of the IRA contribution limit ($4,000 in 2007 and $5,000 in 2008). In other words, contributions to a SEP or SIMPLE IRA don't affect the amount that an individual can contribute to a Roth IRA. However, your contributions to a traditional IRA *do* count toward the limit. We cover SIMPLE IRAs and SEPs later in this chapter.

Conversions to a Roth IRA

Before 2008, you can't roll over money from a tax-qualified plan directly into a Roth IRA, but you can roll it into a traditional IRA. (Chapter 9 has all the info you need on rollovers.) An existing traditional IRA then can be rolled over or converted (we use these terms interchangeably) to a Roth IRA by a taxpayer who has a gross income of less than $100,000 (not counting the conversion amount) for the taxable year of the rollover. Conversions to Roth IRAs aren't available to married individuals filing separate returns.

The funds that you roll over from a traditional IRA into a Roth IRA are taxable in the year of the rollover. For example, if you roll over $50,000 from a traditional IRA into a Roth IRA in 2009, you have to pay tax on the $50,000 in 2009. Even though a conversion to a Roth IRA causes you to pay current taxes on the amount rolled over, the amount will then grow tax-free in the Roth IRA.

Roth IRA rollovers work best if you have funds outside the IRA to use to pay taxes on the rollover. For example, a rollover of $50,000 into a Roth IRA may result in $10,000 in income taxes. It's best to roll over the entire $50,000 and pay the taxes with $10,000 that you have outside your IRA. If you need to take $10,000 from your traditional IRA to pay the taxes, you wind up with only $40,000 left to roll over into the Roth IRA.

A traditional IRA can be converted to a Roth IRA in one of three ways:

- **Rollover:** Assets from a traditional IRA can be contributed (rolled over) to a Roth IRA within 60 days after their distribution.

- **Trustee-to-trustee transfer:** The financial institution holding the traditional IRA assets provides directions on how to transfer those assets to the trustee of a Roth IRA with another financial institution.

- **Same trustee transfer:** The financial institution holding the traditional IRA assets transfers those assets to a Roth IRA. In this case, the transfer should be simpler because it occurs within the same financial institution.

Here are a few upcoming changes for conversions:

- Effective after December 31, 2007, direct rollovers from the tax-qualified retirement plans we discuss in Chapter 3 to Roth IRAs will be permitted. These rollovers are subject to the same rules that apply to conversions from a traditional IRA to a Roth IRA.

- Effective for tax years beginning after December 31, 2009, the requirement that a taxpayer's gross income not exceed $100,000 to be eligible to convert a non-Roth IRA to a Roth IRA will be eliminated.

✔ A special rule has been established for rollovers to Roth IRAs in 2010. Amounts rolled over into a Roth IRA in 2010 aren't included in your income in 2010; instead, 50 percent of the amount is included in your income in 2011 and 50 percent in 2012. That's quite a deal for the year 2010 because none of the rollover will be included in your income. This deal is something you should seriously consider.

Distribution details

Qualified (or tax-free) distributions from a Roth IRA aren't included in your gross income and aren't subject to the 10 percent tax on early withdrawals. But to be considered qualified, distributions must satisfy a *five-year holding period* and must meet one of four criteria.

What's a five-year holding period, you ask? It's the period that begins with the first taxable year in which you (or your spouse) made a contribution to a Roth IRA. In the case of a rollover or conversion, the five-year period begins with the taxable year in which the conversion was made or, if earlier, the taxable year in which a prior contribution was made to your Roth IRA. In other words, the Roth IRA must have been in existence for at least five years *prior to your distribution.* For example, if the Roth IRA is set up on April 5, 2007, for the 2006 tax year, the initial year of the five-year period is 2006, and the five-year period will be satisfied in 2010.

Distributions that have satisfied the five-year holding period will be qualified if the distribution meets one of the four criteria:

✔ It was made on or after the date on which you become age 59½.

✔ It was made to a beneficiary (or to your estate) upon or after your death.

✔ It's attributable to your disability.

✔ It's a distribution made for qualified first-time home buyer expenses (up to $10,000 over the taxpayer's lifetime).

Any distributions from a Roth IRA that don't meet the requirements to be a qualified distribution aren't taxable until they exceed the total amount of your contributions to the Roth IRA. Because you've already paid taxes on the amount of your original contribution, you don't pay taxes twice, whether or not the distribution is qualified. However, nonqualified distributions that are over and above the amount of your original contributions (in other words, the earnings on your contributions) are treated as taxable income.

The Simplicity of the SIMPLE IRA

A *SIMPLE IRA* is a Savings Incentive Match Plan for Employees. This type of plan applies to small companies (100 or fewer employees) that don't offer a 401(k) or other type of retirement plan. Under a SIMPLE IRA plan, your employer makes contributions to a traditional IRA that's set up for each of its eligible employees (we discuss traditional IRAs earlier in this chapter). You can choose to make tax-deferred contributions to the SIMPLE IRA through convenient payroll deductions. Sounds easy, doesn't it? It is!

SIMPLE IRAs must satisfy certain requirements that include the following:

- ✔ The company must have 100 or fewer employees who received $5,000 or more in compensation during the previous year.

- ✔ The SIMPLE IRA must be the only retirement plan that the employer provides. However, employers that maintain a qualified plan for collective bargaining employees may maintain a SIMPLE IRA plan for their other employees.

- ✔ An eligible employee is one who has earned at least $5,000 per year in any two prior years and who's expected to earn at least $5,000 this year.

- ✔ The contribution limit is the lesser of your compensation or $10,500 for 2007. An additional catch-up contribution of $2,500 is allowed for employees who are 50 or older at the end of the calendar year.

- ✔ Employers must deposit employee deferrals as soon as possible (but no later than 30 days following the month in which the employee would otherwise have received the money).

- ✔ Employers must satisfy one of the following two contribution formulas:

  - They must match 100 percent of employee elective deferrals up to 3 percent of compensation.

  - They must make a nonelective contribution of 2 percent of compensation for each eligible employee (regardless of whether the employee defers compensation into the plan).

- ✔ Employers must deposit matching or nonelective contributions into the plan before the due date, including extensions, of their tax returns.

- ✔ Employers must allow their participating employees to stop making deferrals at any time.

- ✔ Each employee must always be 100 percent *vested* in (have ownership of) all the money in his or her SIMPLE IRA (both employee and employer contributions). See Chapter 7 for more about vesting.

After contributions are made to your SIMPLE IRA account, you're free to roll over the funds to another IRA or to withdraw the funds and pay tax on the distributions at any time. Contributions to a SIMPLE IRA don't affect your deductible contributions to a traditional IRA or Roth IRA.

The distribution rules for the SIMPLE IRA differ in one significant way from those for the traditional IRA and the Roth IRA: If you take a distribution from a SIMPLE IRA in the first two years, it's subject to a 25 percent additional tax.

The Skinny on the Simplified Employee Pension Plan (SEP)

An alternative variety of IRA is known as the *Simplified Employee Pension Plan,* or SEP. SEPs provide a significant source of income at retirement because employers are allowed to contribute directly to traditional IRA accounts set up for their employees. It's up to the employer, year to year, whether it chooses to contribute that year. After the money goes into the account, it becomes your money.

Who's eligible?

Small businesses with a handful of workers typically establish a SEP. In this instance, the owner *and* the workers of the business count as employees for the purposes of the SEP. In addition, a self-employed worker can set up a SEP; the employer and the employee, naturally, are the same person.

The employer must contribute to the SEP on behalf of each eligible employee who meets the following requirements:

- Is 21 years old
- Has performed service for the employer for at least three out of the last five years
- Performed service for the employer during the year that the contribution was made and received at least $450 (adjusted for cost-of-living expenses) in compensation for such year (regardless of whether the employee is still employed at the end of that year)

All eligible employees must participate in the SEP, including part-time employees, seasonal employees, and employees who die or terminate employment during the year.

How much can your employer contribute?

The amount that your employer is allowed to contribute is limited to the lesser of $45,000 (for 2007, subject to cost-of-living adjustments) or 25 percent of each employee's compensation. But remember that no minimum funding standards are imposed for a SEP, and your employer isn't locked into making contributions every year. In fact, the employer decides each year whether, and how much, to contribute to its employees' SEPs.

All amounts contributed to your SEP belong to you. In other words, you're 100 percent vested from the very beginning (see Chapter 7 for more details on vesting).

How can you handle distributions and rollovers?

The rules for taking a distribution from a SEP are the same as those for traditional IRAs (we cover the basics of these distribution rules earlier in this chapter). Money from a SEP can be rolled over tax-free to another SEP, to a traditional IRA, or to another employer's qualified retirement plan (provided that the other plan allows rollovers).

Money withdrawn from a SEP and not rolled over to another plan is taxable. If you withdraw money from a SEP before age 59½, you may also be subject to an additional 10 percent tax on the early withdrawal.

Chapter 6

Monitoring the Investments in Your Pension

So you know that your pension grows into a nice nest egg as you work toward retirement. You also know that the money in your plan comes from either your contributions or your employer's. How all the money in your plan accumulates for your retirement may be less obvious. Your plan, after all, is made up of various investments that (hopefully) grow more and more profitable over your working life, just in time for you to retire comfortably. To ensure that this is the case, this chapter provides you with the basics about the investment process and how to stay informed. Knowledge is protection, and in order to properly monitor your investments you need to understand the financial implications of self-directed versus plan-directed investments.

From the day you're hired to the day you expire, and as soon as you begin to participate in your pension plan, your goal should be to remain focused on the investments in your plan, whether the plan selects them or whether you're in charge:

> ✔ **If you're in a defined benefit plan, investment decisions are out of your control.** This lack of control doesn't mean, though, that you shouldn't stay informed as to how your plan is performing and how well your advisors are doing their jobs.

> ✔ **It's critical to monitor those investments that you choose in a self-directed plan (most defined contribution plans are self-directed).** Sometimes you have to make certain financial decisions that can dramatically affect your retirement nest egg.

In this chapter, we go over both types of plans: those with investments that are made by the plan and those that allow you to select your own investments.

The Form 5500 filed by your plan with the Internal Revenue Service (IRS) contains financial information, including investment information. Get in the habit of reviewing your plan's form and the schedules attached to it every year after the new one is filed. Because the Form 5500 contains a wealth of information on the company's pension plan, the plan is required to provide you with a copy if you ask for it. Request a copy in writing from your plan administrator (see Chapter 8 for details on obtaining plan information). You can also review your employer's Form 5500 online at www.freeerisa.com. If you want to check out a blank Form 5500 and its various schedules, you can do so at the IRS's Web site (www.irs.gov/formspubs); just search by form and instruction number, and then you can easily follow our discussion throughout this chapter.

Staying Alert When Others Decide Your Pension's Investments

If you're part of a defined benefit plan, you can expect plan officials and money managers to always make your investment decisions to ensure that the earnings on those investments are sufficient to pay your plan's promised benefits. In defined contribution plans, some plans make the investment decisions for you while others permit you to choose the investments. In a SEP or SIMPLE IRA, you always direct the investments. But remember, you aren't permitted to self-direct the investments unless your plan documents specifically grant you this right. More on all this later in the chapter.

In a defined benefit plan, no individual account exists for each plan participant. Instead, the pool of money is maintained and managed for the benefit of all participants. Because no separate account exists just for you, you and the other pensioners have no opportunity to make investment decisions.

If you're feeling a bit out of control with all this information, don't worry. In the following sections, we show you how to find out who's investing your pension's money and how they're doing so. We also explain how to check your investments' performance, recognize some warning signs of broken rules, and take action against the plan if necessary.

Checking out who's investing your money

In typical defined benefit plans, and even in some defined contribution plans, you have no say as to where your plan's funds are being invested. Instead, these decisions are made by plan trustees, investment managers, or the plan administrator. As you can imagine, then, it's important for you to know exactly who's managing the plan's money and making these decisions on your behalf.

Why do you need to know this stuff? Because if your employer's Uncle Frederick, whose company Cleenumout and Gotcha has 17 complaints against it for unethical practices, is managing your pension money, you have reason to be worried that there may be a problem in the long run. If you're concerned that the plan's money managers are more interested in lining *their* pockets than yours (as would be the case if Uncle Frederick's company is involved), you can make a complaint to the Department of Labor (DOL), as we explain later in this chapter.

To find out the identities of those who administer and provide services to the plan, you need to review the plan's Form 5500 and the schedules that are attached to the form. In the following list, we explain what to look for on the form and schedules to find out who's managing your plan's money:

- ✔ The plan administrator's name and address can be found on the second page of the plan's Form 5500. The plan administrator may be responsible for investing the funds, but that isn't always the case. It's also possible that the plan administrator may be a committee or board of trustees rather than a single person.

- ✔ If someone other than the plan administrator invests the money, such as an entity outside the plan (for example, a bank, an investment management firm, or an insurance company), look at Schedule C of the plan's Form 5500 to find out the names of those who provided services to the plan.

- ✔ The funds from your pension plan may be thrown into a pot and pooled with other pension plan money. These pooled funds may be maintained and invested by an insurance company or bank. Unfortunately, detailed financial information about pooled money isn't included in the Form 5500. This important information is instead filed by the bank or insurance company with the DOL and is available from the DOL upon request.

  The forms filed with the DOL identify all pooled asset funds that your plan participates in, including the names of the companies involved in the pooling of assets. This information should also be on file with your plan administrator. We provide the DOL contact information in the section "Taking action if you have concerns" later in this chapter.

Many insurance companies receive incredibly high fees to manage your pension money, and part of the problem is that you may be paying fees for items that aren't readily apparent, such as recordkeeping, audits, workshops, legal advice, custodial fees, and revenue sharing. In fact, fees are one of the biggest differences between a bank and an insurance company's management of your money.

If your pension money is being managed by an insurance company or through an annuity contract, you need to look at Schedule A, which is attached to Form 5500. Schedule A provides specific information concerning insurance contract coverage, fees, and commissions, including the amount of the commissions and fees paid and the purpose for the fees. It also includes investment and annuity contract information. If you can't determine what the fees are for or don't understand the form, ask a professional to help you decipher it.

Surveying your plan's selected investments

Depending on the size of your plan — whether it has more than or fewer than 100 employees — you must head to different Form 5500 schedules to discover your plan's chosen investments. If you want to explore why one investment or another was chosen, however, that specific information may be available only from the plan administrator or money managers employed by the plan. To contact outside money managers, ask your plan administrator for the name of the plan's financial advisor and how to contact him or her.

No matter the size of your company, look for diversification in its investment portfolio — you want to see a little of this and a little of that. If 80 percent of your plan is invested in any single investment, be concerned. Your plan must act prudently and with skill to minimize risk by diversifying its investment portfolio. The plan shouldn't be investing heavily in unusually risky investments, such as the following:

- ✔ Penny stocks or those equities that are trading for under a dollar
- ✔ Venture capital deals with no set value
- ✔ Real estate in exotic places or real estate connected to the plan sponsor
- ✔ Collectibles such as antiques, coins, or art
- ✔ Hedge funds

Keep the 10 percent rule in mind: With the exception of Employee Stock Ownership Plans (ESOPs; see Chapter 3 for more details) and certain other defined contribution plans designed to invest in employer stock, your plan shouldn't have more than 10 percent of the market value of its plan assets invested in employer property or employer stock. ERISA generally prohibits the investment of more than 10 percent of the plan's assets in employer stock or employer property in order to reduce the risk of a conflict of interest and to diversify plan investments to prevent significant losses.

If you think that your plan is invested in unusually risky investments, discuss your concerns with your plan administrator or the human resources department. In extreme situations, you can consider contacting the Department of Labor. See the later section "Taking action if you have concerns" for more information.

Plans with more than 100 employees

If your pension plan has more than 100 employees and you want to know what investments the plan owns, you need to go to Schedule H of Form 5500 to find out. There, you should look at Part 1, Item 1(c), where you can find the current value of plan assets. The assets you can expect to find listed include the following:

- ✔ Cash
- ✔ U.S. government securities, such as treasury bills
- ✔ Corporate debt instruments, which are bonds issued by corporations
- ✔ Corporate stocks
- ✔ Partnership and joint venture interests (basically business deals that the plan is involved in)
- ✔ Real estate
- ✔ Loans

The value of these assets will be listed for the beginning of the year and the value at the end of the year. The specific assets won't be listed, so if you want to know, for example, the specific stocks and bonds that the plan owns, you should ask the folks who make your plan's investments, such as your plan administrator or the plan's money managers.

Plans with fewer than 100 employees

Financial information for plans with fewer than 100 employees is found in Schedule I, Part I, Item 3 of the Form 5500. The information for smaller plans is limited to the value of specific assets at the end of the plan year that were held during the plan year. Those assets include the following:

- ✔ Partnership and joint venture interests
- ✔ Employer real property, which is, for example, your company's headquarters or the buildings it owns

✔ Other real estate

✔ Employer securities (this is the stock of the company you work for)

✔ Participant and nonparticipant loans

For more specific information regarding the actual assets, you have to contact the folks who make your plan investments, such as your plan administrator or the plan's money managers.

Keeping track of your investments' performance

You have a couple of methods for checking the performance of your plan's investments: reviewing your benefit statement with an eagle eye and calculating the rate of return. If you have direct contact with the plan's investment advisors, ask them about the performance and risk of the various investment options. If you don't have direct contact, ask your plan administrator or your own financial advisor, if you have one.

Your defined benefit plan has promised to pay you a set amount regardless of your investments' performance, so any ups and downs shouldn't cause you to worry yourself sick. Of course, it's a different kettle of fish if your plan goes belly up, as we explain in Chapter 12.

Reviewing your benefit statement

Examining your benefit statement (which we cover in more detail in Chapter 8) is an easy way to see how your plan's investments are performing, and you don't even have to lift a finger! The Pension Protection Act of 2006 (PPA) has changed the rules as to when plans must provide their plan participants with benefit statements. The type of plan you have determines when you get your benefits statement. Here are the general guidelines:

✔ Participants in plan-managed defined benefit plans receive benefit statements every three years, but you can request a benefit statement every year.

✔ Participants in plan-managed defined contribution plans receive annual benefit statements.

✔ Participants in defined contribution plans with participant-directed investments receive quarterly benefit statements (every three months).

Your benefit statement should provide some very basic information that tells you what you need to know about your investments' performance. As a general rule, the benefit statement should provide you with at least the amount of your vested benefits (see Chapter 7 for more about vesting) and information on the performance of the plan's investments. Your statement may also include the following:

✔ The total value of your assets

✔ The percentage of your account that's vested

✔ The change in value of your assets since the last report

✔ A list of the plan's specific holdings, including the cost and present value of each asset

The rate of return or loss may be provided in the report, but if not, it's simply the percentage of increase or decrease from the previous reporting period. So if you had a total value of $10,000 in your previous statement and jumped to $30,000 in your new statement, you have an increase of $20,000. To get the percentage of increase, divide the new number of $30,000 by the old number of $10,000, which gives you a 300 percent increase.

You also need to take into account the contributions that were made to the plan during the year when calculating investment return. For example, if the total contributions to your plan account during the year were $7,000, the investment gain in the previous example is only $13,000 of the total $20,000 increase in your plan account for the year.

Of course, even though a 300 percent increase is beyond the norm, what you may see instead is a more modest gain or even a loss. If you started with $10,000 but your new statement says that you have only $5,000, you have a $5,000 loss since the previous statement. To get the percentage of loss, you divide the new number of $5,000 by the old number of $10,000 and you come up with a 50 percent loss. In reality, your gains and losses hopefully won't fluctuate so dramatically.

Calculating the rate of return

To determine whether your plan is getting a good return on its investments, look at the financial information that's listed in the plan's Form 5500. To roughly calculate the plan's rate of return, add all the income (assets) and losses (liabilities) for the year, and then divide that number by the net assets from the beginning of the year. Here's how to find this information:

✔ If your plan has more than 100 employees, go to Part I of Schedule H of Form 5500. There, you will find the following:

• Total plan assets

• Total plan liabilities

• Net plan assets

Go to Part II of Schedule H to check out the Income and Expenses Statement. The following information is on this schedule:

- Total income (includes total contributions, earnings on investments, and any other income)

- Total expenses (includes benefit payments and payments to provide benefits, corrective distributions, deemed distributions, interest expense, and administrative expenses)

- Net income or net loss (appears at Line 2k at the end of Part II)

✔ If your plan has fewer than 100 employees, go to Part I of Schedule I of Form 5500. There, you find the following:

- Total plan assets

- Total plan liabilities

- Net plan assets

Here's an example: WAG, Inc., a manufacturer of authentic ancient Egyptian artifacts, has $10 million in its defined benefit plan at the beginning of the year, according to its Form 5500. In 2009, the plan made $600,000 on income from interest, dividends, and rents, but it also lost $100,000 on stock sales. To calculate the rate of return, subtract $100,000 from $600,000 for a total of $500,000. Then divide $500,000 by the net assets from the beginning of the year, which was $10 million. For the 2009 plan year, the rate of return was 5 percent (or 0.05). Make the same calculation for a number of years and you'll have an idea of how your plan's investments are performing.

Your plan should outperform a savings account earning 4 percent yearly interest; on the other hand, if the market was down 11 percent and your plan lost only 7 percent, your advisors didn't do so badly. When it comes to earnings in the market, you need to refer to benchmarks to measure how well or how poorly you're doing.

These standard benchmarks can help you gauge your fund performance. If you're in a managed account with relatively high management fees, you have every reason to expect that your account will outperform index funds that have low fees and low turnover. An *index fund* is a fund that automatically buys a little of this and a little of that to have a balanced and representative sample of securities or fixed-income products. There are index funds for big, medium, and small companies. The index funds include the following:

✔ The S&P 500 Index (SPX)

✔ The S&P Midcap Index (MID)

✔ The S&P Small Cap Index (IJR)

There are also index funds for long-term, intermediate, and short-term fixed income. The point of comparing your fund to other funds is to get an objective measure of your plan's performance and to give you a clue if your investments are doing well, poor, or average comparatively.

If the benchmarks are going one way and your account is going another, you have reason to be concerned. If your plan permits you to choose various mutual funds as investment options, review the investment options available and compare their performance to the appropriate benchmarks. If you're limited by the plan documents to a quarterly switch of plan choices, immediately begin to review the performance of the other options in your portfolio.

Seeing signs that the plan isn't following investment rules

Some things can't be repeated too many times. And this is one of them: You can't protect your pension investments if you don't know the rules (and don't bother to check them out periodically). So, for your own sanity, please take this section to heart.

The following rules are important, and you can check them out (by talking to your plan administrator) if you think that they're being abused:

- **The pension money must be invested for your benefit.** Nobody can use the money for himself or herself, including the bosses, the money managers, or their aunts and uncles.

- **Your plan's money can't be used to reimburse pension employees for treats such as lavish trips, expensive office furniture, or visits to the health spa.** If the pension managers are paid full time by the company or a union, they can get reimbursement only for expenses that were properly incurred.

- **The pension's money managers must diversify the investments.** If all of the plan's money is primarily in a single stock or office building, one poor investment could tank the whole plan. The money managers shouldn't invest too much in any single stock, bond, or real estate. Neither should all property owned by the plan be in one geographical area.

- **Pension fund managers must use skill, care, and prudence when they invest your money.** They can be considered failing in this responsibility if they take unreasonable risks or place the funds in a low- or no-interest bank account.

Beware, because if things are awry, the evidence is likely to be concealed. However, the Form 5500 is a good place to look for possible problems. The following sections list the likely places to find problems if your plan has more than or fewer than 100 employees.

If the plan's Form 5500 raises any questions, ask your plan administrator to explain the entry. If you still have concerns after speaking to him or her, you may want to take matters into your hands; see the later section "Taking action if you have concerns" for more information.

Plans with more than 100 employees

In Part III of Schedule G (Form 5500), you can find detailed information about prohibited transactions with a fiduciary (see Chapter 10) or disqualified person, including who was involved, the amount of money involved, and a description of the transaction.

A disqualified person includes your plan's financial advisors, attorneys, accountants, and actuaries as well as your employer. They're disqualified from certain transactions with the plan because they're so closely connected to the plan that they're in a position to have a big influence on plan decisions.

The following are examples of prohibited transactions:

- Your fiduciary invests the plan's money for his own benefit.
- The fiduciary gets a kickback from a vendor in exchange for doing business with the plan.
- The fiduciary gets involved in a business deal that's contrary to the best interests of the plan.
- A disqualified person lends or borrows money from the plan.
- A disqualified person sells, exchanges, or leases property.

It's to be expected that the plan will have administrative expenses for the day-to-day management of the fund and that it will have to pay fees to financial consultants and money managers. However these expenses must be reasonable. In Schedule H, Part II, Item 2(i), there's a line item for administrative expenses, which lists different categories for such expenses, including professional fees, contract administrator fees, investment advisory and management fees, and a category referred to as "other." If the investment advisory and management fees are more than 3 percent of the money under management, the fees are grossly out of whack. Even 1 percent is high (but acceptable). If any of the other expenses are high, you need to find out why. If you find $100,000 of unexplained expenses, it's a good idea to ask what they're for.

Checking out your plan's financial status with the summary annual report

Your plan must prepare a *summary annual report* (SAR) of the plan's financial status. The Form 5500 is the annual report for the plan; the SAR is a summary of that information. The SAR is usually distributed to employees at work and mailed to retirees on an annual basis.

The SAR contains some important financial information, including the following:

✔ Whether the plan's investments lost large amounts of money in the reporting year

✔ The amount of money spent on administrative expenses for the year

✔ If money loaned by the plan wasn't paid back on time

✔ A list of items regarding the plan's financial transactions

The SAR can signal problems, but remember that it's only a summary. If you see items that raise red flags or if you're concerned for one reason or another, you should look at the plan's complete financial statement and annual report (Form 5500). The SAR explains how to get a copy of the Form 5500. When requesting information, be sure to specify the exact form that you need. (See Chapter 8 for more on the SAR.)

Effective for plan years beginning after December 31, 2007, the Pension Protection Act of 2006 (PPA) has repealed the requirement that defined benefit plans provide a SAR. Instead, under the PPA, participants must be provided with an annual funding notice (for each plan year) that includes more specific information than previously required in the SAR.

The point is this: With a little persistence and some elbow grease, the type of information you need to know is available. It's when things go awry that the information is most difficult to get. The more difficult it is to get the information, the more persistent you should be.

In the same schedule, go to Part III (Accountant's Opinion), which is where the independent accountant can indicate his or her opinion of the plan. If the independent accountant's opinion indicates that the plan is unqualified or adverse, or provides a disclaimer (these are boxes to be marked on the form), find out what caused the accountant to indicate that there is a problem. When it comes to questions about your plan, the first place to make an inquiry is to the plan administrator.

When you're looking at Part IV (Transactions During Plan Year) in Schedule H, a number of items can serve as tip-offs to a problem. For example, consider these:

✔ Item 4(b) is where you find out whether any loans were listed as uncollectible. These types of loans would include those to other businesses that weren't repaid and that the plan can't collect. This item can be a red flag that something is wrong with the way that the funds are invested.

✔ Item 4(d) shows whether there were nonexempt transactions with plan insiders (who are called *parties in interest*), such as an officer of the company selling the real estate he was given by his Aunt Cheryl and Uncle Stanley to the plan.

✔ Item 4(f) explains any losses that the plan had due to fraud or dishonesty.

✔ Items 4(g) and 4(h) note whether the plan holds or receives assets whose value can't be readily determined.

✔ Item 4(j) is where you find out whether any plan transactions exceeded 5 percent of the current plan assets.

Plans with fewer than 100 employees

For the small plan, take a look at Schedule I (of Form 5500) to find where there are some juicy secrets that might signal trouble. In Item 2 of Part I, you can find the plan's expenses. If you see big numbers listed under "other expenses," find out about those items. In other words, a plan with $1 million in assets couldn't have 5 percent of its assets (or $50,000) listed as "other" expenses without a pretty good explanation.

In the same schedule, take a look at Part II, Item 4, which has some important information that could signal problems. Consider these:

✔ Item 4(a) notes whether the plan failed to transmit employee contributions on time.

✔ Item 4(b) shows whether any loans were classified as uncollectible (meaning that the loans won't be repaid).

✔ Item 4(c) shows whether any leases were classified as uncollectible (meaning that the tenant is a deadbeat and the rent is unpaid).

✔ Item 4(d) explains whether there were any nonexempt transactions with any parties in interest.

✔ Item 4(f) states whether any losses were caused by fraud and dishonesty.

Taking action if you have concerns

If you're concerned that your pension funds aren't being handled properly, contact the following government agencies, which are primarily responsible for investigating possible violations, bringing lawsuits, and handing out fines and penalties:

✔ **The Department of Labor:** The Department of Labor (DOL) investigates fund mismanagement. If you're concerned that plan trustees are violating the rules, you should contact the nearest regional field office of the

DOL's Employee Benefits Security Administration (EBSA). These locations can be found online at www.dol.gov/ebsa/aboutebsa/org_chart.html.

If a problem is found, the DOL can ask the plan trustees to return the improperly removed funds and can take the plan fiduciaries to court. The DOL could also ask a court to order penalties of 20 percent of the recovered money and to bar the wrongdoers from ever dealing with pension plans again.

✔ **The Internal Revenue Service:** The Internal Revenue Service (IRS) can investigate and impose penalties against anyone who's taking advantage of a close relationship with the plan by taking out improper loans or making other party-in-interest inside deals. See www.irs.gov for information on who to contact at the IRS.

A written claim for reward (for turning someone in to the IRS) that's filed with the Intelligence Division of the IRS may entitle you to 10 percent of what's collected by a penalty tax.

✔ **Federal Bureau of Investigation:** If actual stealing of pension money or out-and-out embezzlement happens, both the DOL and the Federal Bureau of Investigation (FBI) will step in. The FBI can turn evidence of a crime over to the Department of Justice for criminal prosecution.

If you contact the government, gather the important documents beforehand, and be prepared to provide a clear and concise statement of your concerns. And don't worry: It's unlawful for your employer to fire you or retaliate if you give the government information about your pension investment issues.

The government may not be responsive to your claim — even when your concerns are well-founded. It may not pursue your claim because, given the number of claims and the limitations on resources, the agency doesn't share your concern, or if it does, it doesn't choose to pursue it. Fortunately pension litigation is an area where a private attorney can be effective. In Chapter 19, we provide advice on how to select the proper attorney to represent your pension claim.

It's Up to You: Choosing Your Own Pension Investments

If you're in a defined contribution plan, you may have the opportunity to control your investment decisions. This option is referred to as a *self-directed account* or a *participant-directed investment,* and it allows you to make investment choices from a variety of possible investments.

However, your plan documents must provide that you, as a plan participant, are in charge of choosing the investments. So be sure to carefully read your plan documents (which we cover in Chapter 8) to make sure that you know exactly who has the responsibility for making investment decisions. If you're in a defined contribution plan that doesn't give you the opportunity to make investment choices, your plan officials have the job of investing the plan's assets (as we explain earlier in this chapter).

You always direct the investments in SIMPLE IRAs and Simplified Employee Pension Plans (SEPs; see Chapter 5 for more details).

Plans that provide for participant direction of investments want to satisfy the requirements of ERISA Section 404(c). (ERISA stands for the Employee Retirement Income Security Act of 1974; see Chapter 2 for more details.) In order to satisfy Section 404(c), the plan must do the following:

- ✔ **Provide for diversification by offering at least three different mutual fund options with different risk/return characteristics.** For example, the plan must offer at least one bond fund, one stock fund, and one balanced bond and stock fund.

    Your fiduciary is legally responsible for watching and selecting the investments that you choose from (see Chapter 10 for general info on fiduciaries).

- ✔ **Allow at least quarterly changes in investments by the participants.** The plan also must provide enough information about each investment to allow you to make an informed decision.

    Even though ERISA Section 404(c) only requires that you be permitted to change your investments at least quarterly, most plans with participant-directed investment options provide for 24/7 Internet access so that you can review the investments in your plan account and make changes.

Compliance with Section 404(c) isn't mandatory, and failure to comply with it doesn't cause a plan to violate ERISA. Failure to comply simply means that plan fiduciaries may continue to be responsible under ERISA for participant-directed investments. Fiduciaries need to continue to act prudently in selecting and retaining designated investment alternatives for the plan.

In the following sections, we point the way toward help with your investment options, we explain how to monitor and change your investments, and we warn you of what happens when you do nothing in a self-directed plan.

Getting help in making your investment choices

So how do you know which investments to pick? Our answer to this question is "Don't ask us; we're lawyers." Your best bet is to find a trusted financial advisor who can guide you. This advisor can help you make the best choices by taking into account your:

- ✔ Age
- ✔ Dependents
- ✔ Financial circumstances
- ✔ Health
- ✔ Tolerance for risk

Even though we may not be super at choosing investments, we do know that as a general rule, stocks are riskier than bonds and some stocks are as risky as the blackjack tables in Las Vegas.

Chapter 8 has details on finding a trustworthy financial advisor; be sure to ask why he's making his recommendations, and keep track of what investments you've purchased. Generally speaking, stocks, because of their ups and downs, have to be watched more closely than bonds with fixed interest rates. You can also check out *Personal Finance For Dummies,* 5th Edition, by Eric Tyson, MBA (Wiley), to get a handle on the investment scene. However, we suggest that you not ask your lawyer (or your doctor, for that matter) for investment advice. This is the province of trusted financial experts.

Another option? Ask your plan's fiduciary for help. (In this case, the fiduciary in question is your plan's financial advisor.) In the interest of making advice more accessible to plan participants and prodding participants to take advantage of professionally managed funds, the PPA has relaxed some of the rules regarding plan fiduciaries giving advice on investment choices. Prior to the act, it could be considered a conflict of interest for your fiduciary to use his or her influence to make money as a result of advice provided directly to you, the plan participant.

Now, because of the PPA, your fiduciary is permitted to give financial advice directly to you as long as the following conditions are met:

- ✔ **The fiduciary can't increase his compensation with his advice.** It doesn't matter whether he recommends Fudgalot Hedge Fund or Stikumtuyu Preferred Stock Certificates; as long as the advice results in the same level fees regardless of the investment recommendation you select, the advice is within PPA limits. In other words, if the fees stay the same (or level) and don't go up as a result of the recommendation, it doesn't matter if he wants you to buy stock A or stock B.

✔ **If the fiduciary wants to avoid the level fee restriction, his advice must conform to a computer-designed program.** The idea is that if he's restricted to a predesigned program, it can't be tailor-made to take advantage of you. The computer model must do the following:

   • Use generally accepted investment theories that figure in the returns of different types of assets over time

   • Be relevant to you, your age, your risk tolerance, your other assets, your life expectancy, and so on

   • Not operate in a manner that's biased in favor of the investment advisor or his cohorts

   • Use objective criteria to determine which investment options under the plan are best for plan participants

   • Consider the various options in the plan and properly evaluate them before determining how your account should be invested

If you choose the computer investment model option, all the advice by the financial advisor must be given through the computer model unless, unprompted by your advisor, you independently ask for advice that isn't related to the computer model. Then, and only then, is he permitted to offer unrestricted advice.

✔ **Under the PPA, your investment advisor is obligated to advise you of the amounts and the sources of his fees.** In recent years in the world of investment advice, amounts and sources of fees have often been closely guarded secrets (much too sensitive to be indiscriminately shared with those who are paying them). But luckily, the PPA now requires increased disclosure of both the source and the amount of the investment advisor's fees.

Checking (and changing) your investments

You keep track of investments in a self-directed plan the same way that you do in a plan-managed plan; see the earlier section "Keeping track of your investments' performance" for the full scoop. The main difference is that participants in self-directed plans receive benefit statements to review on a quarterly basis.

If you, like many others, are investing your 401(k) with a broker, you may be able to obtain a daily statement by using the Internet to go to the firm's secure Web site. There, you can look at your account and change investments.

Unlike with plan-managed investments, you have the option of making changes to your self-directed investments on at least a quarterly basis. Your plan is required to provide instructions regarding how to make changes to the account. It must also note any fees from the transactions.

Failing to exercise your investment options

What happens if, given all the possible investment choices, you opt to go spelunking instead of picking an investment option? Well, if you make no choice at all, it's then up to the fiduciary to make the investment prudently on your behalf.

To provide fiduciary protection when a default investment is made on your behalf, the PPA stepped in with a brand-new concept called the *qualified default investment alternative.* This latest addition to the pension alphabet soup is affectionately known by all bureaucrats and investment advisors as the QDIA. A QDIA is treated as if you actually exercise control over the account. In order to avoid investment liability, a QDIA must meet all the following requirements:

✔ You or your beneficiaries had to have the opportunity to self-direct your investments (but for whatever reason, you didn't).

✔ The investments must be diversified.

✔ At least once every quarter, you must have the right to switch without penalty to another investment option offered by your plan.

✔ The investment must be managed by an investment company or fiduciary.

✔ You must receive a notice 30 days before the investment is first made on your behalf and 30 days in advance of the investment being made for each following plan year. The notice must explain your right to direct the investment yourself and explain how the account will be invested if you make no choice. It also must be written so that it can be understood, which is the exception for most financial documents.

✔ The plan must make available all the investment material that it receives from the investment advisors or from the actual investment, such as a mutual fund or stock (and it must send the materials to you upon your request).

Special rules for special investment situations

Sometimes, for a certain period of time, your plan doesn't allow you to make any investment decisions. This downtime in which you're prevented from directing your investment for more than three consecutive business days is referred to as a *blackout.* You may also run into times when the plan is changing its investment options. This is referred to as *mapping,* and it will involve a blackout period. During a blackout period, your plan has to follow some special rules:

✔ Because you have no control during a blackout, in order to avoid liability for losses during this time, your fiduciary must provide you notice of the blackout at least 30 days before it begins.

✔ When it comes to mapping, if the plan changes from one investment option to another and the two options are similar, the plan won't be liable for investment losses as long as notice was provided.

Notice must be given at least 30 days, but no more than 60 days, before the switch. The notice must describe the change and include a comparison with your current investment. It must also advise you of your right to invest in a different investment option under the plan. Unless you make a decision to change the investment, you can't bring a claim against the fiduciary for any losses as a result of the change from the prior investment option to the new mapped investment option.

✔ The investments must be one of the following three types:

- Balanced funds under which the investments are split between stocks (equities) and bonds (fixed-rate investments)

- Managed accounts, which are set up and invested by the plan's investment advisor

- Age-based lifecycle or target funds, which adjust the investment risk to be safer or more conservative as you get older

Part II
Making Sure That You Receive the Pension You Earned

The 5th Wave   By Rich Tennant

"Oh, her? That's Ms. Lamont, our plan administrator. She's going to help me determine your eligibility in our 401(k) plan."

In this part . . .

Contrary to popular belief, pension benefits are frequently miscalculated. For this reason, nothing's more important than making sure that when you retire, you receive all the pension benefits that you're entitled to. In this part, you discover how to be among those retirees who get the right amount right off the bat. First, we explain the basics of eligibility, accrual, and vesting in your pension plan. We then identify some helpful guidelines for planning your retirement while you're still working. Finally, we give you an overview of the rules regarding the distribution of your pension benefits.

Chapter 7

Getting the Scoop on Eligibility, Accrual, and Vesting

In This Chapter

▶ Meeting eligibility requirements for a pension plan

▶ Getting a grip on accrual

▶ Determining when the benefits are yours

*E*ligibility, accrual, and vesting are the Three Musketeers of your pension plan. Unless you meet all the requirements, no pension is on your horizon. Here's how the three work together in a nutshell:

✔ First, you must become *eligible,* or in other words, you must fulfill your company's minimum standards to participate in the plan. Generally, these requirements relate to age and the length of time you work.

✔ As you work, you *accrue* (or accumulate) benefits in the plan. When and how benefits accrue is central to your pension's value. Accrual is like building credit; until the benefits *vest* (or are no longer subject to forfeiture), the money you've accrued remains out of reach.

✔ Finally, and most critically, after your benefits are *fully vested* (in other words, when they can't be taken away from you), you can lay claim (when the time is right) to all you have accrued.

This chapter lays out these bedrock concepts in detail.

Eligibility: Officially Entering a Plan

Your employer's retirement plan can establish both age and service requirements that you must satisfy before you can participate in the plan. The Employee Retirement Income Security Act of 1974 (ERISA), however, doesn't give a plan free reign; it sets minimum standards for age and service. The plan can be more generous than those standards, but not less generous. The first step to determine if you're eligible is to check the plan's language in the summary plan description (SPD). (See Chapter 8 for more about the documents the plan must provide you and how you can request the SPD.)

The following sections outline common minimum standards and help you determine whether you're entitled to participate in your employer's plan.

Meeting age requirements

A plan can establish a minimum age that employees must be to participate in the plan, but it can't set a maximum age. But the plan isn't *required* to have a minimum age requirement for eligibility, so if it wants to, it can permit participation for any employee, regardless of age. Here are the general guidelines:

- ✔ A plan can require that employees be at least 21 years old before they can participate in the plan. However, a plan can't require a minimum age greater than age 21 for plan participation.
- ✔ Even though your plan can exclude employees younger than 21, it can't exclude employees because they're older. For example, your plan can't have a rule that says employees older than 50 aren't eligible to participate in the pension plan.

Surveying service requirements

Your plan can impose certain restrictions on the length of time (known as *service*) you must work before you're eligible to participate in the pension plan, subject to certain limitations. Breaks in service can impact your eligibility, too. We explain years of service and breaks in those years of service in the following sections.

Starting with a year (or more) of service

It's common for qualified retirement plans to require that employees complete a full year of service before they can participate in the pension plan. However, just because you aren't yet eligible to participate in the plan doesn't mean the plan can't count the work you've already performed when you do become eligible.

If the plan has eligibility requirements of age 21 and one year of service, you begin to participate in the plan when you complete the later of the requirements. So if you began working for the company at age 19, you would already have completed your one year of service before you reach age 21 and you would complete your eligibility requirements on your 21st birthday. A plan, in any instance, can't require more than two years of work for eligibility purposes, and it can require this number of years only if the plan provides for full and immediate vesting after the two years (we discuss vesting later in this chapter).

The rules for a 401(k) are different from those for other types of pension plans. If you're in a 401(k) plan, you only need to work one year to meet the minimum service requirement before you can contribute a portion of your salary to the plan. Many 401(k) plans provide for shorter eligibility periods of 30 or 90 days. For general information about 401(k) plans, see Chapter 4.

Your plan can choose one of the following two methods for determining whether you have earned a year of service:

✔ **The actual-hours method of counting service:** The plan may define a year of service for eligibility purposes as up to 1,000 hours worked during a consecutive 12-month period. An hour of work means an hour that you were paid to work or were entitled to be paid (such as paid vacation time). The 12-month period for crediting service for participation is generally either the plan year (which could be a calendar year or a noncalendar fiscal year) or the anniversary of your date of hire. Under this method, your employer must keep track of the number of hours you actually work.

If the plan doesn't want to count actual hours, the Department of Labor has provided alternatives. For example, the plan can count days worked (each day will be worth nine hours) or weeks worked (each week is worth 45 hours). These are known as *hour equivalencies*.

✔ **The elapsed-time method:** Under this method, your employer simply keeps track of the credited time since you started work. You basically get one year of service for each full year you work, no matter how few hours you actually work. But if your employer lays you off or you quit before the end of the year, you don't get a full year of service for that year — even if you've actually worked more than 1,000 hours. This method of counting can really hurt workers if they're fired before the last day of the year in which they would have fully vested in their benefits.

Look at your SPD to see which method your plan uses to calculate service. Check out Chapter 8 for full details about this handy document.

Understanding breaks in service

If you leave work and then return, your plan may consider you to have a *break in service.* A break in service is generally a plan year during which you work fewer than 501 hours. Whether your leave is considered a break in service may depend on why you take the break and how long you're gone. If you take time off to go skiing or help orphans in Africa, you'll have a break in service if you don't work the 501 hours in a plan year.

If you leave and go back to work after military service, however, your time away from the office may not be treated as a break in service. And better yet, you may get credit for the time you were in the military. (Another special exception is maternity and paternity leave; see the next section.)

Sometimes you simply can't help taking a break from your job, but keep in mind that you can lose credit for the years you've already worked, depending on the number of breaks and the previous years you've worked. You don't forfeit prior years worked because of a break in service unless you have at least five consecutive breaks. For example, if you worked three years and then took five consecutive breaks in service (you took time off to scuba dive one year; you spent many weeks caring for a sick relative the next year; you took a leave of absence to complete your MBA; and so on), you could lose the unvested benefits you accrued those first three years. No matter how many breaks in service you have, you won't lose the portion of your plan benefits that was vested prior to the break.

If you work more than 500 hours but fewer than 1,000 hours, that's neither a break in service nor a year of service, and you would essentially be in limbo during each year, neither gaining nor losing benefits.

A special occasion: Going on maternity or paternity leave

Say you're about to be a new mom or dad and you want to stay home for a couple of months with your new son or daughter. Congrats! But the last thing you want to worry about right now is how taking time off from your job will affect your pension. You can relax. The rules for maternity or paternity leave are straightforward.

As a rule, your absence from work must be for one of the following reasons:

- ✔ Your pregnancy
- ✔ The birth of your child
- ✔ An adoption by you
- ✔ Caring for your child right after the birth or adoption

The great thing about taking maternity or paternity leave is that you're considered to have worked at least 501 hours when it comes to determining a break in service. So if you go on maternity or paternity leave for 12 months, that time doesn't count as a break in service.

The total number of credited hours given to you by the company for maternity or paternity leave isn't required to exceed 501 hours. But it must be credited in the year the absence begins, and the credits are necessary to prevent a break in service for that year or the following year.

For example, if you went on maternity leave in 2002 after working 750 hours that year and if you returned to work in 2004, you wouldn't have incurred a break in service for either 2002 or 2003. You don't have a break in service for 2002 because you worked more than 501 hours that year, and you don't have a break in service in 2003 because you were on maternity leave and entitled to one free break in service that year.

To pensioners who took maternity or paternity leave: Check your SPD to find out the company policy on maternity and paternity leave and your individual benefit statement (or whatever document the plan provides you that details your service credit) to see if you were given credit for the time you took off for this reason. The whole idea of maternity and paternity leave is that you can take the time off and not be penalized for it. So if you weren't given the credit you were entitled to, bring it to the attention of your plan administrator for correction.

Checking that your plan follows the eligibility rules

Take a look at your SPD to confirm that your plan follows the rules as they apply to eligibility. Both big plans and small plans make mistakes, so you always need to be on the lookout. One of the main reasons we wrote this book is to provide you with the rules that you need so that you can determine if they're being followed. Here are few guidelines to keep in mind as you're reviewing your SPD:

- ✔ Your plan should specify the method used to compute the eligibility period (actual hours versus elapsed time).

- ✔ If your plan credits hours of service when no work was performed (for example, if you're on a leave as a result of a work-related injury), it should spell out the rules for crediting those hours. Generally, a plan must credit service for all hours that you were paid, including paid vacation or paid personal time.

- ✔ The eligibility period for figuring a break in service should be the same as the one used to figure a year of service. In other words, both time periods should be computed by the same method.

- ✔ Your plan should make clear any age or service requirements.

- ✔ Your plan must provide credit hours to prevent a break in service for maternity or paternity leave (which we cover in the previous section).

If you have questions regarding plan eligibility or you can't understand the explanation in the SPD, contact your plan administrator.

Accrual: The Pension Is Almost Yours

Accrual is when your benefits grow or accumulate in your plan. As your benefits accrue, they accumulate in your pension account. However, until those accrued benefits vest (or are no longer subject to forfeiture), they can still be taken from you (we cover vesting later in this chapter). We explain the basics of accrual and discuss an important anti-cutback rule affecting your pension rights in the following sections.

Grasping the basics of growing your benefits

Your benefits under a defined benefit plan are generally based on a formula that includes your years of service and the level of your compensation. Your benefits under a defined contribution plan are based on your account balance, which includes both employee and employer contributions and investment earnings.

Forfeiture

In order to understand forfeiture, you first need to understand the relationship between accrual and vesting. Accrual allows your account to grow, but the money in the account still isn't exactly yours because it can be taken away from you or *forfeited.* When those accrued benefits vest, they're yours and are available to you when you retire. This is known as *full benefit accrual* (see the next section). After accrued benefits are vested, they're no longer subject to being lost or forfeited, regardless of the reason.

A forfeiture occurs if you terminate employment prior to being fully vested in your benefits under the plan. The nonvested portion of your benefits (accrued but not yet vested) may be forfeited when you terminate employment, and your benefit will consist only of the vested portion of your plan benefits. For example, if you're fired before you're 100 percent vested, you forfeit only the portion that isn't vested. So if you were 25 percent vested with $100,000 of accrued benefits, you would forfeit $75,000 and retain $25,000 — your vested portion.

Any time you put your own money into your pension as part of a defined contribution plan, the money is all yours and can't ever be forfeited.

Full benefit accrual

The size of your benefits and the rate at which they grow depends on the specific type of pension that you have and on whether it's a defined contribution or defined benefit plan (see Chapter 3 for the basics on these plans). To estimate the size of the benefits that you're accumulating, examine your SPD. Make sure you understand how you earn service credit for full benefit accrual and that you're receiving the proper credit for each year.

When it comes to benefit accrual, generally the calculation of your service counts only those years that you worked after you became a plan participant, not from the time you started to work. A defined benefit plan, however, can give you benefit credit for years before you started work in the plan. The most common situation for this is when an employer adopts a plan; it may give benefit credit for service before the plan even started. This credit is known as *past-service credit.*

In order to accrue a benefit for a given year, a defined benefit plan can require that you have 1,000 hours of service during a plan year. To receive a contribution in a defined contribution plan, however, the plan can require that you have 1,000 hours of service during the year *and* that you're employed by the employer sponsoring the plan on the last day of the plan year.

You should be able to review the number of service credits that you've accrued in your plan on your individual benefit statement (see Chapter 8 for details on this document). So that you get what's rightfully yours, always be sure to keep track of the value of your credits and benefits throughout the years that you work. If you think that your benefit statement hasn't properly credited your years of service with the company or doesn't reflect your total compensation, contact your plan administrator or your employer's human resources department.

Avoiding an improper retroactive reduction of your benefits

As a rule of thumb, the *anti-cutback rule* prevents your plan from reducing your benefits after they've accrued. The plan can, however, reduce the rate at which future benefits may accrue. For example, if your plan is amended in 2009, benefits accrued before the date of the amendment in 2009 can't be reduced. Benefits accrued after the date of the 2009 amendment may, however, be modified or reduced.

In addition to the amounts that you've accumulated, your plan can't retroactively reduce or eliminate the following:

✔ Optional forms of benefits, such as the right to take your payment in a lump sum instead of an annuity.

✔ Early retirement benefits, if your plan offers them.

✔ A retirement subsidy, which is when your plan provides an additional perk and absorbs the cost. For example, your plan may decide to let plan participants retire at age 60 and pay them the same benefits as if they had continued working until age 65.

Certain types of benefits, by their nature, may be reduced or terminated without running afoul of the anti-cutback rule. This list includes the following:

- ✔ Social Security supplements
- ✔ Various types of insurance, such as accident, health, or life insurance
- ✔ The ability to take a loan from the plan (see Chapter 13 for more details)
- ✔ Self-direction of your investments (*self-direction* is when you're permitted to make decisions regarding how your pension money is invested)

Carefully look at all reductions of benefits and/or plan amendments to determine if rights you had before the change have been taken away wrongfully. Be sure to read Chapter 12 for a more detailed discussion on plan amendments involving the reduction or elimination of past and future benefits and the notice requirements that your plan must follow.

Vesting: The Pension Is Yours, and No One Can Take It!

The idea behind *vesting* is that at some point, the accrued benefits are all yours and can't be forfeited if you quit, lose your job, or for any other reason. Your plan, whether it's a defined contribution or defined benefit plan, must meet certain minimum vesting periods.

A *vesting schedule* is a time period over which your benefits under the plan become nonforfeitable. Each schedule has two elements: years of vested service (generally based on 1,000 hours in a plan year) and the percentage of your accrued benefit that's vested. All of your years of service with the employer starting at age 18 count for vesting service, even if you weren't yet a participant in the plan. Two types of vesting schedules exist:

- ✔ *Cliff vesting* is all or nothing; you're 0 percent vested until you fall off the cliff and become 100 percent vested.
- ✔ *Graded vesting* provides for different vesting levels for different years of service.

Your plan's vesting schedule is stated in the SPD.

When you receive your individual benefit statement (see Chapter 8 for details), review your accrued benefits and the percentage of your vested benefits to see if the statement is accurate. If the benefits don't seem to be correct, contact the plan administrator.

In the following sections, we describe different types of vesting schedules and potential amendments to those schedules.

Employee contributions to defined contribution plans are 100 percent vested at all times. The money started as yours and remains yours. Benefits under a SEP or SIMPLE IRA are 100 percent vested at all times as well; see Chapter 5 for more about these types of plans.

Looking at accelerated vesting schedules

Effective for plan years beginning after 2006, the Pension Protection Act of 2006 (PPA) has accelerated the vesting of benefits in defined contribution plans. Starting in 2007, contributions must take no longer than three years to vest under a cliff vesting schedule and no longer than six years under a graded vesting schedule. Defined benefit plans that are *top-heavy* also are subject to these accelerated vesting schedules.

A *top-heavy plan* is a plan in which the present value of the accrued benefits of the big, important employees (called *key employees*) is more than 60 percent of the present value of the total benefits under the plan. A top-heavy plan must use a vesting schedule no longer than a three-year cliff vesting or six-year graded vesting schedule. The top-heavy schedules apply to both defined contribution and defined benefit plans.

Under a three-year cliff vesting schedule, you aren't vested at all for the first two years, and then — ba-da-bing! — you're 100 percent vested at the completion of the third year of eligible service. Table 7-1 shows the current post-PPA vesting schedule as of 2007 using cliff vesting.

Table 7-1	Three-Year Cliff Vesting Schedule
Years of Vesting Service Completed	*Percentage of Your Accrued Benefit That Is Vested*
1	0%
2	0%
3	100%

Under a six-year graded vesting schedule, you're 20 percent vested after two years, and then the amount increases by 20 percent each year until you're 100 percent vested after six years. Table 7-2 shows the current graded vesting schedule in use after the enactment of the PPA (as of 2007).

Table 7-2	Six-Year Graded Vesting Schedule
Years of Vesting Service Completed	*Percentage of Your Accrued Benefit That Is Vested*
1	0%
2	20%
3	40%
4	60%
5	80%
6	100%

Viewing less rapid vesting schedules

While employer contributions to defined contribution plans after 2006 are subject to accelerated vesting schedules, defined benefit pension plans are subject to less rapid minimum vesting schedules. An employer may elect to have two vesting schedules under a defined contribution plan: an accelerated schedule for contributions made after 2006 and a longer or less rapid schedule for contributions made before 2007. Because forfeitures of nonvested funds under a plan can be used to offset and reduce employer contributions for the year of the forfeiture, some employers choose to have the longest possible vesting schedule.

The PPA, however, does require that vesting under a cash balance type of defined benefit plan be no longer than three-year cliff vesting.

Table 7-3 shows the cliff vesting schedule for defined benefit plans and for contributions to defined contribution plans before 2007.

Table 7-3	Five-Year Cliff Vesting Schedule
Years of Vesting Service Completed	*Percentage of Your Accrued Benefit That Is Vested*
1	0%
2	0%

Years of Vesting Service Completed	Percentage of Your Accrued Benefit That Is Vested
3	0%
4	0%
5	100%

Table 7-4 shows the graded vesting schedule for defined benefit plans and for contributions to defined contribution plans before 2007.

Table 7-4	Seven-Year Graded Vesting Schedule
Years of Vesting Service Completed	Percentage of Your Accrued Benefit That Is Vested
1	0%
2	0%
3	20%
4	40%
5	60%
6	80%
7	100%

Dealing with multiple vesting schedules

As we mention earlier, the PPA changed the minimum vesting schedules for defined contribution plans. So, depending on when you earned your benefits, your employer may have to keep track of multiple vesting schedules for your account balances. The obvious, immediate impact of this change is that your plan's benefit statement may show more than one vesting schedule, which means that some of your accrued benefits are vesting faster than others.

Due to the confusion that can be caused by using multiple vesting schedules, many employers have elected to amend their plan to apply the three-year cliff or six-year graded vesting schedules to all participants employed in 2007, when the new schedule takes effect.

Review your benefit statement each year to make sure that both your benefits and your vested percentage are properly calculated. If they aren't correct, contact your plan administrator or your company's human resources office.

Amending the vesting schedule

If it chooses, the plan can amend the vesting schedule. A defined benefit plan may choose, for example, to change from a five-year cliff vesting to a seven-year graded vesting schedule or to accelerate vesting with a three-year cliff vesting schedule in order to enhance the value of the plan for its participants.

If the vesting schedule is amended, you aren't without rights. If you have completed at least three years of service, you can elect to remain under the old vesting schedule. If you make no decision, you automatically go into the new schedule, provided that you were notified of the change.

Of course, the plan still has to comply with the minimum vesting requirements imposed by law, and your benefits can never be less vested than they were when the vesting schedule was amended.

Reviewing your plan's vesting policies

Here are some quick (though not complete) guidelines that explain how your plan should deal with vesting issues. By going over these guidelines, you'll see whether your plan is complying with the vesting rules under ERISA (see Chapter 2). Because your plan may have service requirements in order for you to be vested, you'll notice some overlap with the earlier checklists.

- ✔ Your SPD and plan document should clearly spell out how hours of service are credited toward vesting. (We discuss SPDs and plan documents in Chapter 8, and we explain how to go about obtaining them if you don't already have them.)
- ✔ The SPD and plan document should define a break in service.
- ✔ If you leave your job with vested benefits and then return to employment, your prebreak service should be counted when determining your vested benefits from employer contributions.

Vesting problems occur frequently. If you think that your vested percentage is inaccurate (or you have other questions), contact your plan administrator.

Chapter 8

Planning for Retirement While You're Still Working

....

In This Chapter

▶ Estimating your retirement costs

▶ Assembling the right pension information to prepare for retirement

▶ Putting everything together for a clear retirement picture

....

*W*e all know that we need to save money for those things that we want to buy, like a new car, a house, or a fancy, high-end TV set. Everything costs money, and the cost of retirement is no different. In fact, your retirement is one of the most costly things you'll ever pay for. As we continue to live longer, we'll have more years of retirement during which we'll need to be supported. And the more years we live after retirement, the more expensive retirement becomes.

These days, fewer employers are choosing to provide traditional defined benefit pension plans (see Chapter 3) because of the funding requirements and the expenses involved. Often companies instead offer retirement options such as 401(k)s (see Chapter 4), which are paid for primarily by the employee rather than the employer. Or the employer may choose not to offer retirement benefits at all, putting the burden directly on the employee. In this case, the employee must shoulder the responsibility of planning responsibly for retirement.

To know how much you should save for retirement, you need to know what you can expect your pension plan to provide you so that you can calculate how it fits into your overall retirement savings plan. We show you the ropes in this chapter.

Tallying the Cost of Your Retirement

For most American workers, the goal of retirement is to have a secure future. And a secure future means different things to different people. For those people who plan to settle into a modest lifestyle in a less expensive part of the country, retirement will be more affordable than for the person who plans to take lavish vacations and live the high life. Likewise, it will be more affordable for those who are planning to retire closer to the normal retirement age of 65 (or even later) than it will be for those who are planning to retire well in advance of that age. Obviously, the more years you have to save, the better off you are.

We aren't professional financial planners or financial counselors — we'll leave that job to someone else. These types of professionals can help you determine exactly how much money you need to put aside now to ensure a secure retirement later. (And we highly recommend that you consult a professional planner or counselor for this type of help! We show you how to find a pro later in this chapter.) But we can say with certainty that it's difficult to save adequately for retirement if you don't know how much you need to put aside each month. And of course that amount depends on your retirement plans: at what age you plan to retire and what your expectations are for retirement.

To meet the goal of a secure future, it's important to make retirement planning a priority. This planning starts in the following sections with a basic understanding of the costs of retirement.

Calculating your current net worth

Your current financial resources directly affect your ability to reach your retirement goals and your ability to protect those goals from potential financial crises. These resources are all those assets that are available to help you meet life's expected and unexpected occurrences. A good place to begin in the examination of your resources is with a calculation of your net worth. If you're married, don't forget to take into account the net worth of both you and your spouse.

Your *net worth* is the total value of what you *own* (your assets) minus what you *owe* (your liabilities). Your net worth is a picture of your financial health. To determine the approximate value of your assets, add up the current market value of the following:

 ✔ Your personal possessions

   Of course, used clothes and well-worn furniture have little value, while diamonds, expensive watches, collectibles, and art can be worth a bundle. You don't need to list every little item; the value of the pricier items is just one part of your net worth, which is, after all, just an approximation.

✔ Your vehicles (yours and your spouse's)

✔ Your individual and joint checking accounts

✔ Your individual and joint savings accounts

✔ The cash value (not death benefits) of life insurance policies

✔ The current value of investments, including stocks, bonds, certificates of deposit, retirement accounts, individual retirement accounts (IRAs; see Chapter 5 for an introduction), and any pensions that you and your spouse have

✔ The current value of all real estate

To determine your liabilities, add up the following:

✔ The outstanding mortgage on your home

✔ Family credit card debt

✔ Your loans and your spouse's, including student loans, auto loans, income taxes due and owing, and taxes due on the profits of any of your investments (if you've cashed them in)

✔ Any other outstanding bills or debts that you and your spouse have or may have in the future, including the present value of the cost of your children's educations and the present value of taking care of dependent parents

Even though these items may not be current obligations, ignoring them will give you an unrealistic picture of your financial health.

Subtract your liabilities from your assets to arrive at your net worth. Your goal is to have a positive net worth that grows from year to year. You'll rely on this net worth to help support your future, and you can draw on these funds when you're faced with a financial crisis (which, of course, can happen to anyone!).

Considering your retirement age and lifestyle options

A lot depends on when you want to retire and the kind of retirement you want to enjoy — namely, how much you need to save between now and then (don't worry; we get to that in the next section).

If you plan to retire early, before the normal retirement age set forth in your plan, you need to build a larger nest egg than if you retire later. That larger nest egg is necessary because you'll be living on it for a much longer period of time, and early retirement may mean a smaller pension. This scenario is especially true if you don't plan on working during retirement.

You also need to consider your lifestyle options during retirement. Someone who's planning a quiet, modest retirement in a low-cost part of the country needs a lot less money than someone who plans to live in a fancy gated community and to winter on the French Riviera.

Making a decision about your retirement lifestyle may be a bit easier if you consider the following questions:

✔ Do you plan to live in an expensive part of the country (or world)?

✔ Do you plan to travel to foreign countries?

✔ Are you planning to work part time or volunteer?

✔ Are you healthy or do you anticipate a large portion of your retirement going toward medical expenses?

✔ Will you go back to school?

✔ Are you planning to visit with your grandkids regularly or spend time golfing at a country club?

✔ Will you have to support your parents or children or pay for your children's college educations?

✔ Do you want to leave an inheritance for your descendants?

Estimating how much you need to save

Consider the following questions when you begin to calculate how large your retirement nest egg will need to be.

How much retirement income will you need?

The rule of thumb is that you need 70 to 90 percent of your preretirement income in order to enjoy the standard of living to which you've become accustomed. This number is often called the *annual cost of your retirement*. The more caviar and champagne in your retirement plans, the higher the percentage of your preretirement income you'll need.

Everyone's expenses are different, of course, but typically, as a retiree, you can expect that they will decline. However, as usual, there are a number of exceptions to that rule. For example, if you still own a home, have kids in school, have college debts to pay off, or have large medical bills to pay, your expenses are likely to be more than the average retiree's. Taxes are also usually smaller for retirees, and costs related to work usually disappear.

How many years are left until you retire?

The more years you have left, the less you have to save each month, and vice versa.

There's an advantage to saving as much as you can early, though, because you'll benefit the most from the compounding of investment income. You should try to save the same percentage of your income throughout your life and perhaps a larger percentage of your income when you're young.

How long will you live during your retirement?

Obviously, your exact life span isn't really known (or knowable) and you don't have complete control over it, but there are some statistics that can help you with your planning. For instance, these days a man who retires at age 55 can expect to live about 23 years into retirement. A woman who retires at the same age can expect to live about 27 years into retirement. And the likelihood that a male retiree will live at least 20 more years is more than 60 percent. For women retirees, that likelihood is about 75 percent.

These figures are only averages, however. For example, white-collar people tend to live longer, and for every person who lives to the actuarial average, there is another person who dies sooner or much later. You, of course, must plan for your own circumstances. If you die early or haven't made provisions for the possibility of outliving the average life expectancy, you're truly up the creek without a paddle.

And don't forget that the healthier you are, the longer you'll live — especially if you have good genes.

What other sources of income will be available to you when you begin to save for retirement?

Your net worth (which we show you how to calculate earlier in this chapter) will tell you whether you're going to be dependent on your pension to support you during retirement. Income in addition to your wages (for example, if you receive income from rental property or dividends from investments) will help as you begin to save for retirement.

When do you plan to start taking Social Security benefits?

The longer you can delay taking them, the higher they'll be when you start taking them. But keep in mind that the longer you delay them, the longer you have to live in order to receive enough payments to make up for the delay in taking them. Complications also arise if you take your Social Security benefits before you reach the magic age of 65. Before you decide what's best for you, go to your local Social Security office and ask for guidance regarding your particular situation.

Are you making adjustments to savings for inflation?

The less your money will be worth in future years, the more of it you're going to need. Because the annual inflation rate is certain to change over time, your best bet is to assume a higher rate of inflation so that the purchasing power of your available money won't be seriously eroded.

What annual rate of return can you expect on your investments?

Just to play it safe, financial planners often rely on historical rates of return based on the risk of the types of investments you choose. The greater the risk, the bigger your potential return or the bigger your possible loss. In other words, expect less, and then if you get more, you'll be pleasantly surprised.

Gathering the Goods on Your Pension Plan

After you have a clear picture of what your retirement years will look like, you have to decide whether your company's pension plan will be all you need or whether it will just be a part of the solution. This decision depends on not only the size of your pension, but also on the strength of the plan.

Our mission, then, is to help you understand how your pension plan factors into your overall assessment of the income that you need for retirement. The documents and information in the following sections help you determine later on just how much retirement security you actually have and how secure it really is.

The necessary pension plan papers

To find out what type of plan you have and what benefits it will provide, you need to assemble your pension documents. It's important to understand what these documents provide so that you can better understand the relationship between your plan's benefits and your overall retirement picture.

The Employee Retirement Income Security Act of 1974 (ERISA) requires plan administrators to give you the following documents regarding your retirement plan's features and funding. Some documents must be given to you automatically and regularly, while others are available to you upon request. Head to Chapter 2 to find out when you can expect to receive these documents under ERISA regulations.

The summary plan description

One of the most important documents your plan administrator must provide you is called the *summary plan description* (SPD). This summary of the retirement plan gives you the following information:

- ✔ Details of how the plan works, including critical plan information and whether it's a defined benefit or defined contribution plan (see Chapter 3 for details)
- ✔ What benefits it provides
- ✔ When an employee can begin participating in the plan
- ✔ How service and benefits are calculated
- ✔ When benefits becomes vested (see Chapter 7 for more about vesting)
- ✔ When and in what form benefits are paid
- ✔ How to file a claim for benefits
- ✔ Your rights and protections under ERISA

Revisions to the plan

If your retirement plan ever changes, you must be informed through a *summary of material modifications* (SMM) or a revised summary plan description. The SMM is the notice that you're entitled to receive of significant modifications to the plan, such as when an amendment will lower future benefit accruals. The revised SPD incorporates the changes into a new plan document.

The summary annual report and Form 5500

Under federal law, your pension plan must give you information about the plan investments. The plan must automatically provide you, free of charge, with a summary of its finances for each year or a written notice of your right to receive that summary. The summary is called a *summary annual report,* or SAR.

Effective for plan years beginning after December 31, 2007, the Pension Protection Act of 2006 (PPA) has repealed the requirement that defined benefit plans provide SARs. Instead, under the PPA, they must provide participants with an annual funding notice for each plan year that includes more specific information than was previously required in the SAR.

In addition, if you ask in writing, your plan administrator must give you a copy of the full annual report and the financial statements that the plan files with the government, referred to as a Form 5500. The Department of Labor (DOL) and the Pension Benefit Guaranty Corporation (PBGC; see Chapter 12) jointly developed the Form 5500.

The SAR is usually one to two pages long and it summarizes the information that's in the retirement plan's Form 5500 and the more detailed financial statements and schedules. It gives you a sense of how well your pension plan's investments have performed. For example, it shows

- ✔ Whether the plan's investments have lost large amounts of money during a year
- ✔ The plan's total administrative expenses for the year
- ✔ A list of items that can alert you to questionable financial arrangements with individuals or organizations that are closely connected to the plan
- ✔ If any money loaned by the plan hasn't been paid back on time

Your individual benefit statement

The *individual benefit statement* is a statement that describes your total accrued and vested benefits (*benefits earned to date*). Before the PPA, this statement was required to be provided to you upon your written request only once every 12 months.

For plan years starting after December 31, 2006, benefit statements will be provided to participants automatically, on a quarterly basis if you self-direct your investments and on a yearly basis if you don't. (See Chapter 6 for more about self-directed investments.) The PPA has made significant changes to what these statements must provide. It's still not certain exactly what will be required in the benefit statement, and the rules won't be out before August 17, 2007 (after the writing of this book), but expect more detailed benefit information on:

- ✔ Vesting (see Chapter 7)
- ✔ Account-related information regarding rates of return and investments
- ✔ An explanation of the limitations or restrictions on directing investments for those plans that permit participant direction
- ✔ An explanation of the importance of a well-balanced and diversified portfolio
- ✔ A statement of the risk of holding more than 20 percent in the securities of one company
- ✔ A cautionary instruction to take into account all your assets, including savings outside the plan, in deciding how to invest
- ✔ A suggestion to periodically review your investment portfolio and objectives and options under the plan

Before you finally retire and claim your pension distribution, you certainly want to request your latest individual benefit statement so that you can do the following:

✔ Confirm that you're entitled to receive benefits at the point you decide to retire (if it's in advance of your normal retirement age)

✔ Find out the bottom line on what you can expect to receive either through an annuity over the course of your lifetime or through a lump sum payment

Chapter 9 has the full scoop on pension distributions.

Other documents under which the plan operates

In addition to the SPD, SAR, and SMM, other documents are important to track down. These documents include the complete plan document, any collective bargaining agreements, and trust agreements.

For instance, even though the SPD provides a summary of the entire plan document, you still should request the complete plan document. In other words, to be safe, you shouldn't rely only on summaries of the plan; take the time to read the whole plan. There have been instances where the SPD and the plan document are in disagreement or inadvertently contradict each other. The complete plan document is where you can find just about anything you need to know about your plan.

A collective bargaining agreement is a pension plan that's created through employer and employee negotiations and that contains all the terms of the pension (as does a plan created through a trust agreement).

This information is made available to you free of charge for your inspection upon written request, or it can be duplicated for you for a reasonable copying fee.

Disclosure notice in underfunded plans

Pension plans that aren't fully funded must notify their participants of this fact. The PPA modified the levels at which this notice is required, but you still must be notified if the plan isn't 90 percent funded. Many exceptions and qualifications to this rule exist, but if you get a notice, you'll find out at what percentage your plan is underfunded. The PBGC must be notified if the plan is less than 80 percent fully funded. (See Chapter 12 for more information about underfunded plans.)

Troubleshooting when you don't get what you need

If your employer hasn't provided you with a copy of the SPD, SAR, the annual report, or any other previously discussed document that you may have requested informally, you should formally request that your plan administrator provide you with a copy. Make all requests for plan documents in writing, and send your letter by certified mail. Clearly describe the items that you're looking for, and be sure to use your best business manners! The items you're requesting include a copy of the plan document and all amendments, the SPD (including revisions) and the SMM, your individual benefit statement, and copies of all communications between you and the plan. (Figure 8-1 shows a sample request letter.) By law, your plan administrator has 30 days to provide you these documents.

Here are some tips for maintaining records of your contact with a plan administrator:

- If you receive a verbal response to a verbal question, keep a written record of the question and answer (and take names!). Confirm in writing to the plan administrator the answer that was given to you. The idea is to eliminate the possibility that along the way someone will deny that he or she told you something.

- All communications with the plan administrator or other staff members that affect your rights, including your request for documents (refer to Figure 8-1) need to be sent via certified mail, return receipt requested. This move is a safety precaution; if the plan says that it never received a request or a critical document, you'll have proof that it was received, along with the date it was received and the name of the person who signed for the letter.

Figure 8-1:
A letter requesting pension plan documents.

[Date]

Via Certified Mail

[Plan or plan administrator]

[Address]

RE: [Your name, last 4 digits of your Social Security number]
        Request for Release of Retirement Plan Records Pursuant to ERISA

Dear Sir or Madam:

I am writing to formally request that you provide me with a copy of the following documents:

1. A full and complete copy of the existing plan document(s), including amendments and retroactive amendments and any summaries of material modifications.
2. A copy of the current summary plan description for the [corporation name] pension plan and any revised summary plan descriptions.
3. The estimated benefit calculations and/or statement of vested accrued benefits. [If you know the date that you want to retire, you can ask for it as of that date.]
4. Copies of all written communications between us pertaining to the plan or plans, including election forms.
5. A copy of the most recent summary annual report and Form 5500.

Please send the above documents to me at the following address:

                [Your complete mailing address]

Thank you for your prompt attention to this matter.

Sincerely,

[Your name]

If you're unable to obtain a copy of the pension documents to which you're entitled, you may be able to get a copy (for a nominal copying charge) by writing to the U.S. Department of Labor at this address:

> U.S. Department of Labor
> Employee Benefits Security Administration
> EBSA Public Disclosure Room
> 200 Constitution Avenue, NW, Room N-1513
> Washington, DC 20210

Be sure to provide your name, address, and phone number so that the Employee Benefits Security Administration can contact you to follow up on your request. To help locate your plan documents, you should include as much information about the plan as possible, including the name of the plan and the city and state where it's located.

Of course, because it's the law, you would expect that there will be no problem after you make a request for documents. The reality is quite different, though. There may be situations when the plan inadvertently fails to honor your request, and there may be instances when the plan intentionally fails to provide requested documents, fearing litigation. The law provides for a penalty of $110 per day for failure to provide these documents in a timely manner. This is easier said than done, though, because if you want to compel the plan to provide you the documents and pay the penalty, you need to file a court case (see Chapter 20 for the basics of pension litigation).

Your personal information

To confirm the information that your employer has on file for you, you should gather your personal information, such as your birth date and employment dates. This information is important because if, for example, the employer uses the wrong birth date in its calculation of the benefits that you're supposed to receive or if the wrong hire date is used and you aren't credited with enough years of service, your personal files can substantiate the correct information.

Here's the list of personal documents and information you need to dig out of your lock box:

- ✔ Your birth certificate
- ✔ Your spouse's birth certificate
- ✔ Documents reflecting your original date of hire with your employer, such as letters welcoming you to the company or your first pay stub

✔ Documents reflecting any subsequent dates of hire

✔ Papers showing any and all termination dates with all your employers

✔ Records confirming that you worked at least 1,000 hours each year

✔ Memos or letters from your company, union, or bank that relate to your pension plan (these may prove valuable in protecting your pension benefit rights)

These personal items, in conjunction with the various official pension documents referenced in the previous section, tell you what you can expect to receive from your plan benefits and help in determining whether your benefits have been correctly calculated and legally applied.

Other helpful facts to have on hand

In this section, we put together a checklist of additional important information about your pension plan and your benefits that you should keep current. You can find most, if not all, of this information in your plan documents (which we cover earlier in this chapter). As you begin to collect this information throughout your working life, make note of it and then stash it away in a file folder so you aren't scrambling to retrieve it all when you reach retirement.

Here's the list of information that we suggest collecting and continually updating:

✔ The name of your pension plan

✔ The plan's Employer Identification Number (EIN)

✔ The plan's Plan Number (PN)

✔ The name of the plan administrator

✔ How you can contact the plan administrator

✔ The date you'll be vested in the plan

✔ The date you're entitled to take early retirement under the plan

✔ The normal retirement age at which you can retire with full benefits

✔ The date you'll reach normal retirement age

✔ Whether your plan allows you to receive your benefits in a lump sum or as an annuity in monthly installments for life

You must know this information to take advantage of early retirement benefits or a lump-sum distribution if your plan allows them (see Chapter 9 for general distribution information). It's always better to depend on yourself to maintain your own information than to rely on a pension plan that may count you as one of thousands of participants.

Painting a Complete Picture of Your Retirement Income

After you've had a chance to collect and review the information in the previous sections, you'll have a much better idea of how your plan benefits can help support you, along with your other assets, during retirement. We walk you through the process of putting it all together in the following sections.

Combining your estimated retirement costs and your pension benefits

To start completing your full retirement picture, estimate how much money you need to save for your retirement, as we show you how to do earlier in this chapter, and examine your existing financial resources (such as your savings and any forms of income other than your wages). You can add to that amount your anticipated pension benefits; you receive this information in your individual benefit statement, which provides you with your total accrued and vested benefits (see Chapter 7 for more about vesting). The individual benefit statement, which we cover earlier in this chapter, is the best snapshot of what you can expect to receive if you retire as of a particular date.

Next, estimate your expenses in retirement. Don't forget about things like taxes, health insurance, and money to save in case of emergency.

If your future income will comfortably support you in retirement, congratulations! Keep saving for retirement just as you've been doing. If your expenses will outstrip your income, though, consider retiring at a later date or returning to work if you've already retired. Try our guidelines for saving more money to supplement your pension benefits in the following section. And we know you don't want to hear it, but you need to reduce your expenses in tune with the reduction in available spending money that you'll have in retirement. Unlike the U.S. government, you can't float a bond or spend for years with money you don't have.

Most folks don't feel comfortable doing such major calculations on their own, so it's best to consult a financial professional to help you put all your information together. We show you how to find a money guru later in this chapter.

Socking away money to supplement your pension benefits

In order to save for retirement, or better yet, to spend for retirement, spend less than you earn! (Easier said than done, we know.) So how do you reach the goal of building a retirement nest egg if you're living paycheck to paycheck? It's tough, but it's possible if you think of retirement as something you have to buy. Create a budget, taking into consideration your monthly income and expenses. Your retirement should be one of your main expenses at the top of the list.

But what if your expenses exceed your income? Should you cut back on your retirement expense? Hardly! Remember, your retirement is the number one expense on your list, and it's nonnegotiable. Consider your other options, such as cutting back on your other expenses, increasing your income, or both. Here are some suggestions:

- **Pay yourself first.** Have money automatically withdrawn from your checking account every month to go toward retirement savings.

- **Avoid bad debt that doesn't provide a financial payoff.** For example, borrowing money to take vacations or eat out would be considered bad debt. On the other hand, borrowing money to pay for your child's education or to advance your own skills leads to long-term financial benefits.

- **Avoid loans with high interest rates.** Always look before you leap; know what the loan terms are and comparison shop.

- **Comparison shop to help cut expenses.** When you buy a new car and go from dealership to dealership to get the best price, you're *comparison shopping.* You can shop this way for things such as insurance or other big-ticket items.

- **Take a second job or improve your skills and education to increase your current income.** If getting another job or going back to school isn't an option, suggest that your teenager get a job (if he or she doesn't already have one). Having a job not only teaches teens valuable money lessons at an early age, but also gives them extra spending money that they won't hit you up for. All that money that was going toward clothes, movies, and CDs can now be put away for savings.

The number one rule, no matter what, is to start saving as early as you can and as much as you can. Make your money work for you as soon as possible!

Seeking out professional financial advice

Your funds have to last as long as you do. So unless you're planning on managing your own money (which can be difficult), you need to seek out professional advice. A good broker or money manager is an invaluable aid to a successful retirement, but a bad one can mean disaster. Here are just a few suggestions to help you tell the difference between a successful professional and a poor one:

- ✔ Watch out for promises of extravagant returns with little or no risk. If it sounds too good to be true, it probably is.

- ✔ There's no such thing as an investment with no fees — they're there even if you can't find them.

- ✔ Beware of free lunches and dinners where the pitch for insurance products or expensive annuities will cost you a lot more than a steak dinner.

- ✔ Don't be impressed with fancy-colored charts showing impressive returns. In other words, just because a financial professional is good with spreadsheet programs doesn't mean that he's an expert when it comes to finances. And if that doesn't convince you, remember the old adage that goes like this: "Figures don't lie, but liars can figure."

- ✔ Separate the salesmen from the advisors. Use this book to find out if your future financial guru knows anything about pensions or just wants to make a sale. In fact, take the book with you; information is the pensioner's friend. But do rely on the advice of your respected professional as it relates to your case in particular.

  Any financial advisors worth their salt should at least make an informed inquiry as to whether your pension is accurate before rushing to invest your funds.

- ✔ Don't be afraid to negotiate the fees you'll be paying. Preserving your assets is in your best interest; high fees aren't. Fees for money mangers are generally in the range of 1 percent of the total assets under management, but they can also be as high as 3 percent or as low as 0.5 percent.

- ✔ You shouldn't be expected to pay a fee on fixed assets, such as money market accounts or bonds that you expect to hold until maturity. You don't need to pay someone to look at your money.

- ✔ Don't confuse free tickets to your money manager's luxury suite at the ballgame with good advice and sound performance in your portfolio. Put more simply — don't allow yourself to be bribed into accepting shoddy performance.

Good financial advisors look and dress alike. The worst advisors may sound the best. Use trusted friends who've had good steady results for years to make recommendations. Pay no attention to the friend who got a hot tip — even if he quadrupled his money overnight.

There's no one place you can go to find the right financial advisor for you. There is, however, somewhere you can go to find a financial advisor you don't want: the Securities and Exchange Commission. This government agency licenses brokers and maintains a Web site where you can find enforcement actions that have been taken against financial advisors based on misconduct. Go to www.sec.gov/litigation.shtml to find out who to stay away from and perhaps pick up a tip or two about the tricks of the trade employed by unscrupulous brokers.

Chapter 9

Understanding the Rules of Pension Distributions

. . . .

In This Chapter

▶ Deciding when to take your pension

▶ Seeing the differences between annuities and lump sums

▶ Making a claim for your distribution

. . . .

*O*ne of the most important issues with respect to your retirement plan is knowing when and how to receive a distribution of your benefits. But be prepared, because the rules are tricky and confusing. In fact, figuring out how to receive a distribution from your plan is akin to rocket science. But have no fear: We're here to give you the basic rules of distributions in this chapter. We explain the different times when you can take a distribution from your tax-qualified plan and from your individual retirement account (IRA; see Chapter 5 for an IRA introduction) along with their tax consequences, and we also go over the differences between your two payment options: annuities and lump sums. Finally, we get you going on the actual claim process.

Knowing When You Can Take Your Distribution

Timing is everything (as they say), so before you make your claim for benefits, you need to understand the basic rules regarding when you can make your claim. The following sections outline the major categories: distributions at regular retirement age, early distributions, distributions at age 70½, and distributions after your death.

Here are a few general rules to remember up front:

✔ Your distribution always comes from the vested amount in your pension plan. (Chapter 7 has full details on vesting.)

✔ With a few exceptions, all distributions are subject to federal and state income tax whether they're in annuity or lump sum form (we cover these options later in this chapter). Here are the exceptions:

   • Roth IRA distributions (see Chapter 5) and Roth 401(k) distributions (see Chapter 4), which are generally distributed tax-free

   • Distributions of after-tax contributions to IRAs and qualified plans, on which only the earnings are taxable

✔ If you receive a distribution from a retirement plan or an IRA prior to age 59½, the distribution is subject to an additional 10 percent tax unless it fits into one of the exceptions (which we talk about later).

✔ Distributions generally must start by the time you reach age 70½; otherwise excise taxes may apply. The excise tax is 50 percent of the required distribution at age 70½ and thereafter.

All is well: Taking your distribution at regular retirement age

Even though the exact timing of retirement plan distributions is controlled by your plan, the Internal Revenue Code requires that pension distributions be made available to participants by a certain date. For instance, under the code, you're eligible for a distribution no later than the 60th day after the close of the *plan year* (the 12-month period under which the plan operates) in which the latest of the following occur:

✔ The date that you reach the earlier of age 65 or the normal retirement age in your plan (check your summary plan description, or SPD, to see what age your plan requires; see Chapter 8 for more about this and other plan documents)

✔ The tenth anniversary of the year that you started your participation in the plan (for example, if you start in the plan at age 58 and the plan's normal retirement age is 65, your tenth anniversary in the plan is at age 68, which is later than the normal retirement age)

✔ The date that you terminate your service with the employer

If you terminate your employment and your pension benefits exceed $5,000, the plan can't force you to receive a distribution of your plan benefits before the later of either age 62 or the normal retirement age under your plan. If your benefits are less than $5,000, however, the plan can force you to take an early distribution of your benefits as a lump sum when you terminate your employment. (We cover mandatory distributions later in this chapter.)

Tough times: Taking an early distribution

Most folks don't need to take their distribution until they're ready for retirement, but sometimes people need to take an early distribution for whatever reason. In the following sections, we cover two types of early distributions — voluntary and mandatory — and the exceptions to additional taxing on such early distributions.

Voluntary distributions

You may be able to take voluntary pension distributions even while you're still working. Here are some voluntary distribution rules for the most popular types of pension plans:

- ✔ **Defined benefit and defined contribution plans:** For plan years beginning after December 31, 2006, pension plans can, if they choose, provide in-service distributions to participants who are age 62 or older. (An *in-service distribution* is a fancy way to say "a distribution while you're still working.") This change was made under the Pension Protection Act of 2006 (PPA) to permit *phased retirement,* in which individuals may choose to continue to work and receive a portion of their pension benefits at the same time.

  If your pension plan has a normal retirement age prior to age 62, the plan can permit distributions when you reach your normal retirement age. However, most pension plans don't permit in-service distributions before age 70½ (we discuss required distributions later in this chapter).

- ✔ **Profit-sharing plans:** If you're in a profit-sharing plan that allows for in-service distributions, amounts that have been in the account for at least two years may be distributed before retirement or before separation from service. (Check out Chapter 3 for a description of profit-sharing plans.)

- ✔ **401(k) plans:** You can take distributions from a 401(k) plan during employment only if you've reached age 59½ or if the distribution satisfies all the following requirements for hardship distributions:

  - The distribution qualifies as a hardship, which is described by Internal Revenue Service regulations as immediate and heavy financial needs for which you don't otherwise have the resources.

- The hardship withdrawal doesn't exceed the principal portion of your elective deferrals to the plan.

- The plan doesn't allow you to make elective deferrals to the 401(k) plan for six months after receiving the hardship distribution.

See Chapter 4 for general information about 401(k) plans.

In some instances, it may be necessary to get the consent of your spouse before you can take an early distribution. Spousal consent is required for all defined benefit plans and for profit-sharing and 401(k) plans containing annuity forms of benefit. (We discuss annuities in more detail later in this chapter.)

Mandatory distributions

A *mandatory distribution* is a distribution made to a participant, without the participant's consent, before he or she reaches the later of either age 62 or the normal retirement age under his or her plan.

Your plan may provide for a mandatory distribution of your pension, but only if the present value of the total vested benefit doesn't exceed $5,000. In other words, if your account balance under the plan is less than $5,000 and you terminate employment, the plan can distribute your plan benefits to you even if you would prefer to leave them in the plan.

Mandatory distributions of more than $1,000 from a qualified retirement plan to a plan participant (but not to a surviving spouse or alternate payee) must automatically be rolled over into an IRA unless you elect to have the distribution rolled over to another retirement plan or to take it in cash. These automatic rollover rules became effective March 28, 2005. (We provide general rollover information later in this chapter.) Any mandatory distributions that aren't rolled over to an IRA or to another retirement plan are taxable.

Automatic rollover rules apply only to mandatory distributions. These rules don't apply to eligible rollover distributions made to a surviving spouse or a former spouse, nor do they apply to mandatory distributions made to a participant who's reached the later of either age 62 or the normal retirement age under the plan.

Your plan administrator must notify you in writing that your distribution may automatically be rolled over into an IRA 30 to 180 days before the distribution. After receiving that notice, if you fail to elect either a direct rollover to another qualified plan or a cash payment, the plan administrator may complete the necessary documents to establish an IRA on your behalf and to select a financial institution.

Information about the automatic rollover procedures must be provided in your plan's SPD or in a summary of material modifications (SMM). The information must

✔ Describe the investment product

✔ Indicate how fees and expenses will be allocated within the IRA

✔ Identify the distributing plan and the plan sponsor

✔ Identify a plan contact

Many employers have amended their retirement plans to eliminate the provision that requires the plan to make mandatory single-sum distributions to participants, or they've reduced the amount of the mandatory cash-out to $1,000 in order to avoid the application of the automatic rollover rules to their plans (because the automatic rollovers apply only to mandatory distributions greater than $1,000). Check your plan's SPD to see whether the mandatory distribution rules apply.

Exceptions to additional taxing

Most distributions from qualified retirement plans are subject to an additional 10 percent tax if they're made before you reach 59½ and if they aren't rolled over to another qualified plan or IRA. (We discuss rollovers later in this chapter.) The additional 10 percent tax on early distributions is payable at the same time that regular income taxes are due.

However, some exceptions allow you to avoid the 10 percent additional tax on early distributions. The most common exceptions include the following:

✔ Distributions that are paid as monthly, quarterly, or annual payments over your life expectancy or the joint lives of you and your beneficiary (which is typically your spouse). Note, however, that this exception doesn't apply unless you have separated from service.

After you begin receiving distributions under this exception, the payments must continue for five years or until you become 59½ years old (whichever is later). Otherwise, the additional 10 percent tax will apply to all the payments that you've received.

✔ Separation from service with the employer that's sponsoring the plan after you reach age 55. This exception, which doesn't apply to IRA distributions, can also apply to self-employed individuals.

✔ Distributions that are used to pay deductible medical expenses. This exception applies only to the extent that the amounts distributed would be allowable as a deduction (whether or not you itemize your deductions and without regard to other limitations on such deductions).

✔ Distributions attributable to a disability that's a physical or mental impairment that can be expected to result in death or be of a long and indefinite duration.

✔ Distributions to unemployed individuals to pay health insurance premiums. This exception applies to IRAs only.

✔ Distributions for qualified higher education expenses furnished to you (the taxpayer), your spouse, your child, or your grandchild. This exception applies to IRAs only.

✔ Distributions for qualified first-time home buyers. This exemption is subject to a $10,000 lifetime limitation and applies to IRAs only.

✔ Payments that are made to an ex-spouse or other alternate payee under a qualified domestic relations order (QDRO); see Chapter 15 for more info on QDROs.

✔ Distributions made on account of an Internal Revenue Service (IRS) levy on your IRA or tax-qualified retirement plan.

✔ Being a reservist and being called to duty for more than 179 days between the dates of September 11, 2001, and December 31, 2007. The PPA provides this exemption. According to the PPA, you can even contribute the amount you took out of your pension by the later of August 17, 2008, or two years after the last day of active service.

✔ Being a state or local firefighter, an emergency medical person, or a police officer. These folks can avoid the 10 percent penalty when leaving employment as long as they're at least 50 years old.

Better do it: Taking your distribution when you're 70½

If you've reached age 70½, you must begin taking at least a portion of your pension benefits. (This distribution is referred to as a *required minimum distribution.*) The distribution for the year during which you reach age 70½ may be deferred until April 1 of the following year. However, the distribution for all subsequent years must be made by December 31. The minimum amount that must be distributed in any year can be made in a series of installments (versus one large distribution) as long as the total minimum payment is made by the end of the year. Your plan can distribute more than the minimum in a year, but you won't receive credit for the additional amount in any subsequent year. And if you have funds in multiple retirement plans, you're required to receive minimum distributions from each one.

Your benefits may be delayed beyond age 70½ to the date of your actual retirement from the plan sponsor as long as you don't own more than 5 percent of the company that's sponsoring the retirement plan. If you decide to delay the distribution further, your required minimum distribution begins by April 1 of the year following your retirement. If you're a participant in a defined benefit pension plan and delay your distributions beyond age 70½ until the date you actually retire, your accrued benefit must be actuarially increased to reflect the value of the benefits that you would have received if your benefits had started at age 70½. For example, if you should have received $1,000 per month beginning at age 70½ and you instead deferred the payments until your actual retirement at age 73, the $1,000 per month you would have received at age 70½ will be increased to reflect your now shorter life expectancy.

If you fail to take your required minimum distribution in the proper year, you're subject to an excise tax of 50 percent (yes, 50 percent!) of the required minimum distribution that you should've taken.

You aren't required to receive a distribution from each IRA that you own. You're permitted to add the totals from all your IRAs to calculate the required minimum distributions and take the distributions from just one IRA if you choose to. Required minimum distribution rules don't apply to distributions from a Roth IRA but do, however, apply to distributions from a Roth 401(k).

The goal is to spread out your pension over your life expectancy and over your beneficiary's life expectancy, based on the total amount of your benefits. Depending on your ages and life expectancies, the amount of your distribution changes. And as your ages change, your life expectancies do as well, so the IRS has created tables to keep track of this information. You can see these tables — the Uniform Distribution Table, the Single Life Table, and the Joint and Last Survivor Table — in Appendix B.

Life expectancy is simply how long the tables say you can be expected to live. The numbers in the tables aren't arbitrary, by the way; they're based on data that's crunched by actuaries. These tables are relied on for just this purpose.

These life expectancy tables, which contain quite a bit of information, are used to predict how long you and/or your beneficiary will live and how your ages will directly affect your distribution period. Each of these tables is used for a different set of people. For example:

- ✔ The Uniform Distribution Table is used only by plan participants.

- ✔ The Single Life Table is used only by beneficiaries. (This table comes into play only after your death; we cover distributions after death later in this chapter.)

- ✔ The Joint and Last Survivor Table is used only by participants who have a spouse more than ten years younger than the participant.

Using the Uniform Distribution Table

If you've reached age 70½ and want to figure out your required minimum distribution, follow these steps:

1. **Determine your plan account balance on December 31 of the prior year.**

2. **Determine the life expectancy factor from the Uniform Distribution Table based on your age on your birthday in the current year.**

   This factor is based on your birthday in the year for which the distribution is required. For example, if you turned age 70 in the year that you reached age 70½, the factor used is based on age 70. If you turned 71 in the year that you reached age 70½, the factor used is based on age 71.

3. **Divide the balance in your plan account on December 31 of the year prior to the distribution by the life expectancy factor from the Uniform Distribution Table to determine your required minimum distribution.**

   For example, assume that your account balance at the end of the prior year was $400,000, and you turned age 70 in the year that you reached age 70½. The factor in the Uniform Distribution Table for age 70 is 27.4. Your minimum distribution for the year is $400,000 divided by 27.4, or $14,599.

For a defined contribution plan, the annual required minimum distribution must equal at least the amount obtained by dividing your account balance on December 31 of the prior year by the factor from the Uniform Distribution Table for your age for the year of the distribution. For example, if your 75th birthday is in 2010, your minimum distribution for 2010 is your account balance on December 31, 2009, divided by the factor from the Uniform Distribution Table for age 75 (which is 22.9).

Using the Joint and Last Survivor Table

The distribution periods under the Uniform Distribution Table are based on a participant with a beneficiary who's ten years younger than the participant. So, the minimum distribution period at age 70 is based on the calculation for a 70-year-old with a 60-year-old beneficiary. Similarly, the distribution for an 85-year-old is based on the 85-year-old with a 75-year-old beneficiary.

However, if your sole beneficiary is your spouse who's more than ten years younger than you, you can base minimum distributions on the Joint and Last Survivor Table. This table produces a distribution period that's even longer than the ten-year spread contained in the Uniform Distribution Table.

The determination of whether you use the Uniform Distribution Table or the Joint and Last Survivor Table is made annually. So, if your spouse dies before you or the two of you get divorced, you go back to using the Uniform Distribution Table. Similarly, if you marry a much younger spouse after your required distribution date, you can switch, the next year, from the Uniform Distribution Table to the Joint and Last Survivor Table.

Benefiting your loved ones: Distributions after your death

The required minimum distributions after your death are based on the life expectancies of the designated beneficiaries who inherit your benefits. (We cover required minimum distributions in the earlier section "Better do it: Taking your distribution when you're 70½.") If you complete the designated beneficiary form provided by your company and therefore choose a particular person as your beneficiary, he or she is considered your *designated beneficiary*. If you don't complete the form and don't identify your beneficiary, the plan kicks in and designates a beneficiary for you — usually your spouse, if you have one.

If the beneficiary you select isn't a person (for example, you leave your pension to a college), you're deemed to have no designated beneficiary. Your benefits will still be paid to the college, but the time period over which the distribution can be made will be shorter than if you had named a person as your beneficiary.

Your beneficiary selections are fixed at the time of your death, so new beneficiaries can't be designated after you die. It is possible, however, for some beneficiaries to disclaim their benefits in favor of other beneficiaries who were already named by you. For example, if your primary beneficiary is your spouse and your secondary beneficiary is your daughter, your spouse can disclaim her benefits and your daughter will become your primary beneficiary. Your surviving spouse, however, can't disclaim benefits in favor of someone whom you had not named as a beneficiary before your death.

In the following sections, we explain how to use the Single Life Table shown in Appendix B, which determines distribution periods for beneficiaries. We also outline some special rules for distributions, depending on your age when you die. For full details on the benefits that go to beneficiaries after your death, see Chapter 14.

Using the Single Life Table

If your surviving spouse is your beneficiary, the applicable period for the distributions is her life expectancy. Your spouse's life expectancy is recalculated annually while she's alive, but it becomes fixed upon death for a specific term based on her age on her birthday in the year of her death. After your spouse's death, any remaining benefits must be paid to her beneficiaries over the remaining fixed-term life expectancy based on the Single Life Table. The balance of the beneficiary's account on December 31 of the prior year is divided by the life expectancy factor for the current year to determine the required minimum distribution for that year.

Here's an example: If your spouse is age 60 in the year following the year of your death, her life expectancy under the Single Life Table is 25.2 years. The required minimum distribution is the account balance at the end of the prior year divided by 25.2. The required minimum distribution for each subsequent year is based on the account balance for December 31 of the prior year divided by the life expectancy from the Single Life Table for each such year. If your spouse dies at age 76 before all of your pension benefits have been distributed, her beneficiaries must receive distributions based on the 12.7-year life expectancy for a 76-year-old under the Single Life Table. For each subsequent year, the factor will be reduced by one. In other words, the next year's life expectancy would be 11.7, the year after that would be 10.7, and so on down the line.

Instead of receiving a minimum distribution, your spouse may also roll over the benefits to an IRA or to another qualified plan. We cover rollovers later in this chapter.

If your individual beneficiary is someone other than a spouse, the applicable distribution period is his life expectancy. The minimum required distributions are based on the fixed-term life expectancy of your beneficiary based on his age in the year following the year of your death.

Here's an example for when your beneficiary is someone other than a spouse: If your beneficiary is age 60 in the year following the year of your death, his life expectancy under the Single Life Table is 25.2 years, a fixed period that's reduced by one for each subsequent year in order to determine the minimum distribution required for that year. In other words, the life expectancy of the year after the 25.2-year fixed period will be 24.2, the year after that will be 23.2, and so on into the future. As with spousal beneficiaries, the required minimum distribution for a given year is the account balance on December 31 of the prior year divided by the proper life expectancy factor.

Effective for distributions after December 31, 2006, the PPA provides that benefits of a non-spouse beneficiary may be rolled over to an IRA. The IRA is treated as an inherited IRA of the non-spouse beneficiary. Distributions from the IRA must be paid over a period that doesn't exceed the life expectancy of the beneficiary and must commence no later than December 31 of the year following the death of the participant. The benefits must be rolled over to an IRA for your non-spouse beneficiary by December 31 of the year following the year of your death.

Death before age 70½

If you die before age 70½, which is when you would have started receiving your pension, the required minimum distribution from your retirement plan generally must begin no later than December 31 of the year following the year of your death. Here are some special rules on the distribution, depending on who your beneficiary is:

- ✔ If your beneficiary isn't a person or individual (for example, you designate a church or synagogue to receive your retirement benefits after you die), you're deemed to have no designated beneficiary (even though the charity will still receive the money). In this case, your entire pension account must be distributed no later than December 31 of the fifth year following the year of your death (this is called the *five-year rule*). This rule also applies if your retirement benefits are left to your estate.

- ✔ If your spouse is your beneficiary, he or she can delay the commencement of retirement plan or IRA distributions until the year during which you would have reached age 70½ if you had lived.

- ✔ If a non-spouse is your sole individual beneficiary, he or she is required to receive the distributions over a period not exceeding his or her life expectancy.

- ✔ Multiple beneficiaries who are individuals and who haven't established separate accounts must receive the distributions over the oldest beneficiary's life expectancy. If the beneficiaries' accounts are separate, the required minimum distribution is based on the age of each beneficiary. If you have multiple beneficiaries and at least one of the beneficiaries isn't an individual, the entire account must be distributed under the five-year rule.

To avoid using the oldest beneficiary's life expectancy, the various beneficiaries must set up separate accounts with separate accounting for profits and losses no later than December 31 of the year following your death.

These are the minimum distribution requirements. Beneficiaries may elect to receive distributions over a shorter period than their life expectancies.

Death after age 70½

If you die after age 70½, the required minimum distributions for the year following the year of your death are based on the applicable distribution period. These rules are similar to the rules in the previous section for distributions for death prior to age 70½. However, the five-year rule and the special spousal distribution rules described aren't applicable.

Surveying Your Options for Distribution Payments

When you start receiving your pension distributions, you may be faced with the choice between receiving your pension money as an *annuity* (which is a regular stream of payments for as long as you or your beneficiary live) or as a single lump sum. In order to make a wise decision, your first task is to find out whether the amount of money that you'll receive in a lump sum is the same as what you can expect to receive through an annuity that's spread out over your lifetime. After you're sure that the annuity and the lump sum have the same value and offer the same benefits, you have to consider the advantages of each one.

Comparing the values of an annuity and a lump sum

The first and most important consideration in choosing between an annuity and a lump sum is to make sure that both options have equivalent values. To make this determination, you must reduce the annuity to a lump sum by making what's called a *present value calculation.* A present value calculation is used to determine the value, in today's dollars, of a sum of money to be received in a future year, based on a specific interest rate. The higher the interest rate used to convert your annuity to a lump sum, the lower the lump sum.

As an example of calculating present value, imagine that you won $1 million in the lottery. A lottery winner is always given the choice of taking a single payment today, which may be only $600,000, or receiving monthly payments totaling $1 million spread out over ten years. In order to determine that the million bucks has an *actuarial equivalent* (what it's worth today) of $600,000, a number cruncher will use interest rate tables to determine how much money you'd need to receive in a lump sum today to equal $1 million if spread out over ten years.

In determining the lump sum present value of your benefits under a defined benefit plan, the plan's actuary performs calculations similar to those performed for a lottery winner who elects to receive a lump sum, except that the pension plan also looks at a mortality table to take your life expectancy into account in the calculation. (In a defined contribution plan, the lump sum amount is your account balance, so complicated calculations aren't needed.)

The Employee Retirement Income Security Act of 1974 (ERISA; see Chapter 2) has rules that determine the interest rates that plans must use to convert a lump sum to an annuity. If these rules aren't followed, the lump sum payment could be much less than the annuity payments (which, of course, is a lawsuit waiting to happen). Interest rates fluctuate and change, so check with your tax advisor or accountant to verify that the proper interest rate was used by your plan. If you do find that your plan used the wrong interest rate, contact the plan and question whether the calculations are correct.

The PPA provides for a phase-in of higher interest rates from 2008 through 2012. This phase-in is important because as interest rates increase, the value of the lump sum distribution decreases. So if you have the option of taking a lump sum in 2008 or 2009 (rather than in 2012 or later), you may opt for the earlier distribution because it's likely that the interest rates will be higher in 2012.

Analyzing the advantages of annuities

What are the pros of accepting an annuity rather than a lump sum? Check out these major advantages:

- ✔ You can't outlive your annuity — it will keep paying you for life.
- ✔ You can provide a steady income for your surviving beneficiary.

Explaining early retirement subsidies

Defined benefit pension plans of large employers frequently provide for *early retirement subsidies* that lessen the negative impact of receiving distributions prior to the plan's normal retirement age. Without such subsidies, you receive smaller monthly annuity benefits because the lifetime annuity benefits are paid over a larger period of time. Reductions for early retirement benefits are often in the neighborhood of 0.5 percent for each month (6 percent per year) that you receive the benefits prior to the plan's normal retirement age. For example, if the benefit is calculated at a normal retirement age of 65, a benefit payable at age 62 may be reduced by 18 percent (6 percent for each of three years) from the age 65 benefit. For example, if the age 65 benefit is $1,000 per month, the age 62 benefit would be $820 per month.

A plan may provide early retirement subsidies to employees who meet certain criteria. For example, the plan may state that an employee with 30 years of service can receive an unreduced benefit at age 62. In the previous example, the employee would receive an 18 percent early retirement subsidy.

Here's the tricky part. If you elect to receive a lump sum benefit rather than an annuity, the lump sum may be based on the benefit without the subsidy. In other words, using the previous example, if you take the annuity at age 62, you'll receive $1,000 per month (the benefit with the subsidy). If, however, you elect to receive the lump sum benefit, you may receive the equivalent of $820 per month (the benefit without the subsidy). In many cases, the value of the subsidy isn't required to be included in the calculation of the lump sum benefit.

So, if you have benefits with early retirement subsidies, be sure that you have an accountant or financial advisor carefully review the calculations to make sure that you're comparing apples to apples and receiving the correct benefit.

Another advantage is the fact that retirement plans usually offer several different annuity options, including the following:

- ✔ **Straight life annuity:** This type of annuity provides equal monthly payments for your life (and your life only). A straight life annuity provides the maximum monthly payment because it's based on one life with no additional contingent benefits. An example of a straight life annuity payment is $1,000 per month.

- ✔ **Qualified joint and 50 percent survivor annuity:** This annuity provides payments for your life, and then when you die, your surviving spouse (or other beneficiary) receives payments equal to 50 percent of your previous monthly payment. With this annuity, payments end when both you and your spouse (or other beneficiary) die. For example, you would receive $800 per month for your life, and then your spouse would receive $400 per month following your death. (We cover the basics of all types of qualified joint and survivor annuities in Chapter 14.)

- ✔ **Qualified joint and 75 percent survivor annuity:** This annuity provides payments for your life, and then when you die, your surviving spouse or beneficiary receives payments equal to 75 percent of your previous monthly benefit. An example payment: $750 per month for your life and $562.50 per month to your spouse following your death.

- ✔ **Qualified joint and 100 percent survivor annuity:** This annuity provides equal monthly payments to you with unreduced payments to your spouse or beneficiary following your death. An example payment: $700 per month for your life and $700 per month to your spouse following your death.

- ✔ **Life and term certain annuity:** This annuity provides equal payments for your life with guaranteed payments for a specific period of time (for example, 120 months or 180 months) to you or your beneficiary. In other words, it provides payments through the later of either your life or the term specified. An example: You receive $900 per month for your life with 180 guaranteed monthly payments, which your beneficiary would continue receiving if you died prior to the end of the 180-month period. If you live beyond the 180-month period, you'll continue to receive the monthly payments guaranteed through the remainder of your life, but there'll be no payments remaining for your beneficiary.

  In the event that both you and your beneficiary die before the 180-month term certain, your beneficiary's beneficiary will receive the payments — after all, they've been guaranteed for a minimum of 180 months.

Looking at the advantages of lump sums

The major advantage of a lump sum is obvious: You have the entire value of your benefit at once, to do with as you see fit. This can be very good if you invest it wisely or very bad if you spend it foolishly. It's your choice! Consider the additional advantages of lump sums:

✔ You can roll your lump sum into an IRA, where it will continue to grow until you take a distribution from the IRA.

✔ An annuity ends when you (or you and your spouse) die, so if you think you might die earlier than the average (for example, if you have a terminal disease), you may be better off taking the lump sum.

✔ If you have other funds that you can live on during retirement, you can use the lump sum to purchase a house or a condo or to plan an estate to leave to your children.

Getting a Grip on Rollovers

A *rollover* is a term for when you move your money from one tax-deferred place to another without paying taxes. But in order to roll over successfully, you need to know whether the distribution that you receive from a qualified plan is eligible for direct transfer to an IRA (or to a qualified plan, if you're still working), thereby avoiding tax consequences. We give you all the basics you need in the following sections.

What are eligible rollover distributions?

The term *eligible rollover distribution* refers to any distribution that's made to you, an employee, of all (or any portion) of your balance in a qualified pension plan. However, the term doesn't include the following:

✔ Distributions in the form of an annuity (which we cover earlier in this chapter) or any distribution that's one of a series of substantially equal period payments (not less frequently than annually) made for your life or the joint life expectancies of you and your designated beneficiary.

✔ Any minimum required distribution starting at age 70½.

✔ Hardship distributions from your 401(k) elective deferrals or from your 403(b) elective deferrals.

If your distribution doesn't fit into one of the categories previously listed, it's considered an eligible rollover distribution, which means that you may roll over all or part of it into an IRA or a tax-qualified retirement plan. Any part that you don't roll over will be taxable to you when it's distributed.

If property is involved during a rollover, you must roll over the actual property or the proceeds from the sale of the property. You can't retain the property and roll over the fair market value of the distributed property. For example, if your distribution from your employer's plan is stock with a fair market value of $25,000, you can roll over the stock directly to an IRA or you can sell the stock and roll over the $25,000 proceeds from the sale of the stock. But you can't keep the stock and roll over $25,000 from your savings.

Who can roll over a distribution and when?

Your distribution must be either transferred directly to the IRA or other tax-qualified plan (a *direct rollover*) or rolled over within 60 days after you receive it — or after your surviving spouse or a former spouse, pursuant to a QDRO (see Chapter 15), receives a distribution.

Effective for distributions after December 31, 2006, beneficiaries other than a surviving spouse may roll over benefits into an IRA. However, such non-spouse rollovers can be made only from plans that specifically permit such rollovers. In this case, the IRA is treated as an inherited IRA of the non-spouse beneficiary, and distributions from the IRA are subject to the distribution rules applicable to beneficiaries.

The IRS can waive the 60-day requirement for rollovers when a pensioner is serving the military in a combat zone or when the president declares a disaster. You can also receive a waiver of the 60-day rollover period if failure to waive the requirement would be against equity or good conscience. For example, if you transfer the rollover amount to a bank or a broker in a timely manner, but the bank or broker mistakenly deposits the funds into a non-IRA account, it would be unconscionable for the 60-day period not to be waived.

What are the tax consequences of rolling over?

If you want to roll over your benefits to an IRA or to another plan, it's best to have the funds transferred directly to the IRA or plan. Federal income tax is withheld at a 20 percent rate on any eligible rollover distributions that aren't directly rolled over. So, what this means is that if the funds are distributed directly to you (rather than directly rolled over), you'll receive only 80 percent of your benefits because 20 percent will be withheld for taxes. These withholding requirements don't apply to distributions from IRAs.

If after your death, your spouse rolls over your pension assets into his or her own IRA, subsequent distributions from that IRA will be subject to the early 10 percent distribution tax if the surviving spouse is under age 59½ at the time of the distribution and isn't eligible for any other exception. (We cover this tax earlier in this chapter.)

What's the rollover process?

Don't worry: You don't have to guess when it comes to rolling over your pension distribution. Your plan administrator is required to provide you with a written explanation of the provisions. These provisions will likely state that:

✔ You can have your distribution directly transferred to an IRA or to another eligible retirement plan.

✔ You must withhold tax on the distribution if it isn't directly transferred to an IRA or another eligible plan.

✔ The distribution won't be subject to tax if it's transferred to an IRA or other eligible retirement plan within 60 days after the date on which you receive the distribution.

The plan administrator must distribute the notice no fewer than 30 days and no more than 180 days before making an eligible rollover distribution.

All you need to do to finish the rollover process is complete the appropriate paperwork for both the plan you're rolling out of and the plan or IRA that you're rolling the funds into.

Claiming Your Benefits

ERISA requires your plan to establish a written procedure that you and other pensioners can follow when claiming your pension benefits and that the company can follow when providing you with your payments. Your SPD sets forth all the procedures necessary to properly file your claim. You should familiarize yourself with the requirements and assemble whatever documents are necessary. If your plan has failed to establish a claims procedure, make the claim for your benefits to the administrator of the plan.

What happens when you're terminated and your plan loses track of you?

As surprising as it may seem, sometimes plans lose track of their former employees who have vested retirement benefits. Luckily, the Pension Benefit Guaranty Corporation (PBGC), the government agency whose main functions are to take over failed pension plans and to guarantee pension benefits, has a missing participants program. It provides that if the plan administrator of a terminating defined benefit or defined contribution plan can't locate a pension plan member after a diligent search, the plan may satisfy the distribution requirement by purchasing an annuity from an insurer or by transferring the missing participant's benefit to the PBGC. Therefore, if you can't locate your former employer, or if the plan has been terminated, you may be able to contact the PBGC for your benefits.

Chapter 12 has more information about the PBGC and terminated pension plans.

All of your requests should be in writing, and it's important that you keep a copy of everything you submit for your records. It's also a good idea to use certified mail for your benefit application and other correspondence with the plan so that you have proof that the documents were sent.

When you make a claim for your distribution, you also need to have a good idea of what your benefits should be. By the time you're ready to retire, you should know what's in your account balance, how it was calculated, how much is vested (in other words, how much definitely belongs to you; see Chapter 7 for more about vesting), and whether you're entitled to any subsidies or other special benefits. Chapter 17 has details on arming yourself with information before retirement and spotting potential signs of trouble with your distribution.

The plan has 90 days to tell you if your claim was approved. If your plan needs more time to take a look at your claim, it can get an additional 90 days as long as the following occur:

✔ The plan notifies you within the initial 90 days that more time is needed.

✔ The notice tells you why more time is needed and gives you the date that the plan expects to make a decision.

If the 90- or 180-day time period has passed and you receive no notice, use the plan's rules for appealing a denial. The SPD describes the appeal procedure if your claim is denied. (See Chapter 18 for more information on appealing your claim if it's denied.)

Part III
Guarding Your Pension from Your Employer

The 5th Wave   By Rich Tennant

"This option in the pension is a little tricky. You can start collecting benefits when you're 58 years old, as long as you look 58 years old."

In this part . . .

Your company or plan can make many decisions that impact your pension. So, in order to be prepared for possible changes instituted by your plan, you need to understand the plan's basic rights, your basic rights, and the steps you can take to protect your rights (and ultimately your pension).

In this part, we start with an overview of the responsibilities of the plan's fiduciaries to give you a framework of what's okay and what isn't. From there we discuss the various changes that have the potential to impact your plan and your retirement, and what you can do to best guard your pension. These changes include the sale or merger of your company and the amendment or termination of your pension plan. Also included are job changes (voluntary or involuntary), which impact the pension benefits that you've earned up to that point.

Chapter 10

Zeroing In on Fiduciaries

- -

- -

*Y*ou work hard and do a good job for your company. In return, that company provides you with a retirement plan so that when the time comes
to lay down the hammer or turn off your computer, there's still food on the
table. If you have a defined benefit plan, the company has put money into
your retirement plan. If you have a defined contribution plan, you put the
money into the plan, and maybe your company did, too. Presumably this
money in the plan — yours and everybody else's — didn't go into a piggy
bank or get buried in a safety deposit box. Instead, it has been invested. This
chapter, then, is about the people who make the decisions about the investment of your money and who ultimately have a big say in the success of your
pension plan. These people are your fiduciaries.

A *fiduciary* is someone who's entrusted to look after the affairs of a third
person and to act in that person's best interest. A fiduciary can't pass the
buck. In this chapter, we tell you what you need to know to be informed
about fiduciaries. In this case, what you don't know *can* hurt you. Just
remember this: All the retirees in the Enron plan had fiduciaries. Some are
good and some are bad. All bear watching.

Generally speaking, any private employee benefit plan managed by either an
employer or an employee organization is subject to the protections of the
fiduciary rules set by the Employee Retirement Income Security Act of 1974
(ERISA). These plans are regulated by ERISA, and their money experts are
provided specific guidance as to what they can and can't do. (Whether these
experts pay attention to these rules is another story.) We focus on ERISA's
fiduciary rules in this chapter.

Ferraris, temptation, and fiduciaries: A combo that may cost you money

Fiduciaries running wild (and spending lots of cash in the process) aren't sexy, and they can be a highly expensive problem to fix. Everyone has heard of the Enron debacle, but in Ohio they have their own story to tell. The investment advisors of the Ohio Workers' Compensation Fund reportedly bought rare coins at inflated prices and, as the story goes, other expensive collectibles, such as autographs and even Beanie Babies. Guardians of the funds sat by and watched as an investment house lost hundreds of millions of dollars that were set aside for the injured workers of Ohio. Sure, people went to jail, but the money is still gone.

The lesson is this: Know who your fiduciaries are and pay attention to what they do and with whom they do it. You may be the one paying for the cherry-red Ferrari and the 90-foot yacht. For some, access to large sums of money is an irresistible temptation.

Defining Who Is (and Isn't) a Fiduciary under ERISA

The determination of whether someone is a fiduciary is important because a fiduciary is held to special standards of conduct. To find out how the law defines a fiduciary, you have to look to ERISA, the law that regulates tax-qualified pensions. But we're guessing that reading through pages and pages of legalese isn't on your list of fun things to do. So in the following sections, we save you some time by explaining who does and doesn't qualify as a fiduciary.

Understanding who qualifies as a fiduciary

According to ERISA, the term *fiduciary* includes any person or entity (a fiduciary can be a group of people) who:

✔ Exercises any discretionary authority or control with respect to a pension plan.

✔ Exercises any authority or control with respect to the management or disposition of plan assets. This tells you that if somebody has the power to decide how your money is invested, spent, or paid, she is a fiduciary.

✔ Renders investment advice for a fee or some other compensation, or has the responsibility to provide that advice. These people are fiduciaries — even if they're wearing a sign declaring that they aren't.

✔ Has discretionary authority or the responsibility to administer the plan. In other words, if this person has the power, she has the title of fiduciary.

In light of ERISA's definition of a fiduciary, there are certain jobs involving your pension plan that are so important that the people who do them are automatically considered fiduciaries. For example, the following people carry this title:

✔ **Plan trustees:** These trustees are similar to a board of directors. They oversee the plan administrator and set policy for the plan.

✔ **Plan administrators:** These staff members are in charge of the pension plan and are considered chief executives of their respective funds.

✔ **Members of the plan's investment or administrative committee:** These people oversee investment decisions.

✔ **Pension investment consultants:** Pension investment consultants are usually the outside hired gurus who advise the investment committee on how the plan's money should be invested.

✔ **Broker-dealers:** If these dealers are recommended by the pension consultant and have the authority to make investment decisions for the plan, they may be considered fiduciaries.

✔ **Investment managers:** These people are the consultants, individuals, or committees that your plan designates to make investment decisions for the plan's assets.

✔ **The hiring folks:** The people or committees who have the responsibility of choosing and hiring anyone who exercises discretion over the plan's funds are exercising the type of authority that makes them fiduciaries.

Other people can be fiduciaries as well, but we won't list them all here. Just remember that one of the important things to know is that some people are fiduciaries for limited purposes only.

Recognizing who isn't a fiduciary

Being a fiduciary doesn't require consent. The test of who's a fiduciary is a functional test based not only on the title, but also on the job. When you have direct responsibility for someone else's financial security, you are, and should be, held to a higher standard, and you're considered a fiduciary. Not everybody involved with running a pension plan is a fiduciary, however, because not everybody has the discretionary power that can wind up sending you to the poorhouse.

The people who are doing what are considered "routine" or "ministerial jobs" aren't considered fiduciaries. For example, ministerial functions include the following:

- ✔ Applying plan rules for plan benefits (for example, when an accountant or a plan attorney uses and interprets the plan's rules)
- ✔ Calculating benefits
- ✔ Preparing materials to communicate with employees
- ✔ Maintaining service records
- ✔ Preparing required reports
- ✔ Orienting new employees to their plan rights
- ✔ Collecting and allocating contributions to the plan
- ✔ Processing claims

Attorneys, actuaries, consultants, and other advisors generally aren't considered fiduciaries unless — and this is an important *unless* — they're investment advisors or they have authority or control over who is.

Surveying the Duties and Restrictions of a Fiduciary

The plan fiduciary has the power and discretion to exercise authority and control on behalf of a third party. With that power, however, comes a limitation: It can only be exercised on behalf of plan participants. Any time the authority is exercised contrary to those interests, or when the fiduciary places his own interests over and above those of the plan members, it's considered a prohibited activity. In the following sections, we discuss what a fiduciary can and can't do.

Everything's okay: Duties and permitted interactions

The important thing to remember about a fiduciary is that he's supposed to be concerned about you (the plan participant), and he isn't allowed to act in his own best interest. And because he's investing your money, he's also supposed to be competent, thorough, and prudent. A fiduciary must do the following:

- ✔ Act in the interest of plan members and beneficiaries.

- ✔ Act for the exclusive purpose of providing benefits and avoiding unreasonable expenses in the administration of the plan.

- ✔ Act with the care, skill, prudence, and diligence expected of a person with that responsibility.

- ✔ Diversify plan assets and minimize the risk of large losses unless it's clearly prudent not to diversify.

- ✔ Act in accordance with the plan documents except to the extent that the document is inconsistent with ERISA itself.

To ensure that a fiduciary upholds these important obligations, his activities in dealing with the pension plan are heavily restricted to avoid self-dealing (see the following section). There are also restrictions on parties in interest, which is a broader category than a fiduciary.

There are certain interactions, however, that are permitted between the fiduciary and the plan. For example:

- ✔ The plan may deal with parties in interest to get office space and to hire necessary legal or accounting services. A *party in interest* can be, for example, a fiduciary, a provider of services to the plan, the plan's attorney, or the plan sponsor, who, because of his relationship with the plan, is prohibited from entering into certain transactions. (See the later section "Prohibited transactions for parties in interest" for more.)

- ✔ Certain insurance contracts can be entered into between the plan and the employer/fiduciary.

- ✔ After December 31, 2006, a registered pension consultant (such as a bank, an insurance company, an investment company, or a broker-dealer that's registered with the Securities and Exchange Commission) is permitted to give financial advice to plan participants and recommend a financial product that he sells. (See Chapter 6 for more information about a fiduciary's role in investment selection.)

Not gonna do it: Restricted activities

Because fiduciaries have control over your money and could benefit personally if they choose to take advantage of the situation, many restrictions are placed on their activities. We explain these restrictions in the following sections.

Prohibited transactions for fiduciaries

Because fiduciaries, like bankers, hold your money, the law applies special restrictions on what they can do with it. But sometimes they disregard the restrictions and do what they want anyway. These fiduciaries are ignoring the fact that it doesn't matter if the deal is ultimately fair and reasonable, with no bad motives intended and no hint of scandal. Forbidden is forbidden. The line is black and white, not gray, and the penalty for crossing this line is the personal obligation to pay back all profits as well as losses. Here are several examples of prohibited transactions for fiduciaries:

- ✔ A fiduciary isn't allowed to invest the plan's money, which includes your money, in his own account or for his own benefit.

- ✔ The fiduciary can't get involved in a transaction that's against the interests of the plan or the participants of the plan.

- ✔ The fiduciary can't get money or some other perk for his own account from somebody who does business with the plan in connection with the plan's money.

Here's an example of prohibited self-dealing by a fiduciary. Say your pension plan hires Les Honest for investment advice. Les, who is now a fiduciary, recommends the firm of Sleazy, Greedy, and Sneaky to help the plan decide what to buy and what to sell. What Les doesn't mention to the plan is that he (Les) is being paid by the Sleazy firm in exchange for the recommendation. Sounds like Les isn't so honest! Surprisingly, this goes on more than you might think.

Prohibited transactions for parties in interest

Some people are so intimately connected to a pension plan that they're considered parties in interest. A party in interest includes fiduciaries, but all those included as parties in interest may not be fiduciaries. The essential difference is that the fiduciary exercises discretion and control over the plan or its assets, whereas a party in interest can unfairly influence the plan because of his close relationship to the plan without the responsibility of a fiduciary. The two concepts are closely related but not identical. All oranges are fruit, but not all fruits are oranges. In the pension world, the fiduciary is the orange, and the fruit is the party in interest.

The definition of *party in interest* is complicated and broad and covers a wide range of individuals, businesses, and other entities. A plan's financial advisor, for instance, is a fiduciary and is also considered to be a party in interest because of his ability to influence plan decisions. Other parties in interest include your employer and the plan's attorneys, accountants, service providers, actuaries, and other persons or entities that provide services to the plan. All of these parties, while not considered fiduciaries, are prohibited from engaging in certain transactions with the plan because of their ability to influence plan decisions. These prohibited transactions consist of everyday-type activities if they involve your pension plan and include the following:

✔ Selling, exchanging, or leasing plan property (for example, the plan's attorney leasing to the plan the dilapidated building that he owns)

✔ Lending or borrowing money or getting an extension of credit from the plan

✔ Furnishing or receiving goods or services to or from the plan (for example, giving the uncle of the plan's financial advisor the contract to provide copiers and fax machines to the plan's office)

✔ Transferring or using for personal benefit any assets of the plan

Expanding the scope of fiduciary liability

Sometimes things happen that force everybody to take a fresh look at the current situation. For example, in September 2003, a federal judge handling a suit against Enron took the bull by the horns and expanded what a fiduciary could be held accountable for. The court's decision gave some concrete examples that drew a clear line in the sand for fiduciaries who were thinking of conduct in the fuzzy gray areas of what may or may not be permissible. Here's a list of the liabilities that a fiduciary may now be held accountable for:

✔ **Liability for following imprudent directions:** "I was just following orders" is no longer an excuse. A *directed trustee* (a trustee following directions) may be accused of breaching his fiduciary responsibility if he knew or should have known that the directions were imprudent. So, this means that the trustee still has a responsibility to find out if the things he's directed to do are in tune with ERISA's fiduciary responsibility requirements.

Some courts have taken a hard line on this, but others have been a bit more lenient unless the trustee actually was part of a plot. This is an area of the law that's still evolving.

✔ **Liability for imposing a blackout:** A *blackout* occurs when the fiduciary puts a hold or restriction on your ability to make changes to your investments or to make choices regarding your pension funds. Blackouts happen in instances when the plan is changing trustees or recordkeepers. Plan administrators must provide a notice to the plan's participants and beneficiaries at least 30 days in advance of the blackout. This blackout notice must describe the restrictions that are going to be imposed and state how long the blackout period is expected to last. Liability can be imposed, for instance, when the blackout isn't lifted even though it presents an extreme threat to your account balance. Ask the Enron pensioners what blackouts did to their accounts.

The Sarbanes-Oxley Act of 2002 bars company directors and executive officers from trading in employer securities during a blackout period. It prohibits loans to company officers during this time period as well.

✔ **Personal liability of the corporation's board of directors:** This liability almost never happens, but it could. If the corporation you work for serves as your plan's financial decision maker, those officers and directors who provide financial advice to the plan may be held personally liable as fiduciaries. For instance, if the board of directors doesn't clearly delegate authority to another financial advisor, the board is presumed to exercise such authority. So if the investment authority isn't specifically delegated, it may boomerang right back to the directors by default.

✔ **Liability of your employer's auditor:** Creative accounting has been painfully common in recent history. One of the country's largest accounting houses, Arthur Andersen, was actually indicted and disbanded as a result of its accounting practices. So, remember that your employer's auditor may be liable under ERISA for knowingly taking part in a breach of fiduciary duty when the employer is fraudulent in its accounting practices.

Knowing Who Pays for What: Fiduciaries and Lavish Spending

Fiduciaries are in a tough spot when it comes to balancing the administration of the plan along with fees and expenses. The fiduciary's job is to protect the plan's assets from being wasted on extravagant purchases and outrageous fees. The fiduciary must make sure that the plan pays only reasonable fees and expenses. Fiduciaries, however, are increasingly subject to lawsuits for approving fees that are excessive or for failing to uncover hidden fees that the plan ends up paying. All plans must have desks for the plan employees, carpeting on the floor, and funds for the occasional seminar. But when the desk is an antique French collector's item, the carpets are rare Persians, or the seminars are in Oahu, the fiduciary has breached her obligation to protect plan assets.

Plan expenses

ERISA has a basic principle that says plan assets must be used only to pay benefits to the plan members and their beneficiaries. But because the plan has ongoing expenses, that money has to come from somewhere, including occasionally from the plan's assets. While the plan is permitted to spend plan assets on activities that benefit the plan, such as financial or legal advice for the plan, these questions remain: "What expenses can the plan legitimately pay for and what expenses must be eaten by the employer?" When your fiduciaries decide to have fancy $200 lunches and meetings in the Bahamas instead of in their own offices, you shouldn't expect your plan to foot the bill.

As you can imagine, it costs money to run the plan. And it's the job of the plan administrator to oversee the day-to-day plan activities and to pay for those services. The administrator is a fiduciary, so she isn't free to spend as she wishes. All expenses must be reasonable. If you want to see where your company's expenses are being spent, check out its Form 5500, which is a joint tax form used by the Department of Labor and the Internal Revenue Service. In this form, you can find the totals paid to consultants and lawyers (and other such folks), the salaries for the people running the plan, and expenses for things like rent and office supplies. (We explain the Form 5500 in a bit more detail in Chapter 6.)

You can expect the plan to pay certain expenses. And because ERISA permits plans to use plan assets to pay reasonable plan expenses, you can be sure that they will. ERISA provides plan sponsors and fiduciaries with much discretion as to how to allocate plan expenses. As long as the method for charging the plan is provided for in the plan documents and isn't inconsistent with ERISA, the plan can be charged for the following reasonable expenses:

- ✔ Actuarial reports about required minimum payments to plan participants or their beneficiaries

- ✔ Preparation of summary plan descriptions (which we cover in Chapter 8)

- ✔ Liquidation of the plan when it's terminated (see Chapter 12 for more about pension terminations)

- ✔ Qualified domestic relations order (QDRO) charges (Chapter 15 has more details about QDROs)

- ✔ Plan amendments relating to fiduciary functions or requirements because the law changed

Your employer can pay for these expenses if it wants to (and your employer just might pay them because these expenses generally are deductible expenses). But your employer also can shift these expenses to the plan and, in effect, to the employees.

Also, in defined contribution plans, some fees can be charged directly to participants who cause the plan to bear a fee on their behalf. These fees include those caused by the following:

- ✔ Processing hardship withdrawals
- ✔ Calculating benefits under different distribution options
- ✔ Making distributions
- ✔ Processing QDROs

For example, if Mr. Joe Employee gets a divorce, the plan incurs expenses for the processing and administration of a QDRO (see Chapter 15 for more details). If the retirement plan is drafted to provide for this plan expense, the plan can charge Joe's account directly for the QDRO-related expenses.

Employer expenses

Of course, other expenses do come up, but some expenses can't be properly paid with the assets of the plan. So the expense has to be paid by the employer. The employer usually absorbs these costs when the expense benefits the employer rather than the plan or plan participant. Examples of these expenses include

- ✔ Actuarial reports that provide the employer information about the financial impact of the plan on the company
- ✔ Consulting fees to design the plan
- ✔ Decisions to terminate the plan
- ✔ Preparation of plan documents
- ✔ Amendments to the plan if they're about formation of the plan as opposed to management of the plan

Keeping an Eye on Your Plan's Fiduciaries

Improper activities can flourish only when they go undetected. So you do yourself and your fiduciary a favor when you make the effort to find out for yourself exactly what's going on with your plan's assets, investments, and spending. By requesting plan documents, asking questions, and raising concerns with the administrators or trustees, you make the plan administrators and your fiduciaries aware that someone is watching and paying attention to what they're doing. Sunlight not only uncovers some problems, but also serves to remove the temptation to take that trip to Scotland or play that round of golf on the plan's tab. These and other improper activities can be prevented by your watchful eye.

What are the signs of bad fiduciaries?

When you're on the lookout for improper fiduciary activities, you simply have to know the warning signs. Here are some of the most common:

- ✔ Failure to negotiate low fees from money managers

- ✔ Failure to establish appropriate benchmarks for the financial performance of the fund

- ✔ Inappropriate distribution of plan assets for the size of the fund

- ✔ Failure to monitor financial advisors and their performance

The amounts paid to money managers and the allocation of plan assets are listed on the Form 5500 (see Chapter 6 for more information).

Don't be fooled if your fiduciaries tell you that the responsibility for inappropriate investments isn't their problem. A fiduciary can't shake his obligations by delegating the work to someone else.

What can you do to get rid of bad fiduciaries?

If your plan fiduciaries have violated the rules, and if your questions or concerns haven't been resolved, you can take action. You should contact the nearest field office of the Employee Benefits Security Office (EBSA) of the Department of Labor. The EBSA has the authority and power to investigate wrongdoing, and it can take action to correct the problem. Go to askebsa.dol.gov for more information about how the EBSA can help you. You can also contact the EBSA by calling 866-444-EBSA (866-444-3272).

If the EBSA is unable to help, you've reached the pinnacle. You may have to protect your pension with your final recourse: a lawsuit against your fiduciaries. In this case, contact an attorney who can advise you of what steps you need to take (check out Chapter 19 for the scoop on hiring an attorney). These types of lawsuits are becoming much more common in the wake of Enron and other corporate scandals. We address lawsuits further in Chapter 20.

Unlawful party-in-interest transactions, such as cozy loans, are a matter to be reported to the Internal Revenue Service (IRS); it's the IRS that can impose tax penalties on prohibited transactions.

Chapter 11

Dealing with Your Employer's Corporate and Financial Changes

In This Chapter

▶ Understanding the implications when your company is merged or sold

▶ Looking at your options when your employment relationship is terminated

▶ Safeguarding your pension in spite of your employer's bankruptcy

*T*he primary reasons that the Employee Retirement Income Security Act of 1974 (ERISA) exists are to protect the funds that you and your employer deposit into your retirement plan while you're still working and to ensure that you have access to plan information whenever you need it. This protection and access to information is especially helpful if your company is about to undergo major changes.

And let's face it — life happens. You were never given any guarantees that you'd be at the same job your whole life or that your company wouldn't make any changes. This fact is even truer in today's ever-changing world. Our hope, then, is that you'll be armed with the right information to make wise choices when you're presented with some of the most common workplace changes.

To help arm you with the right information, in this chapter we cover such topics as company mergers and acquisitions and the very unfortunate but real possibility that your employer declares bankruptcy. We also address job changes that you decide to make or that are made for you. All these situations impact your pension in some way.

Keeping an Eye on Your Plan When Your Employer Combines with Another

The following two major scenarios can affect your pension plan:

- ✔ Your company merges with another company to create a single new company.

- ✔ Your company is sold to the highest bidder and operates under direct control of the acquiring company.

Whatever change your company ultimately makes, you need to find out what will happen to the benefits that you've already accrued (depending on the type of plan you have), and you need to keep track of all changes so that you fully protect your benefits.

Generally, corporate acquisition can occur in one of two ways:

- ✔ **In a stock deal:** In this type of deal, Company B purchases the stock of Company A and thereby acquires both the assets and the liabilities (debts) of Company A, including its pension liabilities.

- ✔ **In an asset deal:** In this type of deal, Company B purchases only the assets of Company A and therefore is *not* responsible for Company A's liabilities.

What are the possible plan changes after a merger or acquisition?

Your company has the following retirement plan options if it merges with or is acquired by another company:

- ✔ The new company can take over the plans of your company and allow you (and other employees) to continue to be covered under those plans. In this instance, you don't have to deal with any plan changes.

- ✔ The new company can merge your company's plan into its own plan, and you can immediately begin to accrue benefits under the merged company's plan.

- ✔ The new company can terminate your company's plan. In this case, usually you have the opportunity to roll over your plan benefits into the new company's plan or into an individual retirement account (IRA; see Chapter 5 for general information on IRAs).

Also, in this case, the new company may have a choice as to whether it will credit your service with your old employer for purposes of participating in its retirement plan. This means that you may begin to accrue benefits under the new company's plan on your first day (if you're credited with prior service), or you may need to complete the same eligibility requirements as a newly hired employee (if you aren't credited).

When your company merges with or is acquired by another company, you can't lose any of your accrued benefits under your old plan; this rule is known as the *anti-cutback rule* (see Chapter 7 for details). But how the new company handles your accrued benefits after a merger or acquisition differs depending on whether you started with a defined contribution plan or a defined benefit plan (see Chapter 3 for the differences between these two types of plans). For example, consider these common scenarios:

✔ If you were in a defined contribution plan with Company A, which then merges with or is acquired by Company B, and the new company either has or sets up a defined contribution plan, Company A may directly transfer your accrued benefits from the original defined contribution plan to the new one that's sponsored by Company B. Your accrued benefits stay the same, and the transfer shouldn't result in any negative tax consequences to you as long as your plan administrator follows all the rules (which will usually be the case).

It's likely that the investment options under the Company B plan will be different from the options under the Company A plan, so you may be forced out of your old investments.

✔ If you were in a defined benefit plan with Company A, the new company (Company B) is generally liable for the debts of Company A under corporate law principles — but only if it purchased Company A's stock. So if you're worried that Company A didn't make all the contributions that it was supposed to, Company B will now have to follow through on that obligation. In any case, your accrued benefits under the Company A plan shouldn't be reduced as a result of the acquisition.

However, if Company B purchases the assets of your old employer (Company A), it doesn't assume Company A's debts. In this case, you may have to leave benefits under the plan of your old employer (Company A) and accrue further benefits under the plan of your new employer (Company B).

Whenever your employer is acquired by or merges with another company, it's likely that changes to your defined benefit plan will result. Often the benefit formula under the plan will change going forward. The benefit formula may provide future benefits at a lesser rate than under your prior plan or it may have a richer formula and provide better benefits. Or your benefits under the defined benefit plan may be frozen, meaning that you may accrue future benefits under a cash balance formula or under a separate defined benefit plan. The point is that there are a lot of possibilities when an employer merges with or is acquired by another company.

How do you keep track of all plan information and changes?

If your company is involved in a merger or an acquisition, you'll receive certain notices and communications from the plan about the upcoming changes in benefits and investment choices. The notices may explain changes in the benefit formula in a defined benefit plan, changes in employer contributions in a defined contribution plan, or changes in investment options under your 401(k) plan. If your old plan terminates or merges into a new plan, you receive specific notification from your employer or the plan administrator. Review any notices carefully, and if you don't understand them, ask your company's human resources department for some guidance. (See Chapter 12, in which notices regarding plan amendments and terminations are discussed.)

As co-author Jori's husband always says, better to have something and not need it than to need it and not have it. So, if you want to protect the benefits that you've already earned, make it a habit to keep track of your benefits, and maintain a file of all important pension activity. Be sure to keep records of the following:

- ✔ All the places you've worked, including the dates that you started and stopped and your year-end paycheck stubs that indicate your salary or rates of pay

- ✔ Any plan documents that your plan sent you, including the summary plan description (SPD) and plan amendments, the summary annual report (SAR), the enrollment forms that confirm that you and other family members are plan participants, and a copy of the benefit election form (if you were provided an option as to the form of your distributions); see Chapter 8 for general information on these plan documents

- ✔ Your individual benefit statements (request these yearly to find out the value of your account)

- ✔ All notices and communications regarding the plan and the merger or the acquisition of the company (as we describe earlier in this section)

It isn't enough to simply collect these documents like stamps; know what they say about the vesting of your benefits and know when and under what circumstances you're entitled to receive them (see Chapter 7 for general information about vesting). You should also know what the plan documents say about mergers and acquisitions.

One of the basic functions of the plan administrator is to advise participants of their rights and options and to respond to your information requests. So if you have any questions or concerns about what's happening to your plan, ask your plan administrator (or the new plan administrator, if you're inquiring after the fact).

If you find out that your old company will retain control of your retirement plan after a merger or acquisition, make it a point to stay current on your old employer's address and phone number and any changes to its name. It's also always a good idea to make sure that your old company knows how to find you. So be sure to tell your prior plan administrator or human resources department whenever your current address and phone number are going to change (and find out how to notify the company in the future if your address changes again). And of course, continue to save and keep accessible all your plan documents as you continue working.

Considering Your Options When You End Your Relationship with Your Employer

Diamonds may be forever, but unfortunately, not much else is — especially your relationship with your employer. When it comes to your job, one of the following scenarios is bound to happen at one time or another:

- ✔ **Your company decides that you need to go.** Your being let go may be personal (for example, you're being fired) or it may be that you're part of a workforce reduction as a result of your employer's financial troubles.

- ✔ **You decide that you no longer want to continue working with the same employer.** You determine that it's time to move on to bigger and better things.

Regardless of whether your termination of employment is your employer's decision or yours, it shouldn't make a difference in terms of how it impacts the benefits you once enjoyed. Your goals, in either case, are to ensure that you'll have access to your pension funds and that your pension benefit investments are safe.

If you think that your company terminated you in order to deny you benefits — for example, your employer fires you just before you vest in your benefits — ERISA provides you with a cause of action. Check out Chapters 18 and 20 for further information about appealing such matters to your company and about litigation to protect your rights.

As a terminated employee, you'll be allowed to receive your vested retirement benefit when you reach the plan's normal retirement date. However, the plan may permit a reduced early retirement benefit at a date prior to the normal retirement date. The plan may also offer a subsidized early retirement benefit if you meet special requirements, such as reaching age 55 and having 30 years of service. But if the plan requires 30 years of service and you were terminated after 27 years, you may receive a reduced early retirement benefit, but you won't qualify for the subsidized benefit. (See Chapter 9 for general information on pension distributions.)

Defined contribution plans

If you've separated from a company where you had a 401(k), a profit-sharing plan, or another type of defined contribution plan, it's possible that the plan may let you take a lump-sum distribution when you terminate employment. However, you need to check your plan provisions in the SPD carefully to see exactly what it says about the form of the distribution. You may have an option to receive it as an annuity instead (see Chapter 9 for details on these forms of distribution). You also need to find out the date that a distribution becomes available to you. While some plans say that you can't get a distribution until you reach a certain age, others say that you can't get one until you've been separated from the company for a certain amount of time.

If your plan offers a lump sum but also offers an annuity as one of the payment options, both you and your spouse (if you have one) must waive out of the annuity in order for you to receive your distribution as a lump sum.

If you leave your current employer before normal retirement age and the plan permits a lump-sum distribution, you have a couple of options regarding your distribution: You can continue to defer taxes by rolling over your account balance to an IRA or a new employer's plan or you can take your money now and pay taxes on it now. Rolling your benefits over into an IRA or another employer's plan is usually the better choice.

Rolling over your money

If you leave your job and you aren't at the right age to take your retirement distribution (or you just aren't ready to take it yet), your new employer's plan may accept rollovers. In this case, the plan may allow you to roll over your defined contribution plan money from your former employer's plan directly into your new employer's defined contribution plan. If your plan allows it, this option is the best because you don't ever touch the money, meaning that no taxes are withheld and no taxes are owed on the amount directly rolled over.

However, not all plans allow rollovers. So if you can't roll your money into your new employer's defined contribution plan, your next option is to roll over your plan benefits into an individual retirement account, or IRA. If possible, your plan benefits should be rolled over directly to an IRA instead of being paid directly to you so that you deposit the funds (within 60 days) into the IRA.

If your funds aren't directly rolled over, your plan will write you a check for your defined contribution plan account balance, but it will be subject to a mandatory withholding of 20 percent for federal income tax (which your former employer will ship right out to the Internal Revenue Service). You then have 60 days to roll over all or any portion of the distribution to an IRA. Remember, however, any portion that isn't rolled over is subject to income tax as a taxable distribution. The point is, to avoid losing 20 percent of the money you've accrued, roll over your money directly!

Head to Chapter 5 for more details on IRAs and rollovers.

Taking your money now

If you want to take either all or a portion of the vested balance in your account in cash before normal retirement age, you'll be taxed and possibly owe penalties for the early withdrawals. This of course reduces your retirement income down the road, so plan accordingly (see Chapter 8 for general details on planning for your retirement while you're still working).

If you're age 55 or older when you separate from the company where you participate in a defined contribution plan, you can receive your benefits without being socked with the additional taxes on distributions prior to age 59½.

Defined benefit plans

If you're in a defined benefit plan and you stop working for your employer *after* you've become vested in your benefits but *before* the plan's normal retirement age, usually you're required to leave the benefits with the retirement plan until you become eligible to receive them. These types of plans normally don't permit you to withdraw your money early. In some instances, however, your plan may offer early retirement options that may entice you to leave the company sooner than you had planned — and take your benefits with you. Check your SPD or other plan documents to see what they say about early distributions.

If you find that your money will be staying put until you reach the eligible age (which is the most likely scenario), it's important that you heed the pointers that we set out for you in the earlier section "How do you keep track of all plan information and changes?" Most important, you want to make sure that you can track down the company (or that it can track you down) when the time comes for you to retire.

Protecting Your Pension if Your Employer Goes Bankrupt

A bankrupt employer is quite different from a plan that doesn't have enough money to pay its participants, which is called *underfunding* of the plan. (See Chapter 12 for a discussion of that topic.) Generally speaking, if your employer's financial condition is such that it must declare bankruptcy, your retirement plan assets shouldn't be affected. This is because ERISA safeguards your assets by requiring employers to fund the promised benefits and to keep the plan assets separate from their company's assets.

There are typically two ways that your employer can declare bankruptcy:

✔ **Chapter 7 bankruptcy:** This type of bankruptcy is referred to as a liquidation or straight bankruptcy. When a company files for Chapter 7 bankruptcy, it will usually liquidate its assets to pay its creditors, and after that it will cease to exist. In this situation, you can expect that your pension plan will be terminated (see Chapter 12 for full details on plan terminations). Depending on what type of plan you have, different actions will be taken when your company files for Chapter 7 bankruptcy:

• If you have a defined benefit plan, the Pension Benefit Guaranty Corporation (PBGC) will jump in and save the day. The PBGC may assume responsibility for paying the benefits up to a certain maximum amount. For plans terminated in 2007, for example, that maximum amount is $4,125 per month. So, if your monthly pension benefits before the termination of the plan were less than $4,125 per month, you'll receive your full benefits. If they were greater, you'll receive only the maximum amount. However, certain ancillary benefits (such as subsidized early retirement benefits) may not be guaranteed by the PBGC.

• If you have a defined contribution plan, your benefit is your account balance. So your employer's bankruptcy shouldn't negatively impact your benefits under the plan.

 ✔ **Chapter 11 bankruptcy:** This type of bankruptcy is referred to as a reorganization, and it's a bit different from a Chapter 7 bankruptcy. If your company files for Chapter 11 bankruptcy, it may not affect your pension plan. In fact, it's quite possible that your pension plan, whether it's a defined benefit or defined contribution plan, will continue to exist while the company is trying to reorganize its financial situation under the protection of the U.S. Bankruptcy Court. It's likely, however, that future benefits or contributions to the plan will be reduced.

If your company files for bankruptcy, you should immediately contact your plan administrator and ask for an explanation regarding the status of your plan and your benefits. You want to make sure that your accrued benefits are protected. Start with some basic questions like these:

 ✔ Has my company filed for Chapter 7 or Chapter 11 bankruptcy?

 ✔ Will the pension plan be terminated or will it continue?

 ✔ If the plan will be terminated, how will my accrued benefits be paid?

 ✔ Will the plan administrator change during the bankruptcy? Who will be the trustee for the plan? (Get these people's names and numbers so that you can contact them when necessary.)

Don't count on the plan or the company to notify you. Instead, take the initiative and contact the company's human resources department, the plan administrator, or the bankruptcy trustee. If you're in a defined benefit plan, contact the PBGC to make sure that it's aware of the bankruptcy.

Because of ERISA's requirements stating that your employer must make its plan contributions in a timely manner and that its assets must be kept separate from the plan's assets, your retirement funds should be fairly safe from your company's creditors if it declares bankruptcy. On top of that, ERISA requires that the plan's fiduciaries properly manage the fund and not abuse the assets (head to Chapter 10 to find out more about fiduciaries).

Chapter 12

Handling Plan Modifications and Terminations

*F*or your pension plan to be a qualified plan under the Employee Retirement Income Security Act of 1974 (ERISA) and receive preferential tax treatment (see Chapter 2 for details), it had to be established by your employer as a permanent plan when it was set up. However, down the road your employer can amend some of the plan provisions as long as the plan documents allow amendments to be made and as long as the benefits you've accrued (or accumulated) prior to the amendment aren't reduced. Because your benefits can be changed, it's important to know what your protected benefits are at the time that your plan is modified. Knowing this information can help you be sure that your benefits are actually being protected. We give you the full scoop on plan amendments in this chapter.

Under ERISA, plan terminations are handled differently from amendments. We explain in this chapter the three ways that terminations can occur for a defined benefit plan: through a voluntary standard termination, a voluntary distress termination, or an involuntary termination.

The good news is that even if your company runs into financial troubles (and let's face it, we all do), you'll still have your pension. The bad news, however, is that the amount you actually receive may be less than what you had anticipated.

The Particulars of Plan Amendments

If your company changes its pension plan, it must follow certain procedures to make sure that you're properly informed of the intended changes and the nature of those changes. We give you what you need to know in the following sections.

Finding out what your plan can't (and can) change

Your qualified retirement plan contains lots of provisions regarding the benefits that you're entitled to and when you're entitled to them. However, many of these benefits are subject to being amended or eliminated by your employer. In the following sections, we sift through the rules concerning what plan benefits are protected, when they're protected, and when they can be changed.

The summary plan description (SPD), which the plan administrator must provide to you and your beneficiaries, usually contains language that authorizes plan amendments, the elimination of plan benefits, and plan termination. (See Chapter 8, where we discuss SPDs in more detail, including how to obtain a copy if you haven't been provided one.)

Benefits protected from amendments

Under tax law, your accrued benefits are always protected. (*Accrued benefits* are those that you, as a plan participant, have already accumulated and have a right to collect; see Chapter 7 for more information on accrual.) Tax-qualified retirement plans (including defined benefit and defined contribution plans) can't be amended to eliminate or reduce retirement benefits that you've already earned and have a right to.

It gets a little trickier, though, when you're trying to determine the rights and benefits that are protected as part of your benefit accrual. Some of your rights and benefits that are protected include the following:

> ✔ **Early retirement benefits:** ERISA doesn't require pension plans (including both defined benefit and defined contribution plans) to provide participants with the option to retire earlier than at the plan's normal retirement age. But if your plan offers such an option, it generally can't amend its provisions to eliminate your right to begin receiving a retirement-type benefit at a particular date that comes after you stop working and before normal retirement age.

✔ **Retirement-type subsidies:** A protected retirement-type subsidy generally refers to a *subsidized early retirement benefit*. If the plan offers a subsidized early retirement benefit, it pays the same benefit at an early retirement age (for example, age 62) that it would at normal retirement age (for example, age 65). Another type of subsidy is a *subsidized qualified joint and survivor annuity,* which provides the same monthly payment over the joint lives of you and your spouse as over your life alone (see Chapter 14 for more about these annuities). Because retirement-type subsidies are protected, they can't be eliminated retroactively. In other words, the subsidy can be eliminated for benefits earned after the amendment but not for benefits earned prior to the amendment.

Defined contribution plans don't offer these benefits because your employer is placing your contributions (and its own contributions) into an individual account that's yours when you retire.

✔ **Benefit payment rights:** Your defined benefit or defined contribution plan may offer you the right to receive your benefit payment in optional forms. For example, it may provide you the right to receive payment in a lump sum instead of an annuity. Another example is when a plan permits a participant to receive an *in-service distribution* (a distribution that you receive while you're still working for the employer that's sponsoring the plan). Generally, your right to receive an in-service distribution is protected. Certain optional forms of payment may be eliminated, but a plan that offers a lump-sum distribution can never eliminate that lump sum option.

Features subject to amendments

Even though qualified retirement plans can't reduce the benefits that you've already accumulated, they can change the rate at which you earn future benefits. For example, if you're accruing benefits at the rate of $10 per month for your years of service through 2006, your defined benefit plan can be amended to provide that for years of service starting in 2007, benefits will be credited at the rate of $8 per month.

Defined contribution plans are usually funded by both employers and employees, and your employer isn't likely to amend the rate at which you contribute to your plan. The employer may, however, change the amount of the contributions it makes in the future. Depending on the plan terms, the employer may also be allowed to reduce or even eliminate its future contributions to the plan.

Other defined contribution plan features that aren't protected from amendments include

✔ Your right to make contributions at a particular rate on either a before- or after-tax basis

✔ Your right to direct investments (see Chapter 6)

✔ Your right to a particular form of investment (see Chapter 6)

✔ Your right to take a loan from the plan (see Chapter 13)

Understanding the purpose of a determination letter request

If your employer intends to amend a provision of its pension plan, it has the option of seeking an advance determination, called a *determination letter,* from the Internal Revenue Service (IRS). This letter would inform the employer as to whether the plan would retain its tax-qualified status if it were to go through with the amendment. Why an employer wouldn't take advantage of that option is beyond us. It only makes sense that a company would want to be certain that the changes it intends to make to its plan would be approved by the IRS and that the plan would continue to receive favorable tax treatment.

Small employers may decide to forego filing for an IRS determination letter due to the cost involved (primarily legal fees). However, the legal fees and IRS filing fees (called *user fees*) for applying for a determination letter are small when compared to the cost that could arise for an improper amendment that may disqualify a plan.

Even though your employer isn't required to request a determination letter from the IRS to amend its plan, in order to exercise this option, the employer must apply for the determination letter in writing. This request is known as a *determination letter request* (pretty clever, huh?). After it receives the determination letter request from your employer, the IRS will review the plan and the proposed amendment.

A favorable IRS determination means that the IRS believes that the terms of the plan amendment meet the requirements of the Internal Revenue Code and that the plan will continue to receive favorable tax treatment. What this means to you is that you're still participating in a qualified plan that enjoys certain tax advantages, creditor protection, and the things we discuss more fully in Chapter 2.

One of the advantages of the determination letter process is that if the IRS doesn't approve of the amendment, the amendment can be revised to satisfy the IRS before it has an adverse impact on the plan's tax-qualified status. In other words, the IRS may require certain revisions in the amendment before it will issue a favorable determination letter.

Being notified of determination letters and amendments

When your employer intends to apply for a determination letter, the plan administrator is required to give notice to all plan participants. You and all other plan participants must be notified not less than ten days and not more than 24 days before the application is filed.

You're also required to receive advance notice of an amendment that will reduce or modify the future accrual of benefits (called an *ERISA 204(h) notice*). Your employer's failure to provide this advance notice can cause the amendment to be ineffective.

According to IRS Treasury Regulations, notice of a determination letter request must be provided by any method that reasonably ensures that all current employees eligible to participate in the plan and former employees with benefits under the plan will receive the notice in a timely manner. Some acceptable methods include electronic transmission, in person, and by mail. A posting in the workplace is also acceptable. If notice is delivered electronically, it must be through an electronic medium that's reasonably accessible, such as e-mail.

When a pension plan amends any of the information that's required to be included in the SPD, this change is referred to as a *material modification* to the plan. This change must be disclosed to plan participants and beneficiaries through a form called a *summary of material modifications* (SMM) or a *revised summary plan description.*

The SMM must be distributed within 210 days after the close of the plan year in which the change is adopted (a plan year can be a calendar year or any 12-month period that the plan chooses to keep its records). Each participant must receive a hard copy or an electronic copy of the SMM; mere posting of the SMM in the workplace isn't sufficient. (Flip to Chapter 8 for more on the SPD, the SMM, and the other documents that you're entitled to receive.)

If your employer mails a notice to you at your last known address (even if you don't live there anymore), this fulfills the notice requirement. The moral of this ever-so-short story is to keep your plan updated with your current address, phone number, and e-mail address so that you can be sure to receive all disclosures that your employer or plan administrator provides.

The following rules from the IRS apply to electronic notification:

✔ The electronic medium must be reasonably designed to provide the notice in a manner no less understandable to you than a written paper document.

✔ You must affirmatively consent to the delivery of the notice in this manner. In other words, in order to receive an electronic notice instead of a written notice, you must demonstrate that you can access the notice in the electronic form used. You can do this by electronically consenting (which demonstrates that you're able to access the notice) or in writing (but only if you confirm your consent electronically).

✔ When the electronic notice is provided, you must be advised that you may request and receive a hard copy at no charge.

The Standards of Standard Plan Terminations

Unfortunately, all good things come to an end, and pension plans can be affected. Sometimes defined benefit plans go belly up and have to terminate. Most defined benefit plan terminations, however, are *standard terminations,* meaning that the plan has enough assets to pay all the benefits it owes to its employees and beneficiaries. Why, then, would a company terminate a qualified retirement plan? The IRS lists the following as some of the reasons:

✔ There has been a sale, transfer, or merger of companies resulting in a change of ownership.

✔ The employer has liquidated or dissolved.

✔ The employer has undergone some adverse business conditions.

✔ A new plan was adopted.

We give you the nitty-gritty on standard terminations in the following sections. Mostly we talk about the termination of defined benefit plans. (A rarer type of plan termination is a distress termination, which we discuss later in this chapter.)

The rules governing standard terminations apply only to defined benefit plans because these plans are insured by the Pension Benefit Guaranty Corporation, or PBGC. The PBGC, which was established by ERISA, is basically an insurance company for your pension plan. In other words, vested accrued benefits from defined benefit plans (meeting certain requirements of the PBGC), are protected up to a certain amount. So what does this mean if you have a defined contribution plan (which isn't protected by the PBGC)? These types of plans are individual accounts, so whatever is in your account at the time the plan is terminated is your account balance, and you're entitled to these benefits.

Even though the PBGC provides certain protections for defined benefit plans, if the plan is terminating through a standard termination, the PBGC's role is very small at this point. It serves to oversee the termination and confirm that in fact the plan has sufficient assets to pay the anticipated benefits. After that, the PBGC simply ensures that the benefits are distributed and the plan terminated. Later in this chapter, we talk about the PBGC's expanded role in the case of involuntary plan terminations (when the PBGC decides that termination is in order) and distress terminations.

Becoming 100 percent vested

A tax-qualified plan must provide that a participant's accrued benefits become 100 percent vested as of the date of the plan's termination, to the extent funded. The phrase *to the extent funded* simply means the amount that has been paid into the plan by the employer as of the date of the plan's termination. You're always 100 percent vested in your *own* contributions, but when your plan terminates, you're required to be fully vested in your employer's contributions as well. This is a nonforfeitable right to 100 percent of your employer's contributions to your account balance (in the case of defined contribution plans) and to your accrued benefits (in the case of defined benefit plans). See Chapter 7 for more about accrual and vesting.

Finding out about a standard termination

In a standard termination, your plan administrator must first inform you in writing that your pension plan is being terminated. This notice, called the Notice of Intent to Terminate, must be provided at least 60 days and not more than 90 days before the proposed termination date. It must inform you, among other things, that:

- ✔ The plan administrator intends to terminate the plan as of a specific proposed date.

- ✔ The plan assets must be sufficient to provide all plan benefits in order to terminate in a standard termination.

- ✔ Benefit accruals will stop as of the termination date.

- ✔ Annuity contracts, if required, may be purchased from certain insurers, which must be specifically identified.

- ✔ A written statement regarding your specific benefits will be provided to you.

✔ If you're already receiving monthly retirement benefits, your benefits won't be affected. But if your benefits will be affected, you must be given an explanation as to how the amount will be affected.

When your company intends to terminate through a standard termination, it also must notify the PBGC on a form called the Standard Termination Notice Single-Employer Plan Termination. This form, which must be filed no later than 180 days after the proposed termination date, certifies that the plan is expected to have enough assets to provide all benefit liabilities.

The next notice your plan administrator will provide you is called the Notice of Plan Benefits. This notice must be provided no later than the date that the company files its Standard Termination Notice with the PBGC. Here are the requirements for the Notice of Plan Benefits:

✔ It must be written in plain language.

✔ It must tell you the estimated amount of your benefits.

✔ It must tell you the form in which your benefit has been valued (either an annuity or lump sum).

✔ It must include the information used in calculating your benefits, such as your length of service, your age (or your beneficiary's age, if you're deceased), your wages, and the interest rate assumptions.

In general, when a defined contribution plan terminates, the benefits are paid in the form of an annuity unless the plan offers an optional form of benefit, such as a lump-sum distribution, which you select instead.

The following are some other notices that must be provided to you in certain situations:

✔ **The Notice of Annuity Information:** If your benefits can be distributed in the form of an annuity, this notice must be provided to you no later than 45 days before the annuity distribution date.

✔ **The Notice of Identity of Insurers:** The purpose of this notice is to help participants make informed elections between lump sums and annuity benefits. This notice must be provided to you no later than 45 days before the annuity distribution date.

✔ **The Notice of Annuity Contract:** If you decide to receive your plan benefits in the form of an annuity, the plan administrator must send this notice to you no later than 30 days after the contract is available.

Just as with the Notice of Intent to Terminate, these notices must be either hand-delivered or delivered by first-class mail (or even courier service) to your last known address. The notices may be issued electronically if it's reasonably calculated that you'll actually receive them. If you're a participant in a terminating defined benefit plan and you haven't received proper notice of the termination, contact your plan administrator.

Distributing the assets

The PBGC has 60 days from the date it receives notification of the plan's intent to terminate to issue a notice of noncompliance if it determines that it's likely the plan assets won't be sufficient to meet its benefit liabilities or if it determines that the notice requirements haven't been satisfied. If the PBGC issues such a notice, the plan can't terminate at that time and will need to continue until the plan assets are sufficient to cover the benefits under the plan.

Assuming that the PBGC doesn't issue a notice of noncompliance and that your plan qualifies for a standard termination, the PBGC allows the plan administrator to complete the termination and distribute the plan assets by doing either of the following:

- ✔ Purchasing annuities from an insurance company, which then pays benefits to each participant upon retirement
- ✔ Making lump-sum distributions

The deadline that employers must meet to distribute all the participants' benefits is normally the later of the following:

- ✔ 180 days after the end of the PBGC's 60-day (or extended) review period
- ✔ If the plan administrator has timely submitted a valid IRS determination letter request, 120 days after receipt of a favorable determination letter (this deadline may be extended)

After promised benefits are provided through the purchase of an annuity or through a lump-sum distribution, the PBGC guarantee ends. Within 30 days after the last distribution date, the plan administrator must certify to the PBGC that the plan assets and benefits were distributed as required.

If you're entitled to receive a lump sum from your plan when it terminates, you can make a tax-free rollover into an individual retirement account (IRA). But make sure it's a direct rollover from your plan into the IRA so you can defer taxes on your distribution until you begin receiving the benefits from the IRA. See Chapter 5 for more about rollovers and IRAs.

If your plan offers an optional form of benefit, don't jump the gun and decide to take your (lump sum) money and run without first considering this: The calculation of the lump sum may turn out to be less than what the number crunchers consider to be the present value of the retirement fund. Consult a professional before you make this decision (also see Chapter 9, in which we discuss the pros and cons of annuity versus lump-sum distributions).

The Details of Distress and Involuntary Terminations

If your defined benefit pension plan can't satisfy the requirements for a standard termination, it can be voluntarily terminated if your employer meets the requirements for a *distress termination*. Usually this type of termination happens when the plan is *underfunded* (meaning that the plan assets won't be sufficient to cover all benefit liabilities) and the employer is in such financial distress that it can't make up the plan's underfunding. Sometimes, though, an employer is in such chaos that the PBGC takes action on its own without waiting for an employer's application; this type of termination is an *involuntary termination*. We give you the lowdown on these terminations in the following sections.

If you're in a plan that's insured by the PBGC (in other words, if you're in a defined benefit plan), and the plan has been less than 80 percent funded for the past year or two and less than 90 percent funded for several years, your plan administrator is required to give you an annual written notice of the plan's funding situation and the limits on the PBGC's guaranteed insurance. But why wait to find out this information from a yearly plan notice? You have a legal right to obtain information about your plan's funding at any time by requesting the information in writing from your plan administrator. (See Chapter 17 for a more detailed discussion of underfunding as a warning sign that your plan isn't doing well.)

Like those of standard terminations (which we cover earlier in this chapter), the rules governing distress and involuntary terminations apply only to defined benefit plans that are insured by the PBGC.

What can you expect during a distress or involuntary termination?

As we mention earlier, a distress termination is the way your employer may terminate a defined benefit retirement plan that doesn't have enough assets to pay all the benefits. However, to terminate a plan in this manner, the employer must prove to the PBGC that it's in such poor financial condition or the pension costs are so burdensome that the employer can't continue in business and support the plan.

In certain dire financial circumstances (such as when the plan doesn't have enough money to pay benefits when due), you can expect the PBGC to take action on its own to end a pension plan. This involuntary termination happens when the PBGC determines that plan termination is needed to protect the interests of plan participants. In such a termination, the PBGC notifies the plan administrator and often publishes a notice about its action in local and national newspapers.

With either termination, if the plan can pay at least the PBGC-guaranteed benefits, the PBGC authorizes the plan administrator to distribute the plan assets as in a standard termination (we cover the distribution of assets in a standard termination earlier in this chapter). If the plan doesn't have enough money to pay even the PBGC-guaranteed benefits, the PBGC steps in, takes the plan over, and uses PBGC funds to make sure that you receive your guaranteed benefits.

If the PBGC takes over your plan, it guarantees the payment of your vested pension benefits up to the limits that are set by law (which means that you may not receive all the benefits that are due to you). Benefits that aren't guaranteed or that exceed the PBGC's limits may or may not be paid. It all depends on the plan's funding and on whether the PBGC is able to recover additional amounts from the employer.

For plans with a 2007 termination date, the maximum guarantee is $49,500 per year (or $4,125 per month), presuming that you're age 65 with a single life annuity. What does this mean to you? If your plan terminates, the PBGC guarantees that you'll receive up to this amount. The guaranteed limit varies depending on whether you're under 65 (the guarantee is lower) or over 65 (the guarantee is higher). So if you're due more than this amount in benefits, at least you know you'll be getting a good chunk of what has been guaranteed. For most people, these limits tend to be sufficient. For further details on guaranteed limits set by law, head to the PBGC's Web site at www.pbgc.gov.

What is the PBGC's role in distress and involuntary terminations?

In a distress or involuntary termination, your plan administrator sends to the PBGC full information concerning your benefits. At this point, the PBGC becomes trustee of your plan and notifies you (and all other plan participants) of this action. The time schedule in these situations is up to the PBGC.

The process for both distress terminations and involuntary terminations then goes something like this:

1. Initially the PBGC provides you with general information about the pension insurance program and its guarantees.

2. As trustee, the PBGC takes over your records. At this point, it continues making benefit payments to current retirees (without interruption) based on an estimate of the benefits that they should receive under the PBGC insurance program.

3. The PBGC reviews the plan's records, provisions, and assets, in addition to your age and length of participation in the plan. With this information, it calculates your benefits based on the form in which they'll be paid (either an annuity or a lump sum). Then the PBGC notifies you of the amounts that you'll receive and advises you of your right to appeal its benefit calculation.

4. The PBGC begins making benefit payments to new retirees. If you aren't yet eligible for retirement, the PBGC provides you with your plan benefits at the same time that you would have been eligible under the pension plan had it not been terminated.

Freezing benefits as an alternative to a plan termination

In some cases, termination may be the only sensible course of action. In most cases, however, other options, such as freezing the benefits, can be considered before terminating a defined benefit plan. A frozen plan continues to operate and pay benefits to plan participants upon retirement. The only difference is that benefit accruals are frozen as of a future date. In other words, an employer may notify plan participants that no additional plan benefits may be accrued after a certain date.

Another option for the employer may be to freeze participation in the plan but continue to provide future benefit accruals for employees hired prior to a certain date. For example, employees hired before January 1, 2008, may still participate in and receive future benefit accruals under the defined benefit plan. Employees hired on or after January 1, 2008, however, will be excluded from the defined benefit plan (but may be able to participate in a defined contribution plan). If your employer's plan is amended to either freeze benefits or freeze participation, you'll be notified by your employer.

Part IV
Shielding Your Pension from Life's Ups and Downs

The 5th Wave   By Rich Tennant

"That reminds me – I have to figure out how to save for retirement _and_ send these two to college."

In this part . . .

*W*hether you're facing financial difficulties, divorce, or even bankruptcy, in this part we help you understand how these situations affect your pension and the options that are available to shield your hard-earned benefits.

Included in this part is a discussion of how and when you can get a loan from your pension plan. We go over the special hardship situations that make it easier to take money out of your plan. If you're going through a divorce, this part can help you determine how your pension will be allocated. We also explain the survivorship rules so that you know what your spouse can expect to receive from your pension in the event that you die before him or her. And, just in case you run across some serious money issues, we discuss the issue of creditor protection — how best to protect your assets both in and out of bankruptcy.

Chapter 13

Hitting Yourself Up for a Loan

. . . .

In This Chapter

▶ Discovering the risks and benefits of borrowing from your pension plan

▶ Understanding the process of getting a loan from your pension plan

▶ Deciphering loan termination and disqualified plans

. . . .

*L*et's face it: Everybody needs money, and occasionally we need more than our savings accounts can produce. Taking a loan from your pension plan may sound like a good idea when you first say it out loud, but because there are so many ins and outs involved with borrowing from your tax-qualified plan, you may find that it isn't always the best idea. In other words, if you don't know the rules regarding pension plan loans, you may end up making a costly mistake. So protect yourself (and your hard-earned dough) by knowing the rules before you take a loan from your plan. And remember, some plans don't even permit loans. So the first thing you should do is find out whether your plan can grant you a loan. Simply check your summary plan description (SPD) or ask the plan administrator to find out.

In this chapter, we discuss the pluses and minuses of taking out a loan from your pension plan and guide you through the loan process. We also describe what happens when good loans go bad and problems because of loan terminations and plan disqualifications. The same loan rules apply to both defined benefit plans and defined contribution plans.

You can't, under any circumstances, pledge your plan benefits to a bank or any party other than the plan as security for a loan or for any other purpose. Also remember that loans from individual retirement accounts (IRAs) are prohibited. If you borrow money from your IRA or attempt to pledge your IRA as security for a loan, the entire IRA is disqualified and taxable to you. See Chapter 5 for the basics of IRAs.

Surveying the Pros and Cons of Borrowing from Your Pension Plan

In some cases, it may be smart to take a loan from your pension plan, but in more cases than not, it may not be the best idea to use your future retirement to take care of today's debts. The following sections list the advantages and disadvantages to consider.

The benefits

Here's a list of some advantages to borrowing the money you need from your pension instead of taking out a traditional loan:

✔ You can borrow the money for any reason at all. So what if you need $5,000 to enter a poker tournament — no staid banker will be around to give you *the look*.

✔ You can avoid extensive and intrusive paperwork and credit checks.

✔ You'll have more control over when you get the loan. Most banks operate on their timetables, not yours. Presumably your plan will take less time than a bank.

✔ Your interest rate will be a fair and reasonable one (we discuss interest rates later in this chapter).

✔ When you pay back your loan, you're really paying it back to yourself, and depending on the interest rate, your account may have earned more from the interest on the loan to yourself than it was earning in the plan itself. (We cover the repayment of loans later in this chapter.)

✔ A loan from your plan isn't taxable to you as long as you follow the rules and repay the loan in accordance with the loan's repayment schedule.

You may also consider borrowing from your plan if no one else will give you a loan. If you're facing an emergency, need the money, and can't get it elsewhere or soon enough, your pension plan may be the answer as long as you follow the rules.

When you borrow money from your plan, if possible, take it from the investments that are paying the weakest returns. However, keep in mind that depending on your plan, you may have no choice about where the fund takes the money for your loan. For example, in a defined benefit plan, you don't have that option because everyone's money is invested as a group. (See Chapter 3 for the lowdown on defined benefit plans.) But the statement of the investments in your defined contribution plan may show a money market investment earning 4 percent and bonds earning 6 percent. It makes more sense to liquidate the 4 percent investment to generate cash for the loan than anything paying a higher yield.

The risks

While convenience and privacy are nice perks of a pension loan, they may be outweighed by the disadvantages of dipping into your retirement. As we point out in the later section "Recognizing loan requirements," one disadvantage is that you may need permission from your spouse to take a loan from your plan — not good if you want to buy a Harley-Davidson with your loan. Also, the folks who run the plan, who probably include management people from your firm, may know that you're short on cash and borrowing from the plan.

Here are some other disadvantages to consider:

- ✔ If you have only stocks available for liquidation, you may be forced to cash them in at a low price.

- ✔ The interest that you pay on the loan may be at a lower rate than the plan would otherwise earn on its investments.

- ✔ The results of a default on a loan from your pension plan — namely, a taxable pension distribution — can be traumatic. In other words, if you default on a loan, you'll have to pay not only federal and state taxes, but also the 10 percent federal tax penalty if you're under age 59½. (We discuss defaults in more detail later in this chapter.)

- ✔ If you're unexpectedly terminated from your job, you may be faced with a double whammy: You will have lost your job *and* your loan may immediately become due and payable.

- ✔ Loans to certain people who have clout with the plan (for example, the employer that sponsors the plan) can result in harsh extra taxes.

- ✔ The interest on a pension plan loan usually isn't deductible. Instead, consider a home equity loan from a bank; the interest is deductible from your taxable income.

Walking through the Loan Process

If by chance you've concluded that a pension plan loan isn't for you, feel free to skip the rest of this chapter. If, however, you still want that plan loan, you have some work to do.

Loans to plan participants must be specifically provided for in the plan documents that we describe in Chapter 8, and the language in the plan document and the SPD must include the following information:

- ✔ The identity of the person who's authorized to administer the participant loan program (this can be a person who's specially assigned this responsibility, such as the plan administrator, or it can be a loan committee)
- ✔ The procedure for applying for loans
- ✔ The basis on which loans will be approved or denied
- ✔ The limitations (if any) on the types and amounts of loans offered
- ✔ The procedure for determining reasonable rates of interest
- ✔ The types of collateral that may secure a participant loan (in almost all cases, your loan from the plan is secured solely by your vested benefits under the plan)
- ✔ A description of the events that are considered default and the steps that will be taken to preserve plan assets in case of such default

We go into more detail on these topics in the following sections.

If the critical loan information isn't in your plan documents, ask your plan administrator or human resources manager, in writing (certified mail, return receipt requested), to provide you with the missing information.

Applying for a loan

The procedure for applying for a loan from your pension plan is specific to your plan. Consult your plan documents to locate the language describing how to apply for a loan, and follow that procedure to a T. You'll have to fill out loan applications and provide specific information. Keep in mind that this is just like any other loan except that you're borrowing the money from yourself.

Approving (or denying) a loan with certain factors in mind

When making a loan, a plan can consider only those factors that would be considered in the average commercial loan setting. Such factors may include the applicant's creditworthiness or financial need. Here are some other rules that a plan must follow:

- **The interest rate for the plan loan must be reasonable.** In this case, a reasonable rate is basically one that a bank would charge for a similar loan. (See the later section "Determining a rate of interest" for more information.)

- **Your plan can establish a minimum loan amount of up to $1,000.** A loan from a pension plan also has a maximum. (See the later section "The size of the loan" for details.)

- **Loans can't be limited to current employees.** If a plan provides for loans, those loans must be available to all plan participants, including former employees with vested benefits in the plan.

- **Your plan must offer the same loan percentage to everyone.** With this rule, even the fat cats can get loans. Congress intended for plans to lend the same percentage of a person's vested benefits to participants with both large and small amounts of accrued benefits.

To get your plan approved, you need to follow the rules. In other words, if you comply with the procedure for the loan and meet the financial criteria, you should be approved.

The plan can't make exceptions. If you're unable to post adequate security, or if you're already over the dollar limit for a loan, no amount of pleading will change a "no loan for you" decision to a yes.

Recognizing loan requirements

You must take seriously the requirements for borrowing from your pension plan. Failure to follow these rules can have unfortunate consequences, including causing your loan to be treated by the Internal Revenue Service (IRS) as a taxable distribution (see Chapter 9 for more about distributions). So, it's helpful to know the requirements, and it's absolutely necessary to comply with them — no exceptions. Here's a list of the most important requirements that you need to know:

- ✔ The loan must be in writing.

- ✔ The loan documents must constitute a legally enforceable agreement. In other words, it must be evidenced by a document (either in writing or in an electronic medium that satisfies certain conditions), and the terms of the agreement must comply with the requirements for plan loans. Usually the agreement is signed unless it's enforceable under your state law without being signed.

- ✔ The loan must be adequately secured (we cover security later in this chapter).

- ✔ You must establish a true debtor–creditor relationship. In other words, the loan has established terms in writing and is no different than a loan from a bank or credit union, which means that it must be repaid in accordance with the loan terms.

- ✔ The plan must charge a reasonable rate of interest. For example, if the going rate is 7 percent, you can't have a loan at 5 percent. (We discuss interest rates later in this chapter.)

- ✔ A definite repayment schedule, consisting of amortized payments of principal and interest paid at least quarterly (once every three months), must be established (we give you details about repayment later in this chapter).

- ✔ Your pension plan can't discriminate when it comes to the availability of loans. If a loan is available to you, it has to be available to others on a similar basis.

If your plan is subject to the automatic survivor annuity, your spouse's consent for a loan also is required because a portion of your retirement benefit automatically goes to your spouse when you die. Because this survivor portion is a pension right that belongs to your spouse, you aren't permitted to borrow from the fund without your spouse's permission. We address survivor annuities in more detail in Chapter 14.

Looking at loan limitations

Several limiting factors affect a loan from a pension plan: the length and repayment of a loan and the size of a loan. We cover the ins and outs of these factors in the following sections.

The length and repayment of the loan

The term of your loan (in other words, how long you have to pay it off) can't be longer than five years. The term of a loan that's outstanding at the end of a five-year period can't be renegotiated, and the outstanding amount will be treated as a pension distribution (which we cover in Chapter 9).

Double-check your loan paperwork! Even if you pay off the loan in three years, if the loan document inadvertently says it's a six-year loan (rather than a five-year loan), the loan wouldn't meet the following important requirements:

✔ The repayment schedule can't be for a term longer than five years.

✔ The loan must actually be repaid within a five-year period.

This situation still constitutes a pension distribution at the time the loan was made because the loan document violated the five-year rule.

You'll be glad to know that there are a few exceptions to this mostly inflexible five-year time period. But remember that these exceptions still have certain requirements and they apply only if you find yourself in the following extenuating circumstances:

✔ **You're taking a leave of absence:** If you're on a leave of absence without pay, or if you're working at a pay rate that's less than the required loan installments, the payment period may be suspended during the leave of absence (for a maximum of one year). The kicker, however, is that the loan must still be repaid within the five-year period.

✔ **You're in the military:** If you're in the military, your plan can suspend your loan payments while you're away from your job serving the country. Once you resume payment, your plan can give you a choice between increased payments or payments at the old schedule with a balloon payment at the end.

✔ **The loan is being used to build or purchase your home:** If you're buying or building a home, your plan can, if it chooses, cut you some slack. Instead of requiring you to repay the loan in five years, the plan can require you to repay within a "reasonable time." Even though there's no set rule on time limitations, the IRS has approved a 15-year limit. But don't think you can take your sweet time and pay whenever you want to: A time and payment schedule must be agreed on when the loan is made.

✔ **You've gone bankrupt:** Prior to October 17, 2005, if you had an outstanding plan loan and then filed for Chapter 13 bankruptcy before the loan was repaid, bankruptcy law required your employer to discontinue withholding loan repayment amounts from your wages. Because the law required a halt to certain activities, this is called an *automatic stay.* As a result, your loan would go into default (which we discuss later in this chapter) and you would face a taxable distribution and the possibility of an additional early distribution penalty tax. If you filed for Chapter 7 bankruptcy, however, plans could continue to withhold loan repayments from your wages.

Under the new Bankruptcy Act that became effective on October 17, 2005, when a pension plan participant files for Chapter 13 bankruptcy, the employer can continue to withhold payments from the employee's wages to repay the loan — and its withholding of the employee's wages doesn't violate the automatic stay provision. Neither is the loan dischargeable in bankruptcy.

Loans from retirement plans must be repaid by *level amortization* (meaning substantially equal payments) with at least quarterly payments of principal and interest. You can't just make interest payments on the loan and repay the principal at the end of the loan term. Plans often require that loans be repaid by salary withholding payments, with the payments withheld from each of your paychecks until the loan is repaid. The payment schedule, such as monthly or bimonthly, is an agreed-upon term of the loan.

The size of the loan

There are strict limitations on the amount that you're permitted to borrow from your pension plan. The outstanding balance of all your loans from all of your employer's plans may not exceed the lesser of $50,000 or 50 percent of your nonforfeitable accrued benefits (those that you're vested in and entitled to; see Chapter 7 for more about accrual). Despite this rule, the plan may permit you to borrow up to $10,000 even if the loan exceeds 50 percent of your vested interest, provided that you have adequate security for such a loan outside your pension plan. (We discuss adequate security later in this chapter.)

For example, if your pension plan has an accumulated value of $120,000 at the time you take out your loan, 50 percent of the accrued benefit is $60,000. However, that amount would exceed the $50,000 limit, so all you can borrow is $50,000.

If permitted by the plan, you can have more than one loan at a time, but combined, your loans can't exceed the loan limit rules. The $50,000 limitation is reduced by the highest outstanding loan balance during the 12-month period prior to the new loan. For instance, if you had a loan balance of $40,000 within the 12 months preceding a request for a new loan, the maximum permissible loan amount would be $10,000, which is the difference between the $50,000 limitation and the $40,000 balance. It wouldn't matter if, at the time of your request for a new loan, you owed only $20,000, because within the past 12 months you had owed $40,000.

Exceeding a loan limit triggers a distribution — and that's not a good thing, because a distribution is taxable. The good news is that your failure to comply with the limitations on loans results in a distribution only to the extent that the dollar limitation is exceeded. So if you could have borrowed $30,000, but you instead borrowed $40,000, only the extra $10,000 is subject to being a taxable distribution. (See Chapter 9 for more about pension distributions and taxes.)

Bankruptcy 101

You may think that bankruptcy is bankruptcy. Honestly, you're right — no matter how you look at it, bankruptcy is never fun. But, in reality, the two main types — Chapter 7 and Chapter 13 — are quite different. Here are the important differences:

✔ In a Chapter 7 bankruptcy proceeding, you're able to *liquidate* all your debts in exchange for the liquidation of your assets. (*Liquidation*, in layman's terms, is simply wiping out your debts through the bankruptcy.) A trustee is appointed to your case, and that person sells your property and distributes the proceeds to your creditors. After your assets are sold, your debts are officially wiped out.

✔ In a Chapter 13 proceeding, a repayment plan is established so that your debtors can be paid in full or in part over a three- to five-year period. During this repayment period, your creditors must suspend their collection efforts.

Determining a rate of interest

An appropriate interest rate is determined by competitive bank rates for a similar loan. If a bank would make the loan at 7 percent, that amount would be considered an appropriate rate. The plan's loan policy typically ties the loan interest rate to a specific bank prime rate and usually states that the plan loan rate is 1 percent or 2 percent over prime.

The Department of Labor believes that when interest rates are an issue, the problem generally isn't with interest rates that are too high. Instead, the problem is with interest rates that are too low. Loans at interest rates that are too low may be viewed by the IRS as a violation of the plan's nonalienation rules (plans can't assign or alienate their benefits). This could result in the loss of the plan's tax-qualified status.

Ensuring adequate security

The requirement of *adequate security* for a loan is satisfied if the liquidation of the security will pay off the loan. To determine whether a participant has adequate security to take out a pension plan loan, the plan looks at the type and amount of security that's required in an otherwise identical transaction in an average commercial setting. Simply put, if a $10,000 loan has security that could be sold for $10,000, the security is adequate for the loan.

In almost all cases, your plan loan will be secured by 50 percent of your vested interest under the plan. Because your plan loans are generally limited to 50 percent of your vested interest under the plan, your vested benefit is adequate security for your plan loans.

The only time that it would be possible for your plan loans to exceed 50 percent of your vested interest is if your total loans are less than $10,000. Most plans don't adopt the $10,000 exception and won't let your loans exceed 50 percent of your vested interest. If a plan does permit your loans to exceed 50 percent of your vested interest (under the $10,000 exception), your loan must be adequately secured by security other than your vested benefit.

The plan administrator and trustee must take great care to ensure that your loans are adequately secured. For example, if you borrow more than 50 percent of your vested accrued benefits under the plan and the loan is secured solely by 50 percent of your vested accrued benefits under the plan, the loan is inadequately secured. The penalty for an improper loan is that the loan will be treated as a distribution and will be taxable. You can avoid the problem only by taking loans from the plan that are less than 50 percent of your vested interest.

Defaulting on a loan

A loan from your own pension plan is just like a loan from a hard-nosed bank: After you receive your loan, you have to pay it back in the appropriate repayment time frame. In fact, in some ways the penalties for being late or failing to repay a pension loan are worse then a bank's. For instance, if you don't pay your loan back on time, the loan is considered a distribution from your pension, called a *deemed distribution.*

Late loan payments can cause your loan to be *in default.* Your loan is in default when you aren't complying with the terms of the loan (such as not making your payments on time). However, IRS regulations permit a *grace period* (extra time in which to pay on the loan) for late payments before a plan loan is considered to be in default. The grace period can't extend beyond the end of the calendar quarter following the calendar quarter during which the loan payment was due.

For example, imagine that your loan payment is due on May 15, 2008. The calendar quarter during which this payment is due ends on June 30, 2008. So, if the missed May 15, 2008, payment hasn't been paid by September 30, 2008 (which is the end of the calendar quarter following the calendar quarter during which the payment was due), the loan is in default. And because it's in default, the entire balance due on the loan and the accrued interest through the date of default is a deemed distribution and taxable to the plan participant.

Even though the defaulted loan was taxable to you as a deemed distribution, the loan is still considered by the plan to be outstanding for purposes of determining amounts available to you for future plan loans.

If for some reason you fall behind, make sure you get back on track before the IRS grace period has passed you by. If you fail to make up any missed payments by the end of the grace period, the plan has no choice but to consider your defaulted loan to be a taxable distribution to you.

Understanding Loan Termination and Plan Disqualification

Over-the-top abuses of plan assets can cause your plan to be disqualified as a legitimate pension plan. Or your plan may decide that with all the rules and risks involved, providing loans to its pensioners isn't worth the headache. Both situations are unpleasant, but don't worry, because the next sections give you the basics.

When the plan stops providing loans

You may ask yourself why your plan makes it so difficult to borrow what should be your own money. Before you get too furious, though, remember that your plan does *not* have to provide the right to receive a loan against your accrued pension benefits. Under certain circumstances your plan can even stop allowing you and other participants to borrow from your pensions. If your plan decides that permitting participants to borrow from a pension plan is administratively burdensome, or if there have been questionable loans, the loan provisions can be removed for future loans. But if the loan provisions are removed, any current outstanding loans must still be repaid in accordance with their terms.

When the plan is disqualified

Your company president can't just borrow from the pension plan and then turn around and loan the money to the company. Neither can the president take the company's pension money and loan it to herself (unless she's a plan participant and complies with all of the rules for participant loans discussed in this chapter). If she does pull a sneaky move like one of these, the plan can be disqualified, which means that all of the assets in the plan will become currently taxable to you and the other plan participants. Further, you would be unable to roll over money from a disqualified plan into a qualified plan or into an IRA. These are serious consequences that can cost you your retirement.

Plan disqualification is different from plan termination (see Chapter 12 for more on plan terminations). With plan disqualifications, the IRS has revoked the ability of the plan to take advantage of the tax benefits for pension plans.

Even loans to employees who aren't disqualified persons can cause problems for a pension plan. For example, the IRS once disqualified a plan for permitting loans to plan participants at below-market rates of interest. Even a loan to a rank-and-file employee can violate the rules. The moral is that you must be careful about participant loans.

In the end, the most important thing to remember is that the money in your company's pension plan belongs to its participants, and it must be used for their exclusive benefit. So, when money from the retirement plan is used for any purpose other than paying pension benefits, the plan may be disqualified by the IRS. Everyone (you *and* the company president) must adhere to the strict loan requirements that we list earlier in this chapter. The rules aren't created just to make it difficult for you to borrow from your pension plan; they were created to protect your money from being abused by those in charge. The best protection against abuse of plan assets is to pay attention to your plan. Review your plan's Form 5500s for monkey business, and don't be afraid to ask questions if something doesn't look right to you.

Chapter 14

Surveying Survivorship Benefits

. . . .

In This Chapter

▶ Beginning with basic facts about survivorship benefits

▶ Checking out survivorship benefits before and after retirement

▶ Knowing how and when to waive survivorship benefits

▶ Understanding how tough circumstances affect survivorship benefits

. . . .

*N*o one likes to think about his or her own death, but it's smart to do whatever you can right now to protect your loved ones. In this chapter, you find out how to extend your pension benefits to your spouse and loved ones after you die. These benefits, called *survivorship benefits,* are paid by your pension plan to your designated beneficiary — usually a spouse — when you die. Survivorship benefits are typically elected to protect your spouse's interest in your pension. Now, for the first time, some survivorship benefits have been extended to same-sex couples and other non-spouse beneficiaries. You can thank the Pension Protection Act of 2006 (PPA) for this extension of benefits.

The rules of survivorship benefits are pretty tricky. For starters, they're different depending on whether you die before or after you retire. Have no fear, though; we break down what you need to know and why you need to know it in this chapter.

Keep in mind that all annuities are benefits, but not all benefits are annuities. Survivorship benefits from defined contribution plans consist of your account balance in the plan when you die, which aren't necessarily paid out in an annuity. Survivorship benefits from defined benefit plans, however, are generally paid in the form of annuity payments for the life of your spouse or other beneficiary. So the information in this chapter regarding the various types of survivor annuities relate primarily to defined benefit plans. (See Chapter 3 for the basics about defined benefit plans and defined contribution plans.)

Understanding the Basics of Survivorship Benefits

In 1984, the Retirement Equity Act (REA) became law. One of the primary goals of the REA was to protect the rights of a pensioner's spouse in a tax-qualified pension plan. Before the REA, you could elect, without consulting or obtaining consent from your spouse, to provide no pension benefits to your spouse when you died. Now, after the passage of the REA, your spouse has automatic rights to a pension payment after you die.

The REA changed the Employee Retirement Income Security Act of 1974 (ERISA; see Chapter 2) in several important ways. For example, the REA stated the following provisions:

✔ When you die, your surviving spouse has an absolute right to an annuity (or payment) of no less than 50 percent of your vested pension benefit, if it's more than $5,000. (If your vested benefit is less than $5,000, you can do what you want with it.) For your spouse to be entitled to the 50 percent, however, the plan can require that the two of you were married at least one year prior to your death.

Under the PPA, your plan has to provide the right to elect a 75 percent survivor annuity if you and your spouse prefer that option to the 50 percent survivor annuity. But the cost of this option is that the plan will pay lower benefits during your life; in other words, your spouse receives more if she outlives you, but you receive less while you're alive.

✔ You and your spouse can waive the 50 percent entitlement, but you both have to agree to it. (You find out more about waiving rights later in this chapter.)

In the following sections, we discuss some additional fundamentals of survivorship benefits, such as the basics of annuities, the plans that offer survivorship benefits, the ways to find the details of such benefits, and the process of designating a beneficiary for such benefits.

Focusing on annuity fundamentals

To understand survivorship benefits, you need a basic grasp of the concept of annuities. An *annuity* provides a series of regular payments under a contract paid over a period of years.

In defined benefit plans, the benefit formula tells you how much the annuity is worth. If you start the annuity before the plan's normal retirement age, it may be reduced to reflect the longer period of payout. In a defined contribution plan that offers an annuity form of payment, the size of the annuity depends on the available funds in your account when the annuity is purchased.

Here are some basics about annuities:

- ✔ The amount of the annuity depends on the value of your pension at the time that the annuity is purchased. In other words, your vested benefits determine the dollar value of your particular pension. (Chapter 7 has more information about vesting.) The annuity payments are based on the current lump sum value of your benefit and a projection of the interest that the plan will earn on the funds while it's paying you your benefits.

- ✔ You have to meet the plan's eligibility requirements to get pension benefits. (See Chapter 7 for more about eligibility.)

- ✔ Some pension plans will subsidize your annuity in some form or another (we discuss subsidized annuities later in this chapter).

- ✔ Several types of annuities exist, including these:

    - **Fixed-period annuities:** These annuities provide definite benefit amounts at regular times for a fixed period of time (such as 20 years) and can end before your death.

    - **Annuities for a single life:** With these annuities, you receive regular payments for your life, and they end at your death. In other words, when you die, your benefits can't be passed on to a spouse or other loved one.

    - **Joint and survivor annuities:** These annuities provide payments for the lives of two people (in this case, these people are called *annuitants*). The first annuitant receives a fixed amount during his life. After he dies, the surviving annuitant receives the same amount or a smaller amount at regular intervals for the rest of her life. (We cover these types of annuities in detail later in this chapter.)

- ✔ Before January 1, 2007, you had to choose the type of payment within 30 to 90 days prior to the beginning of your first payment. With the enactment of the PPA, and after January 1, 2007, you now have 30 to 180 days prior to the payment commencement date to elect a payment option (such as one of the different types of annuities or a lump sum; see Chapter 9 for more about lump sums).

Knowing which plans offer which benefits

Only certain plans are required to offer survivorship benefits and annuities. Here's a list of the survivorship benefits that each of the different plans offer:

- ✔ **Defined benefit plans must offer post- and preretirement survivor annuities.** Keep in mind that the survivor annuity rules cover only benefits that you (the employee) were entitled to and that you were actually vested in before death. *Vested benefits* are those benefits that you're entitled to receive from the plan.

✔ **Defined contribution plans don't have to offer survivor annuities in all circumstances.** If your defined contribution plan doesn't provide for an annuity form of payment (meaning that you'll receive your retirement benefits in a lump sum), the plan doesn't have to offer a survivorship benefit. If, however, one of the benefit options under your plan is an annuity for your life, and that's the option you choose, the qualified and joint survivor annuity rules apply (we cover this type of annuity later in this chapter).

Defined contribution plans that require mandatory employer contributions (such as money purchase plans or the very rare target benefit plans) must offer annuity forms of benefit and survivor annuities.

Defined contribution plans such as 401(k) plans, profit-sharing plans, and stock bonus plans may choose to offer an annuity as an optional form of benefit. Any plan that provides for any type of annuity must also provide for survivor annuities.

In a profit-sharing plan, your spouse has no right to your benefits prior to your death, but he or she is entitled to 100 percent of them after you die.

✔ Your spouse has no rights in individual retirement accounts (IRAs), SIMPLE IRAs, or SEPs (see Chapter 5 for more about these types of plans).

For plans that offer an annuity form of payment, the plan can't pay you your benefits without your spouse's consent, and your spouse is entitled to 50 percent of the benefits at the time of your death. For plans that don't offer an annuity form of payment, the plan can pay you your benefits without your spouse's consent, but your spouse is entitled to 100 percent of the benefits when you die.

Finding out the details of your benefits

Survivorship rights are tricky, and they all have financial implications that aren't always apparent. Because of this difficulty, the law requires your plan to give you (and your spouse) an explanation of the various survivorship options in your plan documents (see Chapter 8 for details about these documents). The law also requires your plan to explain the relative value of the different options, such as a 50 percent or a 75 percent survivor annuity. Your plan also must advise you of the eligibility requirements and must tell you whether the plan subsidizes any of the options (when there's no change in cost to you because the plan is making up the difference). Generally speaking, you're entitled to all this information before the annuity starts.

The written explanation provided by your plan must meet the following requirements:

✔ It must explain your rights to waive the qualified joint and survivor annuity (we discuss waivers later in this chapter).

✔ The explanation of the impact of the various options must be written in a way intended to be understood by the average plan participant.

✔ It must provide a comparison of the value of your choices, and the comparisons must show the financial impact of the optional benefits at various time periods (for instance, in the middle and at the end) so you can see the pattern of the option's values. You should be able to compare the various benefits without a slide rule and without reference to tables and charts.

✔ It should inform you of the amount that you can expect under a normal benefit, such as a single life annuity.

✔ If you choose to waive the qualified joint and survivor annuity, your spouse must consent, in writing, on a spousal consent form provided by your plan administrator that explains, in plain language, the effect of a waiver. Your spouse's consent must acknowledge the effect of this waiver.

Now that you know you're entitled to this information, make sure you have it and understand the financial impact of your survivorship options before you and your spouse make any decision. This information is mandated, so only plan oversight or error would explain your failure to receive it. A request to the plan administrator should correct the problem.

If your plan fully subsidizes the survivorship benefit, the plan generally doesn't need to provide the explanation. You find out more about subsidies later in this chapter.

Designating your beneficiary

Your plan has a designation of beneficiary form that's available from your human resources department or pension office. It's in your best interest to fill out the form as soon as you know who you want to designate as your beneficiary. This way, if you're hit by the proverbial truck on your way home from work, your beneficiary will be protected. You also must keep the form current because as a result of death or divorce, your beneficiary can change. Without a completed designated beneficiary form, your spouse is automatically your beneficiary.

The PPA made some changes regarding distributions to non-spouse beneficiaries. For example, the PPA allows a plan participant's retirement benefits to be rolled over not only by a spouse, but also by a domestic partner or any other non-spouse beneficiary, such as siblings, parents, and children. Before the PPA, only you or your spouse could roll benefits over to an IRA (see Chapter 5 for more about IRAs). Now the surviving partner (or other beneficiary) can avoid taxes by rolling over the pension benefit to an IRA. The benefit can be distributed over the beneficiary's life.

Under the old rule, the plan could require that a participant's pension be taken as a lump sum, resulting in immediate taxes. In this case, the pension could put the survivor into a much larger tax bracket because it would be considered taxable income to the surviving beneficiary in the year that it was distributed.

Plans aren't required to provide for rollovers by non-spouse beneficiaries. If your employer's plan doesn't provide for this option, ask your employer to amend the plan to include rollovers for non-spouse beneficiaries.

Spelling Out the ABCs of Specific Survivor Annuities

How much your spouse can receive when you die depends on the following factors:

- Whether you die before or after eligibility for retirement
- If you die before retirement, whether you were eligible to retire at the time you died
- Whether your pension plan is a defined benefit or a defined contribution plan
- The percentage of survivorship benefits you and your spouse choose

Based on these factors, you can have one of the following survivor annuities provided by ERISA:

- A qualified joint and survivor annuity (QJSA)
- A qualified preretirement survivor annuity (QPSA)

We discuss the features of both types of survivor annuities in the following sections.

The qualified joint and survivor annuity

If you, the plan participant, are alive on the *annuity starting date* (the date you're entitled to begin receiving your benefit payments), the annuity is known as a *qualified joint and survivor annuity* (QJSA). In other words, this type of annuity typically kicks in if you die *after* you retire. In the following sections, we explain the amount and timing of benefits that a spouse receives with a QJSA.

The following changes take effect January 1, 2008, under the PPA (if you're part of a collectively bargained plan, these options are mandated after the earlier date of January 1, 2009, or the expiration of the current contract):

- ✔ If a plan provides for the automatic 50 percent survivorship benefit, the plan must provide the choice for participants to elect a 75 percent benefit option.

- ✔ If the plan already offers a 75 percent option, it must provide an option to elect a 50 percent survivorship benefit.

The amount of benefits

A QJSA is an annuity or series of payments paid over your life and your spouse's life if you die *after* you retire. Because a QJSA takes into account your life as well as that of your spouse (who will continue to receive benefits after you die), the amount of these payments to you will be smaller than if they were going to be paid for only your lifetime.

However, after you die, the plan must provide an annuity to your spouse in payments no less than 50 percent of the amount payable to you while you were alive. For example, imagine that your annuity was $2,500 a month while you were alive. After your death, your spouse gets one half of that amount, or $1,250.

Even though the minimum payment to a surviving spouse is 50 percent, some pension plans do provide for survivor monthly payments of up to 100 percent of the monthly benefit that the plan participant received while he or she was alive.

Some pension plans do this for everyone automatically. Other plans give you a choice. But in such plans, the higher the survivorship benefit, the lower the benefit during the life of you, the employee. Generally, under the PPA, all plans subject to these rules must offer both 50 percent and 75 percent survivor annuity options.

The timing of benefits

While you're alive, you're entitled to receive payments as soon as you reach the earliest retirement age under your plan. If your plan provides for voluntary distributions when you leave the company, however, you could leave the company and receive a payment. In that case, the plan documents must be reviewed to determine how soon you would be eligible to receive your pension.

The qualified preretirement survivor annuity

If you, the plan participant, die before the annuity starting date (in other words, typically *before* retirement), and if you have vested benefits from either employee or employer contributions to your plan, your spouse is entitled to receive survivorship benefits in the form of a *qualified preretirement survivor annuity* (QPSA). A QPSA is an annuity for the life of your surviving spouse.

The calculation of the QPSA depends on when you die and on what type of pension plan you have. In the following sections, we outline several scenarios in which a spouse receives a QPSA.

Death after reaching the earliest retirement age in a defined benefit plan

If you die after reaching the earliest permitted retirement age in your plan (but before you've actually retired), the payment to your surviving spouse under the QPSA can't be less than the survivor payment that your spouse would have received if you had retired with a QJSA the day before you died. (We explain QJSA basics earlier in this chapter.)

For example, assume that your plan at Intergalactic Shipping is a defined benefit plan that required you to work ten years and reach age 55 before retiring. Also assume that you died on August 2 (before you actually got around to retiring) after working 12 years and after reaching age 55.

Because you could have retired after working ten years, and because you had already reached age 55, you died after the earliest date that you could have retired. So, for purposes of calculating your spouse's survivorship benefits, your plan pretends that you retired with a QJSA on the day before you actually died — August 1. For your surviving spouse, then, the QJSA is worth 50 percent of what you would have received while alive. In other words, your surviving spouse will get 50 percent of what you would have been eligible to receive after working 12 years and retiring with a QJSA. For instance, if you were entitled to $1,000 per month, your spouse will get $500 per month for life.

Death before reaching the earliest retirement age in a defined benefit plan

If you die before you reach the earliest permitted retirement age in your defined benefit plan, the payment will be based on the assumption that you lived until the earliest permitted retirement date. But remember, your beneficiary can't receive an annuity until the date when you could have first retired.

In this example, we change the facts slightly from the previous one, but do presume that the plan's requirements of working ten years and reaching age 55 stay the same. This time, however, assume that you die after working eight years at Intergalactic Shipping.

In this scenario, the plan assumes that you left service at the date of death but lived until the earliest time that you could have retired. So, the retirement annuity is calculated on your working eight years and surviving to year ten. But remember that your spouse has to wait two years before the annuity is payable since that's the earliest you could have retired if you had lived.

The amount your spouse receives is still 50 percent of what you would have received, but retiring at the earliest time permitted (depending on the plans rules) ordinarily results in a reduced benefit for a plan participant. Therefore, your spouse receives 50 percent of a lower annuity.

If your surviving spouse doesn't live the two years until you would have been eligible to take your retirement, your defined benefit plan can deem the benefit forfeited (in other words, that money couldn't subsequently be passed on to another beneficiary). Similarly, if your spouse chose to delay the payment of the annuity until five years after your death and he or she suddenly died in the fourth year, the plan can cancel the annuity.

Differences in a defined contribution plan

If you're in a defined contribution plan, you need to be aware of some of its differences when it comes to annuities:

- ✔ If your defined contribution plan has an annuity option, the preretirement survivor annuity must have a value that's at least 50 percent of your vested account balance as of the date of your death.

- ✔ Your account balance can't be lost — even if your surviving spouse dies before the money in the account is used to purchase the annuity.

  Your vested account balance in a defined contribution plan is your money. If you die before you receive all your benefits in a defined contribution plan, the balance in your account will be paid to your beneficiaries.

- ✔ The plan must permit your surviving spouse to direct the plan to pay the money within a reasonable time after your death.

Now let's assume that you work at Suburban Canoe and have a defined contribution plan. At the time of your death, you have $200,000 in your account. An annuity can be purchased for your survivor with the $200,000, or the survivor can direct that a lump sum payment of $200,000 be paid.

Subsidized annuities

An annuity for two lives ordinarily is more expensive to buy than an annuity for one life. Your plan ordinarily passes this cost on to you by paying you less while you're alive if you have a survivorship benefit. However, if your plan wants to, it can fully subsidize your QJSA or QPSA survivorship benefits.

When your plan subsidizes your benefits you'll experience no decrease in the benefits. This is because your plan is making up the difference between the cost of an annuity for one life and the extra cost of an annuity for two lives (referred to as *subsidizing the benefit*) out of the plan's pocket.

For example, with a fully subsidized QJSA, if your annuity pays you $100 per month, the survivorship benefit is guaranteed not to decrease when you die. So, your spouse can also count on receiving $100 per month.

If your company offers this benefit (your plan documents will explain the benefit if that's the case), it obviously loves its employees.

Steps for a beneficiary to take when received payments are incorrect

If a beneficiary's survivorship benefits are incorrect, the first step is to notify the plan administrator and ask for a correction. Your beneficiary should provide any documents or other items in possession to fully explain why he or she believes the benefit amount is incorrect.

If your beneficiary isn't persuasive enough and the plan administrator won't budge, the next step is to file an administrative appeal. The administrative appeal is done in-house to the plan administrator or whoever is designated to handle such matters. Remember that there are specific time periods to follow regarding how the appeal is handled. See Chapter 18 for more about appeals.

If your beneficiary still can't get any satisfaction and the administrative appeal is denied, the last resort is filing a lawsuit. These are the same rights that plan participants have. We explain the litigation process in Chapter 20.

"Waiving" Goodbye to Survivorship Benefits

Before the REA came on the scene in 1984 (we describe its arrival earlier in this chapter), you, the plan participant, could waive spousal survivorship benefits without first notifying or getting permission from your spouse.

However, after the REA's enactment, spousal consent became a requirement. So now, by law, you can't give up your spouse's right to receive survivorship benefits unless your spouse first signs a waiver with respect to such benefits. In the following sections, we discuss reasons to waive benefits, explain what needs to be in a waiver, and cover circumstances in which a waiver may be challenged.

Checking out reasons to waive survivorship benefits

Survivorship benefits aren't for everyone. In the following list, we review the reasons why you may want to waive them:

- ✔ If your spouse has more than enough money to support himself or herself after you die, it's probably advantageous for you to waive the spousal survivor annuity, because then you'll be able to receive the maximum annuity payment. (If your spouse is set to receive survivorship benefits, you'll receive a smaller benefit amount each month once you retire.)

- ✔ If the same financial protection can be provided to your surviving spouse at a lower cost through the purchase of an insurance policy on your life (rather than through a joint annuity), consider waiving the spousal survivor annuity. By taking out an insurance policy at a lower cost, you're saving money, and you'll receive more money down the road (as we explain in the previous bullet).

- ✔ If it's unlikely that your spouse will outlive you (because of age, health, or bad genes), it may be a good decision to waive the survivorship benefit because then your annuity won't be reduced later.

Meeting mandatory requirements in a waiver

The QJSA is now automatic unless both you and your spouse waive these rights. So, if you and your spouse decide that you want to waive the spousal benefits, your waiver must meet these requirements:

- ✔ It must explain the effect of the waiver in easy-to-understand language.

- ✔ You must waive the benefit in writing.

- ✔ Your spouse must consent to the waiver in writing.

- ✔ You must designate a new beneficiary on a form that may not be changed without the consent of your spouse. If your spouse has signed a waiver in favor of a specific beneficiary, you can change your designated beneficiary only if your spouse signs a new consent to the waiver. (You can find out how to designate a beneficiary earlier in this chapter.)

- ✔ Your spouse's consent to waive survivorship rights must acknowledge the full effect of that decision (for example, your spouse needs to acknowledge the fact that the waiver will diminish his or her survivorship benefits that would otherwise apply).

- ✔ Your spouse's consent must be witnessed by a representative of your plan or it must be notarized.

Beware of waivers in prenuptial agreements

In today's fast-paced world, with a 50 percent divorce rate, prenuptial agreements are pretty common. These agreements, which are entered into prior to marriage, provide for a division of marital assets in the event of a divorce or death. Some couples put waivers of survivorship benefits in their prenuptial agreements without thinking things through legally. In other words, they don't realize that these waivers aren't valid! If a spouse wants to waive survivorship rights, he or she has to be a spouse at the time of the waiver. So, the problem here is that a waiver of survivorship rights in a prenuptial agreement is invalid because the waiver wasn't signed by your spouse — it was signed by your soon-to-be spouse (because the signing took place before the nuptials). Simply put, survivorship rights can't be waived in a prenuptial agreement. The solution? Properly execute the waiver *after* you're married.

Say you die before you retire and your spouse receives a QPSA. Just as with the QJSA, if you and your spouse don't want this benefit, you both must waive your rights it.

The waiver of a QJSA or a QPSA must be made after the pension plan participant reaches the age of 35. If a waiver was made before age 35, another one is necessary after the plan participant reaches age 35.

A spouse's consent to waive survivorship benefits isn't required if:

✔ You have a court order that confirms that your spouse can't be found.

✔ Your spouse has been declared incompetent by a court of law and his or her guardian consents to the waiver.

✔ You have a court order establishing that you're legally separated or abandoned.

The election of a previous spouse as a beneficiary doesn't have any effect on the rights of a current spouse. If you and your current spouse haven't waived the survivorship benefits, the claim of your current spouse defeats any beneficiary you named before your marriage to your current spouse.

Challenging a waiver

A waiver can be challenged by your spouse only if the waiver was unclear and not understood by your spouse at the time of signing or if your spouse signed under pressure. Otherwise, your spouse can't revoke the consent to the waiver. In other words, if a spouse changes his or her mind after waiving his or her survivorship benefits (for example, in favor of the kids from the plan participant's first marriage), it's too late!

After the death of the plan participant, however, the surviving spouse may elect to change the payment schedule of the annuity or to elect a lump sum payment if it's in fact permitted by the plan.

Looking at the Impact of Life's Unpleasantries on Survivorship Benefits

If it's not one thing, it's another. Life is filled with challenges and obstacles, and while some of these hardships can be anticipated, others can't. This section is an overview of some of life's low points and how they can impact your spouse's survivorship rights.

Your plan is changed or terminated

Many things can happen to a pension plan. For instance, your company may be sold and the pension plan taken over by another company. Or the plan may be terminated or become underfunded and not have sufficient assets to pay the benefits provided under the plan. In these cases, the plan may be taken over by a government agency called the Pension Benefit Guaranty Corporation (PBGC). This agency guarantees benefits in defined benefit plans.

If any of the previously mentioned situations happen to come up with your pension, there are protections for your spouse's survivor annuity. For example, consider the following:

- ✔ Even if your company is merged or spun off to a company with a pension plan that doesn't offer survivor annuities, your spouse's annuity is still good. (For more on mergers, see Chapter 11.)

- ✔ If your pension plan is modified or terminated, the survivor annuity is still good. (For more on plan modifications and terminations, see Chapter 12.)

- ✔ If the PBGC takes over your busted plan, the PBGC will pay your spouse's survivorship benefits. (For more on plans going belly up and being taken over by the PBGC, see Chapter 12.)

You have unpaid taxes

You can't escape Uncle Sam. In other words, if you don't pay your taxes, the Internal Revenue Service can place a lien on your ERISA pension benefits to satisfy your unpaid tax liability. However, this authority doesn't extend to spousal annuity survivorship benefits (unless the tax lien also applies to your spouse). So if you want to get your hard-earned money, be sure to pay your taxes.

You go through a divorce

Just when you think that your divorce can't get any messier, your spouse decides that he or she wants to claim the survivorship benefits that are due to him or her. The basic rule in this case is that if your soon-to-be ex-spouse wants to receive survivorship benefits, he or she must first obtain an order called a *qualified domestic relations order,* or QDRO, through the divorce proceedings. This issue is discussed in much greater detail in Chapter 15.

If you and your spouse separate but don't actually divorce, your spouse still gets the survivorship benefits.

Chapter 15

Dividing Your Pension between You and Your Ex

*I*f you have a pension and are divorced or considering divorce, this chapter is a must. In the event of a divorce, a state divorce judge decides all the issues surrounding the divorce, such as custody, alimony, and the division of assets. Your qualified pension plan is one of those assets that must be divided between you and your ex. Because the Employee Retirement Income Security Act of 1974 (ERISA; see Chapter 2) preempts and trumps state law, state court judges can't divide up pension assets. But Congress, in its vast wisdom, provided the *qualified domestic relations order,* or QDRO. A QDRO is a court order that's approved by a plan administrator and that divides your benefits between you and your ex-spouse. It allows a state judge to allocate federally regulated pension rights subject to a number of restrictions and limitations.

If you have a pension governed by ERISA and you get divorced, it's likely that you'll have a QDRO as part of your divorce. If you can't escape a QDRO, it's best to face it head on. So in this chapter, we give you the lowdown on QDROs, including how they affect you, your ex, and your pension. Be sure to read this chapter before you meet with your divorce lawyer!

Checking Out the Basics of a Qualified Domestic Relations Order

As a general rule, ERISA doesn't allow you to assign or in any way alienate your interest in your pension plan to somebody else. The purpose of ERISA is to make sure that your money is still yours when you retire and that it isn't lost in that poker match called life. An exception is made for the assignment of pension benefits through a QDRO.

A QDRO is used exclusively to allocate pension benefits. A QDRO can be created to allocate pension benefits in a divorce, to provide marital support from a pension, and to collect unpaid child support. Pension assets are part of what you and your spouse have accumulated during your marriage and are therefore a marital asset to be fairly divided in a divorce and available for child support. Because federal law (through ERISA) controls most private pensions, and state court judges applying state law grant divorces and arrange for alimony and child support, the QDRO provides a way for a state court domestic relations judge to reconcile state and federal law in order to divide pension assets.

The order issued according to state law starts off as a *domestic relations order* and then becomes qualified, or a QDRO, only after meeting all the criteria and being approved by the pension plan trustee or administrator (we walk through the steps of qualifying an order later in this chapter). It isn't necessary that each party (the plan participant or the ex-spouse receiving the benefit) endorse or approve the QDRO.

In the following sections, we explain a few basic facts about QDROs, such as the folks they benefit, their common formats, and the details they include. We also discuss the limitations of a QDRO.

Who benefits from a QDRO?

The QDRO is for the benefit of a person called an *alternate payee,* which is just another term for your ex-spouse, soon-to-be ex-spouse, any other ex-spouses, children, or other dependents. So the QDRO grants benefits not to you, but to your ex-spouse or dependents. For instance:

- ✔ A separation agreement (an order of support while you're still married) awarding a portion of your pension benefits to your spouse can be a QDRO.

- ✔ If you have a second divorce, any QDRO in place for your first ex-spouse can't be altered or changed. A second QDRO can divide only benefits that haven't been allocated in a prior QDRO.

- ✔ Any child or other dependent who's recognized by the court can be entitled to all or a portion of your pension benefits. The QDRO can order the benefits to be paid to a state child support agency on behalf of a child, but the child, not the agency, is still the alternate payee. The QDRO can be used to pay child support even if no divorce is pending.

What are the different forms of a QDRO?

QDROs are used to either divide marital property or provide support payments. These different objectives can result in different choices regarding the method used to divide the assets in your pension plan. Here are the two basic approaches to dividing retirement benefits through a QDRO:

- ✓ **Separate interest:** In this method, the QDRO divides the plan participant's retirement benefit into two separate portions. This allows the alternate payee the ability to receive a portion of the retirement benefit at a different time and in a different form from that chosen by the plan participant. The funds can be paid out to the alternate payee before the earliest retirement date if the plan permits such a payout.

- ✓ **Shared payment:** In this method, the alternate payee doesn't receive any payments until the plan participant is eligible to begin to receive payments. The benefit payments are split, with a portion paid to the alternate payee and a portion paid to the participant.

Either of these approaches can be used for support purposes, for the division of marital assets, or to allocate benefits from a plan, depending on the type of retirement plan you have:

- ✓ Many defined contribution plans permit a lump-sum distribution from the plan to be paid to the alternate payee when the QDRO is approved.

- ✓ Defined benefit plans often permit distributions to an alternate payee only when the plan participant is also receiving his or her plan benefits.

See Chapter 3 for details on the differences between these plans.

Doling out benefits to your ex if your plan isn't covered by ERISA

If you get a divorce and your pension plan isn't covered by ERISA (which includes most if not all government employees, schoolteachers, and other public employees), your pension assets will be handled differently depending on the state you live in. Most states, however, have implemented procedures similar to the QDRO to provide for the distribution of pension benefits to the ex-spouse. Your divorce lawyer can tell you what the pension divorce distribution rules are for your state and how they impact your pension.

What information appears in a QDRO?

Any QDRO must include all of the following information:

- ✔ The last known name and address of the pension plan participant.

- ✔ The last known name and address of the alternate payee (spouse, ex-spouse, or child or dependent).

- ✔ The amount or percentage of the participant's benefit that's payable to the alternate payee or the method used to calculate the amount or percentage to be paid.

- ✔ The number of payments or the period to which this QDRO applies. (An order to pay the benefits immediately takes care of this requirement if the plan permits lump-sum distributions.)

- ✔ Identifying information for each pension plan to which the QDRO applies. (Keep in mind that it's possible to have more than one pension plan.)

- ✔ Information noting that the order is a court judgment, decree, or order.

- ✔ Information showing that the order is issued by a court of competent jurisdiction and is signed by the judge.

What can't a QDRO do?

The power of the QDRO is limited. To a large degree it's confined by the terms of your pension plan. But here are the basics. The QDRO can't

- ✔ Require the pension plan to pay benefits that aren't provided under the plan. For example, if the plan provides benefits only in the form of an annuity, the QDRO can't require the plan to pay benefits to your ex-spouse in a single lump sum payment. If, however, the plan provides for a choice between an annuity and a lump sum under the separate interest approach, each of you can make a different choice.

- ✔ Increase the benefits otherwise provided under the plan.

- ✔ Require the plan to change actuarial assumptions. *Actuarial assumptions* are factors used by actuaries to project future financial conclusions, and they may take into account life expectancies as well as interest rates in order to make certain calculations.

- ✔ Change the QDRO benefits provided to an earlier payee when another payee comes into the picture. For example, your second ex-spouse can't get any of your pension benefits previously awarded by a QDRO to your first ex-spouse.

- ✔ Make one alternate payee pay another alternate payee. The QDRO can't, for instance, require your pension plan to pay your ex-spouse's current spouse or a subsequent ex-spouse of your ex-spouse.

✔ Provide for a payment earlier than the date the plan received the order. In a shared payment, the QDRO can't give your ex a payment before the earliest date that you'll reach retirement age or an earlier date permitted by the plan.

Your earliest retirement age is the earlier of these two dates:

- The earliest date you can take a distribution under the plan

- The date you reach 50 or the first date you could get benefits if you left work (whichever is later)

Qualifying a Domestic Relations Order

To transform itself from just an order by a domestic relations judge to a QDRO, the order must be *qualified*. By qualification, we mean that before an order can divide pension benefits, it must conform to the various safeguards in place to protect federally regulated pensions. Until it's qualified, the order has no effect on your pension and no money can be distributed. The plan administrator disperses the money and determines whether the domestic relations order graduates to become a QDRO.

In the following sections, we show you the steps required to carry out the qualification of a domestic relations order.

Sending the order to the plan administrator

Because the QDRO must be consistent with the terms of your divorce decree or settlement, the attorney who's responsible for preparing the proposed QDRO needs to make sure that the language and terms of the QDRO reflect your settlement agreement. Your attorney and your spouse's attorney will negotiate how your retirement benefits will be allocated and which attorney will prepare the QDRO. Usually the attorney who prepares it makes sure that your plan administrator gets a copy of the proposed QDRO after it's issued and signed by the court.

Knowing everyone's responsibilities during the qualification process

Different people with different responsibilities play roles in the process of qualifying a domestic relations order. In the following sections, we outline the duties of the plan administrator and the plan participant (that's you, of course). Chapter 2 has more information about the general duties of a plan administrator.

The responsibilities of the plan administrator

A plan administrator has several important duties during the qualification process:

- ✔ The administrator provides a copy of the QDRO procedures that are in place for your pension plan and advises everyone involved of their rights to receive all correspondence regarding the QDRO. The possible alternate payee is entitled to all relevant plan documents and your benefit statements. Your attorney needs this information to draft the QDRO.

- ✔ Of course, the administrator is in charge of determining the validity of the order. To accomplish this task, the administrator must review the QDRO and make sure that it clearly identifies the plan that the order covers, that it provides only benefits permitted under the plan, that the benefits are going to a person entitled to them, and that it specifies the number of payments and the method of determining the amount of the payments. To assist in this process, the administrator may send the QDRO to the plan's attorney to determine whether the QDRO meets all the necessary requirements for qualification. The administrator should make every effort to avoid unnecessary expenses and adopt policies that are designed to make the administrative process more efficient.

- ✔ The QDRO review should be completed within 60 days. If an attorney, at the request of the administrator, has to review the QDRO, the review should be completed within 75 working days of receipt of the QDRO. You and any alternate payees are entitled to be notified in writing of the reason for the delay and the decision date of the validly of the QDRO.

- ✔ After a QDRO is determined to be valid, the plan administrator must implement the QDRO in conformity with the plan provisions.

- ✔ According to ERISA, the plan administrator is responsible for making sure that the alternate payee receives the same information that you, the plan participant, receive — even if the plan is terminated.

Your responsibilities as a plan participant

Your first responsibility is to provide your attorney with any and all plan documents and plan information regarding your retirement benefits so that he or she better understands what you're entitled to. It's difficult to resolve property and support issues if your attorney doesn't have an appreciation of the extent of your assets; your pension benefits are part of those assets, and a QDRO can't be properly drafted without such information.

Your second responsibility is to make sure that your plan administrator knows of any special circumstances, such as other QDROs you may have with a prior spouse. You should continue to provide information that may affect the QDRO as it becomes available.

You also need to do the following:

✔ It's important that you and the alternate payees make sure that the plan administrator has copies of any orders amending the QDRO. If the plan administrator isn't aware that the QDRO has been amended, it will prevent him or her from properly complying with the QDRO.

✔ You have an ongoing obligation to give the administrator your current address and to provide releases for necessary information that the administrator may require.

✔ It's your responsibility to submit information you believe may be important to the plan administrator. And you have to do this within 15 days of receiving the initial receipt letter.

✔ You're responsible for all the administrative expenses of qualifying an order. If the plan incurs expenses in processing or administering your QDRO, your account could be charged as long as the expenses are reasonable. Any charges must be explained to you in advance. This is the current position of the Department of Labor, which reverses an earlier position that stated that QDRO charges couldn't be charged to your pension account. Now, if the plan so chooses, it can pass these costs on to you, the plan participant.

Consider yourself forewarned! The agencies that issue the rules can and do change their minds.

Following up with the qualification decision

In the following sections, we explain what happens after an order is or isn't qualified. If your plan administrator approved the order, it's determined to be qualified, and this means that the plan administrator has certain tasks to do. If the QDRO isn't approved (and therefore not qualified), the plan administrator must notify the parties and segregate the funds that would have been subject to the QDRO.

Implementing a qualified order

If the plan administrator determines that the QDRO is qualified, the following steps must be followed to implement the order:

1. **The plan administrator sends a qualification letter via first-class mail to you (the plan participant) and each alternate payee, stating the amount of the benefit and when it will be available for distribution.**

2. **Payments begin as provided for in the QDRO.**

   Before payments begin, however, the plan administrator must have a copy of the signed court order by the domestic relations judge. One of the things you pay your attorney to do is to make sure that the plan administrator receives the right documents in a timely manner.

The payments under a QDRO stop either when the QDRO says they stop or upon receipt of a court order that terminates the payments. If you're the plan participant and you die, payments to your ex-spouse stop unless the QDRO provides for survivorship benefits. The QDRO should also state what happens to the benefits if your ex dies before you. (See the later section "What if my ex dies?" for more information on survivorship benefits.)

If language in the QDRO would terminate the benefits under certain conditions such as a new marriage, it's your responsibility to notify the plan administrator so the appropriate modification can be made.

Determining that an order isn't qualified

If the plan administrator decides that the proposed QDRO isn't qualified, a disqualification letter is sent by first-class mail to you (the plan participant) and each alternate payee. This letter lists the reasons the proposed QDRO doesn't meet the standards for qualification.

If the plan administrator approves an order that doesn't meet the requirements for qualification, the mistake can result in sanctions such as plan disqualification (meaning that the plan could lose its tax-deferred status). So, your plan administrator needs to make sure any order received properly meets the requirements for qualification before he or she approves it.

Disputing the validity of an order

If you question the validity of the QDRO, payouts won't begin until the dispute is resolved. The following actions occur at this time:

1. **The assets being disputed with the QDRO should be segregated by the plan administrator.**

   The *segregated assets* are those monies that are subject to being paid from your pension plan to your ex-spouse if the QDRO had been determined to be qualified.

2. **After the assets are separated, they're placed in an escrow or specialized distribution account.**

   The money is held in safekeeping in this special account until it's decided where it should go and who gets it.

3. **If the QDRO is determined to be valid and qualified, the administrator pays your ex the segregated money, plus interest, at the time the payments are to begin.**

   If payments to your ex-spouse should have already begun, the first payment becomes due on or after the date the qualification is made. After the payments begin, no future accrued benefits go to your ex.

4. **If after 18 months the QDRO still hasn't been qualified by the administrator, the administrator must pay the assets back to the plan, or to you if you're retired, as though an order hadn't been provided to the plan administrator.**

Reviewing an order all over again

Some circumstances can cause the plan administrator to make a new review of the qualification of a QDRO after an initial determination of its validity has been made. Here are examples of these instances:

✔ If no payments are made to the ex-spouse or alternate payees for an extended period of time after the QDRO is qualified, another determination or qualification may be made before payments begin. The administrator, for example, may have lost the QDRO or may have failed to process it in a timely fashion. If changes were made to the plan documents during the intervening time period, the QDRO must comply with these changes.

✔ If the QDRO is amended, the administrator must determine its qualified status, as amended.

Handling Taxes on Qualified Domestic Relations Orders

Whether you expected it or not, you have to remember that Uncle Sam socks you with taxes when you receive benefits under a QDRO. The following are some important tax effects on QDRO distributions:

✔ Federal income tax must be withheld from the designated distribution under the QDRO unless you elect not to have the withholding rules applied. The withholding rules are applied for a QDRO as if the alternate payee were the employee.

✔ Your ex-spouse may roll over an eligible QDRO distribution to an IRA or other qualified plan.

✔ For *eligible rollover distributions* payable under a QDRO to a spouse or ex-spouse, federal income tax is required to be withheld at a 20 percent rate unless the distribution is paid (rolled over) directly to another qualified plan or to an IRA. (Chapter 5 has information about IRAs; Chapter 9 has more information about rollovers.)

✔ Distributions to an ex-spouse are taxable to the ex.

✔ Distributions under a QDRO to a non-spouse alternate payee (a child, for example) will be taxable to you and can't be rolled over by the alternate payee. These distributions also aren't subject to the 20 percent withholding rules.

✔ If the QDRO orders child support paid to your ex, it's taxable to your ex. However, if the child support is paid to your child, it's taxable to you.

For general rules about tax effects on pension distributions, check out Chapter 9.

Protecting Your Rights If You're the Ex

If you're trying to tap into your ex's pension plan, remember this: Until the plan administrator approves the QDRO, it's just you and your attorney attempting to navigate the complex world of pensions. To protect your rights, you must be extra vigilant. So, in the following sections, we explain how you, the soon-to-be former spouse, can protect your rights to your ex's pension benefits.

Ensuring that your divorce attorney is familiar with pensions and QDROs

Many attorneys aren't familiar with the drafting of QDROs. In fact, many attorneys rely on outside consultants to assist them in the preparation of your QDRO. Even though receiving outside help may mean that your QDRO meets all the technical hurdles of the qualification process, it also means that your attorney may not have obtained all the pension benefits that you were entitled to receive. Some plans offer early retirement benefits or other options that can increase the value of the plan. If a QDRO doesn't take these features into account, the administrator isn't going to pay them to you if they kick in. Your attorney must be sophisticated enough to understand the impact of benefit provisions that may be obscure or not easily recognizable in order to make sure that they're factored into the equation.

To protect yourself, find out from your attorney how many QDROs he has drafted or whether he has a consultant prepare them. Also make sure that your attorney is aware of the type of benefits that your ex's plan provides (or that he can find out). Here are some questions you can ask your attorney:

- How will I be impacted if my ex dies?

- What happens if I remarry?

- Can my ex do anything to stop my benefits after the proposed QDRO becomes a court order and is qualified by the plan administrator?

- What happens if my ex fails to apply for a pension, is injured, or waives his or her pension?

As we point out in Chapter 19, for your attorney to be effective, he first must be knowledgeable. In fact, when you first interview a prospective attorney, it's perfectly reasonable to determine what your attorney knows about QDROs, because if your spouse has a pension, it's going to be involved in the divorce.

The attorney is supposed to have answers to these all-important questions, so consider yourself forewarned if he can't answer them.

Obtaining plan information

You and your attorney have the right to receive all the documents from your ex's plan. This includes the summary plan description (SPD), which is a condensed version of the full plan document. You and your attorney also have a right to the entire plan and all its amendments (as opposed to just the SPD). To draft a proposed QDRO (which may be your attorney's responsibility to prepare), your attorney needs to know the type of plan that your ex-spouse participates in (defined benefit or defined contribution; see Chapter 3 for more details) and be familiar with the plan's provisions and benefits. It's possible that the SPD and the plan document may be inconsistent, and if that's the case, make sure that your attorney knows how to resolve the inconsistencies if she's drafting the QDRO.

You need to know the procedure that your ex's plan has for handling QDROs. And remember that your attorney needs to have this information from the benefits office *before* the QDRO is drafted. If the plan has a procedure in place to expedite qualification of the QDRO, your attorney should follow the procedure (if she's drafting the QDRO) or make sure that your ex-spouse's attorney is following the procedure (if she's not responsible for drafting it). Your attorney should also get any model QDROs from the plan administrator and feel free to call the plan administrator, who generally is helpful in answering questions. In addition, many plans are willing to take a look at a proposed domestic relations order before it's presented to your domestic relations judge.

The number of years your soon-to-be-ex has worked for the company, his or her salary, and the plan amendments can all impact the value of the pension benefits. So we recommend that you and your attorney retain an expert to review all the plan documents to determine the true value of the available retirement benefits. There are pension gurus out there who know the ins and outs of pensions and can assist your attorney in analyzing your plan and ferreting out some less-than-obvious provisions that can affect the cash value of the pension. The whole point of the QDRO is to allocate pension benefits, but before you can even begin to divvy up the pot, you have to know what it's worth.

Asking a few "what if" questions

In the following sections, we answer some important "what if" questions that you, the soon-to-be ex, may ask during the QDRO qualification process. Some situations may be more likely to occur than others; you should be prepared for them and understand their consequences.

What if my ex's pension plan fails?

As an alternate payee, you'll receive a proportionally reduced benefit if your former spouse's plan tanks or can't pay the benefits that have been promised. Here's why: A failed pension plan may be insured by the Pension Benefit Guaranty Corporation (PBGC), which is an agency that insures tax-qualified defined benefit pension plans up to a certain amount. (Flip to Chapter 3 for more on tax-qualified plans.) Defined contribution plans aren't generally covered by the PBGC. If your ex-spouse's pension plan is under the jurisdiction of the PBGC (meaning that it's likely a defined benefit plan in which the benefits are insured), any domestic relations order needs to be approved by the PBGC.

In the event of a plan bankruptcy, the PBGC will proportionately adjust the benefits to take into account the reduced benefits provided by the PBGC (as long as no provisions prohibit this adjustment). When the PBGC has to take over a failed plan, it usually provides only a portion of the benefits that the pensioner would otherwise receive. When the PBGC takes over a plan in which the plan administrator has already determined a QDRO to be qualified, but before any payments are made, the PBGC must also evaluate the order to see if it qualifies as a QDRO.

Chapter 12 has the full scoop on failed pension plans and the PBGC.

What if my ex has more than one pension?

Keep in mind that if your ex has a 401(k), was in a defined benefit plan from a previous job, or has retirement savings, all these plans will be part of a QDRO. It's critical for your attorney, then, not only to assemble all your ex's pensions, but also to thoroughly understand their features. For example, he needs to know answers to questions like "Does the plan provide for a cost-of-living adjustment?" and "Does your ex have the right to early retirement benefits or to receive benefits in a lump sum?" If the plan provides for benefit increases that the QDRO doesn't take into account, the plan administrator won't pay out such increases. In short, if all the benefits aren't determined before the QDRO is qualified, you may be shortchanged. So, you should make sure that your attorney has all the documents necessary to ferret out all the goodies in your ex's plans.

What if my ex dies?

Make sure *survivorship benefits* are included in your ex's plan. Otherwise you may be in for an extra shock if your ex dies prematurely. In other words, if survivorship benefits aren't included, your payments stop.

The *qualified joint and survivor annuity* (QJSA) is the procedure put in place to provide benefits to a spouse after a pensioner dies. But the QDRO is so powerful that it can defeat a subsequent spouse's survivorship right under the pension plan. The QDRO generally coordinates with the QJSA annuity requirements that exist at the time the QDRO takes effect to protect the retirement rights of the former spouse (you) as well as the current spouse (your ex's new partner). If survivorship rights are made a part of your QDRO, a new spouse won't be able to get a survivorship benefit because it was already guaranteed to you, the former spouse, by the QDRO.

Here are three situations that could change who receives the survivorship benefit under the QJSA:

- ✔ If the plan participant dies, the plan pays the surviving spouse a monthly survivorship benefit unless the QDRO specifies otherwise.

- ✔ If the plan participant dies after a divorce, the divorced spouse loses the survivorship protection unless it's preserved by the QDRO.

- ✔ If the plan participant remarries after a first divorce, the new spouse gets the survivorship benefit unless the QDRO states otherwise.

But a QDRO can change these results. The QDRO can award the survivorship benefit to the former spouse. For instance, if you didn't waive your survivorship rights to your ex-spouse's pension plan while you were married, your QDRO can provide that you, the alternate payee, be treated as the surviving spouse for purposes of survivorship benefits. So, the QDRO can defeat the survivorship rights of your ex's current spouse in favor of you, the former spouse, if you provide for it in your QDRO. And the plan administrator can't be forced to pay the survivorship benefits to the current spouse when the QDRO already requires that such payment be made to you, the former spouse.

If there's more than one divorce, any subsequent QDRO can grant only what's left from any previous QDRO.

If you think this is confusing, you're right. That's why it's tough for even lawyers and judges to get the QDRO right — all the more reason to be sure that your attorney has a command of these tricky issues. A good attorney can advise you of these possibilities and help you get the results you want.

Check out Chapter 14 for more details on survivorship benefits.

Being vigilant throughout the qualifying process

If the proposed QDRO doesn't strictly follow the rules, the plan administrator will reject the QDRO. You can skip all this uncertainty by asking the plan administrator to approve the QDRO in advance. This is a common practice. Even after a preapproved QDRO is signed by the court and sent to the plan, your attorney must follow up to make sure that it wasn't lost and that the plan administrator is implementing the order. Vigilance is the word when you're dealing with pensions and, in particular, QDROs.

Also important to remember is that your ex's plan must accept the QDRO as qualified before you can receive a distribution from the pension fund, and you can't receive a distribution from the fund until your spouse retires or becomes otherwise eligible to receive plan benefits. In other words, before you get too excited, you must look to the plan procedures and information to see what it says about the payout of benefits.

Chapter 16

Protecting Your Retirement Funds from Creditors and Bankruptcy

....

In This Chapter

▶ Distinguishing your protections if you're not in bankruptcy

▶ Understanding your protections if you're in bankruptcy

▶ Taking action to protect all your retirement funds

....

*I*t's bad enough when your financial situation hits rock bottom and creditors are knocking at your door. But when you add in the worry about whether you'll lose your retirement benefits as well as everything else you've managed to save, the night sweats and anxiety attacks really come on strong.

But, thanks to provisions set forth in the Employee Retirement Income Security Act of 1974 (ERISA) and the Internal Revenue Code (IRC), your tax-qualified pension plan receives extensive protection from creditors. And you can give even more thanks to the bankruptcy law enacted in 2005, which broadened bankruptcy protection for your retirement funds and individual retirement accounts (IRAs).

In this chapter, we cover the protections that your retirement funds receive and steer you toward more help in protecting your money from creditors.

Inside or Outside? Looking at Levels of Creditor Protection

You have different levels of creditor protection depending on whether you've filed for bankruptcy. The terms *outside of bankruptcy* and *inside of bankruptcy* are common and pretty simple:

  ✔ The term *outside of bankruptcy* means that the individual (in this case, the plan participant) who's in financial trouble isn't under the jurisdiction of the federal bankruptcy court because he or she hasn't filed for bankruptcy.

Creditors, however, can still go after these folks. Luckily, though, the provisions of ERISA and the IRC apply to and protect individuals outside of bankruptcy, although the protections are a bit different.

✔ *Inside of bankruptcy* is the term used when an individual (now called the debtor) has filed for bankruptcy; at this point, the debtor is within the control of federal bankruptcy laws, and his or her assets are considered part of his or her bankruptcy estate. (A *bankruptcy estate* is the property that you own when you file for bankruptcy; pensions are included in a bankruptcy estate.) The 2005 Bankruptcy Act protects the assets of individuals inside of bankruptcy.

The provisions of ERISA and the IRC don't protect pension benefits that have already been distributed; the provisions only keep your benefits from being reduced by creditors before they're distributed. After the benefits are distributed from the plan, a creditor's rights are enforceable against the plan participant but not against the plan itself. In other words, the plan is still protected, but the benefits you've received are fair game for your creditors. Same goes for the benefits that are distributed from an IRA (see Chapter 5); they're also fair game for creditors. However, as a result of the 2005 Bankruptcy Act, eligible rollover distributions are protected from creditors of those folks who are inside bankruptcy. But remember, these eligible rollover distributions may be protected for only 60 days after they're distributed if they aren't rolled into an IRA or a qualified plan.

Finding Protection Outside of Bankruptcy

Your tax-qualified pensions and IRAs receive different types of protection when you're outside of bankruptcy; in general, qualified pensions receive federal protection, and state law may protect IRAs. The state law protection varies from state to state. (See the State Laws Protecting IRAs chart we provide in Appendix B for some guidance.) We sift through the differences in the following sections.

Tax-qualified pension plans

Both ERISA and the IRC require that tax-qualified pension plans (generally, the ones we list in Chapter 3) contain provisions that prohibit the assignment or alienation of plan benefits (these provisions are known as *anti-alienation clauses*). In other words, your benefits under a tax-qualified plan have been insulated from creditors' claims; your creditors simply can't take away your pension to pay off your debts.

As we say throughout this book, most rules have exceptions, and this one's no different. The following are considered exceptions to the rule; in these circumstances, the assets in your tax-qualified plan may not be protected from certain creditors:

- ✔ **Federal criminal penalties and fines:** Within the past few years, several federal courts have held that the general anti-alienation rules of ERISA and the IRC don't protect retirement plan assets from fines or penalties that are imposed when you commit a federal crime. For example, if you're convicted of a federal drug offense, it's possible that your retirement plan assets could be seized to pay criminal penalties.

- ✔ **Federal tax levies and judgments:** The Internal Revenue Service (IRS) can go after your retirement plan assets to enforce judgments against you for taxes and penalties.

- ✔ **Fiduciary violations against the retirement plan:** If you're a plan fiduciary and commit a crime against the plan (such as a theft of the assets of the plan), your benefits under the same plan may be offset to repay the plan for the crime you committed against it. (Chapter 10 has general information about fiduciaries.)

- ✔ **Qualified domestic relations orders (QDROs):** Retirement plan assets are marital assets that are subject to division in divorce, and they may be ordered to be distributed for child support. (See Chapter 15 for more information about QDROs.)

Not only is your tax-qualified plan protected from your own creditors, but it's also protected from your employer's creditors. The rationale behind this rule is that a qualified retirement plan is established for the exclusive benefit of employees and their beneficiaries. Because your employer doesn't have any significant rights with respect to your assets, your employer's creditors don't either.

Traditional and Roth IRAs

As we explain in the previous section, individuals who are outside of bankruptcy can generally rely on federal law protections under ERISA and the IRC to protect their retirement plan assets from the claims of creditors. No such federal law protections apply for assets in IRAs, though. Instead, IRA owners must look to state law to see if their IRA assets are protected from creditors. Appendix B features a table that reviews the state laws for all 50 states and that notes whether traditional IRAs and Roth IRAs are protected in each state.

In most cases, even when the state law protects IRAs from creditors, the IRA assets are still subject to division in divorce, attachment for child support, federal tax levies, and federal criminal penalties.

Simple IRAs and SEP Plans

SIMPLE IRAs and Simplified Employee Pension Plans (SEP Plans), which are employer-sponsored, are treated differently from individually created and funded traditional and Roth IRAs. ERISA defines a pension plan under its jurisdiction as any "plan, fund or program that is established or maintained by an employer that provides retirement income to employees." Typically the pensions that we cover in Chapter 3 qualify. But the courts and the Department of Labor say that even though the contributions are immediately allocated to the employee's IRA, SEP and SIMPLE IRAs also are ERISA pension plans because they're arranged by the employer.

The fact that SEPs and SIMPLE IRAs are considered ERISA pension plans can create serious problems for debtors outside of bankruptcy because ERISA and the IRC provide no creditor protection for IRAs. So outside of bankruptcy, IRAs are governed by state laws for creditor protection. However, state laws may be preempted by ERISA with respect to SEPs and SIMPLE IRAs. This preemption can put SEPs and SIMPLE IRAs in the unusual position of having neither federal nor state law protection from creditor claims outside of bankruptcy.

If you live in a state that protects traditional IRAs but not SEPs or SIMPLE IRAs, you may want to roll over your funds from those plans to a traditional (rollover) IRA, because the traditional IRA is likely to have a better chance of being protected from the claims of creditors. Talk to the custodian of your SEP or SIMPLE IRA about rolling over the assets to a traditional IRA.

Understanding Protection Inside of Bankruptcy

The Bankruptcy Abuse Prevention and Consumer Protection Act of 2005 (also known as the 2005 Bankruptcy Act) made noteworthy changes in the bankruptcy rules and added specific protections for both tax-qualified retirement plans and IRAs in bankruptcy.

If you go into bankruptcy, the assets in the tax-qualified plans that we list in Chapter 3, including Section 403(b) plans and Section 457 plans, are protected from creditor claims against your bankruptcy estate. In other words, your creditors can't touch those assets even though you own them. Assets in SIMPLE IRAs and SEPs also are protected from your creditors in bankruptcy.

The rules are different for traditional and Roth IRAs; these plans are protected to $1 million. For example, if you have $500,000 in either a traditional or Roth IRA, creditors definitely can't touch your money. However, if you have $1.2 million in a traditional or Roth IRA, creditors can take up to $200,000 (the difference over $1 million).

SEPs and SIMPLE IRAs are exempt without a dollar limitation. Rollovers into IRAs from qualified plans, Section 403(b) plans, and Section 457 plans aren't subject to the $1 million exemption limitation either.

Here are a few other rules in the 2005 Bankruptcy Act:

- ✔ Pending retirement plan contributions (such as amounts withheld from your wages) are excluded from your bankruptcy estate; they don't count as part of the property you own when you file for bankruptcy, so creditors can't touch them.

- ✔ Eligible rollover distributions retain their exempt status after they're distributed from the plan. But such distributions may be protected for only 60 days if they aren't rolled over to another retirement plan or IRA. So act fast when you make a rollover!

- ✔ Pension benefits that were awarded to a plan participant's former spouse through a QDRO — before the participant filed for bankruptcy — are excluded from the participant's bankruptcy estate. The benefits subject to the QDRO are treated as if they're the benefits of the former spouse rather than the plan participant. QDROs filed after you're in bankruptcy may be stayed pending the conclusion of your bankruptcy. (See Chapter 15 for more details about QDROs.)

Planning for Protection from Creditors

It's true: You can do things to protect your pension from creditors, but you have to be proactive, and you need professional help to make sure you avail yourself of all the protection options available. Depending on your particular situation, you may need to meet with a pension attorney, a civil defense/trial attorney, or a creditor protection/bankruptcy attorney. For example:

- ✔ If you currently have no creditor claims against you, you should meet with a retirement plan attorney or someone at your employer's human resources department to ensure that your retirement benefits are in a tax-qualified retirement plan that's protected both inside and outside of bankruptcy. Find out what creditor claims will be protected and when, based on the type of plan you have. Even though your employer's plan is probably tax-qualified and protected from creditors, it doesn't hurt to ask. (Chapter 3 has the full scoop on tax-qualified plans.)

- ✔ If you're in serious financial difficulty and can't pay your creditors (who you fear will sue you, but they haven't yet), even though you aren't in bankruptcy, now's the time that you should meet with an attorney who specializes in creditor protection and bankruptcy matters. Try to pursue all possible settlement options *before* filing for bankruptcy, because bankruptcy will negatively impact your ability to obtain credit for many years down the road.

✔ If you aren't in bankruptcy but creditors have filed claims against you, you need to hire an attorney immediately to defend you from such claims or lawsuits. Failure to respond to the suit doesn't mean that it will just go away. In fact, if you don't respond in a timely manner (generally within a month or so after the suit is filed against you, unless you've been given an extension of an additional month or so), your lack of action may result in a judgment being taken against you. At that point, you lose your ability to settle the claim at a lower amount, and liens may be filed against you and your assets.

Whomever you meet with, discuss the issues regarding protection of your retirement plan and IRA assets, and make sure the attorney is familiar with the new rules.

To find bankruptcy, creditor rights, or pension attorneys who are practicing in your area, contact your local bar association for referrals or check Web sites such as www.martindale.com and www.findlaw.com. Check out Chapter 19, where we discuss how to find a lawyer in more detail. You may also want to consider debt counseling or consumer creditor counseling services that can assist you in getting your financial situation under control. These services are usually listed in your phone book.

Part V
Taking Action When Bad Things Happen to Good Pensioners

The 5th Wave   By Rich Tennant

"Isn't that our plan administrator?"

In this part . . .

In this part, we help you deal with the unexpected (and unfair) situations that crop up regarding your pension plan, and we show you how to investigate whether you've been shortchanged. If your plan has done you wrong, we help you determine when you should be concerned. We also explain the resources available to help you fight back, including how to use the appeal process and how to successfully maneuver litigation. We also help you find the right attorney, and we explain the differences between suing your plan individually and suing as a class representative in a class action suit.

Chapter 17

Looking Out for Potential Distribution Problems

In This Chapter
▶ Surveying common pension errors
▶ Watching for red flags that indicate possible problems
▶ Going over your pension benefits
▶ Finding help from a variety of folks

*I*n the pension world, there's a tremendous gulf between the power and knowledge of the plan and the power and knowledge of the average pensioner. Consider the advantages of the company and the plan:

✔ The company employs pension actuaries who are familiar with the Employee Retirement Income Security Act of 1974 (ERISA; see Chapter 2) and who fully understand the implications of the present value calculations and the life expectancy tables (see Chapter 9 for more about these items).

✔ The company hires attorneys who advise the company regarding new legislation and how pending cases impact on the rules. These attorneys also lobby on behalf of the company to have an impact on legislation that's pending before Congress. Even your own authors have won a case in court only to find that special legislation in Washington, D.C., threatened the verdict.

✔ The pension plan employs a full-time administrator and staff not only to run the plan, but also to keep the plan out of trouble.

The most common perception, or perhaps misperception, is that you and the plan are on the same team. But to your pension plan, you're just a debt, not a lovable old-timer who's faithfully served your company. The plan has its team, and you have only, well, yourself. The plan's experts have spent their careers learning the intricacies of pensions while you've been doing your job. They know the rules, and they also know that you probably don't. What you have here, then, is a David and Goliath situation. But as you know, David won that battle. You can win the same way David did. You can't expect to memorize all the pension laws and review all the court decisions, but you can be aware of the red-flag situations. And you can take action if you discover an error in your pension distribution. It's all very doable, and by the end of this chapter, you'll have a bag of stones for your slingshot.

If you're still working, you're more vulnerable to upheavals in your pension plan than if you're already retired, so it's extra important for working folks to watch out for the potential problems that we outline in this chapter.

Checking Out Common Mistakes in Calculating Pension Distributions

When their long-awaited retirement finally arrives, most pensioners want to take their money and move on. Few, if any, ever question whether their pension distribution is correct. And maybe they should have. We say this because the government estimates that up to 30 percent of all pension calculations are incorrect. Math mistakes can be made, or the plan may simply record the wrong information, which results in your pension calculation being incorrect. Systemic violations can also affect every person in the plan. What we're getting at is that you must be on high alert so that you aren't among the millions who retire with less money than they're entitled to receive. A good place to start is to identify some of the most common errors, which we do in the following sections.

Careless recordkeeping mistakes

Pension plans commonly make a number of just plain careless or negligent mistakes when calculating your benefits. These mistakes have two things in common: They aren't usually discovered, and they can cost you a lot of money. The list of potential errors is as long as your imagination, but that list certainly includes the following errors:

- Your wages aren't properly reported or recorded.
- Your company doesn't give you credit for all your years of service.
- You were on maternity leave sometime during your employment, and service prior to your leave isn't credited when you retire.

✔ Commissions, bonuses, or overtime aren't credited, even though your plan documents say that they should be.

✔ Your plan ignores new vesting requirements or increases in pension benefits.

✔ Credit for work in a prior company isn't included.

✔ The plan staff or the computer program muffs up the math.

✔ Your birth date or Social Security number is incorrect.

✔ The assets in your plan are incorrectly valued or valued on the wrong date (for example, you're in a defined benefit plan and your benefits are to commence on August 1, 2009, but the value of your benefits is calculated as of August 31, 2008).

✔ Your company merges or goes out of business, and no one is sure which benefits you're entitled to (Chapters 11 and 12 have information on what happens to a pension during mergers, bankruptcies, and other difficult circumstances).

✔ The company loses your records and is having trouble re-creating your file.

Mistakes made by pensioners

Sure, you can get angry when your company makes mistakes, but remember that you can make them as well. Here are some examples of mistakes you may make one day:

✔ You may fail to update your human resources office about your divorce, your new marriage, or a death in your family. For example, if you're married and your spouse is listed as your beneficiary, your spouse will be your beneficiary until he or she is removed. If you divorce and fail to mention this fact to your company, and if you fail to advise your company that your ex is no longer your beneficiary, he or she will have a claim to your money when you die. (See Chapters 14 and 15 for more information about survivorship benefits and the effect of divorce on your pension.)

✔ You may discover an error in your personnel file but do nothing about it and tell no one. If you notice, for example, that the wrong year is recorded for your birth or that the year you started working is off by a year or two (or ten!), your benefits will be directly affected. The mathematical formulas used to calculate your benefits are based on, among other things, your age and years of service (see Chapter 7 for details). The longer you've worked, the higher your benefits, and likewise with your age. So if you notice this error, don't keep it a secret, or you're likely to be the one who'll suffer.

If you discover a mistake in your personnel file, bring it to the attention of someone in your human resources department or advise the plan administrator. Ask him or her to fix it pronto; we suggest that you do this in writing, keeping a paper trail just in case you need it down the road. This doesn't mean you can't call first. Just remember to follow it up in writing to make sure the correction is made.

When it comes to pension mistakes, silence isn't golden. Instead, it's the squeaky wheel that gets the oil.

Major (and really expensive) mistakes

The mistakes that we discuss in this section are those big mistakes that affect everyone in the plan. If and when these mistakes are uncovered, they can cost the plan millions. Chances are that if the company miscalculated your benefits based on one of the following errors, the mistake was made across the board for other retirees as well. Multiply the mistake on your behalf by the number of other retirees, and the number adds up quickly! Here's a list of the most common mistakes:

✔ The plan administrator uses an incorrect or illegal formula to calculate everyone's benefits (therefore paying everyone more or less than they're entitled to). But keep in mind that we seldom hear about errors in which the plan pays more benefits than it should; the calculations almost always seem to err on the side of the employer.

✔ Your plan reduces your benefits for service already performed. In other words, your plan doesn't provide you with benefits that you earned prior to the plan being changed. Even though the plan is amended to no longer offer a benefit it previously provided, after you've earned it, it's yours, and you're entitled to receive it.

There's a little something called the *anti-cutback rule* that says, in a nutshell, that it's okay to take away benefits in the future, but benefits can't be reduced retroactively. Suppose that your plan offers a subsidy to employees who take early retirement. Under the subsidy, if you retire early, your plan pays you a lump sum amount totaling the amount you would have been entitled to if you hadn't taken early retirement. If the company eliminates the subsidy after you've worked under this premise for 20 years, it can't touch the subsidy for the 20 years that you've already worked. It can, however, amend the plan for the remaining years that you work before retirement.

Making plans to have your money last as long as you do

Consider what co-author Bob Gary's slightly ancient but lovable brother Gene likes to say: "I have all the money I will ever need to retire as long as I die next month." He has the right idea; the goal of your pension is for your money to last at least as long as you do. Interestingly, studies show that women underestimate their life expectancy, while men overestimate. On average, women live five years longer than men of the same age. But you should also know that the Internal Revenue Service (IRS) life expectancy tables (see Chapter 9 for more information) are unisex tables that don't differentiate between men and women.

Your mantra must be to plan and save to meet and even exceed a typical life expectancy, and to pack that life with the activities of your choice. Today's 75 is yesterday's 60. We expect that many people out there intend to mount a motorcycle rather than a rocking chair in their retirement. The secret to life is to never stop living it. (Gene would tell you that if you were to ever bump into him in Las Vegas.) Only you can choose to seize the moment. Climb Mount Kilimanjaro, scuba-dive in the Great Barrier Reef, or take your grandchildren fishing at a nearby lake. While the spark of life runs on human energy (which is free), the ticket to the play requires money and income. Much in this world requires planning and sacrifice, and your secure retirement is no different. So you need to ensure that you receive all you're entitled to.

✔ Your traditional defined benefit plan converts to a cash balance plan (which we cover in Chapter 3), and your account balance is now smaller than it was before the conversion.

✔ Your pension isn't paid within a reasonable amount of time after you file your request for benefits. As a general rule, you should start receiving your distribution within about 45 days after your application is made (which is done after you retire).

✔ Cost-of-living increases aren't properly credited.

✔ You take a lump sum rather than an annuity, and the plan uses an inflated interest rate to calculate your lump sum (resulting in an amount that's lower than you're entitled to).

✔ À la Enron, your company is overinvested in shaky company stock.

✔ The boss is illegally dipping into the fund.

✔ The company delays making payments into your 401(k), and you lose some investment earnings.

✔ As a result of improper investments or your plan's failure to follow your investment instructions, your fund is short of money.

Recognizing Red Flags That Signal Trouble Ahead

Most prospective pensioners are sailing blissfully toward retirement with the full expectation that if they do their jobs well and avoid being canned or getting hit by a truck, they'll make it to their retirement day and all will be fine. And while that attitude may sound like a good one to have, you have to remember that the unexpected can happen at any moment. Consider, for example, the iceberg that sank the unsinkable *Titanic*; no one was aware of that icy rock hidden under the surface. Similarly, where your pension is concerned, it's your job to be aware of the red flags that signal that an iceberg is ahead. Sometimes your gut can tell you when something is awry, but being on the lookout for problems is the best way to avoid them.

Warning signs in defined contribution plans

The following is a short list of warning signs indicating that your pension may be in trouble and that you may not receive all the money that you've earned. These red flags are most relevant to defined contribution plans (see Chapter 3 for more about this type of plan):

- Your pension plan is always switching managers and financial consultants.
- You find investments in your portfolio that you didn't authorize.
- Your company doesn't provide your individual benefit statement with the regularity required under new pension rules, resulting in fines to the company.

  Starting in 2007, the plan is required to:

  - Distribute quarterly benefit statements to participants who can direct the investment of their benefits under the plan
  - Distribute annual benefit statements if the trustees direct the investments under the plan
- Your account balance appears to be wrong.
- You have a big, unexplained drop in your account balance.
- Your employer has financial problems.
- Former co-workers are having trouble collecting their benefits.

> ✓ Your account statement shows that contributions from your paycheck are late in being made or aren't being made at all to your 401(k). Your elective deferrals are supposed to be contributed as soon as reasonably feasible, which the Department of Labor (DOL) interprets as a week after deferral from your salary. Chapter 4 has the basics about 401(k) plans.

If you notice these errors, you should first contact your plan administrator or human resources department for an explanation. If you still believe that the plan has serious problems, you can contact a DOL pension attorney. (We give you contact information for the DOL later in this chapter.)

Underfunding in defined benefit plans

Under a traditional defined benefit plan, the level of benefits you receive at retirement is fixed, but the employer's contributions in any given year are *not* fixed. The benefit you're promised to receive at retirement is set forth in your summary plan description (SPD) and calculated by actuaries based on factors such as your age, salary, and years of service. (See Chapter 3 for the basics of defined benefit plans.)

To better understand how the current underfunding crisis came about (which estimates that American defined benefit plans face a debt of about $600 billion), a bit of explanation is in order. ERISA and the Internal Revenue Service (IRS) established minimum funding rules to ensure that employers fund the retirement benefits earned by their employees. Friendly accountants and actuaries cooperate with optimistic assumptions for what these plans will earn over time and crunch numbers to determine the cost of these benefits. However, prior to the Pension Protection Act of 2006 (PPA), employers weren't required to fund their defined benefit plans at 100 percent; in fact, it was sufficient if your plan was only 90 percent funded. So, your company's insatiable desire for a happy balance sheet may have cost you your future pension. The more a company assumed that its pension portfolio would earn, the less it contributed to fund the plan. In 2000, for example, the stock market went down, but the pension obligations to present and future retirees marched on.

In an effort to solve this underfunding problem, the PPA has made the funding requirements much more rigid. Effective for plan years beginning after 2007, single-employer defined benefit plans must make contributions to meet 100 percent of their funding obligations. Plans currently underfunded have been given three years to meet this funding requirement and seven years to make up all shortfalls — quite a heavy obligation for an underfunded plan. In order to reduce their funding obligations under defined benefit plans, many employers are freezing benefits under defined benefit plans and providing for future benefits under 401(k) plans that are funded in part by you. The PPA also imposes new requirements so that plan participants receive notice within 30 days after their plan has become subject to a restriction based on its funding status. If you receive such a notice, it's a red flag that your plan is in trouble.

What about the plan you participate in? Is it underfunded? Here's how to get the information you need to find out:

1. **Ask your human resources department or plan administrator for a copy of your company's Form 5500, which is a required DOL financial report about your pension plan.**

   If this tactic doesn't work, you can check online for the form. If you know the name of your plan, you can go to www.freeerisa.com for a copy of the Form 5500. (See Chapter 8 for more about this form.)

2. **When you have the Form 5500, go to Schedule B and find and make note of the Current Value of Assets and Accrued Liability lines.**

   These lines show you the value of the plan assets and what it owes.

3. **Divide the current assets by the accrued liability.**

   The result is the percentage of your plan that's actually funded. If your plan is less than 100 percent funded, it has to increase funding to comply with the new 100 percent funding rules. Most plans currently aren't more than 90 percent funded. If your plan's funding level is less then 80 percent, it's considered endangered and at risk, while less than 65 percent funded is considered to be at critical status.

There's a strong possibility that a seriously underfunded plan will freeze all future benefits. This suspension of benefits may be the prelude to eliminating your defined benefit plan.

Some troubled companies have their pension plans taken over by the Pension Benefit Guaranty Corporation (PBGC). See Chapter 12 for more about this organization and for full details about underfunding.

Reviewing Your Pension Distribution for Mistakes

It's not rocket science to know that when you retire, another set of eyeballs (besides the plan's) needs to confirm that everything is hunky-dory — and those eyeballs, my friend, would be yours. Unfortunately, this task fits into the category of easier said than done. So, in the following sections, we give you a few pointers on this all-important job.

Arming yourself with important information

In anticipation of a battle, any good general would make a list of the necessary weaponry to carry that day. The same goes for looking over your pension information. You should, at a minimum, have familiarity with the following as you double-check your distribution papers:

- ✔ The plan documents, particularly as they relate to vesting, accrual of benefits, distribution, early retirement, and lump sum issues (see Chapter 8 for more about plan documents)

- ✔ All plan amendments, particularly those amendments that have altered the benefits package

- ✔ The tables and assumptions that were used to calculate your pension benefits (check out Chapter 9 for more on these important calculation tools)

- ✔ Whether your plan is a defined benefit plan or a defined contribution plan, know the difference and know all the types of plans that you've participated in during your employment, including individual retirement accounts (IRAs; Chapter 3 introduces you to the wide array of retirement plans out there)

- ✔ Mergers, terminations, and bankruptcy — none of these should escape your vigilance (as you find out in Chapters 11 and 12)

- ✔ All the critical information regarding your work history, including rates of pay, breaks in service, survivorship information, and divorce history (and make sure that the plan has this same information recorded correctly)

Confirming a few facts before you retire

We recommend that you determine, prior to retiring, that:

- ✔ Your plan distribution complies with ERISA and any other rules that may impact the size of your pension. See Chapter 9 for the full scoop on distributions.

- ✔ Your plan has all the necessary information, that it's correct, and that the proper tables were used and the math calculated correctly. The calculations need to conform to the benefit formula stated in the plan, and the factual information needs to be correct. In Chapter 8, we explain the necessary information that your plan should have.

Moving forward when you think you've found an error

If you believe that there's an error in any of the factual data in the calculation of your pension benefit, bring it to the attention of your plan administrator or your human resources department; it will usually be corrected. If you have other concerns regarding the benefit calculations, or if the plan administrator doesn't properly address your concerns, review the procedures in your SPD for appealing your benefit calculations. See Chapter 18 for more information about the appeal process.

Getting Guidance from the Right Places

You probably don't have the time, nor is it necessary, to become a pension expert in order to receive what you've rightfully earned. Instead, like David fighting off Goliath with his slingshot, you must know where to focus your attention. And you have to know who to go to when you run into trouble that you can't handle alone. Described in the following sections are private and public organizations, along with pension professionals, that can assist you in resolving issues with your pension plan. You can even consult fellow pensioners for advice.

As the need for these resources becomes more apparent, the list of public and private resources to aid pensioners is growing. But remember, the indispensable component is *you*. You must be willing to stand up and ask questions to determine that you're receiving the proper pension, and you must be prepared to challenge your plan if it becomes necessary to do so. Some of the organizations listed in the following sections may be able to assist you in determining whether your pension is correct.

Private groups

The following organizations have experience in reviewing pension benefit issues and providing recommendations for government agencies or professionals to contact to further review the issues or claims.

The Pension Rights Center

The Pension Rights Center in Washington, D.C., is developing an Internet database that provides information and assistance to pensioners and serves as a referral resource.

Pension Rights Center
1350 Connecticut Avenue, NW, Suite 206
Washington, DC 20036-1739
Phone: 202-296-3776
Fax: 202-833-2472
Web site: www.pensionrights.org

The National Center for Retirement Benefits

The National Center for Retirement Benefits is a private company that assists those pensioners who have retired or who are preparing to retire.

National Center for Retirement Benefits
666 Dundee Road, Suite 1200
Northbrook, IL 60062
Phone: 800-666-1000
Fax: 847-564-4944
Web site: www.ncrb.com

Regional pension counseling projects

Six regional pension counseling projects were designed to help individual pensioners with their particular pension problems. They include the following:

✔ Great Lakes Pension Rights Project (Mich., Pa., Ohio, and Ky.)

- Serving Michigan and Pennsylvania:
  Elder Law of Michigan, Inc.
  3815 W. St. Joseph, Suite C200
  Lansing, MI 48917
  Phone: 517-485-9164
  Fax: 517-372-0792
  Web site: www.elderslaw.org

- Serving Ohio and Kentucky:
  Pro Seniors, Inc.
  7162 Reading Road, Suite 1150
  Cincinnati, OH 45237
  Phone: 800-488-6070
  Fax: 513-621-5613
  Web site: www.proseniors.org

✔ Mid-Atlantic Pension Rights Project (N.Y. and N.J.)

The Public Advocate's Office
1 Centre Street, 15th Floor
New York, NY 10007
Phone: 212-669-7200
Fax: 212-669-4701
Web site: www.pubadvocate.nyc.gov

✔ Midwest Pension Rights Project (Mo., Kans., Ark., Miss., and Ill.)

2165 Hampton Avenue
St. Louis, MO 63139
Phone: 877-725-1516
Web site: www.midwestpension.org

✔ New England Pension Assistance Project (Conn., Maine, Mass., N.H., R.I., and Vt.)

Gerontology Institute
University of Massachusetts–Boston
100 Morrissey Boulevard
Boston, MA 02125-3393
Phone: 888-425-6067
Fax: 617-287-7080
Web site: www.pensionaction.org

✔ Pension Information, Counseling and Assistance Project of the Southwest (Tex., Okla., and N. Mex.)

Phone: 888-343-4414
Web site: www.tlsc.org/Pension%20Counseling.htm

✔ Upper Midwest Pension Rights Project (Minn., N. Dak., S. Dak., Wis., and Iowa)

• Serving Minnesota, North Dakota, and South Dakota:
Minnesota Senior Federation
1885 University Avenue W., Suite 190
St. Paul, MN 55104
Phone: 877-645-0261
Fax: 651-641-8969
Web site: www.mnseniors.org

• Serving Wisconsin:
Coalition of Wisconsin Aging Group
2850 Dairy Drive, Suite 100
Madison, WI 53718
Phone: 800-366-2990
Fax: 608-224-0607
Web site: www.cwag.org

• Serving Iowa:
Iowa Legal Aid
1111 9th Street, Suite 230
Des Moines, IA 50314
Phone: 515-243-2151
Web site: www.iowalegalaid.org

Government agencies

The following government agencies oversee and regulate pension plans and assist plan participants. We provide additional contact information for government agencies in Chapter 2.

The Internal Revenue Service and the Department of Labor

The Internal Revenue Service (IRS) and the Department of Labor (DOL) have developed a number of publications on various pension issues. The Securities and Exchange Commission is also a valuable resource for saving and investments. Go to www.irs.gov to reach the IRS home page, and from there, click on Retirement Plans Community. You also can go directly to www.irs.gov/retirement/participant/index.html to find out more about almost any pension topic and to view publications. You can visit the DOL at www.dol.gov.

The Employee Benefits Security Administration

The Employee Benefits Security Administration (EBSA) oversees private pensions and is responsible for administering and enforcing ERISA's provisions. It has 15 regional and district offices to answer questions from retirees. The regional offices often will help you get documents and will sometimes offer other help as well. The EBSA is part of the DOL and has an Office of Participant Assistance.

Go to askebsa.dol.gov to find out how to send your inquiry via e-mail. You also can reach a benefit advisor via telephone at the Employee and Employer Assistance Hotline at 866-444-EBSA (866-444-3272).

The Pension Benefit Guaranty Corporation

The Pension Benefit Guaranty Corporation (PBGC) provides benefits to retirees if their pension plans fail. The PBGC also has a missing pensioner program. Visit www.pbgc.gov, or go directly to the page earmarked for workers and retirees at www.pbgc.gov/workers-retirees/index.html to find out more about the services that the PBGC provides and the basic benefits that it guarantees.

Pension professionals

If you run into problems regarding your pension, it often helps to get in touch with a pension professional. These professionals, who have the necessary skills to even the playing field between you and the company, include the following:

  ✔ **Pension lawyers:** As we like to think, in the pension world the right lawyer is like the Colt pistol in the Old West — both are the great levelers. A good pension attorney can cause your employer to treat your pension claim more seriously. (Head to Chapter 19 for details on finding a lawyer.)

✔ **Pension actuaries:** These professionals calculate retirement benefits and can review your pension benefit to see if it's calculated properly.

✔ **Accountants:** Sharp accountants can spot when a company has overstepped its bounds and trashed the rules.

Fellow pensioners

As a member of a pension plan, you aren't alone; you can always look to your fellow pensioners for help and advice. Chances are that one of them will have come across a similar problem to yours at one point in their lives. So remember, take advantage of your fellow pensioners (and we mean that in a good way). Here are a few suggestions:

✔ Form a retirees group, exchange e-mail and home addresses, and encourage the discussion of pension issues.

✔ Set up a Web site where you and other pensioners can post questions and receive answers from other retirees who have had similar problems.

✔ Make a point of sharing pension issues, and encourage your co-workers to do the same.

✔ If you need to hire a professional (like those we list in the previous section) to answer a question that affects the group, encourage the other pensioners to split the expenses. You should also ask your fellow pensioners whether they have experience with a professional who's knowledgeable regarding pension issues.

The bottom line is to talk to your co-workers about your pension. They can learn from you, and you can learn from them. When it comes to a pension question or concern, you're never alone.

Chapter 18

Tackling Denied Claims

In This Chapter
▶ Understanding claims denied in full and in part
▶ Appealing a denial of your claim

*E*very pension plan governed by the Employee Retirement Income Security Act of 1974 (ERISA; see Chapter 2) is required to set up and maintain a procedure that you follow to claim your pension, along with a procedure to appeal the decision if your claim is denied. This chapter discusses the importance of following the appeal procedure and what to expect along the way.

Oh, No! Discovering That Your Claim for Benefits Has Been Denied

All plans governed by ERISA have set procedures for filing claims for benefits, and your plan must tell you what these procedures are. This information is usually outlined in your summary plan description (SPD), which you should review before you file your claim. A claim is considered filed when you meet the plan's requirements of a "reasonable claim-filing procedure." In other words, simply follow the plan's directions; for instance, if the plan specifies where to file your claim or with whom to file your claim, do just that. Keep a copy of what you file, and remember to mail it via certified mail, return receipt requested, so you have proof. If you don't know how or where to file your claim, ask your plan administrator. (See Chapter 8 for a review of how to request the SPD or any other documents that you need; Chapter 9 has details on the general process of filing a claim.)

If your plan hasn't set up a formal filing procedure, your claim is considered filed when you make, or your representative (someone acting on your behalf with your consent) makes, an oral or written request for benefits. This request must be made to someone from the plan who has the proper authority to receive claims for pension benefits, such as your plan administrator or someone to whom he or she has delegated the authority to accept the paperwork for the request. (Remember, even though ERISA requires plans to set forth claims procedures, it doesn't mean your plan has done so. That's why ERISA provides that your claim will be filed simply upon your request for benefits.) So, after waiting eagerly to hear about your claim, you find out that you've been denied. Two types of denials exist:

- ✔ **Denial in full:** In this case, your claim may be denied because you aren't eligible for benefits under the plan. For example, maybe you haven't been a participant in the plan for enough years, or maybe you aren't the required age. (Chapter 7 has the scoop on ensuring that you're eligible to receive benefits from your plan.) Your claim may also be denied because you haven't provided sufficient information that the plan requested from you to complete your claim. (This is an important reason you need to file your claim according to your plan's procedures!)

- ✔ **Denial in part:** If your claim is denied in part, this generally means that the plan calculated your benefits at a lower amount than you had expected to receive based on your account statements or on the individual benefit statements you received in the past.

If your claim has been denied in full or in part, your plan administrator must inform you of this denial through a written notice, in language that you can understand. (As we discuss in Chapter 2, the plan administrator is the guy or gal who runs your pension plan, determines your eligibility to participate, and decides whether to accept your claim for the distribution of your benefits.) At a minimum, the written notice must outline the following:

- ✔ The specific reason or reasons for the denial

- ✔ Specific reference to plan provisions on which the denial is based

- ✔ A description of any additional material or information necessary for you to correct your claim, and an explanation of why this material or information is necessary

- ✔ Appropriate information as to the steps that you need to take if you or your beneficiary want to submit the denied claim for review (see the following section for details)

If you don't receive notice from your plan that your claim was denied *or* accepted, don't assume that no news is good news. In this case, if notice isn't given to you within 90 days of your filing, the claim is considered denied — unless, of course, special circumstances exist that would justify extending the time period to process your claim. The plan can get a 90-day extension, but to do so, the plan must

- ✔ Notify you within the initial 90 days that more time is needed

- ✔ Tell you why more time is needed and the date that the plan expects to make a decision

If 90 more days go by and you receive no answer, you can consider the claim to have been denied.

Undergoing an Appeal after Your Claim Is Denied

If you feel that your claim for pension benefits was wrongly denied (denied in full) or incorrectly calculated (denied in part), you have an important weapon at your disposal: an appeal. In the following sections, we explain the appeal process and help you decide whether pension litigation is in your future.

The appeal process can be tricky, so it's important that you follow not only your plan's requirements to appeal the denial, but also the specific time periods set forth by your plan for doing so. Generally, you have 60 days to appeal the denial of your claim, but if you need more time, the plan may extend this time period. However, remember that if you file beyond the 60 days without first requesting an extension, you may have waived your right to appeal. The plan may provide the procedure for requesting an extension. However, you should always put requests in writing, retain copies, and send your request via certified mail, return receipt requested. It's critical that you present your claim properly and follow all the rules for appealing the decision exactly as the plan requires. This is known as *exhausting your administrative remedies.* If you fail to go through this process properly, a court may have reason enough to dismiss any related lawsuit that you file down the road. The reason for this possible unfortunate outcome is that courts require you to take advantage of the plan's appeal process before you file a lawsuit.

The appeal process is known as an *administrative appeal* because it's part of the company's overall appeal process, as opposed to a formal court procedure. Likewise, the term *administrative remedies* refers to the company's detailed rules that must be followed in order to have the decision changed (and your claim remedied).

The proper presentation of your claim from the start not only affects your appeal, but also may impact your chances for success in any later litigation regarding your pension. Given all these factors, we strongly recommend that you hire an attorney to assist you in the administrative appeal process. The right attorney can properly present the basis for appealing your claim, protect your rights, and preserve the record in case of a lawsuit. And your attorney may be able to find additional claims for benefits that you didn't even know existed. (We discuss the process for hiring the right attorney in Chapter 19.)

Gathering and submitting critical information

First things first: Make sure that your denial letter complies with the requirements that we set forth earlier in this chapter. This way, you know what you're appealing and how to appeal it. If the denial letter doesn't include everything it should, contact the plan administrator (or whoever signed the denial letter) and ask that the missing information be provided to you immediately.

Even though you may request the information missing from the denial letter face to face or over the phone, confirm in writing all conversations you have regarding the missing information (send all correspondence via certified mail, and request a return receipt). Also make sure to keep a copy of all the letters that you send and receive on this matter. Creating a paper trail is always a good idea!

The denial letter from your plan should refer to the section of the plan on which the denial is based. It's important for you to have this information so you understand why the plan denied your claim; without it, you have no way of knowing what to submit to ask the plan to reconsider. If a copy of this particular section isn't provided to you, you may be able to find it in the SPD; if you can't, ask the plan administrator for a copy of the section. And remember that the denial of access to this information, in some cases, is enough for a court to find that you were denied a full and fair review. (This is fancy language for whether you got a fair shake during the appeal process.)

Got all the information you need from the denial letter? Good! Now you can move forward based on that information. If your plan asks you to provide additional information for an appeal, you should by all means collect that information and provide it. For example, your plan may request a certified copy of your birth certificate because your age needs to be confirmed. If you think that additional information or evidence will benefit your case, provide that also. The plan may not consider the additional information you submit to be helpful, but you can submit whatever you or your attorney think will help substantiate your claim. The main point is this: Make sure that you do what's asked and that you provide the requested information or materials within the time limits set forth in the denial letter or the SPD. And don't miss any deadlines!

Checking out the basic review procedure

Your plan must put a procedure in place for you or your representative (such as an attorney) to appeal your claim to a duly appointed fiduciary (we discuss fiduciaries in detail in Chapter 10). So who's the duly appointed fiduciary who will decide whether you eat steak or hot dogs in your retirement? The plan's procedure should set out who's designated to fulfill this responsibility.

Generally, the plan administrator is responsible, but the plan can designate another person to review and make decisions regarding claims for benefits and claim denials. Check the SPD or the plan document (the unabridged document that the SPD summarizes) to find out who will be reviewing your appeal. It never hurts to know who's going to rule on your claim. It could be an ally, a foe, or someone who's never heard of you.

The person or committee conducting the review looks at all the additional information you've submitted, along with everything you provided when you initially made your claim. The reviewer also looks at additional information that he or she considers relevant, such as a plan amendment or part of your work record. The reviewer considers all the facts, the language of the plan and its amendments, and the law, and then makes a determination.

The decision given after the review is either an acceptance of your claim (great!) or yet another denial (not so great). It must be issued in writing and be in language that you can understand, and it needs to include specific reasons for the decision. You're required to receive a decision no later than 60 days after your plan receives your request for a review. In some cases additional time may be needed, such as if the plan determines that a hearing is necessary. In no case, however, should the decision be issued later than 120 days after the plan receives your request. If the plan extends its decision beyond the 60 days, you'll receive a written notice of the extension before the expiration of the 60 days. If you hear nothing for 120 days, you should follow up with your plan administrator. If the plan administrator doesn't take action on your appeal, you can contact the Department of Labor (DOL) or a private pension attorney to take further action. (Chapter 2 has contact information for the DOL.)

Hearings on your appeal are rarely requested by the plan administrator or fiduciary, so if one is requested, we suggest that you consider hiring an attorney at this stage. Why? A hearing may signal that the plan is unsure of the correct response to your appeal and is looking for more information or clarification of some point. (You can find more on hiring the right attorney in Chapter 19.)

It's a good idea to have an attorney help you at the plan-review stage, but keep in mind that fees for this purpose may have to come from your pocket, because courts generally won't award fees for time or expenses incurred before a lawsuit is filed.

Deciding whether to litigate if the appeal fails

If your plan reviews your appeal and decides to stand by its decision to deny your claim, you're left with one option: Take the plan to court. As a plan participant or beneficiary, you have the right to bring a civil action in court to enforce your rights. For many, though, going to court and suing their employer's pension plan is an emotional and difficult decision. After many years of working for the benefit of your employer and trusting that your employer is acting in your best interests, litigation against that employer's pension plan presents a personal challenge. Take a personal inventory before you move on to litigation by answering the following questions:

- ✔ Is the financial impact of the plan's adverse decision significant to you? In other words, will you receive just a few bucks less a month, or will you receive half the amount you think you should?

- ✔ Do you have the temperament and patience to participate in litigation that can go on for years?

- ✔ Can you separate your experiences over the span of your work life with the company and then challenge that same company in court?

- ✔ Can you give your attorney control of your fate as it relates to your pension?

- ✔ Can you accept the fact that just because you're right doesn't always mean you'll win?

- ✔ Can you avoid getting too emotionally involved in your case? The fact is that it isn't healthy when your case consumes and reduces your quality of life.

After you consider these questions, if you conclude that you want to litigate rather than accept what you consider an unfair result, the next and perhaps only step available is getting started with the litigation.

If the civil action to enforce your rights is brought under ERISA, the action will be brought in federal district court. However, an action involving a claim not governed by ERISA may be brought in a state court according to the applicable state law. (For more about pension litigation, head to Chapter 20.)

Chapter 19

Hiring and Working with an Attorney

. . . .

In This Chapter

▶ Looking for a lawyer who meets your needs

▶ Picking a winner through the interviewing process

▶ Getting started by looking at a few important numbers

▶ Developing (or ending) the relationship with your attorney

. . . .

*W*e'll say it up front: Many people are uncomfortable with lawyers, and nobody ever wants to have to hire one. Assume that you've done everything you can to avoid confrontation or even a lawsuit against your pension plan. However, if you feel you've reached the end of your rope and believe you're entitled to more benefits, you may have no other choice but to shop for a legal representative. In this chapter, we explain how to find and choose the best attorney for your needs. Your attorney will serve as your advocate — a defender of your rights and a champion for your cause — to help you get the benefits you believe you deserve. (Head to Chapter 20 for full details on preparing for pension litigation.)

Searching for the Best Attorney for Your Needs

All attorneys went to law school, but that's where their similarities end. There's an attorney for just about any situation. So, to find the best attorney for your situation, you have to know three things:

- ✔ The type of pension plan you have
- ✔ The kind of attorney you need and the experience of that attorney
- ✔ Where to look to find acceptable candidates

In the following sections, we explain what you should know about searching for an attorney while keeping these three considerations in mind.

Identifying the type of attorney you need

Attorneys specialize in all sorts of fields, and it's no different when it comes to pension law. Some pension attorneys practice exclusively in federal court, and some practice exclusively in state court. Many attorneys have experience in both. The type of plan you have determines whether your case will be heard in state or federal court. You want an attorney who's familiar with the state or federal court procedure that applies to your plan. But no matter which court your case is in, the most important skill for your attorney to have is experience litigating pension cases.

In the United States, we have the federal court system, with one set of rules, and the state court system, in which each state has its own set of rules. Here's a rundown on the two types of courts:

- ✔ **Federal court:** These courts have *jurisdiction,* or authority, over private, tax-qualified pension plans that are covered by ERISA. (ERISA stands for Employee Retirement Income Security Act of 1974; see Chapter 2 for more information.)

- ✔ **State court:** These courts have jurisdiction over public employee pension plans covering employees of state and local governments. State pension plans are a creation of a particular state's legislature. So, for example, if you're in the New York state teacher pension plan, New York state courts will interpret and enforce the New York pension laws.

So, you need to know whether you have a private, tax-qualified plan or a plan regulated by state law (a public employee plan) before you hire an attorney. You ideally want to find an attorney who's both familiar with your type of pension plan and experienced in practicing in the court that has jurisdiction over your plan. In the following sections, we help you figure out the kind of plan you have and give you a few pointers on the type of attorney you need based on your plan.

What kind of plan do you have?

You shouldn't have too much trouble figuring out what type of plan you have. Simply look at any plan documents that you've received about your pension plan (we describe these documents in detail in Chapter 8), and then follow these guidelines:

- ✔ If your employer is a private company, you most likely have a tax-qualified private pension plan. To verify this fact, flip through the first few pages of your plan documents, including the summary plan description

(SPD). Typically, the word *ERISA* will appear in the table of contents or the overview section.

Knowing the name of your plan is helpful in determining whether it's a private plan. For example, if your plan name is The Sydney Michael Designer Watch Company Profit-Sharing Plan, you can be sure that your employer is a private company.

✔ If you're a government or public school employee, chances are that your plan is a public plan (governed by state law) or a federal plan (governed by federal law), and neither type of plan is covered by ERISA. The biggest clue is where you work. Just remember that ERISA was created to regulate the private sector's pension plans — from your podiatrist's plan to IBM's — not the plans for local firefighters or state troopers.

If you're still unsure whether you're in a private or public plan, just ask your company's human resources manager. We're sure that he or she will be glad to tell you. Also, go to www.freeerisa.com and type in your company name to find out what plans it offers. Or do a Web search for your company and add *pension plan* to the search criteria. Many companies have information posted on their Web sites about their pension plans. This type of info, such as whether your company is involved in any current litigation regarding its pension plan, is useful for your initial meeting with your attorney. The claims in other cases may be relevant to your claims, or they may affect them in some way.

What skills should your attorney have, based on your plan?

Your attorney must know how to *litigate* a pension claim (present your claims in a lawsuit filed in court). You wouldn't go to a heart doctor for brain surgery. This is no different. You need a pension litigator, not a personal-injury attorney, even if the personal-injury attorney is the best of the best in his field.

Your attorney should have experience in litigating ERISA claims if you have a private pension plan or state claims if you have a public pension plan. The rules aren't the same for each, so, preferably, your attorney should be skilled in the type of plan you have.

Pension litigation is unique because the case often depends on a complicated legal analysis, not on the facts. Typically, your entire case will be decided on whether the specific language of your plan documents conforms to the law governing your plan (either federal or state). Your attorney needs to be more than a smooth talker; she must understand this complicated area of the law, be able to clearly communicate and write complex ideas, and have litigation experience.

For more details about the skills and experience a pension attorney needs, see the later section "Asking the right questions during the interview."

Finding a few good candidates

In your search for a capable pension attorney, many resources are available to guide you and assist you in the process. We suggest that you start with attorneys who come personally recommended. After that, continue with the other options in the following sections, doing your research online first, not only because it's quicker and easier, but also because it provides you with the most options. If you don't have access to the Internet, later we also provide phone numbers to assist you.

Federal pension law (ERISA) is the same in every state, so the right attorney can be located anywhere. Don't be discouraged if you can't find an appropriate attorney in your area; you can cross state lines in your search if you have to. In this case, if necessary, the attorney can obtain permission from the court to handle a case in a court that he isn't admitted to practice in. If you're in a public pension and your claim involves state law, your attorney must be licensed in that state. Otherwise he must get permission from the trial judge to represent you for just the one case.

Do not — we repeat, *do not* — go to your local Yellow Pages in search of an attorney. The cute, young attorney from the phone book who won Aunt Minnie $500 when she slipped at the supermarket isn't for you. You need an attorney who has both barrels loaded with the right stuff. That means experience in pension litigation dealing with the type of pension plan you have and the ability to communicate effectively. Because the Yellow Pages directory merely lists names, addresses, and phone numbers, you have no way of finding out anything more concrete about your choices. The phone book isn't bad for looking up phone numbers, but don't expect it to provide more information than that.

Personal recommendations

Personal recommendations from respected attorneys or accountants (or even friends who may have had similar problems) are your first option. Ask around — you may be surprised by the resources and recommendations that the right questions to the right person will uncover. Because it's probably safe to assume that you'd trust the recommendations of these people, listen to what they tell you about their own personal experience and whether they'd hire a particular attorney again. Was the attorney responsive to their needs, such as promptly returning phone calls? Was the attorney responsive to their concerns (for example, fear of retaliation)? Does the attorney personally spend time with clients, or was their contact usually with a paralegal, secretary, or junior attorney? Finally, you should ask whether the attorney was successful in the case.

If you're lucky enough to receive recommendations of some attorneys in the pension-rights field, you can check them out further on the Internet (as we discuss in the later section "General online resources") or in books and articles that can be found at your local library. Some books rate attorneys and identify the type of practice they have. And your prospective attorney may have published an article (or a book), which can give you even more background her. Ask the librarian for help with this. Your librarian may also be able to help you find the Martindale-Hubble directory for your state.

Organizations that provide pension counseling services

These types of organizations usually network with pension attorneys who provide advice, serve on advisory boards, and even offer free legal services when requested by the organization. Because these organizations are actively following the legal issues that affect seniors and retirees, they generally know who's knowledgeable in the field. Here are two of the most common organizations that provide pension counseling services:

- ✔ **The Pension Rights Center:** This organization protects and promotes retirement security through its regional Pension Information and Counseling Project. This project consists of six private, nonprofit programs, broken down geographically throughout the United States and primarily funded by the U.S. Administration on Aging. To find out more, go to www.pensionrights.org/help/counseling.

  If you'd rather get in touch with the center through the mail or by phone, here's the contact info: Pension Rights Center, 1350 Connecticut Avenue, NW, Suite 206, Washington, DC 20036-1739; phone 202-296-3776.

- ✔ **Pension Action Center:** Like many of these organizations, the Pension Action Center provides no-cost referrals to attorneys or other professionals who can advise retirees and assist them with legal issues involving their pensions. To find out more about the Pension Action Center, go to www.pensionaction.org/npln.htm.

  To write or call this group, use this contact information: National Pension Lawyers Network, Gerontology Institute, University of Massachusetts, 1000 Morrissey Boulevard, Boston, MA 02125-3393; phone: 617-287-7324.

Because these are grass-roots organizations, they may have only certain hours that someone is answering phones, but the Web sites are helpful in making contact as well.

Bar associations

Contrary to their name, bar associations don't serve alcohol, but attorneys. There are local and state bar associations as well as a national bar association. Each level provides different services to the legal profession. The local bar association may provide a lawyer referral service and may process grievances against attorneys. The state bar may act as a liaison to the courts, maintain publications on the law, and process grievances. The American Bar Association (ABA), which is the national association, sets policy for attorneys and publishes on topics of importance to attorneys.

If your local bar association maintains an attorney referral service, it will direct you to an attorney in your area who's in good standing with that state's bar association (usually this means that the attorneys haven't been disbarred). It can also specify attorneys who are experienced with pension issues. Local bar associations have the best referral information because they're local to your community.

But the ABA (www.abanet.org) also maintains a registry of lawyers by field of practice. At the home page, you can click on the Find Legal Help link, or you can go directly to the ABA page for lawyer referrals (www.abanet.org/legalservices/lris/directory). Both of these Web addresses display a map of the United States. When you click on the state in which you're employed and/or live, you're taken to a Web page that lists your state's bar association's office phone numbers. If any are available, the site also lists hyperlinks to Web sites with further information. From there, you can look for an attorney who handles pension issues, employee benefits, or retirement plans.

You can also contact the ABA at 321 N. Clark Street, Chicago, IL 60610; phone 312-988-5000.

We can't assure you that all local bar association offices have Web sites, and we can't assure you that all bar associations that do have Web sites are contained on the ABA's link. In fact, while writing this chapter, we discovered that our local bar association, which has quite a terrific Web site (loraincountybar.org), isn't listed on the ABA's Lawyer Referral page. If your local bar association isn't on the Web, you can always call your local bar association and ask if it provides a legal referral service.

General online resources

The Internet can be quite helpful when you're looking for an attorney or when you want to check out a recommendation from a friend. Here are some resources that we recommend:

- The Martindale-Hubble directory (which you should be able to find at your local library) and its online service (www.martindale.com) are often used by attorneys to find out about their opponents, but it's also a good resource for anyone who's looking for an attorney. This directory is excellent because it's organized geographically and by type of practice. It also rates attorneys.

- Search engines, such as Google and Yahoo!, are great when you want to search by keyword. For example, you might go to www.google.com

and search for *pension law attorney.* You can also search by typing in an attorney's name or law firm.

Remember that the more specific you are, the more you narrow the search. If your search is turning up too many hits, narrow it by state and city or even by adding the words *defined benefit plan* to the search.

✔ FindLaw (`www.findlaw.com`) is helpful when you want to find out more about an attorney you're thinking about hiring. At this Web site, you simply type in the criteria you want to search for and then settle in to review the results.

Using the Web to find anything is an art form, and the best way to master it is to just give it a try.

Interviewing a Prospective Attorney

After you've identified a few pension attorneys who may be able to help you, set up your first appointment with the one who comes most highly recommended and who also appears in one of the other resources outlined in the previous section. In the first meeting, you'll get to know this person a little and will get a sense of whether you can work with her. A smooth working relationship is necessary because, after all, some of these cases go on for years. The discussion of the circumstances of your case should also help you assess how knowledgeable the attorney is about your problem. You have no obligation to hire an attorney in the first meeting, so don't feel pressured to make a decision on the spot.

In the following sections, we walk you through the all-important interviewing process. If the first interview is positive, you won't need to proceed to your second choice.

Calling to set up the interview

A phone call to set up an initial meeting with an attorney shouldn't be difficult or time-consuming. Just follow these steps:

1. **When you call, ask the secretary or receptionist if you can speak directly with the attorney; this is an acceptable and expected request.**

   Be prepared to give the secretary, the attorney, or both a brief explanation that includes your name, your employer's name, the length of time of your employment, your age, and whether you've already retired. Gather all your pension and employment information before you place the call in case the attorney asks what documents you have.

2. **When you're actually speaking with the attorney, explain the nature of your concerns about your pension and what you've already done to address those concerns.**

    You want the prospective attorney to confirm that he handles issues such as yours. Ask if the attorney maintains a Web site, and if so, ask for the address. Checking the site can help you figure out the focus of the attorney's practice.

3. **If it sounds like the attorney can handle your complaint, schedule an appointment to meet and ask specifically what you should bring with you.**

4. **Ask whether you'll be charged for this appointment.**

    Most good pension attorneys won't charge a fee for this initial meeting (often called an *initial consultation*), but if you're advised that you'll be charged, find out what the charge is, and ask how long you can expect your appointment to last.

You should expect to be scheduled within a week or two; if not, the attorney may be too busy to work on your case (unless she's out of town, and that, of course, is an exception). Presuming that your appointment is scheduled in a reasonable period of time, you need to get ready for the face-to-face meeting.

Preparing for the interview

Keep in mind that your first meeting with an attorney is an interview, so you should act like an interviewer. After all, *you* are interviewing the attorney to hire him. Take a list of questions with you (see the following section) so you can find out what the attorney knows about pensions and whether he's the right choice for you.

Even if you want to hire the attorney, the attorney may decide that he doesn't want the case. It could be that the attorney isn't familiar with the law or that he feels that the two of you may not be a good team. Or the attorney may feel that there's a conflict of interest between you because of a prior case he has handled.

Before you make the trip to the attorney's office, you need to be familiar with the questions on your list. You can group them by category or topic, or you can put an asterisk by the questions you consider most important.

Don't forget to take the documents that the attorney identified in your initial call. At the very least, take the following items with you to this meeting:

✔ The SPD and any amendments made to it

✔ Your individual benefit statement and your payout schedules

✔ Any communication from the plan regarding the problem with your pension or the calculation of your benefits

If you have them or can easily get them, it's also helpful to bring along the following items:

✔ Your pay stubs

✔ If applicable, your collective bargaining agreement

✔ The plan's Form 5500, which provides a summary of the plan's financial information

✔ Your employee personnel manual

If in doubt about whether to bring a document to the meeting, just bring it. It's better to have it and not need it than to need it and not have it.

Asking the right questions during the interview

During the initial consultation, you find out about the attorney's background, skills, and qualifications, and whether the attorney has any conflicts of interest in regard to your case. Equally important, you can use the interview to get a better understanding of what you can expect from the litigation process.

The most important question you can ask during an interview is "What are my chances of recovery?" In other words, does the attorney think you'll win? You don't just want happy talk. You want an attorney who will tell you the unvarnished truth, particularly if your case is a long shot. Although it's most likely too soon for the attorney to have an opinion about the odds of your winning (after all, you do want her to do her homework and research the facts and legal issues before jumping to conclusions), she may able to tell you if there are elements to your claim that are flat-out losers. If the attorney doesn't think you'll win, even after looking into your claims further, she may take a pass on your case and refer you to someone else. Then you'll have to decide if the risk of going to court is worth it.

Potential conflicts of interest

At your interview, you want to make sure that your potential representative doesn't have a *conflict of interest* that may arise if he has previously represented your plan or a financial institution that invests money for your plan. In other words, you want an attorney who's going to look out for your best interests, not the plan's best interest. If he has been involved as an attorney with any aspect of your pension plan, he should disqualify himself. If he doesn't disqualify himself, do it for him, and end the interview at this point.

The questions you can ask to determine whether your case could be a conflict of interest for the attorney are pretty straightforward:

- ✔ Have you ever acted as the attorney for my pension plan, my company, or any of the big shots at my plan or company?

- ✔ Do you have a personal relationship or friendship with any of the key people at the plan or company?

- ✔ Is there any reason you might have a conflict of interest if you took my case?

Pension litigation experience

Because you need to find out about the prospective attorney's experience in the field of pension litigation, you can uncover this information by asking the attorney for details about her background. Here are some examples of questions you can ask and why you would ask them:

- ✔ **How many years have you been doing work in the area of pension law?** Obviously, someone who has been involved in pension work for several years is a better choice than someone who tells you that you're going to be his first pension client. The more years of experience, the better. We don't suggest hiring an attorney with fewer than five years of experience.

- ✔ **What percentage of your practice is involved in pension litigation?** You don't want someone to gain the bulk of her pension litigation experience on your case. You ideally want someone who has active pension cases on her *docket* (a list of cases that an attorney is currently handling) and who's handled at least five pension cases in the past. The preferred attorney is someone whose practice focuses mostly on pension issues.

  If because of location your choices are somewhat limited, find an attorney who has litigation experience with sophisticated issues. If she handles important civil (not criminal) matters and has litigated at least some pension cases with good results, this attorney may be okay. As we mention earlier, it is possible to go across state lines to recruit an attorney, but do remember that it may be difficult to find a qualified attorney who's willing to travel to your location (unless, of course, your case is of special interest to the attorney).

- ✔ **Have you handled matters involving public pension plans and/or private plans governed by ERISA?** As discussed earlier in the section "Identifying the type of attorney you need," you want someone who's familiar with the type of plan that you have. Make sure the attorney understands your type of plan and can explain to you the significant legal issues that are typical with it. If he can't, it's the blind leading the blind. After all, you're buying expert advice, not just a cheerleader.

✔ **Do you have courtroom experience?** You want an attorney who not only is familiar with pension plan documents, but also has courtroom experience litigating pension claims.

✔ **What types of claims have you litigated?** Find out the types of claims your attorney is familiar with and how her experience relates to your possible case. For example, if your claim involves the plan's violation of ERISA, you need an attorney who can handle those specifics. On the other hand, an attorney who brings cases concerning the types of investments that plans make won't necessarily be as familiar with claims that involve violations of ERISA.

You won't know her claims credentials unless you ask. In other words, don't be afraid to flesh this out during the interview. Simply ask how her experience litigating bad investment claims, for example, makes her qualified to bring an ERISA violation claim. You might be surprised.

✔ **Have you litigated claims on behalf of pensioners as well as employers?** If you find an attorney who has represented only employers in the past (not employees), before hiring the attorney, be sure that he's committed to your claim. You should ideally hire someone who understands and is sympathetic to employee issues and concerns. You want someone with a track record demonstrating that he's looking out for the little guy or gal. There are plenty of qualified employer-side attorneys, and you might find the right one for your claim, but generally, pension attorneys represent one side or the other.

✔ **What has your success rate been?** If the attorney has handled a number of pension cases and never won, before you say "Thanks, but no thanks," find out why she has never won a case. And keep in mind that just because an attorney has won 'em all doesn't mean she's the best around — she may take only the easy ones. Consider asking the attorney to tell you about the cases she's won and lost; attorneys like to share war stories, and you'll get a sense of how easy or complicated her victories or defeats were.

✔ **Have any of your cases produced published decisions?** A *published decision* comes about when a case has gone to trial, the court has ruled, and the decision is important enough that the court decides it should be published. More commonly, however, published decisions are *appellate* decisions, meaning that a trial court's decision has been appealed to a higher court called the Court of Appeals. If any of the attorney's cases have been published, this confirms that he's been involved in important pension litigation.

Don't forget to show the attorney the documents that she requested in order to review your case. If you don't already have an extra copy of these items, ask the attorney if she can make a copy of them so that you can keep the originals. Sometimes the documents may be too lengthy to copy at that moment, so if you can't wait for them, ask if you can pick them up later or if they can be returned to you by mail.

The working process

Make sure that you can work well with the attorney by asking the following questions:

- ✔ **What sort of communications can I expect from you?** You want someone who, at a minimum, returns your phone calls. You also want someone who's up front with how he expects to communicate with you. In other words, will he send you monthly or bimonthly updates even if nothing has happened in that interim?

  It's important to know what's going on, as it's going on, and you should find an attorney who will keep you up-to-date. Sometimes that means you won't hear anything for a while, and sometimes that's okay. The important things are that your attorney communicates with you when something happens and that he sends you copies of important correspondence and *pleadings* (the documents that are filed with the court). Litigation in general can take an extended period of time, and pension litigation is no exception. No matter how long the case takes, you should ask and expect your attorney's assurance that you'll be kept up-to-date as things happen and that your phone calls will be returned within 24 hours.

- ✔ **Can I expect that you'll be handling my case yourself, or will another attorney from your firm handle it instead?** If your prospective attorney is going to hand you off to another attorney, this may not necessarily be a bad thing. If the other attorney is just as experienced as your first choice, you're okay, but you need to know. Sometimes the entire law firm has similar experience, and you end up with an attorney who has more time to work on your case, not less. So, if another attorney is going to be involved, meet that attorney and ask her all the previous questions.

Miscellaneous info

You will, of course, have other questions about how long the case will take, what's expected of you as the client, and even the consequences of winning or losing. The anatomy of a pension suit is discussed in Chapter 20, but here are some of the questions that all clients should ask their attorneys:

- ✔ **What is the estimated value of my claim?** After your attorney has determined that you have a claim, a pension actuary usually calculates the estimated value of your claim (see the later section "Crunching Your

Pension Plan Numbers after You Hire an Attorney"). But estimates can change after your attorney has all the information. If your estimate changes, be sure to ask your attorney why.

✔ **How long will my case take?** Your attorney can give you an estimate based on experience, but much depends on unknowns, such as which judge is assigned to your case and whether opposing counsel is cooperative or fights every issue. From personal experience, we can say that pension cases go faster than most court cases, but that can still mean years.

✔ **What will I be expected to do?** For the most part, your attorney will take care of the case, but you may be expected to appear in court for pretrials or settlement conferences. You'll usually be required to provide written answers to questions posed by the other attorneys and to provide live testimony under oath to the opposing attorneys about the case. This is called *discovery.* If the case actually goes to trial, you'll have to take the stand and testify. (See Chapter 20 for details about your participation in the discovery process and trial.)

Discussing payment options

As you consider hiring an attorney, you might be thinking, "Who's going to pay for all this fine talent? Everyone knows you can't spend $10 to collect $7." Attorneys are paid two ways: by the hour and by contingency contract. The client often has the option to choose the preferred method of payment. So, specifically ask the attorney about his fees and then base your follow-up discussion on his answer and your preference.

The fees you pay no matter what

The litigation expenses and court costs are the same whether you hire an attorney on an hourly basis or on a contingency basis. A litigation expense isn't the same as the attorney's fee for time spent working on your case. You need to know what's included in litigation expenses, and make sure that the contract you're asked to sign (if you hire the attorney) spells this out. Some of the larger expenses will be incurred for pension actuaries or other experts as well as court reporters and deposition transcripts (see the later section "Crunching Your Pension Plan Numbers after You Hire an Attorney" for more about actuaries). You'll be expected to pay these expenses.

Ask the attorney if she'll pay these bills for you as they come in (referred to as *advancing the expenses*) or whether you'll be expected to pay them at that time. Most attorneys will advance payment on the larger expenses, but do find this out in advance. The contract usually indicates that the attorney is reimbursed for the expenses she advances out of your portion of the recovery. Some of the smaller expenses that you might be charged for include, for example, photocopy charges, postage, and long-distance phone calls.

As far as court costs are concerned, the first court cost you'll incur, if your case is filed, is the filing fee. This is a set rate, depending on the court you're filing in. And each time a motion or pleading is filed with the court, regardless of who files it, charges are incurred. The court clerk keeps track of these charges. If the case doesn't settle and goes to trial, additional charges are incurred. Presuming that you win the case or settle it in your favor, the other side typically pays (or reimburses) the court costs.

The hourly rate attorney

If your attorney is going to charge you by the hour, find out:

- **What items she charges for and what items she doesn't.** Will you be charged for time spent on phone calls, even if you only talk briefly? What if you run into your attorney at a restaurant or on the golf course and ask a question? Will you receive a bill in the mail? You need to understand what goes into the hourly rate.

- **An estimate of the charges and what they're based on.** Although an attorney may not be able to estimate specifically the amount of time he will spend, the attorney should be able to give you a ballpark guess as to how much time he'll spend on each stage of your case. You may want your attorney to assure you that you won't be charged an hourly rate until it's determined that in fact you have a case. Otherwise, you'll want an estimate as to how much money it will cost you to find out whether you have a case. If it's going to cost too much money (more than you have or are willing to pay) to make that determination, it may not be worth it. That's a choice you have to make.

- **How attorney time is billed (for example, by a tenth of an hour, a sixth of an hour, and so on).** If the attorney responds that you'll be charged, for example, by *a sixth of an hour,* that means that every time the attorney works on your case, you'll be charged a minimum of ten minutes time (a sixth of an hour), regardless if two minutes, eight minutes, or ten minutes of time are spent. On the other hand, if you'll be charged by *a tenth of an hour,* that means you'll be charged a minimum of six minutes time (a tenth of an hour), regardless whether two minutes or six minutes are spent. The result is obvious: You want someone who bills in the smallest increments possible so you don't pay for time that's not spent on your case.

- **When you will be billed.** Some attorneys send a monthly bill, and some wait until the case is over. Find out when you can expect to lay out cash. Your attorney may also want an up-front payment or retainer. A *retainer* is typically a payment for the attorney to get started and shouldn't be payment for all work and expenses in advance.

As with just about everything in life, hiring an hourly-rate attorney has its pros and cons:

- ✔ **Pros:** If your case is resolved quickly, you end up paying an hourly-rate attorney a lot less money than the contingency attorney because the earlier the case settles, the less attorney time you're paying for.

- ✔ **Cons:** The meter is always running. You'll feel constrained to check on your case if you're charged for your call to the attorney. Top attorneys charge from $300 to over $500 per hour. At those prices, some attorneys may worry that they're spending too much time on your case, while others may run up your bill just because they can. These concerns are avoided with the contingency attorney.

It's often expensive to hire an attorney on an hourly basis. If your claim isn't a sure thing, and if the attorney needs to do a lot of research to make the determination, you can spend a lot of money only to discover that you don't have a case.

The contingency attorney

The attorney who works on a contingency is a totally different animal from one who works on an hourly rate. Attorneys usually love contingency contracts, and generally clients do too. If an attorney offers to handle your case and proposes taking a percentage of your recovery, this is known as a *contingency fee contract.* Simply put, the attorney gets paid only if you win the case, which is why clients prefer contingency contracts. Attorneys favor them because they get a percentage of the recovery in the end. And the larger the recovery, the more the attorney (and the client) receive. It's a win-win situation for everyone. Because attorneys don't usually handle cases on a contingency basis if they don't think they'll win, they can devote as much time as necessary to ensure victory and not worry that their clients think they're running up the tab.

The typical range for contingency contracts is 25 percent to 40 percent of the recovery. That means the attorney's fee will be that percentage of however much money your case settles for or that you win in your lawsuit. But if there isn't a settlement, and you lose the case in court, you won't owe attorney's fees, and the attorney doesn't get paid for her time. So if the attorney takes your case, obviously she thinks your case is a winner.

In a typical contingency case, there's no charge for the attorney's time, but you're still responsible for the expenses that will be deducted from your portion of the recovery. Some states allow contingency attorneys to advance litigation expenses and agree to waive their repayment at the end of the suit, or even to assume the expenses of litigation. Ask the attorney whether that's permitted in your state and whether he'll agree to waive the repayment of these expenses in the event that you lose the case and have no means of repaying them.

In a contingency contract, your attorney risks not earning a fee; therefore, if you do win, the fee will likely be higher than on an hourly basis.

Generally, an attorney agrees to a contingency contract if your potential for recovery is high and/or if she can serve as counsel on behalf of many people who have a claim similar to yours. This is known as a *class action lawsuit*. You can read more about class actions in Chapter 20. If your case is a class action and you're the class representative, the fees are awarded by the court, and the expenses wind up being apportioned among all the members of the class. So if there are 1,000 class members, each one is responsible for a small part of the total expenses.

If you and your attorney are in agreement that the fee will be paid on a contingency, make sure you read the contingency contract closely and understand its provisions. Be sure you know who's responsible for the expenses and how they're to be paid in the event of a win or a loss. Many contingency contracts provide a sliding fee scale in which the contingency percentage increases if the case goes to trial. In other words, the attorney receives a lower percentage for a settlement and a higher percentage when the case proceeds to trial.

Whether you make a decision that day or not, ask to see the contract that you'll be asked to sign. If there's something in the contract that you don't like or don't want to agree to, don't be afraid to ask if the attorney is willing to negotiate the terms. This isn't an unusual request.

Making your decision

After your first interview is completed, if you feel this attorney meets your needs, you can select this person. If you have any hesitation, however, or simply want to have two candidates to compare, return to your list of attorney choices and repeat the interview process with choice number two from your list.

Trust your instincts. If you've done your homework and your prospective attorney seems to know his stuff, you're comfortable with him, and your instincts tell you he has your best interests at heart, you've probably made a good choice. But if from the get-go, something about the attorney makes you uncomfortable, trust yourself and move on to your second choice, because once you're in the midst of litigation it may be too late to switch.

If you've decided *not* to hire this attorney, don't forget to let him know (and thank him for his time, of course). But if you've made the decision that this is the attorney you want to hire, keep reading to find out what happens next. If you didn't sign the attorney–client contract (also called a *retainer agreement*) in your first meeting with the attorney, call and tell him that you want to retain his services, and then schedule an appointment to get the ball rolling.

At that appointment, you'll sign the retainer agreement, which officially authorizes the attorney to proceed on your behalf. The agreement spells out the fee and expense arrangement, as we discuss in the earlier sections. Even though some contracts include an appeal, many won't. If an appeal isn't included, this can be handled through a new contract if and when the need arises. Finally, both you and your attorney should be clear as to what the agreement requires of each of you.

Crunching Your Pension Plan Numbers after You Hire an Attorney

After interviewing your potential attorney candidates and selecting one that fits the bill, what's the attorney going to do for you? First, she'll collect the pension plan documents that we hope you've retained over the years and perhaps brought with you to the interview. These may include any or all of the following (which are more fully explained in Chapter 8):

✔ Benefit election form

✔ Collective bargaining agreement (if you're in a union)

✔ Individual benefit statement

✔ Summary annual report (SAR)

✔ Summary of material modifications (SMM) or a revised summary plan description

✔ Summary plan description (SPD)

✔ The trust agreement

✔ The full plan document

✔ Written correspondence, such as the following:

  • Letters from the plan advising of modifications to the plan

  • Letters informing you that you won't be receiving a benefit

  • Notices regarding the plan's funding status

  • Copies of written inquiries that you made to the plan requesting information or action regarding your pension

If you haven't previously requested or received the preceding information or haven't kept these items, your attorney sends a letter to the plan administrator (which every plan is required by law to designate) requesting whatever documents are missing. The administrator has a limited period of time to provide certain requested information.

Upon receipt of the necessary plan information, your attorney meticulously reviews the plan documents and compares them with the SPD to determine whether the language between the plan and the SPD is consistent. The attorney also reviews your plan documents to determine whether they're consistent with the federal or state laws that govern your plan.

If your attorney concludes that the plan violated the law, he must then determine whether you have a lawsuit. Your attorney may need to send your information to an expert number cruncher (called an *actuary*) to determine whether you've suffered a loss, and if so, how much you've been damaged.

A pension actuary has very specialized training to calculate the value of pension benefits. He examines your pension plan and *benefits calculations* (what you're receiving or what you expect to receive based on the formula in the plan) and compares those benefits with what you should have received if the law was properly followed or the numbers correctly crunched. Ultimately, the pension actuary figures out whether you lost any money and the tentative amount of damages you may have suffered. This helps determine the potential value of your case, which in turn helps your attorney determine whether your case is worth bringing.

Based on what the attorney learns from the actuary, if the attorney determines that you indeed have a case, it's time to move forward, either with an individual claim or a class action suit. Chapter 20 has the full scoop.

Keeping an Eye on Your Relationship with Your Attorney

It goes without saying that you attract more bees with honey. So if you treat your attorney with TLC, your positive attorney–client relationship can take you a long way. If your attorney doesn't respond to your TLC, you can take steps to put your working relationship back on track. But if that doesn't work and all else fails, you can always end things and hire another attorney.

Giving a little TLC

Treat your attorney with TLC: Trust, Look, and Concern. For instance:

- ✔ **Trust the attorney's advice.** Let your attorney develop the legal arguments and deal with the pension plans. Don't send letters to the plan or the judge, offering your two cents. Your attorney is your legal representative, and all communications are now her responsibility.

✔ **Look at the work that your attorney produces for you.** This includes the complaint he drafts on your behalf that sets forth the basis of your claims and any motions, pleadings, or briefs that he files with the court.

Reviewing his work gives you the opportunity to see that all the proper facts and information have been set out correctly, and it also assures you that your attorney is actually doing the work.

✔ **Show concern on an ongoing basis about the outcome of your case.** This is part of the squeaky-wheel maxim. Good attorneys are busy; you want an attorney to resist the temptations to put your case at the bottom of the pile. Although your lawyer is likely busy, she'll still expect you to call in every few weeks to see what's happening. After all, even though your attorney may have many cases, she knows that this is your only case and will therefore understand your concern.

Although it may be amusing to the public to compare attorneys to sharks, the simple truth is that without your own personal shark, you can't navigate the waters of the legal system. You aren't hiring a predator; you're hiring a dedicated advocate who's familiar with the deep waters you now find yourself in. He'll navigate the shoals, protect your interests, and defend your rights. Your attorney will commit his skill, time, and heart to righting your wrong. Most often an attorney's motivation is not just a fee, but also a passion for justice. You'll be amazed at how much your attorney will treasure a simple "thank you" for a job well done.

Seeing signs that your big shot is a big flop

Your lawyer works for you — not the reverse. Repeat after me: "The attorney works for *me.*" Although no attorney likes to admit that bad attorneys are out there, it's true. As in every profession, there are good eggs and bad eggs. The trick is to identify a bad egg before it spoils your breakfast. Here are some warning signs:

✔ Your phone calls aren't being returned.

✔ When you do reach your attorney, you find out that it's been many months since anything has happened, and the only explanation offered is "I've been busy."

✔ Your case has been filed in court, and the attorney has been on the losing end of most of the battles.

Losing a *motion* (a request to the court to rule in your favor on a particular matter) doesn't necessarily mean that your attorney is a bad egg, but the combination of not winning and poor communication indicates that something isn't right.

If you reach the point that you're concerned about your lawyer, whether it's early on or down the road, it's best to address your concerns with her head on. Do this *before* you make the difficult decision to replace your attorney in the midst of litigation. She may be able to resolve your concerns and assure you that your fears were misplaced. Or she may be willing and able to make an adjustment to resolve the problem. On the other hand, after discussing your concerns with your attorney, it may become obvious that it's time for a change.

If you terminate your attorney–client relationship after the litigation has begun, you must be certain that you have a replacement. A lawsuit without an attorney is like a ship without a rudder. All cases have to be filed within certain periods of time. So if you fire your lawyer just before the time is about to run out to file your case, you may not be able to find an attorney to prepare a complaint and get your case filed in time.

Terminating the relationship

If you're dissatisfied with your attorney's services and haven't received a satisfactory response to your concerns, send the attorney a letter terminating his services. Make sure you do the following:

- ✔ Include a brief summary of your case, including all outstanding matters that you're aware of. Request that the attorney advise your new counsel of any important deadlines in your case.

- ✔ Ask for a bill for services (if you're paying by the hour) and a list of all expenses to date.

- ✔ Obtain a release of your obligations under the contract, and be certain that once your relationship is terminated you don't owe him anything else. If the dismissed attorney claims he's entitled to something in the event that your next attorney wins your case, clarify in writing what he claims he's entitled to. Likewise, release your attorney of his obligations under the contract so that you can hire another attorney.

- ✔ Ask the attorney to prepare your file so you can pick it up.

If your attorney acts unethically or unprofessionally, you can file a complaint with the grievance committee of your local bar association.

Chapter 20

Dissecting a
Pension Lawsuit

. . . .

In This Chapter

▶ Getting a grip on ERISA's rules for pension lawsuits

▶ Tracking a typical pension lawsuit from start to finish

▶ Examining the process of payment

. . . .

*W*hen diplomacy has failed, and you've done everything to follow the
rules in order to receive your rightful pension (and whether you
haven't seen a penny or have been collecting the wrong benefits for years),
your final recourse is a lawsuit. But believe us when we say that a lawsuit is
the legal equivalent of an armed conflict. It isn't always pretty.

At this point, you've probably done the following to try and get what belongs
to you:

✔ You've filed your request for a pension distribution (see Chapters 9 and
17), but the plan said, "Sorry, Charlie." It had a different idea about the
amount you should get.

✔ You've filed your administrative appeal (see Chapter 18), and to that the
plan said, "Hit the road, Jack."

✔ You've decided that despite the plan's refusal to see it your way, you're
right, and the plan is wrong. So you followed the steps in Chapter 19 and
found a qualified pension attorney who's chomping at the bit to champion your cause.

Now that you're ready for a lawsuit, this chapter takes you on a tour of what
to expect.

Examining ERISA's Rules for Pension Lawsuits

The Employee Retirement Income Security Act of 1974 (ERISA; see Chapter 2) governs the tax-qualified pension plans that we describe in Chapter 3, so it only makes sense that it has a say in how lawsuits against those pension plans are carried out. In the following sections, we explain what you can sue for and what your employer can't do to you if you choose to sue under ERISA's provisions.

What does ERISA allow you to sue for?

If you're a participant or beneficiary of a tax-qualified pension plan that's governed by ERISA, you can initiate a civil action in court to enforce certain rights. In other words, you can sue in order to do the following:

- ✔ Recover benefits owed to you and enforce your rights under the plan

- ✔ Gain access to plan documents that you requested in writing and that weren't provided within 30 days (you can find a list of these documents in Chapter 8)

- ✔ Clarify your right to benefits that you have yet to receive

- ✔ Obtain relief from a breach of fiduciary duty; if the plan's fiduciaries are squandering the money that should be used for your pension, you can go to court to put a stop to it and recover lost funds (see Chapter 10 for details about fiduciaries)

- ✔ Require the plan to give you a statement of your vested benefits after leaving work (Chapter 7 has the scoop on vesting)

- ✔ Get an injunction to prevent or restrain the plan from violating its own provisions or ERISA

- ✔ Get a review of an action by the Pension Benefit Guaranty Corporation (PBGC) that has harmed you (see Chapter 12 for more about the PBGC)

- ✔ Get a review of a final action of the Department of Labor (DOL) in order to either restrain the DOL or force it to take action according to ERISA

The Secretary of Labor has discretion to join in lawsuits filed in federal court to enforce ERISA rights. In other words, if the government thinks that the issues in your case are important enough or will have a wide-ranging impact, it can choose to get involved in your lawsuit in order to have a say in the outcome.

Legal wins by the little guys

You can find example after example of pensioners taking on their plans and recovering the distributions that they were entitled to receive. They may have required more than a slingshot, but here are a few examples of David, the pensioner, bringing down Goliath:

✔ A class of pensioners brought a case against a bank, claiming that the bank violated its fiduciary obligation to the plan. The pensioners recovered $15.45 million.

✔ Pensioners initiated a case against an employer, claiming that their lump sum payments violated the anti-cutback rule. More than 5,000 pensioners recovered $48.5 million.

✔ Pensioners filed a claim that their lump-sum distributions, which were paid from a cash balance plan, weren't the same as if they had elected an annuity. Several thousand pensioners recovered $240 million.

✔ A class of pensioners filed suit against their plan for miscalculation of benefits, and they recovered $2.9 million.

✔ Former employees sued their employer because the plan used the wrong interest rate to calculate their lump sums. Twelve thousand pensioners won and recovered $51 million.

✔ Employees sued because their company attempted to get out of its pension obligation by laying off employees who were close to retirement. The employees won, and 2,500 workers were awarded $415 million.

✔ Pensioners brought an action against directors of a bank because corporate insiders sold stock to an employee stock ownership plan at inflated prices. Five hundred employees received $9.35 million.

✔ Participants in a pension plan sued their company for wasting plan assets and improperly paying certain investment expenses out of the plan. Hooray for the pensioners — 40,000 recovered $141.73 million.

✔ Pensioners sued their company and its pension plan because they overestimated Social Security benefits and violated certain provisions of ERISA. Yet again, the pensioners were victorious, and 75,000 received $80.9 million.

✔ Early retirees (represented by your authors and their law firm) sued their cash balance pension plan because the lump sum benefits they received weren't the actuarial equivalent of the benefits they would have been entitled to receive at age 65. Judgment in the amount of more than $46 million (the amount of the underpaid benefits plus prejudgment interest) was upheld by a court of appeals on behalf of more than 1,200 pensioners.

The point is this: A plan can find a host of opportunities and reasons to not pay the benefits that it owes (and to which you're entitled!). From the previous examples, you can see that the reasons and opportunities range from using the wrong interest rate in the calculation of lump sums to laying off employees to avoid paying them their pension benefits.

And remember that when pensioners sue as a class, collectively they have the muscle to bring about significant victories. This list is far from complete, so don't be fooled into thinking that because the plan and company are big and powerful, they can't be beat. In a lawsuit, one side wins and one side loses; in pension litigation, however, the law and the facts win out. If you've been wronged, don't be afraid to fight for what you've earned.

Should you worry about retaliation from your employer?

When contemplating whether you should sue your employer's pension plan, you won't be the first employee to be concerned about possible retaliation. Luckily, you don't have to be concerned, because according to ERISA, your employer can't take any of the following actions just because you or your beneficiary are attempting to enforce your rights under your pension plan:

- ✔ Terminate your employment
- ✔ Fine you
- ✔ Suspend you
- ✔ Expel you from the workplace
- ✔ Discipline you (for example, by writing you up as a bad employee or docking your pay)
- ✔ Discriminate against you

Neither can your employer take any of the previously listed actions against you for testifying or providing information in a proceeding related to ERISA. In fact, the use of force or violence to restrain, coerce, or intimidate you is a criminal offense and punishable by a fine of up to $10,000 and/or a year in jail. If your employer steps over the line with force, you can turn him in to law enforcement, and if he fires you, you can sue him. As a practical matter, your employer knows that you have rights and usually will leave you alone.

Before You Begin: Preparing to File a Complaint

Before you even file a complaint (which is the first document you file to start your lawsuit), you and your attorney must put in some prep time. You need to hand over a lot of important paperwork, and you and your attorney must make an important decision: whether to file your complaint individually or on behalf of the many people in the same circumstance as you.

Sharing your documents with your attorney

Your attorney needs certain documents from you in order to get started on your case. These documents include the following critical plan records that we mention in Chapter 8:

- ✔ The summary plan description (SPD)

- ✔ The plan document (the unabridged pension plan document, including all its provisions, that's summarized by the SPD)

- ✔ All plan amendments (usually found in a revised SPD or a summary of material modifications)

- ✔ Your individual benefit statement, along with any and all documents prepared by the company to explain what you'll receive when you retire

- ✔ Any legal documents that the plan asked you to sign, such as a *release of claim* (also known as a *waiver of your rights*)

- ✔ Any correspondence between you and the plan

- ✔ All the records that were submitted in your administrative appeal

- ✔ All opinions from the plan regarding your administrative appeal

Before your attorney can determine whether you have a case, he or she must review what the plan says you're entitled to receive. The attorney will have to assess whether you're getting what you've been promised or whether the plan's method of calculating your benefits somehow violates ERISA. To reach these conclusions, the previously listed important plan papers must be carefully reviewed by your attorney (and perhaps a pension actuary) for further analysis. When it comes to pension litigation, it's all about the documents. Pension law is complex, but almost all the necessary information is available before you start a lawsuit.

Deciding whether to file solo or as part of a class action

It's likely that if you had problems receiving the proper payout from your pension plan, a number of other people are in the same boat as you. Your attorney can determine whether your claim is unique to you or is the type of error that will impact other pensioners the same way it impacts you. In this case, one of the issues that you have to consider is whether to file a lawsuit that pertains to just you or to participate in a lawsuit that you file on behalf of all others who are similarly situated. This type of lawsuit is referred to as a *class action.*

Essentially, with a class action, you're asking the court to consider your case to be filed on behalf of all plan participants who have suffered the same type of loss as you have. Class actions are quite common in pension litigation because the plan usually treats all pensioners the same, so a mistake made in the calculation of your benefits may very well apply to a number of other people.

So how do you decide whether to file as an individual or participate in a class action suit? The primary advantages to filing an action on your own behalf include the following:

- ✔ The particular procedures that are part and parcel of class action litigation can be avoided, which may mean that your case will proceed more quickly. (We cover these particular procedures later in this chapter.)

- ✔ If you file your case individually, you'll be more in control of the outcome. In other words, if you decide to settle, it's your decision alone, and that decision won't affect hundreds or thousands of other people and require court approval.

There are, however, powerful benefits to filing your pension case as a class action. For example, consider these advantages:

- ✔ When you're part of a large group of people, it's less likely that your company can wear you down or stonewall the litigation.

- ✔ Top attorneys who have the necessary skill and resources to litigate against major corporations will be more willing to represent your claim on a contingency basis when they can represent hundreds or thousands of people at one time through one lawsuit. Even though the attorney won't receive compensation if you lose the case, that's a gamble that he or she is willing to take because if you win, the attorney may be awarded a substantial fee by the court. When a case is filed individually, however, the attorney usually asks to be paid on an hourly basis. (Chapter 19 has more information on paying an attorney.)

- ✔ Ultimately, the costs of the case may be spread out among the entire class rather than being paid by just one person.

- ✔ If your case can be brought as a class action, your attorney may request additional compensation for you, as the class representative, to reflect the extra work that you'll have to do. However, it's within the discretion of the court whether to award you that additional compensation. We discuss the responsibilities of a class representative later in this chapter.

Exactly what will you be getting yourself into if you decide to file a class action suit and become a class representative? You'll be expected to respond to inquiries (known as *discovery*) from the pension plan's attorney. These inquiries will help him or her determine whether your claim is the same as the claims of the other plan participants you want to include in your case. (We elaborate on discovery later in this chapter.) Suffice it to say that as a class representative, it's your responsibility to participate in this process, to look out for the interests of the other class members, and to follow through with the lawsuit until its conclusion.

Get Ready to Rumble: Filing a Complaint

Every case starts with the filing of a complaint by an attorney. The *complaint* is the legal document that describes your claims and puts your pension plan (also known as the *defendant*) on notice of the claims being asserted against it. Whether you're filing on your own behalf or as a class representative, every complaint must include certain basic components, which we discuss in the following sections.

The essential elements of any complaint

Along with the name of the plaintiff (that's you) and the identity of the defendant (your pension plan), a complaint always has the following crucial components:

- ✔ **The nature of the claim.** For example, if your plan used the wrong interest rate to convert your annuity to a lump sum, the complaint needs to say so.

- ✔ **An explanation noting that the complaint is being filed as a class action suit.** So, if your claim is being asserted on behalf of all other pensioners in your plan with the same problem, the complaint must say so, and the identities of the retirees who make up the class must be specified. (See the following section for more about class action complaints.)

- ✔ **A list of the errors made by the plan, a calculation of these damages, and what you hope to recover from the lawsuit.** What we mean is that you must make note of the compensation that you (and the group or class that you hope to represent) are seeking for the shortfall in your pension, including your claim for interest and attorney's fees.

- ✔ **The identity of the court in which your case is being filed.** For example, if ERISA regulates your pension plan, a federal statute is involved, and your case will presumably be filed in a federal court, such as the U.S. District Court for the Southern District of Ohio. If your pension plan is a creature of state law, such as a state teachers' or police pension fund, the complaint will be filed in state court.

The particulars of filing a class action complaint

As you can imagine, filing a class action suit can be complicated and time-consuming. And, of course, as with any legal process, you have plenty of rules to follow. So, in the following sections, we go over the process of filing a class action complaint: meeting some special requirements, requesting class certification, and distributing a class notice if your request is granted.

Meeting the requirements of a class action complaint

To be valid, a class action complaint must meet the following requirements:

- ✔ A sufficient number of pensioners must have the same problem. For example, class actions typically range in class size from 30 up to tens of thousands.

  If the wrongdoing that's alleged in your complaint is continuing, at some point during the lawsuit the court will require your attorney to establish a cutoff date for determining the members of the class. Without such a date, you would never be able to determine the class's size or its damages and therefore would never be able to resolve the case.

- ✔ At some point in the lawsuit, the class members must be able to be identified. If the members can't be identified, you can't make a claim on their behalf. Usually the attorney filing the lawsuit must determine all the people who are part of the class. This determination is easily accomplished from the plan's records because the plan keeps track of all its participants. If the court rules that your case can go forward as a class action, all members of the class must be notified in writing about the case. (We discuss this notice later in the chapter.)

- ✔ All the pensioners must have the same legal problem. This concept is called *commonality*. An example is "all pensioners who worked at the company during a certain stated period of time, who took their pension benefits in a lump-sum distribution as opposed to an annuity, with their benefits having been calculated with the wrong interest rate."

- ✔ The claims stated in the complaint on behalf of you, the class representative, must be the same as or typical of the claims of the other pensioners whom you assert are part of the class. To be the class representative, you must have a claim that's the same as everyone else's. This is called *typicality*.

- ✔ The court must be convinced that your interest in bringing the case is in the best interests of the rest of the group and that you picked a lawyer who not only knows what he or she is doing, but also has class action experience.

✔ A class action must be the best way to handle these claims, and the common issues must be more significant than any differences that exist. In other words, there's no better way for the pensioners to assert their claims; for example, it may be cost prohibitive for them to file their own individual cases.

If you meet the special requirements to bring a class action, you don't need permission from the individual class members to proceed on their behalf.

Seeking class certification

If your complaint states that you're seeking class action status, one of the first pleadings that your attorney will file is called a *motion to certify the class* (certification of the class is necessary for the case to proceed as a class action). Attached to that motion will be a memorandum that demonstrates how your case satisfies all the requirements in the previous section. The more information and documentation that your attorney includes to prove fulfillment of the requirements, the better your chances that the court will certify the class. The SPD and the other plan documents you submitted to your attorney (we cover this task earlier in this chapter) indicate whether your problem impacts an entire group or is a mistake that applies only to you.

As part of the U.S. judicial system, the opposing party (in this case, the pension plan) has the opportunity to oppose the motion to certify, and most times it will do so after taking your deposition and after conducting other discovery to refute your class action allegations. (We dive into the details of discovery later in this chapter.) The party opposing the motion to certify will file a motion with the court arguing that you haven't met the requirements for your case to be considered a class action. This battle between the attorneys and the court will decide which side wins.

After the motion to certify has been successfully filed, the court has the option to hold a hearing for further argument on the issue of class certification. After any hearings take place, the court will rule on the motion to certify the class. Obviously, the earlier you know, the better, because then you have an idea of how to proceed with your lawsuit:

✔ If the court determines that you haven't met all the elements to support class certification, your case will proceed on your individual behalf and for your claims only.

✔ If the court decides that you've satisfied the requirements for a class action and that you're a satisfactory class representative, the judge will certify the class, and your lawsuit will proceed as a class action.

✔ The court may find that the case can be a class action but that the person bringing the case (that's you) isn't the right person to represent the class because your particular claim is different, you have some agenda that makes your interest incompatible with the class's interest, or your attorney isn't experienced enough to represent the class. In many of these situations, the problem can be corrected by using, if available, a more suitable class representative or adding an experienced class action attorney to the legal team.

Check with your lawyer to determine whether you can appeal the court's ruling on class certification. The answer may differ depending on whether you're in state court or federal court.

Sending out a notice

After the court certifies your case as a class action, it will send out a notice to all the people who are part of your proposed class and who will be affected by any decision made in the case. So, if 2,000 people are in the class, the court will send out 2,000 notices telling every pensioner about the case and giving them a chance to opt out of the case if they don't want to be included. The notice must

- ✔ Be sent by first-class mail to the last known address of each class member

- ✔ Describe the nature of the claims and define the class generally (for example, "All participants in the ABC Pension Plan who retired between January 13, 2005, and March 17, 2007")

- ✔ Provide specific procedures for opting out if anyone decides not to participate in the litigation

- ✔ Explain that if the class member stays in the case, he or she will be bound by the result

- ✔ Identify the attorney (or attorneys) for the class

- ✔ Provide a method or person to answer the class members' questions; the attorney's name and telephone number are included in the notice so that potential class members can contact him or her with any questions

- ✔ Be published in local newspapers in a shorter form to notify those people who fail to receive the notice by mail

Understanding the Plan's Response to the Complaint

Your pension plan usually has the following two choices when responding to the complaint, whether it's an individual case or a class action:

✔ **Filing a motion to dismiss:** By filing a *motion to dismiss,* the plan can ask the court to toss out your case, alleging that the complaint doesn't set out a legitimate claim that entitles you to compensation. It's unusual for a court to grant this motion and dismiss a case on the initial filing by the plan, but it does happen. If such a motion is filed, you have 20 days to respond; your attorney will file a brief with the court setting out the legal reasons why your case shouldn't be dismissed.

✔ **Filing an answer:** If the pension plan doesn't file a motion to dismiss, or if the court denies the plan's motion to dismiss, the plan must file an answer to the complaint.

The purpose of an answer to a complaint is to allow a plan to admit or deny the specific allegations that are set forth in your complaint and to raise its defenses. The plan must assert certain defenses now, or it loses its right to raise them later. Defenses include such things as filing the case too late or having previously signed a release, forever waiving your rights to a claim.

Whatever option the plan chooses, the response must be filed in federal court within 20 days of receiving the summons and the complaint. In state court, this period of time may be a bit longer. But everyone knows, either from personal experience or from those experiences of friends or families, that if these short time periods were actually adhered to, litigation wouldn't drone on for years. So don't be surprised when the plan requests an extension of time to respond (and kindly remember that you may need additional time to respond to a motion down the road as well).

Getting the Goods: The Discovery Process

After the pension plan files its answer to your complaint, the next stage of litigation is called *discovery.* Your participation in discovery will be an important part of the case, either as an individual plaintiff or as a class representative. Each party (both you and the pension plan) has the right to conduct discovery, and each party is governed by the same rules. The purpose of discovery is to find out what the other party knows about the claims and defenses asserted, to get all the details that will make or break your case, to nail down people's testimonies, and to gather all the critical documents. Discovery is conducted in two ways: in writing (with interrogatories and requests for production of documents) and orally (with depositions). Both methods are described in the following sections.

Interrogatories and requests for production of documents

Two types of written discovery are at your disposal:

- ✔ **Interrogatories:** This type of discovery is in the form of written questions, which are submitted by the lawyers to the opposing parties. As the plaintiff, you're expected to answer the questions. Your lawyer then reviews your answers for accuracy and responsiveness to the questions. In addition, if any questions are considered inappropriate, your attorney objects to them and states the basis of the objection (such as the question is beyond the scope of what the plan is allowed to ask you). Your answers are then submitted in a timely manner to the defendant pension plan, usually within the 30-day time period allotted (unless an extension of time is requested).

  Each party may submit more than one set of questions during the course of the litigation. For example, the plan's attorney may ask you to specify your financial loss and ask you why you claim the plan is responsible.

- ✔ **Requests for production of documents:** The purpose of a *request for production of documents* is to find out what documents the other party has to support their claims or defenses. As a plaintiff, you'll most likely be asked to produce all the documents that you initially provided to your attorney, such as your benefit statement and SPD, even though the plan already has copies of these documents. The attorney for the plan wants to know what your lawyer relied on to file your complaint. (We describe the documents that you must provide to your attorney earlier in this chapter.) You'll likely be asked to provide other records relating to your claim as well. These records may include your birth certificate (to confirm your age) and employment records from another job (if you had a break in service during your employment). Your attorney will guide you in deciding which documents you need to produce in response to the plan's request.

Just because the attorneys submit interrogatories and requests for production of documents doesn't guarantee that either side will provide the sought-after information. For instance, the attorneys may object to providing the information if they determine that the request is too broad or burdensome or that the information isn't relevant to the lawsuit. In the case of pension litigation, keep in mind that it's the plan that has most of the documents, so it's the plan's attorney who will be doing most of the objecting. And remember that as the plaintiff, all the documents that you have are frequently documents that the plan has as well, so you have nothing to hide.

If either party refuses to provide relevant documents after good-faith attempts to get the party to do so, the other party has one weapon to possibly turn things around: It can file a *motion to compel* with the court. The purpose of this motion is to ask the judge to compel the refusing party to answer the interrogatories or to produce the requested documents. As with other motions that are filed with the court, the opposing party is provided a limited period of time to respond to your motion (usually less than a month, depending on whether you're in federal court or state court). The court then issues its order and either grants the motion and orders that the documents or information be provided, or denies the motion and refuses to compel the other party to produce anything.

The battles that take place between the attorneys will be handled by the attorneys, so the best advice that we can give you is to let your attorney do his or her job and not let yourself get aggravated.

Depositions

In addition to the requests for production of documents and the interrogatories, the other type of discovery available to the parties is known as the *deposition*. A deposition, which is the oral form of discovery, is when the opposing attorney asks you questions, under oath, about the claims asserted in your lawsuit. During the testimony, a court reporter records your answers on a special machine that's made just for this purpose (the reporter frequently also records the testimony digitally via a computer). Your attorney is present at the deposition to make sure the opposing attorney asks you only proper questions. If the opposing attorney does ask any inappropriate questions, your attorney will pipe up before you answer and object.

Attorneys take oral depositions because they can get longer answers and explanations to their questions and attempt to trip up the *deponent* (the person answering the questions). Because you're answering on the spot, with little time to prepare an answer, it enables the attorney to judge your credibility and see how believable a witness you'll be in court. After the testimony is completed and transcribed by the court reporter, the deponent gets the opportunity to review, but not change, his or her testimony.

Being deposed is a bit daunting, especially if you haven't ever been through a deposition, but your attorney is there to help you. He or she will fully explain the routine in advance, do a bit of role-playing to help you feel comfortable, and remind you to carefully listen to the question that's being asked before you answer it. Your attorney will also stop the other attorney from bullying or intimidating you. But by far the best advice that your attorney will give you is to always tell the truth.

In It to Win It: Stating Your Case to the Court

After the discovery phase is concluded, you've reached a critical junction in your pension case. At this point, essentially all the facts are known (they've been discovered), and either or both parties may be eager to file a *motion for summary judgment* with the court, asking that judgment be rendered in their favor, without a trial. This motion saves time and further expenses. But even if your attorney opts to file this motion, you still may find yourself going to trial and even having to appeal a decision against you. But of course, we hope your lawsuit ends with an acceptable settlement in your favor. In the following sections, we walk you through the process of going to court.

Moving for summary judgment

When a party files a motion for summary judgment, it must allege that based on the law and the facts, it's entitled to judgment at that point because:

- ✔ No material facts are in dispute.
- ✔ The law supports their position and not their opponent's.

Pension cases are somewhat different from other lawsuits, because both parties usually agree on the facts but disagree about whether the facts constitute a violation of the law. So, many pension cases are decided based on a legal interpretation of whether the plan or the conduct of the plan violated ERISA or some other law. The other side is always given the opportunity to respond to the motion, and because this motion can ultimately end the case, the opposing party usually has no fewer than 30 days to respond (this time period can vary depending on whether your case is in federal court or state court). Additional time is frequently extended to the parties.

If the court grants summary judgment, the party that filed the motion wins the case, and the other side may appeal the decision (we discuss appeals later in this chapter). If the court doesn't grant summary judgment, the case proceeds to trial.

Going to trial and awaiting judgment

Anyone who has a TV has likely seen a jury trial. Most pension cases, however, are tried without a jury because ERISA doesn't provide for a trial by jury. At a pension trial, you and the pension plan present the witnesses and evidence gathered during the discovery process (which we cover earlier in this chapter) to the court. At the conclusion of the testimony, the judge renders a decision, and the following happens:

- ✔ If the decision is in favor of the defendant (the pension plan), you, the plaintiff, lose, but you have the right to appeal.
- ✔ If the judgment is in favor of the plaintiff or the plaintiff class (that's you), you win. The pension plan can appeal the decision.

The losing party has a limited period of time — usually 30 days — to file an appeal. We discuss appeals in more detail later in this chapter.

Accepting a settlement if you win

As a practical matter, if you win the lawsuit, don't expect the pension plan to pull out its checkbook and simply write a check for the amount that it owes. This rarely occurs. If there's a judgment rendered against a plan, the plan usually attempts to compromise and settle at a lower amount. The motivation for you to consider a settlement is to avoid the risk of the judgment being overturned on appeal, which is always a very real risk. (See the following section for more about appeals.) It's the job of your attorney, not you, to negotiate any settlement, and it's the attorney's obligation to keep you informed about the progress of the negotiations. The trial court has no say as to whether you settle or not.

If you choose, you (in an individually filed case) can order your attorney to settle even if he or she thinks it's a bad idea. However, what's the point of hiring a good attorney and then ignoring the attorney's advice? We recommend that you listen to your attorney for the best results.

If after much negotiation, you're ready to accept a settlement in an amount less than the judgment, you're free to do so as long as you're proceeding as an individual plaintiff in your own individual case (rather than as a class representative). In fact, you're free to settle at any amount that you deem acceptable and that the plan agrees to pay.

If your case was initially certified as a class action, however, settlements are a different story. It's not your decision as the class representative to accept a settlement offer. Your attorney is certainly free to negotiate with the plan to see what it's willing to pay to resolve the claims, but you don't have the right to accept a settlement. This is because as a class representative, you have an obligation to proceed in the best interests of the class. And even though you may not like the offer extended, it's possible that the court will determine the offer to be in the best interest of the class.

If your attorney believes that the plan's offer may be in the class's best interest, it's up to the court to make the ultimate determination, and it will do so through a *Fairness Hearing*. This hearing determines whether you, as the class representative, and your attorney have protected the best interests of the class. To assure fairness to everyone, a hearing is held so that class members can learn the details, and if they don't approve, they have a chance to be heard. Here's a bare-bones outline of the typical hearing process:

1. A notice of the proposed settlement is sent to all class members describing the terms of the settlement.

2. The members of the class are given the date of the Fairness Hearing, and then they have the opportunity to object to the settlement.

3. Each member of the class is given a chance to review all the court filings and find out how much he or she will receive.

4. The court takes testimony and evidence at the Fairness Hearing and determines whether the settlement is fair. The court also awards the attorney's fees and expenses.

Appealing the decision if you lose

So you've lost your lawsuit and want to appeal the decision. First things first: If your original case was in a U.S. District Court, according to ERISA, you appeal to the U.S. Court of Appeals for that district. Likewise, state cases that took place in state trial courts will be appealed to state appellate courts.

If you lose and your case is a class action, the whole class loses, too. To appeal your loss, your attorney must file a notice of appeal (either on your behalf, if your case was filed on an individual basis, or on behalf of you and the class, if it was filed as a class action) and order that the record of the case be sent to the appropriate appellate court. Then your attorney has to file a legal brief with the court of appeals that specifies why the lower court's decision was wrong. The plan files an opposing brief. No new evidence is offered, and the case is decided on whatever evidence was in front of the trial court (which is why the entire record is sent to the appeals court).

If the plan loses the lawsuit and chooses to appeal, it must post a bond to ensure that the judgment can be paid if it loses the appeal. If the plan loses the appeal, and it's an ERISA case, the final recourse is an appeal to the U.S. Supreme Court (which chooses to hear very few cases). State pension cases (in other words, non-ERISA cases involving state funds, teacher unions, and so on) can be appealed to their respective state Supreme Courts, and after a loss at that level, an appeal may be made to the U.S. Supreme Court. Your attorney will keep you informed during the appellate process, but because all the evidence has already been submitted to the trial court, there's nothing more for you to do but wait for the decision.

Take the Money and Run: Getting Paid after Winning Your Lawsuit

After winning your court case, it's almost time to enjoy the fruits of your labor. In the following section, we cover the basics of receiving your payment from your pension plan.

Paying out the money in different types of lawsuits

As you find out in the following sections, the process of payouts differs in individual and class action lawsuits.

Individual cases

If your case was filed on an individual basis and if you settle or win at trial or on appeal, the defendant (the plan) writes a check. The money is usually sent to your attorney, who disburses it to you after he or she deducts expenses and legal fees according to your contract (see Chapter 19 for more about attorney contracts).

Class action cases

Upon the successful conclusion of a pension class action suit, the amount of money awarded may be in the tens of millions of dollars. To dole out this money correctly and efficiently to the class members, the court usually appoints an administrator to oversee the distribution.

In a pension class action case, each participant usually receives a different payout amount because each class member is impacted differently. However, the calculations are made using the same factors that are used in pension calculations. These factors include age at retirement, length of time at the job, salary, and so on.

A pension plan payment is taxable, so approximately 20 percent of the payment will be withheld. If you have questions about the taxability of your payment, we strongly recommend that you consult your accountant or a tax attorney.

After the money has been disbursed to all the class members, a report is made to the court accounting for the final distribution, which tends to be lower than the actual award. Less money is usually distributed because it isn't unusual, given the age and mobility of the class members, that some people entitled to funds can't be located. Their money is held in a special account while the attorneys try to locate those missing class members.

If the case was settled, provisions usually are made for redistributing any unpaid monies when missing class members, after a thorough search, can't be located. These unpaid funds may

✔ Be paid out to the identified class members in proportion to their original payment from the lawsuit. For example, if $1 million is undistributed due to missing class members who, despite all efforts, can't be found, the million bucks can be paid out in a second distribution to those who've already received payments.

There are a number of methods to calculate how much extra money each class member should receive. One way is to pay each class member the same percentage of the total award that he or she received in the first distribution. In other words, if a member's initial payment is 2 percent of the total amount, he or she is paid 2 percent of the undistributed million dollars in a second distribution.

✔ Escheat to the state, which means that the money goes back to the government because the proper recipient can't be found

✔ Be returned to the pension plan

✔ Be held in an account for a set number of years until heirs can be located

✔ Be paid to a charity by order of the court

Including prejudgment and postjudgment interest

The payment you receive from your victorious lawsuit usually consists of your share of the judgment amount plus interest (in an amount determined by the court) from the time that your first pension distribution was due until the date the initial judgment was rendered in your favor. This interest is called *prejudgment interest,* and it's calculated into your judgment amount. After all, the plan continued to earn interest on the money that it didn't pay out when it should have. So, you're entitled to the interest that you would have earned on it.

Paving the way for future pensioners

Most pension mistakes aren't discovered, and even if a lawsuit is filed, the plan can delay payment by fighting the lawsuit. In the meantime, the plan has the use of your money for free. Lucky plan; poor you.

For example: If a plan loses the lawsuit and is ordered to pay interest at the statutory rate (the interest that a defendant pays after losing a lawsuit is set by law so the court knows what interest rate to apply), this amount is most likely to be less than the plan has been earning on its investments. So the plan has little to lose and a lot to gain by not paying the plaintiff right off the bat.

Your own authors were involved in a class action case in which the pensioners challenged the plan's payment of interest at the statutory rate, and the pensioners won. The decision from this case can potentially benefit you if you decide to sue your plan. The court in our case ruled that the pension plan must pay the greater of the statutory interest rate or the interest that the plan actually earned on the money while it was wrongfully withholding it. As a result, the plan didn't benefit from holding the money, and it had to pay what it earned on that money, which amounted to an extra $13 million!

The moral of the story? If you bring a lawsuit against your plan, your legacy may be that you've improved the lot for all pensioners, not just yourself.

During the appeal process and until all appeals have been exhausted, a judgment amount, inclusive of prejudgment interest, continues to earn interest, known as *postjudgment interest*. So in addition to prejudgment interest, the plan must pay postjudgment interest from the date that judgment was rendered until the date that the money is finally paid.

Awarding attorney's fees

If you hired your attorney on a contingency basis (see Chapter 19 for more information about this setup), keep in mind that while your lawsuit ground on for years, your attorney worked for free, perhaps passing on other cases because he or she was too busy working on yours. After winning your case, you can stop feeling sorry for your lawyer; ERISA allows an award of attorney's fees and costs for the prevailing party. The court has discretion to award attorney's fees in a couple of different ways:

- ✔ The *common fund award* is a percentage of the total recovery (usually between 20 percent and 33⅓ percent).
- ✔ The *lodestar and multiplier* is a method in which the attorney is paid his or her hourly rate (the lodestar) times a multiplier (for example, two or three times his or her hourly rate) that the court determines.

The court can also award money based on a blend of both of these methods.

Part VI

The Part of Tens

The 5th Wave   By Rich Tennant

"According to our lump sum pension payout plan, you're eligible to take anything from the first three shelves."

In this part . . .

*H*ere in this part, we identify ten important issues as they apply to each of the following three groups of pension participants:

- ✔ Pensioners who are still working
- ✔ Retirees and employees who are getting ready to retire
- ✔ Small business owners

We want to help prepare you for potential pension issues, no matter where you fall on the spectrum. Forewarned is forearmed.

Chapter 21

Ten Key Pension Issues for People Still Working

*O*ne of the biggest changes in your life comes about when you leave the workforce and enter retirement. And there's nothing like a little advance preparation to make the transition go smoothly. The best time to get set for this next stage of your life is while you're still working. This chapter gives some suggestions to get you ready for the big day when you say sayonara to the daily grind.

Be Familiar with Special Requirements for Participating in Your Plan

Your plan may require that you work 1,000 hours during a consecutive 12-month period to be eligible for participation in your pension plan that year. The plan may also tell you that you have to be employed on the last day of the year or meet a certain sales figure to be eligible. Whatever the rules are, you need to know them. Why? If there are years that you aren't eligible for participation, you have to know why so that you're able to verify whether your benefit package is correct when it comes time to receive your distribution. See Chapter 7 for full details on eligibility, accrual, and vesting.

Keep Your Pension Documents Safe and Accessible

If we were to say, "Go get your summary plan description," and your response was "Give me a few days to find it," you need to read on. However, if you immediately go get the key to your strongbox, you can skip this section. You've done your job!

Your pension documents serve as your contract with the plan regarding your pension. Keep these documents together in a safe place where you can easily get to them. It doesn't need to be a safety deposit box or even a lock box; a desk drawer, file folder, or any special place in your home will do. Over the years there will be amendments to the plan, communications from the plan, benefit statements, Form 5500s, and other documents yet to be created by the Washington bureaucracy. This is all important stuff. Keep everything. There's a good chance that you'll need these documents down the road. (Check out Chapter 8 for more about these documents.)

If you've lost or tossed some of these papers, request copies from your plan administrator. Make this request in writing, and send it certified mail, return receipt requested.

Fill Out Those Pesky Beneficiary Designation Forms

If you get hit by a truck tomorrow, your pension beneficiaries will be consoled by their memory of you and, well, by the survivorship benefits that they'll get because of you. But wait — you never filled out the forms. Or just as bad, your former wife is still listed as your beneficiary.

To prevent a similar scenario in which your only legacy is that you were forgetful and scatterbrained, don't procrastinate! Fill out the proper beneficiary forms, and if your circumstances change, be sure to make the necessary changes to the forms; your beneficiaries will love you for it. See Chapter 14 for more information.

Take Advantage of Any and All Investment Advice Available to You

The recent trend appears to be that companies are switching from defined benefit plans to self-directed 401(k) plans, and the big fear with that switch is that without expert advice, pensioners may make bad investment decisions. But never fear — you aren't alone. Your plan may have financial advisors that you can consult prior to making any investment decisions. Take advantage of that advice, but be sure to develop a relationship with an independent financial advisor whom you can consult to get a second opinion.

Long before retirement, you should begin meeting with financial advisors to find one you trust and who's best suited to your financial needs. There's usually no charge for an initial meeting. In fact, the advisors will be more than happy to meet with you, and they'll probably buy you lunch as well. Also, your company's retirees may have an organization that can provide you with the names of financial advisors and keep you posted on what's going on with your pension plan from the retiree's point of view. Head to Chapter 6 for more information about investments in pension plans.

If Your Plan Invests in Employer Stock, Determine Whether You Can Diversify

Your pension plan may, for any number of reasons, be invested in your company's own stock. But just because you work for the company doesn't mean that it's necessarily a good investment. So, for many different reasons (for example, the future of the company may not be bright, or you've just realized that it isn't a great idea to have all your eggs in one basket), you may want to diversify your pension portfolio in other stocks.

Prior to the Pension Protection Act of 2006 (PPA), it was up to the company whether you could diversify out of employer stock, except for Employee Stock Ownership Plan (ESOP) special rules (see Chapter 3 for more about ESOPs). Now, post-PPA, you can diversify your investments without the company's permission. The PPA provides that after three years of service, you can diversify 100 percent out of company stock. This new choice is being phased in over three years. For company contributions in employer stock after three years of service, the following rules apply during the phase-in period:

- ✔ In 2007, you can diversify ⅓ of your investments out of company stock.
- ✔ In 2008, you can diversify ⅔ out of company stock.
- ✔ In 2009, you can diversify 100 percent out of company stock.

The bottom line is this: If you're holding mucho company stock, you may want to consider hedging your bet by diversifying out of it. A balanced portfolio of high- and low-risk stocks and bonds becomes even more important as you grow older. And this is why you should have a financial consultant you trust to help you with these decisions.

Know Whether You Can Check Plan Benefits or Change Investments Online

You're living in the age of the Internet. In fact, you can do just about anything online — find a date, shop for groceries, watch the news, pay bills, and the list goes on and on. And it may just be that your plan has established a way for you and other participants to monitor and check your plan benefits online.

This online access to your pension plan is a terrific advantage for you because now the information is as close as your computer; you no longer have to wait for communication from the plan. And there's no need to worry about having to access your account during the normal nine-to-five workday (when you may be at work as well), because you can usually access your account 24 hours a day and seven days a week. Your plan may have also established a mechanism for you to change your investments online. If that's the case, take advantage of the technology. Ask your plan administrator if these features are available.

Get the Help of a Financial Advisor

Find a trusted financial advisor right now. If you don't have a good financial advisor, investment mistakes can sweep your retirement down the drain. The trick is to find an advisor who's more interested in you than in the fees that you create. However, remember that these top-notch advisors are much more difficult to find than the average money-hungry ones. So, when searching for the right advisor, you have to ask lots of questions, and you have to remain skeptical. Chapter 8 helps you find a financial advisor.

Know How Much You're Really Saving for Retirement

Discuss with your financial advisor how much money you'll need when you retire. Whether you need $50,000 or $500,000, you simply need to make a plan to set aside money. And when you're making that plan, take into account the number of years you have until retirement, your available savings, and the realistic projections by your financial advisor as to what your money can earn. Here are a couple of considerations to keep in mind (head to Chapter 8 for more about planning for retirement):

- ✔ **Beware of taxes.** When you look at your retirement account balance, it may look pretty healthy. But you have to remember that those are pretax dollars that you're counting. In other words, your final amount may be significantly less, depending on the tax rate.

    For instance, when you retire, the tax rate may be higher than it is now, even though your personal tax rate may decline if your income is lower after retirement. There's not much you can do about taxes except pay them and remember that you may need to leave a safety cushion to account for changes by the Internal Revenue Service (IRS).

- ✔ **Keep inflation in mind when you look into the future.** If you have ten years until retirement, an inflation rate of 3 percent can have a big impact when spread over those ten years. So, when you talk to your financial advisor, make sure that you take a look at some inflation-resistant investments, such as equities. You may be too young to have all your eggs in a fixed-income basket.

Remember, the earlier you start saving, the better because of the interest buildup. So, start putting money aside for retirement today — unless, of course, it's after 6 p.m. In that case, start tomorrow.

Max Out Matching Contributions in Your 401 (k)

If a genie offered you an extra dollar for every dollar you put in the bank, we're guessing that you would scrape together every dollar you could. Better yet, if that same genie could make a special deal with Uncle Sam that every dollar you and the genie socked away would grow tax-free, you would be, and should be, ecstatic.

Matching, tax-deferred genies don't exist, but matching, tax-deferred 401(k)s do. Don't greet this news with a yawn or with excuses why you don't have money to set aside. This special tax treatment is a gift from Uncle Sam; take advantage of it. You owe it to the sweet old person you'll become someday to take 100 percent advantage of matching contributions. Skip the steak dinner and the trip to the Bahamas if that helps you take advantage of matching contributions.

Even without a match, your 401(k) is one of the best deals going. If you can, contribute the maximum, which in 2007 is $15,500 (if you're over 50 and your employer allows catch-up contributions, the maximum goes up to $20,500). Tightening the belt today can save you from a diet of cold beans in your golden years.

Head to Chapter 4 for full details on 401(k)s.

Confirm That the Pension Benefit Guaranty Corporation Insures Your Plan

Defined benefit plans are insured by the Pension Benefit Guaranty Corporation (PBGC) in case they experience financial problems and can't pay your pension. If this happens, the PBGC will pay you up to $49,500 a year starting at age 65, if your plan terminates in 2007 (the limit may increase during subsequent years). However, if your plan is financially shaky, the PBGC may want your company to pay a risk premium in order to get insurance from the PBGC. So, check with your plan administrator to confirm that your plan is in fact insured by the PBGC. See Chapter 12 for the full scoop on the PBGC.

Church-sponsored defined benefit plans; federal, state, or local government plans; and defined benefit plans offered by professional-service employers (doctors and lawyers, for example) with fewer than 26 employees usually aren't insured by the PBGC.

Chapter 22

Ten Key Pension Issues for People Getting Ready to Retire

In This Chapter

▶ Making sure that your employer is using the right information for your benefits

▶ Knowing the implications of the choices that you make regarding your retirement

*Y*ou must consider several pension issues before you retire. An obvious biggie is whether the amount that your employer says you'll receive for your retirement is the correct amount. If your plan has fancy bells and whistles, such as subsidies for early retirements or lump sum payment options, you need to know whether these options are in your best interest — and certain factors will play into this decision. For example, you may want to work past retirement age or go back to work after you retire. This chapter has tips on all these issues and more.

Make Sure the Facts on Which Your Pension Is Based Are Correct

The natural reaction to this suggestion is usually "Nah, I don't need to know these facts. The pension plan office knows all that stuff." But don't be so sure that your pension plan has it right; a mistake can cost you big money. Many parts and pieces go into your pension calculation, and not surprisingly, your plan has more than just you to worry about.

Even though calculating your pension distribution requires some work on your plan's part, you also have to make sure that you do your part. For example, here are some questions you want to be sure to answer:

> ✔ If you were under different vesting tables for the time that you worked, has your company applied the correct schedule to the correct time periods?

✔ Has your company credited you for time off for military service or for maternity or paternity leave?

✔ Does the plan have your correct birth date, marital status, and total time with the company?

✔ Did you tell the plan if you divorced or selected a different beneficiary?

✔ Does the plan have your correct salary for the entire time that you worked with the company?

Make sure that your plan has everything right before you walk out the door. You'll save yourself a lot of aggravation. Chapter 8 has checklists of all the information that you should verify with your pension plan before you retire.

Verify That the Plan Is Using the Proper Formula to Calculate Your Benefits

To calculate your benefits, your pension plan takes all your information and applies it to the plan formula. For your own protection, you need to know what that formula is. Compare the provisions in the unabridged plan document with those in the summary plan description (SPD) to confirm that they're the same.

The next step is to verify that the company is applying the correct formula to your pension benefits. It's quite possible that your company, if big enough, has more than one pension plan and more than one formula. If the wrong one is used, you could end up receiving substantially less money than you should. Or if the right formula is used but applied incorrectly, the same thing could happen.

When in doubt, hire an attorney (see Chapter 19) or an actuary to verify that your plan is using the right formula (and following the law regardless of the formula).

Be Sure the Plan Had the Right to Reduce Your Benefits (If They've Been Reduced)

As the years roll on, plans inevitably make amendments to the pension benefits it provides. Some of these changes result in your pension becoming less valuable to you. But just because the plan decides to eliminate a subsidized benefit or stick in some additional hurdles for you to jump before you get your pension doesn't mean that it's permitted to do so. There's a fundamental rule stating that the plan can't take away what you've already earned.

To find out whether your plan is staying within the law, keep a copy of all plan amendments, especially those that have in any way made your pension less valuable to you. Then determine when that change took effect. If the reduction of your benefits is retroactive and eats into benefits that you earned for service or work already performed at the time of the change, your plan may have violated the anti-cutback rule. This violation, which is more common than you may realize, is a big deal and can cost you thousands of dollars in lost benefits. Head to Chapter 7 for more about the anti-cutback rule and Chapter 12 for more about legal and illegal plan amendments.

Select Your Own Investments If Your Plan Gives You the Opportunity

As you approach retirement, you must be increasingly vigilant in order to properly position your investments to best serve your own needs. The older you get, the more important your investment choices become. The right investment for a 25-year-old isn't necessarily the right investment for a 55-year-old. The older you are, the less risk you should be taking with your money.

If your plan allows you the opportunity to select your own investments and you don't make a selection, the plan will make the investment choice for you. This is referred to as a *default investment.* Having someone else make the decision for you isn't ideal, because only you know which options best suit your situation. If you don't exercise your freedom to choose, you have no voice. And believe us when we say that the insurance companies and investment firms want to get their hands on the probable billions of pension dollars that are invested by default when pensioners don't make their own choices. If you wind up in a high-risk, high-fee fund run by Feesaplenty Insurance Co. by default, you can blame only yourself.

With the advent of the Pension Protection Act of 2006 (PPA), your fiduciary now is permitted to give financial advice directly to you as long as the fiduciary doesn't increase his or her compensation based on his or her investment recommendations (meaning that the fees must stay the same as a result of the recommendations made). However, if the fiduciary wants to avoid the level fee restriction, his or her advice must conform to a computer-designed program.

See Chapter 6 for much more information about investments in pension plans.

Know What Fees You're Paying

As you approach retirement, your investments and retirement distributions will replace your salary and become your primary sources of income. So, the steady drip, drip, drip of fees will become even more important for you to bring under control. Make sure that you uncover all the fees that you're paying to your advisors. Whether the fees are hidden or not, they're there (and you're paying big bucks for them!). There's no such thing as a free lunch, and if you select an investment, someone is making money on it — and that someone probably won't be you.

When your broker tells you about a great risk-free investment paying 6½ percent, you'd better think twice if the fees for that low-risk investment are 3 percent. At these numbers, the investment has to earn 9½ percent just to get your promised 6½ percent — which is highly unlikely. If you think your fees are too high, tell your broker. Fees, like everything else in the world of money, can be negotiated.

Under the PPA, your investment advisor is obligated to advise you of the amounts and the sources of his or her fees. In recent years in the world of investment advice, amounts and sources of fees have often been closely guarded secrets (much too sensitive to be indiscriminately shared with those who are paying them!). Luckily, however, the PPA requires increased disclosure of both the sources and the amounts of the investment advisor's fees.

The bottom line is this: It's wrong for all fees not to be disclosed, and it's your right to insist that they are.

Choose Carefully between a Lump Sum and an Annuity

If you're given the option to select the form of your pension distribution, you may be wondering whether you should choose a lump sum or an annuity. The question is simple; the answer, however, is not. If you're ill or expect to have a short life expectancy, you're probably better off taking your pension benefits in a lump sum. If, on the other hand, you expect to live a long life, chances are that taking your benefits in the form of an annuity will deliver a bigger bang for your buck.

For example, $1,000 per month for life is worth a lot more if you live for 20 years rather than five. Your accountant can tell you how long you have to live to make the annuity worth more than the lump sum. This information is worth knowing before you decide on the form of your pension distribution. You also have to figure in survivorship benefits; if you and your spouse are both healthy and have good genes, for instance, an annuity with a spousal survivorship benefit may be better over the long haul.

The PPA, passed in August 2006, increases the interest rate used to calculate the lump sum equivalent of an annuity. As interest rates go up, lump sums go down. So, lump-sum distributions calculated after the PPA will be less than lump sums calculated prior to the PPA. This change makes lump-sum distributions a less attractive alternative to annuities than they were prior to the PPA.

Additionally, the PPA has eliminated certain calculations (called *whipsaw calculations*) that previously had to be performed before a participant received a lump-sum distribution from a cash balance plan. For distributions after August 17, 2006, a cash balance plan is permitted to pay the individual's hypothetical account balance as a lump-sum distribution (see Chapter 3 for more on cash balance plans and hypothetical account balances). If you received a lump-sum distribution from a cash balance plan before August 17, 2006, however, there's a good chance that it wasn't calculated properly and that you received less than you should have. Consult a pension attorney to review the lump sum calculations for distributions from cash balance plans prior to August 17, 2006.

Check out Chapter 9 for more about annuities and lump sums.

Take Advantage of Rollovers

One of the great benefits of having funds in a tax-qualified pension plan is that in many situations, they may be rolled over into another tax-qualified plan or an individual retirement account (IRA). What this means to you is that you can continue to have your retirement funds grow in a tax-deferred account and not pay taxes on the money until it's distributed to you. However, remember that this perk applies only to eligible rollover distributions made to you, of all (or any portion) of your balance in a qualified pension plan. It doesn't apply to distributions made in the form of annuity payments, minimum required distributions made at age 70½, or hardship distributions.

Your plan administrator must tell you in writing that your upcoming lump-sum distribution may be rolled over into another tax-qualified plan or into an IRA. Your distribution must be either transferred directly to the IRA or other tax-qualified plan or rolled over within 60 days after you receive it — or after your surviving spouse or a former spouse, pursuant to a qualified domestic relations order (QDRO), receives the distribution (see Chapter 15 for more on QDROs).

It's best to have the funds transferred directly to the IRA or tax-qualified plan. (This type of transfer is called a *direct rollover.*) Federal income tax is withheld at a 20 percent rate on any eligible rollover distributions that aren't directly rolled over. So, this means that if the funds are distributed directly to you (rather than directly rolled over), you'll receive only 80 percent of your benefits because 20 percent will be withheld for taxes.

Effective for distributions after December 31, 2006, beneficiaries other than a surviving spouse may roll over benefits into an IRA. However, such non-spouse rollovers can be made only from plans that specifically permit such rollovers.

We tell you a lot more about what rolls into what and when in Chapter 9.

Have a Plan for Drawing Down Your Lump Sum Payout

The purpose of your pension plan is to provide sufficient funds for the rest of your life. Spending the money in your account in a defined contribution plan or an IRA is referred to as *drawing down.* When drawing down your account, you have to consider what *withdrawal rate* (the percentage of your total account balance that will be distributed to you each year) will provide you with sufficient living expenses without breaking the bank when you select a lump sum payout. For example, if you have $400,000 in your plan, a withdrawal rate of 3 percent will give you $12,000 per year. It doesn't matter if your withdrawal rate is a conservative 3 percent or a risky 6 percent; you still need a plan. The rate can be adjusted if you live a long life, or it can be based on portfolio performance.

You may need expert financial advice to help you form a realistic picture of what your investments can realistically earn over your life. If your investment portfolio is projected to earn 8 percent, you can take more out each year than if it will only earn 4 percent. As a rule of thumb, many investment advisors suggest that you withdraw 4 percent of your account each year if your account is invested in a balance of stocks and fixed-income investments. But play it safe, because your investment advisor's opinion as to how much you'll earn over a period of years may not always be on the money.

Look Before You Leap and Take Early Retirement

Some companies offer incentives to older workers to retire before they had originally planned to. These incentives include *subsidized early retirement benefits,* which give senior employees the same monthly benefit at age 60, for example, that they would get at age 65.

If the company offers a lump sum form of payment option in addition to the annuity, it's possible that the lump sum will be based on the unsubsidized early retirement benefit rather than on the subsidized early retirement benefit. (See Chapter 9 for more about the differences between lump sum and annuity payments.) In this case, the lump sum payment will be worth a lot less than the subsidized annuity payments.

Before you take early retirement, make sure that the company has provided you with plenty of information, in easy-to-understand language, about the relative benefits of the various early retirement and payout options. If the costs and benefits of the options are unclear to you, have an attorney or accountant review them and explain what you're getting yourself into. In the end, the money that you use to hire an attorney or an accountant will be money well spent.

Find Out How Returning to Work after Retirement Affects Your Pension

After three weeks of playing golf and watching television, many retirees get a bit bored and decide that working wasn't so bad. If you feel this way and want to return to your job (and the company in fact wants you back), you need to find out whether the time you work after retirement increases your pension. You also want to find out whether you can draw your pension if you do return to work. These are questions for your company's human resources manager (or the pension plan administrator, if your company doesn't have a human resources department).

If you return to the workforce at a new company instead of your old one, ask your new human resources manager (or plan administrator) whether going back to work will have any positive or negative impact on your retirement benefits.

Chapter 23

Ten Key Pension Tips for Small Business Owners

. . . .

In This Chapter

▶ Knowing how much you can afford to contribute to your employees' retirements

▶ Attracting new employees and keeping good ones with your offer of retirement benefits

▶ Selecting your administrator and investments

. . . .

*A*re you a small business owner in search of a smart pension plan? Here's the key: To look out for your employees, you also need to look out for yourself. This chapter is devoted to you, the small business owner, to help you make retirement plan decisions that you can afford in order to attract and keep the best employees.

Before you select the best pension plan for your small business, keep the following information in mind:

✔ Charts in Appendix B provide an overview of the variety of different plans and dollar limits. These charts enable you to compare features.

✔ Professional fees vary, depending on the type of plan you select. At a minimum, you'll incur expenses for legal services (to set up a retirement plan and submit the required documents to the Internal Revenue Service for plan qualification), accounting services, and actuarial services (if you implement a defined benefit plan).

✔ Before you settle on a retirement plan, be sure to consult an attorney, an accountant, an actuary, and/or a financial advisor to help you pick the plan that best meets your objectives and to guide you through the ropes as you introduce the plan into your business.

Be Certain You Can Afford a Retirement Plan for Yourself and Your Employees

As a small business owner you can contribute $4,000 to a traditional individual retirement account (IRA) in 2007 ($5,000 in 2008), and if you're over the age of 50, you can contribute an additional $1,000 catch-up contribution. If you have a spouse, you also can contribute on his or her behalf. So potentially, you can put somewhere between $8,000 and $10,000 into an IRA, tax-free, in 2007. This is your starting point. If you can't afford to put this much away for yourself (and your spouse, if you have one), regardless of how desirable a retirement plan is for your employees, you won't be able to fund it. However, if you can contribute more than this amount and want to do so, you have several plan options; keep reading.

Think about a SIMPLE IRA If You Have Fewer Than 100 Employees

If you have fewer than 100 employees who received at least $5,000 in compensation in the preceding year and you don't sponsor any other type of qualified plan, you can set up a SIMPLE IRA. In this type of plan, your employees can defer up to $10,500 per year in addition to a catch-up contribution of $2,500 if they're over age 50 (these are the maximums for 2007; check out `www.irs.gov/retirement/article/0,,id=96461,00.html` for future rates). As the employer, you have a choice of two contribution formulas:

- ✔ You can match 100 percent of an employee's contributions up to 3 percent of his or her compensation.
- ✔ You can make a nonelective contribution of 2 percent of compensation for each eligible employee.

The major advantage of SIMPLE IRAs for employers is that they usually have lower annual administration costs than other types of qualified plans. The plans are easy and inexpensive to set up and operate, and no discrimination testing is required. You generally have no filing requirements, and the annual reporting required for qualified plans (Form 5500 series) isn't required for SIMPLE IRAs. Usually, the financial institution or broker that holds the plan's SIMPLE IRAs handles most of the other paperwork.

If you can afford to put away $10,500 for yourself plus the $2,500 catch-up contribution if you're over age 50 (and the same amounts for your spouse, if you're married and your spouse is employed by your business), and if you can afford to make contributions to your employees' accounts, a SIMPLE IRA may be the plan for you. You're still providing your employees an option to save, and for the vast majority of employees, $10,500 per year may be sufficient.

Head to Chapter 5 for details on SIMPLE IRAs.

Consider a 401 (k) Plan to Attract and Retain Good Employees

Employees have come to expect their employers to, at a minimum, sponsor a 401(k) plan that allows them to make their own tax-free contributions. In addition to providing your employees with this opportunity to save their own funds, you can consider offering to match your employees' contributions (if you can afford it, of course). These matching contributions will serve as incentives to retain current employees and to attract new ones. A 401(k) is an option that you should consider if you can contribute more than $10,500 per year to a plan for yourself.

Under a 401(k), which is a type of defined contribution plan, you set up a plan in which your employees may elect to defer a portion of their compensation to their 401(k) plan, tax-free. They can defer up to $15,500 per year (in 2007) plus $5,000 as a catch-up contribution if they're over age 50. If an employee earned less than $15,500, he or she is permitted to contribute up to 100 percent of his or her compensation.

When you establish a 401(k) plan, you have the option to decide whether your company will contribute to your employees' accounts. If your company will contribute, you also choose how the contributions are made. For example:

- ✔ You can match your employees' contributions at an amount that you determine (so if they don't contribute, you have nothing to match).

- ✔ You can contribute up to a certain percentage of their income (called a *nonelective contribution*). This percentage must fall within the current legal limits.

- ✔ You can put both of the previous options in place.

The limit in 2007 for total contributions to all defined contribution plans offered by an employer is 100 percent of compensation up to $45,000 per year (plus an additional $5,000 catch-up contribution if the employee is over 50). Total contributions are those from both the employee and you, the employer.

Even if you set up a 401(k) plan, you can also set up other retirement plans, such as the profit-sharing plan we discuss in the next section. Also, your business can be any size and still be eligible to set up a 401(k).

The major advantages for you (the employer) are the following:

✔ If cash flow is an issue, you have the flexibility to change the amount of your nonelective deferrals each year as well as your match, because your contributions are discretionary.

✔ If you offer either a match or a nonelective contribution to your employees, you're a good guy, but if you offer to do both, you're a *really* good guy. This gesture goes a long way toward employee satisfaction and provides major incentives to your employees to save for their own retirements.

Even though you have the discretion to change your contribution amount (or to even decide not to contribute), professionally speaking, it isn't a good idea to do this to your employees. If you tell your employees at the beginning of the year that you'll match their deferrals up to a certain percentage, you should follow through. In some cases, your decision to change your contribution may not be a violation of the Employee Retirement Income Security Act of 1974 (ERISA), but it may quite possibly be a breach of contract to renege after your employees have relied on your word.

Check out Chapter 4 for full details about 401(k)s.

Add a Profit-Sharing Plan to a 401(k) for Extra Benefits

Another defined contribution plan option is the profit-sharing plan, which is the most flexible of all retirement plans. When you set up a profit-sharing plan in addition to a 401(k), the combo will be an attractive benefit incentive for your employees because it provides them with extra retirement savings that are completely contributed by you. It's a bonus for you as well, because:

✔ You aren't obligated to make contributions to the plan.

✔ You can make a year-by-year determination whether you want to contribute or not.

✔ If you decide to contribute, you can contribute any amount between 0 percent and 25 percent of your covered employees' compensation.

✔ Your contribution amounts can vary year-to-year. If you do make contributions, you must make them according to a set formula written into the plan for determining how profit-sharing contributions will be made.

Keep in mind that the maximum amount for 2007 that can be contributed to each covered employee's defined contribution plan (both employee and employer contributions, and for all defined contribution plans that you establish) is the lesser of 100 percent of the covered employee's compensation or $45,000 per year (plus a $5,000 catch-up for those folks over 50). So, if you can contribute $45,000 for yourself (or $50,000 if you're over 50) and have the ability to do so for your employees, a profit-sharing plan, along with a 401(k), is an option that you can look into.

Find out more about profit-sharing plans (and other defined contribution plans) in Chapter 3.

Consider Defined Benefit Plans for More Sizeable Contributions

If you can afford to contribute more than $50,000 per year for yourself to a retirement plan and can also afford to contribute that much to your employees' plans, you may want to consider a defined benefit plan. With this type of plan, the level of benefits is fixed, and the contributions are determined by an actuary.

Defined benefit plans, by their very nature, are more complicated than defined contribution plans. So, unless you want to contribute more than $45,000 (or $50,000 if you're over age 50), there's no reason to take on the additional administrative costs and expenses of setting up and running a defined benefit plan.

Because defined benefit plans can provide greater benefits for you and your employees than defined contribution plans in a shorter period of time (because you're contributing more), the advantage to you is that you can deduct more than you can with other retirement plans (your actuary can provide you with your actual deduction limits). Also helpful is the fact that your plan can provide different levels of benefits to different classes of employees.

Flip to Chapter 3 for general information about defined benefit plans.

Weigh the Pros and Cons of Fixed versus Flexible Contributions

As an employer, you may be in the type of business in which profits fluctuate yearly, making it difficult or impossible during the down years to contribute toward your employees' retirements. If you find yourself in that situation, consider a retirement plan in which you have the ability to make flexible (rather than fixed) contributions. What's the difference? Consider the following:

- ✔ With *flexible contributions,* you can decide each year how much to contribute to the retirement plans that you've chosen to set up. For example, a profit-sharing plan is an example of a flexible contribution; you, the employer, can decide to contribute somewhere between 0 percent and 25 percent of your employees' compensation.

- ✔ A *fixed contribution,* on the other hand, is a mandatory contribution that you must make each year. For instance, even if you have a bad year financially, you still have to contribute at year's end to a defined benefit plan.

Encourage Your Employees to Contribute

Generally speaking, all employees appreciate matching contributions. In fact, your matching contributions actually encourage them to save even more for their own retirement (otherwise, they may not even save a penny!).

But even if you can't afford to provide matching contributions for your employees, you should encourage your employees to contribute to a 401(k) plan to save for their own retirement. Your employees who think on a more long-term basis will appreciate the opportunity that you're providing them to save pretax dollars in a 401(k).

It also doesn't hurt to remind your employees that they'll pay no current income taxes on the contributions they make to the plan and that their accounts will continue to grow, tax-free, until the benefits are distributed to them. If you're providing your employees with the option to direct their own plan investments, you may also explain that self-direction puts them directly in control of their own futures and destinies.

Carefully Select a Third-Party Administrator

In small companies, the plan administrator is usually the owner or an officer of the company. Because ERISA requires that fiduciaries (such as the plan administrator) administer and manage their plans prudently and in the interest of the plan's participants and beneficiaries, expertise in areas that are outside the plan administrator's professional knowledge are frequently required. If you lack the expertise to manage and administer your retirement plan, you must hire someone with the professional knowledge to carry out this function, such as a certified public accountant (CPA) or a third-party administrator (TPA). TPAs are typically firms that do nothing but administer retirement plans (because they deal with nothing but retirement plans, they know the ins and outs like no one else). A TPA performs the following tasks as a part of administering a retirement plan:

✔ Determines the manner in which contributions will be allocated

✔ Prepares the necessary forms, such as the Form 5500s, the annual returns, and the participant benefit statements (see Chapter 8 for more about pension plan documents)

✔ Distributes and files the necessary forms and notices

The TPA you're looking for is going to administer your plan in a proper and professional manner at a reasonable price. Survey a number of potential TPAs, asking for the same information and providing the same requirements, so you can make a meaningful comparison and selection. It's always helpful to talk to other business owners who have retirement plans to see who they use, and consider referrals from your attorney or CPA.

Examine All Investment Options

As far as investment options for your plan are concerned, you want to offer primarily mutual funds because they provide diversified investments. (Diversified investments are great because you lessen the risk of a loss if any one investment goes down in value.) If your plan is a defined contribution plan that provides for participant direction of investments, your options will likely be limited to a selection of mutual funds that offer different investment characteristics.

When examining your investment options, look at the *expense ratio* of the funds compared to the annual cost to operate the fund. Expense ratios are usually expressed in terms of *basis points;* a basis point is 1/100 of 1 percent. For example, if a fund has an expense ratio of 125 basis points, this means that 1.25 percent of the assets goes to expenses each year. So if a mutual fund has a gross investment return of 7 percent but an expense ratio of 1.25 percent, the net investment return to your account will be 5.75 percent. Most actively managed funds typically have expense ratios of between 50 to 125 basis points. Generally speaking, you don't want the highest investment return because it comes with the highest risk.

As a small business owner, the type of plan you select is partly determined by how much it's going to cost. And how much it's going to cost depends on the investment fees and plan administration expenses that the service provider charges. You need to ensure that informed cost–benefit decisions are being made so that the plan and your employees aren't paying for a service that they don't need or that's not financially justified.

Check the various fees attached to different funds, and examine their performance history. Check out sites such as www.morningstar.com to look at the investment performance volatility and expense ratios of the various funds. Go to www.dol.gov/ebsa/pdf/401kfefm.pdf to view a sample 401(k) Plan Fee Disclosure Form.

Avoid annuity contracts as often as possible (they have high fees attached). Also generally try to avoid funds with *front-end loads* (investment fees that you pay up front) and funds with surrender charges or *back-end loads* (fees that you pay at the end).

Just as with the selection of TPAs (see the previous section), you want to seek out referrals for investments advisors. Talk to your attorney, your accountant, and other business owners whom you know and trust. They're usually the ones who can provide the best recommendations. See Chapter 6 for general information about investments.

Uncover Hidden Fees

Most employers find it necessary to hire an outside pension consultant who usually recommends a money manager for your plan. You should carefully choose this consultant by interviewing several choices and finding out about their fees. Make sure that the fees are transparent and that there are no hidden or undisclosed fees. Ask the consultant whether he or she has a relationship with the recommended money manager and whether he or she receives any payment from the money manager. This is the type of fee that's frequently not disclosed, and it can have a big impact over the life of a pension.

If the pension consultant doesn't disclose such information, you need to know whether there are recordkeeping or administrative fees that also aren't disclosed. Hidden fees can be very expensive. Protect your plan participants by requiring full disclosure of all fees and transparency of all business relationships from your pension consultant.

Part VII
Appendixes

The 5th Wave   By Rich Tennant

"I've been working over 80 hours a week for the past two years preparing for retirement, and it hasn't bothered me OR my wife, what's-her-name."

In this part . . .

In Appendix A, you find a glossary of all the technical pension words and phrases that you need to know to successfully navigate through this book. Use this glossary also to help yourself decipher the alphabet soup of retirement terms that you're sure to come across when discussing your pension plan.

In Appendix B, we provide you with some charts and tables to help you better understand some of the concepts that we discuss throughout this book.

Appendix A

Glossary

In this glossary are the major terms that you need to know for protecting your pension. Even though the important words and phrases are defined within the first chapter in which they appear, this glossary serves as a handy reference in case you forget what a word means or what an acronym stands for. These definitions are found on Web sites and in publications of the Department of Labor (DOL), the Internal Revenue Service (IRS), and the Pension Benefit Guaranty Corporation (PBGC), and within legal statutes and regulations.

accrued benefit: The portion of an employee's normal retirement benefit that has been earned at any given point during his or her career.

alternate payee: A person other than a plan participant — such as a spouse, former spouse, child, or other dependent of the participant — who's identified in a domestic relations order as having the right to receive all or some of a participant's pension benefits.

annuity: A series of regular payments made to a retiree or beneficiary over a period of years at evenly spaced intervals that usually continue for the lifetime of the recipient.

anti-cutback rule: A rule stating that once you've earned certain rights or benefits, your plan can't take them away from you retroactively. The plan may change your rights going forward, however.

bankruptcy estate: The property you own when you file for bankruptcy.

beneficiary: Any person or entity designated to receive your plan benefits when you die, such as a spouse, child, or significant other. In tax-qualified retirement plans, your spouse is your beneficiary unless you and your spouse agree to a different beneficiary.

beneficiary designation form: A form that you complete and return to your employer to designate your beneficiary. If you don't complete the form, the plan kicks in and designates a beneficiary for you, usually your spouse. See *designated beneficiary.*

blackout: The period of time when a fiduciary puts a hold on your ability to make changes to your pension investments. A blackout can be caused when there's a change in the plan's investment advisors, trustees, or recordkeepers or when the plan undergoes a merger or acquisition. During this time period, plan participants can't access their accounts.

break in service: A time period in which you're absent from work. For example, working fewer than 501 hours in a consecutive 12-month period designated by the plan is considered a one-year break in service in most plans.

catch-up contribution: An additional contribution for plan participants who are over age 50 (or who turn age 50 within the plan year) and who want to put away more money before retirement. If your plan permits catch-up contributions, you can increase your contributions over and above the regular 401(k), 403(b), or IRA contribution limits.

class action lawsuit: A lawsuit in which one pensioner (or a few pensioners) files on behalf of all others who have suffered the same type of loss. Class actions are common in pension litigation because the mistakes made in the calculation of benefits usually apply to a number of pensioners.

cliff vesting: A type of vesting schedule in which an employee is considered 100 percent vested in the company's contributions after a specific number of years but is 0 percent vested prior to reaching that specified number of years.

collective bargaining agreement: A contract between an employer and its union employees that governs the terms and conditions of employment for a stated period of time.

cost-of-living adjustment: An adjustment to a retiree's qualified retirement plan that reflects cost-of-living increases. These adjustments typically result in small, incremental increases in retirement benefits in order to keep benefits in line with inflation.

deemed distribution: A distribution from your pension plan that's treated as if it's a payment from your plan, thus creating a taxable event. For example, if you take out a loan from your plan and don't pay it back on time, the money you received is considered a distribution from your pension and is subject to taxation at the time you default on the loan.

default investment: An investment decision made by your plan (instead of by you). When you don't choose an investment option provided by your plan, your plan will choose the investment for you.

defined benefit plan: A plan that guarantees a certain payout at retirement according to a formula that takes into consideration the employee's salary and years of service in the plan. The plan defines (or calculates) the benefit as an annuity at retirement age.

defined contribution plan: A plan that provides a payout at retirement that's dependent upon the amount of money contributed by the participant, the employer, or both, to the participant's individual account provided by the plan. The final benefit depends on the performance of the investments. These plans are also referred to as individual account plans.

denial in full: A denial of your claim for pension benefits because you aren't eligible for benefits. Your claim may be fully denied for a number of different reasons, such as you haven't been a participant in the plan for enough years, you aren't the required age to receive benefits, or you didn't provide sufficient information to the plan to calculate your benefits.

denial in part: A partial denial of your claim for pension benefits because the plan didn't approve of some part of your claim or incorrectly calculated your benefits. A denial in part generally means that your benefits will be lower than you had expected to receive based on individual benefit statements or account statements you received in the past.

Department of Labor (DOL): The agency that's responsible for administering the provisions of Title I of ERISA, which regulates the administration of pension and employee benefit plans.

designated beneficiary: An individual or an entity designated as a beneficiary under the plan, whether you designate the beneficiary or not. In the event that you don't designate a beneficiary, the terms of the plan designate a beneficiary for you. See *beneficiary.*

discretionary contribution: A contribution to a retirement plan (such as a profit-sharing plan) where the amount is determined each year by the employer sponsoring the plan. See *flexible contributions.*

discrimination test: A test in the field of pension law that ensures that plans don't discriminate between highly compensated employees (HCEs) and non–highly compensated employees (NHCEs).

disqualified person: Someone who, because of his or her relationship with a plan, isn't permitted to enter into certain transactions with the plan. This person is also referred to as a party in interest and can include a plan fiduciary, a plan sponsor, and plan service providers. See *parties in interest.*

distress termination: A procedure that allows your employer to voluntarily terminate a defined benefit pension plan that doesn't have enough assets to pay the promised benefits. After termination, the plan is taken over by the PBGC.

distribution: Any payout from a retirement plan.

early retirement benefit: The option to retire earlier than the normal retirement age set forth in your plan.

early withdrawal: Any withdrawal that's made prior to reaching age 59½. Early withdrawals may be subject not only to income taxes, but also to a 10 percent penalty imposed by the IRS unless they satisfy certain exceptions.

elective deferrals: The employee contributions that you make on a salary reduction basis, pretax, to a defined contribution plan. The formula and limit of the amount that you elect to defer are set forth in the plan documents and usually expressed in the form of a percentage of income.

eligible rollover distribution: A distribution from a qualified retirement plan that may be rolled over (transferred) to another qualified retirement plan or an IRA.

eligibility: The green light to participate in your employer's pension plan. If you're eligible to participate, that means you've met the plan's requirements, such as age and years of service.

Employee Benefits Security Administration (EBSA): A division of the DOL that's responsible for enforcing the rules governing the conduct of plan managers, the investment of plan assets, the reporting and disclosure of plan information, and the fiduciary provisions of ERISA.

Employee Retirement Income Security Act of 1974 (ERISA): The major pension legislation enacted in 1974 to protect the rights of participants and beneficiaries of employee benefit plans. For a plan to be considered tax-qualified, plan sponsors must design and administer their plans according to ERISA's qualification standards and fiduciary responsibilities.

exhaustion of administrative remedies: The rule stating that in order to file a lawsuit when your company denies your request for benefits, you must first comply with all the plan's administrative requirements for an appeal. Your failure to do so can be reason to dismiss a subsequent lawsuit.

fiduciary: Any person who exercises any discretionary authority, responsibility, or control over a plan, the administration of a plan, or the management or disposition of a plan's assets, or anyone who renders investment advice regarding a plan's assets for a fee.

fixed contributions: The mandatory contributions set by a pension plan that an employer must make each year.

flexible contributions: Contributions that are considered flexible because the employer can decide each year how much to contribute to its chosen retirement plans. See *discretionary contribution.*

forfeiture: The loss or surrender of your nonvested benefits. Your vested benefits are nonforfeitable. All or a portion of your plan benefits may be forfeited if you haven't completed the required number of years stated in the plan's vesting schedule.

Form 5500: An annual financial report that most retirement plans must file with the DOL. You're entitled to receive a copy of this document yearly and free of charge.

graded vesting: The type of vesting schedule that allows employees to earn the right to employer contributions made on their behalf gradually (usually over a set period of years).

individual account plans: A type of retirement plan in which the employee or the employer contributes to an individual account on behalf of the employee. Those contributions are then invested on the employee's behalf. Eventually, the employee receives the balance in his or her account based on how much has been contributed and how much the account balance has fluctuated based on the investments' gains or losses. Individual account plan is another name for a defined contribution plan.

individual benefit statement: A statement prepared by the plan administrator that describes your total accrued and vested benefits.

individual retirement account (IRA): A type of account that individuals can set up in order to make contributions. An IRA isn't sponsored by an employer, but is created and funded by the employee. Contributions to a traditional IRA are tax-deductible when they're made; distributions from a Roth IRA are distributed tax-free.

in-service distribution: A plan distribution paid to a participant while he or she is still working for the employer that sponsors the retirement plan.

inside of bankruptcy: The term that's used when a debtor has filed for bankruptcy; at this point, the debtor is within the control of the federal bankruptcy laws, and his or her assets are considered part of the bankruptcy estate.

Internal Revenue Service (IRS): The branch of the U.S. Treasury Department that's responsible for administering qualified retirement plans and other retirement accounts and for enforcing the Internal Revenue Code. If you fail to pay your taxes, the IRS serves as the tax collector.

involuntary termination: A termination of a defined benefit pension plan initiated by the PBGC if it determines that plan termination is necessary to protect the interests of plan participants (such as when a plan doesn't have enough money to pay benefits when they're due).

lump sum: A form of distribution in which all your pension benefits are paid to you at one time in a single payment.

mandatory distribution: A distribution made to a plan participant, without the participant's consent, before he or she reaches the later of either age 62 or the normal retirement age under his or her plan.

match: The most popular type of employer contribution to a 401(k) plan, in which your employer contributes to your account, based on a percentage of your contribution, up to a certain maximum amount set by the plan or by law.

multiemployer plan: A plan to which two or more unrelated employers contribute according to a collective bargaining agreement.

optional benefits: Those benefits that a plan may offer its participants, such as the option to retire earlier than the plan's normal retirement age.

optional forms of benefits: The different ways in which you can receive your pension distribution, such as through annuity payments or in a lump sum.

outside of bankruptcy: The term that's used when a debtor isn't under the jurisdiction of the federal bankruptcy court (and so the bankruptcy act and rules don't apply). The term usually implies that the person is in financial trouble but hasn't (yet) filed bankruptcy.

parties in interest: Those people who are so intimately connected to a plan that they're considered to have an interest in the plan. These folks may include a plan fiduciary, a plan sponsor, and plan service providers. See *disqualified person.*

Pension Benefit Guaranty Corporation (PBGC): The federal agency that was established pursuant to ERISA for the purpose of insuring private defined benefit pension plans. The PBGC takes over and runs failed plans, providing payments to retirees if their plans terminate and are unable to make the payments.

pension fund: The fund that's made up of employer and employee contributions. This fund must be kept separate from the employer's assets.

pension investment consultant: The independent consultant who's hired to advise the investment committee on how the plan should invest its money.

pension plan: An arrangement to provide people with an income or pension during retirement when they're no longer earning a steady income from employment. Pension plans, which are also called retirement plans or plans, may be set up by employers, the government, unions, or institutions such as employer associations. They're typically classified as defined benefit plans or defined contribution plans, depending on how the benefits are determined.

Pension Protection Act of 2006 (PPA): The notable pension legislation adopted in 2006. This act significantly alters employer-sponsored defined benefit plans by amending sections of ERISA and the Internal Revenue Code. It affects defined contribution plans as well. The act includes new notice requirements and other requirements to ensure that plans are properly overseen and implemented.

plan administrator: The individual, group, or entity named in the plan document that's in charge of day-to-day operations of an employer's plan.

plan document: The complete written document that describes all the terms and conditions for the operation of the retirement plan sponsored by your employer.

plan participant: Any individual who's participating in a pension plan and has an account in the plan by virtue of his or her employment with an employer that offers this benefit.

plan sponsor: The company, employer, or firm that establishes a retirement plan on behalf of its employees.

plan trustee: A person or organization with the duty to receive, manage, and disburse the assets of a plan. Plan trustees are similar to a board of directors.

plan year: A period of 12 consecutive months designated by the plan for keeping its records. It can be a calendar year or a noncalendar fiscal year.

present value: The value, in today's dollars, of promised future payments.

present value calculation: A calculation that's used to determine the value, in today's dollars, of a sum of money to be received in a future year. The calculation is based on a specific interest rate stated in the plan or required by the IRS.

pretax basis: Those contributions that are made to your account prior to taxes being paid. Because the monies weren't included in your taxable income at the time that they were deferred or contributed to the plan, they'll be included in your taxable income when they're eventually distributed to you from the plan.

prohibited transactions: Those activities that fiduciaries or parties in interest can't participate in because of the possibility of pension insiders benefiting from their relationship to the fund or because they may be able to exercise undue influence over the fund. ERISA prohibits transactions with parties in interest.

qualified default investment alternative (QDIA): An investment option that plans use when you fail to choose an investment in a plan that permits you to choose investments for yourself (thus forcing your plan to invest your funds for you). A QDIA must meet certain requirements, such as diversification, in order to avoid liability. QDIAs must be managed by an investment company or a fiduciary, and they must allow you to switch to another investment at least every quarter.

qualified domestic relations order (QDRO): An order made by a state court judge that divides a plan participant's retirement plan benefits with a soon-to-be ex-spouse (in cases of divorce). The order becomes a QDRO only after it meets certain criteria and is approved by the pension plan trustee or plan administrator. The person who approves the QDRO also qualifies the order.

qualified joint and survivor annuity (QJSA): An annuity or series of payments paid over your life and your spouse's life if you, the plan participant, die first. Because a QJSA takes into account your life as well as that of your spouse, the amount of these payments will be smaller than if they were just going to be paid through your lifetime.

qualified preretirement survivor annuity (QPSA): An annuity that's available for the life of your surviving spouse. For example, if you, the plan participant, die before you retire and have vested benefits, your spouse will be entitled to receive survivor benefits in the form of a QPSA. The plan can require that this annuity not take effect until the plan participant would have been eligible to receive benefits under the plan, or it can permit an immediate annuity for the life of the spouse.

rate of return: The amount of money that you're earning annually on your investment. This rate is expressed in terms of a percentage. For example, if you're earning $1,000 per year based on a $10,000 investment, your rate of return would be 10 percent.

required minimum distribution: The minimum amount that must be paid each year to a plan participant starting at the required beginning date (age 70½).

Retirement Equity Act (REA): An act designed to safeguard the rights of a participant's spouse in a qualified plan. The act requires that benefits be paid only in a form other than a QJSA if the participant's spouse consents.

retirement plan: See *pension plan.*

retirement-type subsidy: An additional benefit paid under a plan that's above and beyond the benefit paid under the plan's normal benefit formula. Your employer can't retroactively eliminate these types of subsidies, which usually include subsidized early retirement benefits or subsidized qualified joint and survivor annuities.

revised summary plan description: See *summary of material modifications.*

rollover: A tax-free transfer of your pension money from one tax-deferred place to another. For example, you may move your money from one employer-sponsored plan to another or from an employer-sponsored plan to an IRA.

self-directed account: An account in a defined contribution plan under which the investments are selected by the plan participant. The investment elections are usually limited to a specific selection of mutual funds chosen by the plan administrator.

single-employer pension plan: A plan in which a single employer contributes to a plan covering its own employees.

standard termination: A termination of a defined benefit pension plan approved by the PBGC where the plan has sufficient assets to pay all the benefits due under the plan.

summary annual report (SAR): A summary of the Form 5500 Annual Financial Report, which most retirement plans must file with the DOL. This document must be given to you yearly and free of charge. For plan years beginning after December 31, 2007, the SAR will be replaced with an annual funding notice that includes more detailed information than required in the SAR.

summary of material modifications (SMM): A document that informs you of a change in your retirement plan. This document must be given to you free of charge.

summary plan description (SPD): A summary of the retirement plan document that tells you what the plan provides and how it operates. This is one of the most important documents you're entitled to receive. If your retirement plan is ever changed or amended, a revised SPD or a summary of material modifications will be sent to you.

survivorship benefits: Pension benefits that are extended (after you die) to your spouse under a defined benefit plan. Your benefits under a defined contribution plan (and under some defined benefit plans) may be left to anyone whom you designate as your beneficiary. If you're married, however, you need spousal consent to designate a non-spouse beneficiary.

tax-deferred contribution: A contribution that's made into an account on your behalf without any tax obligation being due from you at the time the contribution is made. With this type of contribution, you're deferring the taxes until you withdraw the money. Being able to have a portion of your compensation paid directly (deferred) into a pension plan account each year is considered to be an employee benefit because it allows you to put money away for your retirement.

tax lien: A hold placed by the IRS on pension benefits to satisfy a plan participant's unpaid tax liability.

tax-qualified plan: Any plan that qualifies for favorable tax treatment according to the applicable sections of the Internal Revenue Code and its regulations.

third-party administrator (TPA): A firm selected by the plan sponsor that administers retirement plans. To administer plans, the firm determines eligibility and the manner in which pension contributions will be allocated, prepares the necessary forms (such as the Form 5500s, the annual returns, and the participant benefit statements), and distributes and files the necessary forms and notices.

underfunded: A defined benefit plan that doesn't have plan assets sufficient to pay the benefits accrued under the plan.

vested: A term meaning that your accrued benefits belong to you, even if you leave the company before retirement age. The amount of time that you must work before you're vested depends on your plan's vesting schedule.

voluntary distribution: A distribution that you've requested from the plan. With limited exceptions, distributions can't be made prior to your termination of employment with the employer sponsoring the plan.

year of service: A plan year during which you work or are paid for at least 1,000 hours. For most plans, 1,000 hours in a plan year is considered a year of service for eligibility, vesting, and benefit accrual purposes.

Appendix B

Tables and Charts

● ●

*A*ppendix B contains a variety of tables and charts that we reference throughout this book and that serve to provide you with more complete information on different pension topics:

✔ The Comparison of Types of Tax-Qualified Retirement Plans chart can help you navigate through the various retirement plans that we describe in Chapter 3. The chart helps you quickly find the features of the type of tax-qualified plan that you're interested in.

✔ The Retirement Plan Dollar and Percentage Limits chart provides you comparative information on contribution limits by dollars or percentage of income. (Chapter 3 has more information about contribution limits.)

✔ The Uniform Distribution Table is used to determine the distribution period for required minimum distributions to an employee from a retirement plan or an individual retirement account (IRA). We discuss this table in Chapters 5 and 9.

✔ The Single Life Table is used to determine the life expectancy of a beneficiary of a deceased plan participant for purposes of required minimum distributions from a retirement plan or IRA following the death of the participant. See Chapter 9 for more about this table.

✔ The Joint and Last Survivor Table is used to determine the joint and last survivor life expectancy for purposes of determining required minimum distributions for a participant and a spouse who's more than ten years younger than the participant. Head to Chapter 9 for more about this table.

✔ Because the laws regarding IRA exemptions from creditors vary state by state, we include the State Laws Protecting IRAs chart, which provides an analysis of the treatment of IRAs as exempt property for each state, including yours. We talk about this chart in Chapter 16.

COMPARISON OF TYPES OF TAX-QUALIFIED RETIREMENT PLANS

PLAN ELEMENTS:	PROFIT-SHARING	401(K)	CROSS-TESTED PROFIT-SHARING	MONEY PURCHASE PENSION	DEFINED BENEFIT	COMMENTS:
1. Contributions:						
(a) Employer-Mandatory	No	No	No	Yes	Yes	Generally, employer contributions for profit-sharing and 401(k) plans are discretionary.
(b) Employer-Discretionary	Yes	Yes	Yes	No	No	Contributions for profit-sharing and 401(k) plans can range from 0-25% of aggregate eligible compensation.
(c) Employee-Pre Tax	No	Yes	No	No	No	Generally, "elective deferrals" for 401(k) are limited to the lesser of 100% of compensation; $15,500 for 2007. Nondiscrimination testing limits elective deferrals for highly compensated employees to a multiple of the non-highly compensated employees elective deferrals.
(d) Employee-After Tax	Yes	Yes	Yes	Yes	Yes	Subject to nondiscrimination testing.
(e) Employer-Matching	Yes	Yes	No	No	No	Employer may proportionately match employee elective deferrals or after-tax contributions, subject to nondiscrimination testing.
2. Overall Limitation on Contribution Based on Eligible Compensation:						
(a) On Employer Contribution (§404)	ϖ25%	ϖ25%	ϖ25%	25%	Limitations Based on Benefits, Not on Contributions	Limitation does not include employee elective deferral contributions.
* (b) On Allocation to Each Employee (§415)	Lesser of ϖ100% of Comp. or $45,000	Lesser of ϖ100% of Comp. or $45,000	Lesser of ϖ100% of Comp. or $45,000	Lesser of ϖ100% of Comp. or $45,000	Annual Benefit Limit is Lesser of 100% of Comp. or $180,000	Limitation aggregates employer contributions, matching contributions, employee contributions, and forfeitures.
3. Eligibility to Participate Maximum Restrictions:						
Age	21	21	21	21	21	Additional exclusion available for employees covered by a collective bargaining agreement. Any additional exclusion of employees is subject to nondiscriminatory coverage and participation testing.
Service	2 Years	1 Year	2 Years	2 Years	2 Years	
***4. Maximum Vesting Schedules of Employer Contributions:						
(a) If 1 Year of Service	5 Year Cliff / 7 Year Graded	5 Year Cliff / 7 Year Graded	5 Year Cliff / 7 Year Graded	5 Year Cliff / 7 Year Graded	5 Year Cliff / 7 Year Graded	Employee contributions and elective deferrals are always fully vested. Employer matching contribution can be subject to vesting schedule.

PLAN ELEMENTS:	PROFIT-SHARING	401(K)	CROSS-TESTED PROFIT-SHARING	MONEY PURCHASE PENSION	DEFINED BENEFIT	COMMENTS:
*** Top Heavy matching contribution (eff. 2002) all defined contribution plans (eff. 2007)	3 Year Cliff 6 Year Graded	3 Year Cliff 6 Year Graded	3 Year Cliff 6 Year Graded	3 Year Cliff 6 Year Graded	3 Year Cliff 6 Year Graded	
(b) If 2 Years of Service	2 Year Cliff	N/A	2 Year Cliff	2 Year Cliff	2 Year Cliff	
** See Summary of Vesting Schedules Below						
*** The top heavy schedules (3 year cliff or 6 year graded) are the maximum vesting schedules for all DC plan contributions made on or after the first day of the 2007 plan year.						
5. Participant Loans	Yes	Yes	Yes	Yes	Yes	Optional plan provision. Generally, a loan cannot exceed lesser of $50,000.00 or 50% of participant vested benefit. Loan is generally repaid by monthly or quarterly payments over 5 year term at market interest.
6. Distribution of Vested Benefits Upon:	Death Disability Retirement Employment Termination	Death Disability Retirement Employment Termination	Death Disability Retirement Employment Termination	Death Disability Retirement Employment Termination	Death Disability Retirement Employment Termination	
7. In-Service Distributions:	Yes	Hardship Age 59½	Yes	Only Upon Attainment of Plan's Normal Retirement Age	Only Upon Attainment of Plan's Normal Retirement Age	Profit-sharing plans may permit in-service distributions as an optional provision. IRS regulations define the events qualifying for hardship distributions from 401(k) plans. Hardship distributions are limited to participant elective deferrals. In-service distributions from all plans must commence at age 70½.
8. Benefits Subject to PBGC Coverage:	No	No	No	No	Yes	
9. Participant Individual Accounts:	Yes	Yes	Yes	Yes	No	
10. Plan Benefit at Retirement or Other Termination of Employment:	Vested Account Balance (Employer and Employee Contributions, Forfeitures, and Investment Gains and Losses)	Vested Account Balance	Vested Account Balance	Vested Account Balance	Vested Accrued Benefit Based on Plan Benefit Formula	Maximum annual benefit from defined benefit plan is lesser of 100% of Average Compensation or $165,000.00 (adjusted by COLA).

PLAN ELEMENTS:	PROFIT-SHARING	401(K)	CROSS-TESTED PROFIT-SHARING	MONEY PURCHASE PENSION	DEFINED BENEFIT	COMMENTS:
11. Plan Contributions/Benefits Weighted in Favor of Older and/or Long Service Employees:	No	No	Yes	No	Yes	Contributions under a defined contribution plan (other than a cross-tested profit-sharing or a target benefit plan) are generally allocated based on a participant's compensation, without regard to age or service (e.g. a 50 year old employee with 20 years of service and a 30 year old employee with 5 years of service will receive the same contribution if they have the same compensation). Cross-tested and target benefit plans take the participant's age into account and test contributions for nondiscrimination purposes based on future projected benefits.
12. Level of benefits paid to participants is affected by Plan's investment performance:	Yes	Yes	Yes	Yes	No	In a defined contribution plan, income, expenses, gains, and losses with respect to plan investments affect the value of the participants' individual accounts. In a defined benefit plan, investment income, etc. affect the funding standard account only -- not the ultimate amount of benefits paid to an individual participant.

* Profit-Sharing, 401(k), Cross-Tested Profit-Sharing, and Money Purchase Pension Plans are all classified as defined contribution plans and are subject to many of the same restrictions.

₪ Limits effective commencing in 2002.

**Vesting Schedule

	Immediate	2 Year Cliff	3 Year Cliff	5 Year Cliff	6 Year Graded	7 Year Graded
Year 1	100%	0	0	0	0	0
2		100%	0	0	20	0
3			100%	0	40	20
4				0	60	40
5				100%	80	60
6					100%	80
7						100%

Richard A. Naegele, JD, MA

RETIREMENT PLAN DOLLAR AND PERCENTAGE LIMITS

	2001	2002	2003	2004	2005	2006	2007
Annual compensation for plan purposes (for plan years beginning in calendar year) 401(a)(17)	$170,000	$200,000 indexed in $5,000 increments	$200,000	$205,000	$210,000	$220,000	$225,000
Defined benefit plan, basic limit (for limitation years ending in calendar year) 415(b)	$140,000	$160,000 indexed in $5,000 increments	$160,000	$165,000	$170,000	$175,000	$180,000
Defined contribution plan, basic limit (for limitation years ending in calendar year) 415(c)	$35,000	$40,000 indexed in $1,000 increments	$40,000	$41,000	$42,000	$44,000	$45,000
401(k) / 403(b) plan, elective deferrals (for taxable years beginning in calendar year) 402(g)	$10,500	$11,000	$12,000	$13,000	$14,000	$15,000 indexed in $500 increments	$15,500
457 plan, elective deferrals (for taxable years beginning in calendar year)	$8,500	$11,000	$12,000	$13,000	$14,000	$15,000 indexed in $500 increments	$15,500
401(k) / 403(b) / 457, catch-up deferrals (for taxable years beginning in calendar year) (Age 50+) 414(v)	Not available	$1,000	$2,000	$3,000	$4,000	$5,000 indexed in $500 increments	$5,000
SIMPLE plan, elective deferrals (for calendar years) 408(p)	$6,500	$7,000	$8,000	$9,000	$10,000	$10,000 indexed in $500 increments	$10,500
SIMPLE plan, catch-up deferrals (for taxable years beginning in calendar year) (Age 50+) 408(p)	Not available	$500	$1,000	$1,500	$2,000	$2,500 indexed in $500 increments	$2,500
Defined contribution plan §415 percentage of compensation contribution limit 415(c)	25% of compensation	100% of compensation					
Profit sharing plan §404 percentage of compensation deduction limit	15% of compensation	25% of compensation					
Elective deferrals	Count against §404 deduction limits	Do not count against §404 deduction limits					
SEP contribution / deduction limit 408(k)	15% of compensation	25% of compensation					
IRA contribution limit 408(a)	$2,000	$3,000	$3,000	$3,000	$4,000	$4,000	$4,000 2008: $5,000
IRA catch-up contribution (Age 50+)	Not available	$500	$500	$500	$500	$1,000	$1,000
Highly Compensated Employee 414(q)	$85,000	$90,000	$90,000	$90,000	$95,000	$100,000	$100,000
SEP Coverage 408(p)	$450	$450	$450	$450	$450	$450	$500
FICA Covered Compensation	$80,400	$84,900	$87,000	$87,900	$90,000	$94,200	$97,500

Richard A. Naegele, JD, MA

UNIFORM DISTRIBUTION TABLE APPLICABLE DURING LIFETIME*

Age of the Participant	Distribution Period
70	27.4
71	26.5
72	25.6
73	24.7
74	23.8
75	22.9
76	22.0
77	21.2
78	20.3
79	19.5
80	18.7
81	17.9
82	17.1
83	16.3
84	15.5
85	14.8
86	14.1
87	13.4
88	12.7
89	12.0
90	11.4
91	10.8
92	10.2
93	9.6
94	9.1
95	8.6
96	8.1
97	7.6
98	7.1
99	6.7
100	6.3
101	5.9
102	5.5
103	5.2
104	4.9
105	4.5
106	4.2
107	3.9
108	3.7
109	3.4
110	3.1
111	2.9
112	2.6
113	2.4
114	2.1
115 or Older	1.9

*Per final regulations issued April 17, 2002

Richard A. Naegele, JD, MA

SINGLE LIFE TABLE

AGE	LIFE EXPECTANCY		AGE	LIFE EXPECTANCY		AGE	LIFE EXPECTANCY
0	82.4		38	45.6		76	12.7
1	81.6		39	44.6		77	12.1
2	80.6		40	43.6		78	11.4
3	79.7		41	42.7		79	10.8
4	78.7		42	41.7		80	10.2
5	77.7		43	40.7		81	9.7
6	76.7		44	39.8		82	9.1
7	75.8		45	38.8		83	8.6
8	74.8		46	37.9		84	8.1
9	73.8		47	37.0		85	7.6
10	72.8		48	36.0		86	7.1
11	71.8		49	35.1		87	6.7
12	70.8		50	34.2		88	6.3
13	69.9		51	33.3		89	5.9
14	68.9		52	32.3		90	5.5
15	67.9		53	31.4		91	5.2
16	66.9		54	30.5		92	4.9
17	66.0		55	29.6		93	4.6
18	65.0		56	28.7		94	4.3
19	64.0		57	27.9		95	4.1
20	63.0		58	27.0		96	3.8
21	62.1		59	26.1		97	3.6
22	61.1		60	25.2		98	3.4
23	60.1		61	24.4		99	3.1
24	59.1		62	23.5		100	2.9
25	58.2		63	22.7		101	2.7
26	57.2		64	21.8		102	2.5
27	56.2		65	21.0		103	2.3
28	55.3		66	20.2		104	2.1
29	54.3		67	19.4		105	1.9
30	53.3		68	18.6		106	1.7
31	52.4		69	17.8		107	1.5
32	51.4		70	17.0		108	1.4
33	50.4		71	16.3		109	1.2
34	49.4		72	15.5		110	1.1
35	48.5		73	14.8		111+	1.0
36	47.5		74	14.1			
37	46.5		75	13.4			

Richard A. Naegele, JD, MA

JOINT & LAST SURVIVOR TABLE

AGE	70	71	72	73	74	75	76	77	78	79	80	81	82	83	84	85	86	87	88	89	90
30	53.5	53.5	53.5	53.4	53.4	53.4	53.4	53.4	53.4	53.4	53.4	53.4	53.4	53.4	53.4	53.3	53.3	53.3	53.3	53.3	53.3
31	52.5	52.5	52.5	52.5	52.5	52.5	52.4	52.4	52.4	52.4	52.4	52.4	52.4	52.4	52.4	52.4	52.4	52.4	52.4	52.4	52.4
32	51.6	51.6	51.5	51.5	51.5	51.5	51.5	51.5	51.5	51.5	51.4	51.4	51.4	51.4	51.4	51.4	51.4	51.4	51.4	51.4	51.4
33	50.6	50.6	50.6	50.6	50.5	50.5	50.5	50.5	50.5	50.5	50.5	50.5	50.5	50.5	50.5	50.4	50.4	50.4	50.4	50.4	50.4
34	49.7	49.6	49.6	49.6	49.6	49.6	49.6	49.5	49.5	49.5	49.5	49.5	49.5	49.5	49.5	49.5	49.5	49.5	49.5	49.5	49.5
35	48.7	48.7	48.7	48.6	48.6	48.6	48.6	48.6	48.6	48.6	48.5	48.5	48.5	48.5	48.5	48.5	48.5	48.5	48.5	48.5	48.5
36	47.8	47.7	47.7	47.7	47.7	47.7	47.6	47.6	47.6	47.6	47.6	47.6	47.6	47.6	47.6	47.5	47.5	47.5	47.5	47.5	47.5
37	46.8	46.8	46.8	46.7	46.7	46.7	46.7	46.7	46.6	46.6	46.6	46.6	46.6	46.6	46.6	46.6	46.6	46.6	46.6	46.6	46.6
38	45.9	45.9	45.8	45.8	45.8	45.7	45.7	45.7	45.7	45.7	45.7	45.7	45.6	45.6	45.6	45.6	45.6	45.6	45.6	45.6	45.6
39	44.9	44.9	44.9	44.8	44.8	44.8	44.8	44.8	44.7	44.7	44.7	44.7	44.7	44.7	44.7	44.6	44.6	44.6	44.6	44.6	44.6
40	44.0	44.0	43.9	43.9	43.9	43.8	43.8	43.8	43.8	43.8	43.7	43.7	43.7	43.7	43.7	43.7	43.7	43.7	43.7	43.7	43.7
41	43.1	43.0	43.0	43.0	42.9	42.9	42.9	42.9	42.8	42.8	42.8	42.8	42.8	42.8	42.7	42.7	42.7	42.7	42.7	42.7	42.7
42	42.2	42.1	42.1	42.0	42.0	42.0	41.9	41.9	41.9	41.9	41.8	41.8	41.8	41.8	41.8	41.8	41.8	41.8	41.8	41.7	41.7
43	41.3	41.2	41.1	41.1	41.1	41.0	41.0	41.0	40.9	40.9	40.9	40.9	40.9	40.9	40.8	40.8	40.8	40.8	40.8	40.8	40.8
44	40.3	40.3	40.2	40.2	40.1	40.1	40.1	40.0	40.0	40.0	40.0	39.9	39.9	39.9	39.9	39.9	39.9	39.9	39.9	39.8	39.8
45	39.4	39.4	39.3	39.3	39.2	39.2	39.1	39.1	39.1	39.1	39.0	39.0	39.0	39.0	39.0	38.9	38.9	38.9	38.9	38.9	38.9
46	38.6	38.5	38.4	38.4	38.3	38.3	38.2	38.2	38.2	38.1	38.1	38.1	38.1	38.0	38.0	38.0	38.0	38.0	38.0	38.0	38.0
47	37.7	37.6	37.5	37.5	37.4	37.4	37.3	37.3	37.2	37.2	37.2	37.1	37.1	37.1	37.1	37.1	37.0	37.0	37.0	37.0	37.0
48	36.8	36.7	36.6	36.6	36.5	36.5	36.4	36.4	36.3	36.3	36.3	36.2	36.2	36.2	36.2	36.2	36.1	36.1	36.1	36.1	36.1
49	35.9	35.9	35.8	35.7	35.6	35.6	35.5	35.5	35.4	35.4	35.4	35.3	35.3	35.3	35.3	35.2	35.2	35.2	35.2	35.2	35.2
50	35.1	35.0	34.9	34.8	34.8	34.7	34.6	34.6	34.5	34.5	34.5	34.4	34.4	34.4	34.3	34.3	34.3	34.3	34.3	34.3	34.2
51	34.3	34.2	34.1	34.0	33.9	33.9	33.8	33.7	33.6	33.6	33.6	33.5	33.5	33.5	33.4	33.4	33.4	33.4	33.3	33.3	33.3
52	33.4	33.3	33.2	33.1	33.0	33.0	32.9	32.8	32.8	32.7	32.7	32.6	32.6	32.6	32.5	32.5	32.5	32.5	32.5	32.4	32.4
53	32.6	32.5	32.4	32.3	32.2	32.1	32.0	32.0	31.9	31.8	31.8	31.8	31.7	31.7	31.7	31.6	31.6	31.6	31.6	31.5	31.5
54	31.8	31.7	31.6	31.5	31.4	31.3	31.2	31.1	31.0	31.0	30.9	30.9	30.8	30.8	30.8	30.7	30.7	30.7	30.7	30.7	30.6
55	31.1	30.9	30.8	30.6	30.5	30.4	30.3	30.3	30.2	30.1	30.1	30.0	30.0	29.9	29.9	29.9	29.8	29.8	29.8	29.8	28.9
56	30.3	30.1	30.0	29.8	29.7	29.6	29.5	29.4	29.3	29.3	29.2	29.2	29.1	29.1	29.0	29.0	29.0	28.9	28.9	28.9	28.9
57	29.5	29.4	29.2	29.1	28.9	28.8	28.7	28.6	28.5	28.4	28.4	28.3	28.3	28.2	28.2	28.1	28.1	28.1	28.0	28.0	28.0
58	28.8	28.6	28.4	28.3	28.1	28.0	27.9	27.8	27.7	27.6	27.5	27.5	27.4	27.4	27.3	27.3	27.2	27.2	27.2	27.2	27.1
59	28.1	27.9	27.7	27.5	27.4	27.2	27.1	27.0	26.9	26.8	26.7	26.6	26.6	26.5	26.5	26.4	26.4	26.4	26.3	26.3	26.3
60	27.4	27.2	27.0	26.8	26.6	26.5	26.3	26.2	26.1	26.0	25.9	25.8	25.8	25.7	25.6	25.6	25.5	25.5	25.5	25.4	25.4
61	26.7	26.5	26.3	26.1	25.9	25.7	25.6	25.4	25.3	25.2	25.1	25.0	24.9	24.9	24.8	24.8	24.7	24.7	24.6	24.6	24.6
62	26.1	25.8	25.6	25.4	25.2	25.0	24.8	24.7	24.6	24.4	24.3	24.2	24.1	24.1	24.0	23.9	23.9	23.8	23.8	23.8	23.7
63	25.4	25.2	24.9	24.7	24.5	24.3	24.1	23.9	23.8	23.7	23.6	23.4	23.4	23.3	23.2	23.2	23.1	23.1	23.0	22.9	22.9
64	24.8	24.5	24.3	24.0	23.8	23.6	23.4	23.2	23.1	22.9	22.8	22.7	22.6	22.5	22.4	22.3	22.3	22.2	22.2	22.1	22.1
65	24.3	23.9	23.7	23.4	23.1	22.9	22.7	22.5	22.4	22.2	22.1	21.9	21.8	21.7	21.6	21.6	21.5	21.4	21.4	21.3	21.3
66	23.7	23.4	23.1	22.8	22.5	22.3	22.0	21.8	21.7	21.5	21.3	21.2	21.1	21.0	20.9	20.8	20.7	20.7	20.6	20.5	20.5
67	23.2	22.8	22.5	22.2	21.9	21.6	21.4	21.2	21.0	20.8	20.6	20.5	20.4	20.2	20.1	20.1	20.0	19.9	19.8	19.8	19.7
68	22.7	22.3	22.0	21.6	21.3	21.0	20.8	20.6	20.3	20.1	20.0	19.8	19.7	19.5	19.4	19.3	19.2	19.2	19.1	19.0	19.0
69	22.2	21.8	21.4	21.1	20.8	20.5	20.2	19.9	19.7	19.5	19.3	19.1	19.0	18.8	18.7	18.6	18.5	18.4	18.3	18.3	18.2
70	21.8	21.3	20.9	20.6	20.2	19.9	19.6	19.4	19.1	18.9	18.7	18.5	18.3	18.2	18.0	17.9	17.8	17.7	17.6	17.6	17.5
71	21.3	20.9	20.5	20.1	19.7	19.4	19.1	18.8	18.5	18.3	18.1	17.9	17.7	17.5	17.4	17.3	17.1	17.0	16.9	16.9	16.8
72	20.9	20.5	20.0	19.6	19.3	18.9	18.6	18.3	18.0	17.7	17.5	17.3	17.1	16.9	16.7	16.6	16.5	16.4	16.3	16.2	16.1
73	20.6	20.1	19.6	19.2	18.8	18.4	18.1	17.8	17.5	17.2	16.9	16.7	16.5	16.3	16.1	16.0	15.8	15.7	15.6	15.5	15.4
74	20.2	19.7	19.3	18.8	18.4	18.0	17.6	17.3	17.0	16.7	16.4	16.2	15.9	15.7	15.5	15.4	15.2	15.1	15.0	14.9	14.8
75	19.9	19.4	18.9	18.4	18.0	17.6	17.2	16.8	16.5	16.2	15.9	15.7	15.5	15.2	15.0	14.8	14.6	14.5	14.4	14.3	14.2
76	19.6	19.1	18.6	18.1	17.6	17.2	16.8	16.4	16.0	15.7	15.4	15.1	14.9	14.7	14.4	14.3	14.1	13.9	13.8	13.7	13.6
77	19.4	18.8	18.3	17.8	17.3	16.8	16.4	16.0	15.6	15.3	15.0	14.7	14.4	14.2	13.9	13.7	13.5	13.4	13.2	13.1	13.0
78	19.1	18.5	18.0	17.5	17.0	16.5	16.0	15.6	15.2	14.9	14.5	14.2	13.9	13.7	13.4	13.2	13.0	12.9	12.7	12.6	12.4
79	18.9	18.3	17.7	17.2	16.7	16.2	15.7	15.3	14.9	14.5	14.1	13.8	13.5	13.2	13.0	12.8	12.5	12.4	12.2	12.0	11.9
80	18.7	18.1	17.5	16.9	16.4	15.9	15.4	15.0	14.5	14.1	13.8	13.4	13.1	12.8	12.6	12.3	12.1	11.9	11.7	11.5	11.4

Richard A. Naegele, JD, MA

STATE LAWS PROTECTING IRAs

STATE-BY-STATE ANALYSIS OF INDIVIDUAL RETIREMENT ACCOUNTS AS EXEMPT PROPERTY*

STATE	STATE STATUTE	IRA EXEMPT	ROTH IRA EXEMPT	SPECIAL STATUTORY PROVISIONS
Alabama	Ala. Code §19-3-1(b)	Yes	No	
Alaska	Alaska Stat. §09.38.017	Yes	Yes	The exemption does not apply to amounts contributed within 120 days before the debtor files for bankruptcy.
Arizona	Ariz. Rev. Stat. Ann. §33-1126(B)	Yes	Yes	The exemption does not apply to amounts contributed within 120 days before a debtor files for bankruptcy.
Arkansas	Ark. Code Ann. §16-66-220	Yes	Yes	A bankruptcy court held that the creditor exemption for IRAs violates the Arkansas Constitution — at least with respect to contract claims.
California	Cal. Code of Civ. Proc. §704.115	No	No	IRAs are exempt only to the extent necessary to provide for the support of the judgment debtor when the judgment debtor retires and for the support of the spouse and dependents of the judgment debtor, taking into account all resources that are likely to be available for the support of the judgment debtor when the judgment debtor retires.
Colorado	Colo. Rev. Stat. §13-54-102	Yes	Yes	Any retirement benefit or payment is subject to attachment or levy in satisfaction of a judgment taken for arrears in child support; any pension or retirement benefit is also subject to attachment or levy in satisfaction of a judgment awarded for a felonious killing.
Connecticut	Conn. Gen. Stat. §52-321a	Yes	Yes	
Delaware	Del. Code Ann. Tit. 10, §4915	Yes	Yes	An IRA is not exempt from a claim made pursuant to Title 13 of the Delaware Code, which Title pertains to domestic relations order.
Florida	Fla. Stat. Ann. §222.21	Yes	Yes	
Georgia	Ga. Code Ann. §44-13-100	No	No	IRAs are exempt only to the extent necessary for the support of the debtor and any dependent.
Hawaii	Haw. Rev. Stat. §651-124	Yes	Yes	The exemption does not apply to contributions made to a plan or arrangement within three years before the date a civil action is initiated against the debtor.
Idaho	Idaho Code §55-1011	Yes	Yes	The exemption only applies for claims of judgment creditors of the beneficiary or participant arising out of a negligent or otherwise wrongful act or omission of the beneficiary or participant resulting in money damages to the judgment creditor.
Illinois	Ill. Rev. Stat. Ch. 735, Para. 5/12-1006	Yes	Yes	
Indiana	Ind. Code §34-55-10-2	Yes	Yes	
Iowa	Iowa Code §627.6	Yes	Yes	
Kansas	Kan. Stat. Ann. §60-2308	Yes	Yes	
Kentucky*	Ky. Rev. Stat. Ann. §427.150(2)(f)	Yes	Yes	The exemption does not apply to any amounts contributed to an individual retirement account if the contribution occurred within 120 days before the debtor filed for bankruptcy. The exemption also does not apply to the right or interest of a person in individual retirement account to the extent that right or interest is subject to a court order for payment of maintenance or child support.

STATE	STATE STATUTE	IRA EXEMPT	ROTH IRA EXEMPT	SPECIAL STATUTORY PROVISIONS
Louisiana	La. Rev. Stat. Ann. Sects. 20-33(1) and 13-3881(D)	Yes	Yes	No contribution to an IRA is exempt if made less than one calendar year from the date of filing bankruptcy, whether voluntary or involuntary, or the date writs of seizure are filed against the account. The exemption also does not apply to liabilities for alimony and child support.
Maine	Me. Rev. Stat. Ann. Tit. 14, §4422(13) (E)	No	No	IRAs are exempt only to the extent reasonably necessary for the support of the debtor and any dependent.
Maryland	Md. Code Ann. Cts. & Jud. Proc. §11-504(h)	Yes	Yes	IRAs are exempt from any and all claims of creditors of the beneficiary or participant other than claims by the Department of Health and Mental Hygiene.
Massachusetts	Mass. Gen. L.Ch. 235, §34A	Yes	Yes	The exemption does not apply to an order of court concerning divorce, separate maintenance or child support, or an order of court requiring an individual convicted of a crime to satisfy a monetary penalty or to make restitution, or sums deposited in a plan in excess of 7% of the total income of the individual within 5 years of the individual's declaration of bankruptcy or entry of judgment.
Michigan*	Mich. Comp. Laws 600.6023	Yes	Yes	The exemption does not apply to amounts contributed to an individual retirement account or individual retirement annuity if the contribution occurs within 120 days before the debtor files for bankruptcy. The exemption also does not apply to an order of the domestic relations court
Minnesota	Minn. Stat. §550.37	Yes	Yes	Exempt to a present value of $30,000 and additional amounts reasonably necessary to support the debtor, spouse, or dependents.
Mississippi	Miss. Code Ann. §85-3-1	Yes	No	
Missouri	Mo. Rev. Stat. §513.430	Yes	Yes	If proceedings under Title 11 of United States Code are commenced by or against the debtor, no amount of funds shall be exempt in such proceedings under any plan or trust which is fraudulent as defined in Section 456.630 of the Missouri Code, and for the period such person participated within 3 years prior to the commencement of such proceedings.
Montana	Mont. Code Ann. §31-2-106(3)	Yes	No	The exemption excludes that portion of contributions made by the individual within one year before the filing of the petition of bankruptcy which exceeds 15% of the gross income of the individual for that one-year period.
Nebraska	Neb. Rev. Stat. §25-1563.01	Yes	Yes	The exemption only applies to the extent reasonably necessary for the support of the Debtor and any dependent of the Debtor.
Nevada	Nev. Rev. Stat. §21.090(1)(q)	Yes	No	The exemption is limited to $500,000 in present value held in an individual retirement account, which conforms with Section 408.
New Hampshire	N.H. Tit. 52 §511:2	Yes	Yes	Exemption only applies to extensions of credit and debts arising after January 1, 1999.
New Jersey	N.J. Stat. Ann. 25:2-1(b)	Yes	Yes	

STATE	STATE STATUTE	IRA EXEMPT	ROTH IRA EXEMPT	SPECIAL STATUTORY PROVISIONS
New Mexico	N.M. Stat. Ann. §42-10-1, §42-10-2	Yes	Yes	A retirement fund of a person supporting another person is exempt from receivers or trustees in bankruptcy or other insolvency proceedings, fines, attachment, execution, or foreclosure by a judgment creditor.
New York	N.Y. Civ. Prac. L. and R. §5205(c)	Yes	Yes	Additions to individual retirement accounts are not exempt from judgments if contributions were made after a date that is 90 days before the interposition of the claim on which the judgment was entered.
North Carolina	N.C. Gen. Stat. §1C-1601(a)(9)	Yes	Yes	
North Dakota	N.D. Cent. Code §28-22-03.1(3)	Yes	Yes	The account must have been in effect for a period of at least one year. Each individual account is exempt to a limit of up to $100,000 per account, with an aggregate limitation of $200,000 for all accounts. The dollar limit does not apply to the extent the debtor can prove the property is reasonably necessary for the support of the debtor, spouse, or dependents.
Ohio*	Ohio Rev. Code Ann. §2329.66(A)(10)	Yes	Yes	SEPs and SIMPLE IRAs are not exempt.
Oklahoma	Okla. Stat. Tit. 31, §1(A)(20)	Yes	Yes	
Oregon	OR. Rev. Stat. 18.358	Yes	Yes	
Pennsylvania	42 PA. Cons. Stat. §8124	Yes	Yes	The exemption does not apply to amounts contributed to the retirement fund within one year before the debtor filed for bankruptcy.
Rhode Island	R.I. Gen. Laws §9-26-4	Yes	Yes	The exemption does not apply to an order of court pursuant to a judgment of divorce or separate maintenance, or an order of court concerning child support.
South Carolina	S.C. Code Ann. §15-41-30	No	No	The debtor's right to receive individual retirement accounts and Roth accounts are exempt to the extent reasonably necessary for the support of the debtor and any dependent of the debtor.
South Dakota	S.D. Cod. Laws 43-45-16; 43-45-17	Yes	Yes	Exempts "certain retirement benefits" up to $250,000.00. Cites §401(a)(13) of Internal Revenue Code (Tax-Qualified Plan Non-Alienation Provision).
Tennessee*	Tenn. Code Ann. §26-2-105	Yes	Yes	
Texas	Tex. Prop. Code Ann. §42.0021	Yes	Yes	
Utah	Utah Code Ann. §78-23-5(1)	Yes	Yes	The exemption does not apply to amounts contributed or benefits accrued by or on behalf of a debtor within one year before the debtor files for bankruptcy.
Vermont	Vt. Stat. Ann. Tit. 12 §2740(16)	Yes	Yes	
Virginia	Va. Code Ann. §34-34	Yes	Yes	The exemption does not apply to the extent that the interest of the individual in the retirement plan would provide an annual benefit in excess of $25,000.00. If an individual has an interest in more than one retirement plan, the limitation is applied as if all retirement plans constituted a single plan. The Code provides a table from which the annual benefit may be determined.

STATE	STATE STATUTE	IRA EXEMPT	ROTH IRA EXEMPT	SPECIAL STATUTORY PROVISIONS
Washington	Wash. Rev. Code §6.15.020	Yes	Yes	
West Virginia	W.Va. Code §38-10-4	Yes	No	
Wisconsin	Wis. Stat. §815.18(3)(j)	Yes	Yes	The exemption does not apply to an order of court concerning child support, family support or maintenance, or any judgments of annulment, divorce, or legal separation.
Wyoming	Wyo. Stat. §1-20-110	No	No	

*Kentucky, Michigan, Ohio, and Tennessee: The U.S. Court of Appeals for the Sixth Circuit in Lampkins v. Golden, 2002 U.S. App. LEXIS 900, 2002-1 USTC par. 50,216 (6th Cir. 2002) held that a Michigan statute exempting SEPs and IRAs from creditor claims was preempted by ERISA. The decision appears to be limited to SEPs and SIMPLE-IRAs.

Richard A. Naegele, JD, MA

Index

• *M* •

• *N* •

• *Q* •

• T •

● **W** ●

Notes

BUSINESS, CAREERS & PERSONAL FINANCE

0-7645-9847-3

0-7645-2431-3

Also available:
- Business Plans Kit For Dummies
  0-7645-9794-9
- Economics For Dummies
  0-7645-5726-2
- Grant Writing For Dummies
  0-7645-8416-2
- Home Buying For Dummies
  0-7645-5331-3
- Managing For Dummies
  0-7645-1771-6
- Marketing For Dummies
  0-7645-5600-2

- Personal Finance For Dummies
  0-7645-2590-5*
- Resumes For Dummies
  0-7645-5471-9
- Selling For Dummies
  0-7645-5363-1
- Six Sigma For Dummies
  0-7645-6798-5
- Small Business Kit For Dummies
  0-7645-5984-2
- Starting an eBay Business For Dummies
  0-7645-6924-4
- Your Dream Career For Dummies
  0-7645-9795-7

HOME & BUSINESS COMPUTER BASICS

0-470-05432-8

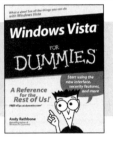

0-471-75421-8

Also available:
- Cleaning Windows Vista For Dummies
  0-471-78293-9
- Excel 2007 For Dummies
  0-470-03737-7
- Mac OS X Tiger For Dummies
  0-7645-7675-5
- MacBook For Dummies
  0-470-04859-X
- Macs For Dummies
  0-470-04849-2
- Office 2007 For Dummies
  0-470-00923-3

- Outlook 2007 For Dummies
  0-470-03830-6
- PCs For Dummies
  0-7645-8958-X
- Salesforce.com For Dummies
  0-470-04893-X
- Upgrading & Fixing Laptops For Dummies
  0-7645-8959-8
- Word 2007 For Dummies
  0-470-03658-3
- Quicken 2007 For Dummies
  0-470-04600-7

FOOD, HOME, GARDEN, HOBBIES, MUSIC & PETS

0-7645-8404-9

0-7645-9904-6

Also available:
- Candy Making For Dummies
  0-7645-9734-5
- Card Games For Dummies
  0-7645-9910-0
- Crocheting For Dummies
  0-7645-4151-X
- Dog Training For Dummies
  0-7645-8418-9
- Healthy Carb Cookbook For Dummies
  0-7645-8476-6
- Home Maintenance For Dummies
  0-7645-5215-5

- Horses For Dummies
  0-7645-9797-3
- Jewelry Making & Beading For Dummies
  0-7645-2571-9
- Orchids For Dummies
  0-7645-6759-4
- Puppies For Dummies
  0-7645-5255-4
- Rock Guitar For Dummies
  0-7645-5356-9
- Sewing For Dummies
  0-7645-6847-7
- Singing For Dummies
  0-7645-2475-5

INTERNET & DIGITAL MEDIA

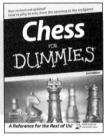

0-470-04529-9

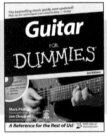

0-470-04894-8

Also available:
- Blogging For Dummies
  0-471-77084-1
- Digital Photography For Dummies
  0-7645-9802-3
- Digital Photography All-in-One Desk Reference For Dummies
  0-470-03743-1
- Digital SLR Cameras and Photography For Dummies
  0-7645-9803-1
- eBay Business All-in-One Desk Reference For Dummies
  0-7645-8438-3
- HDTV For Dummies
  0-470-09673-X

- Home Entertainment PCs For Dummies
  0-470-05523-5
- MySpace For Dummies
  0-470-09529-6
- Search Engine Optimization For Dummies
  0-471-97998-8
- Skype For Dummies
  0-470-04891-3
- The Internet For Dummies
  0-7645-8996-2
- Wiring Your Digital Home For Dummies
  0-471-91830-X

* Separate Canadian edition also available
† Separate U.K. edition also available

Available wherever books are sold. For more information or to order direct: U.S. customers visit www.dummies.com or call 1-877-762-2974. U.K. customers visit www.wileyeurope.com or call 0800 243407. Canadian customers visit www.wiley.ca or call 1-800-567-4797.

SPORTS, FITNESS, PARENTING, RELIGION & SPIRITUALITY

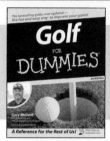
0-471-76871-5

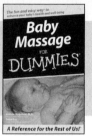
0-7645-7841-3

Also available:
- Catholicism For Dummies
  0-7645-5391-7
- Exercise Balls For Dummies
  0-7645-5623-1
- Fitness For Dummies
  0-7645-7851-0
- Football For Dummies
  0-7645-3936-1
- Judaism For Dummies
  0-7645-5299-6
- Potty Training For Dummies
  0-7645-5417-4
- Buddhism For Dummies
  0-7645-5359-3

- Pregnancy For Dummies
  0-7645-4483-7 †
- Ten Minute Tone-Ups For Dummies
  0-7645-7207-5
- NASCAR For Dummies
  0-7645-7681-X
- Religion For Dummies
  0-7645-5264-3
- Soccer For Dummies
  0-7645-5229-5
- Women in the Bible For Dummies
  0-7645-8475-8

TRAVEL

0-7645-7749-2

0-7645-6945-7

Also available:
- Alaska For Dummies
  0-7645-7746-8
- Cruise Vacations For Dummies
  0-7645-6941-4
- England For Dummies
  0-7645-4276-1
- Europe For Dummies
  0-7645-7529-5
- Germany For Dummies
  0-7645-7823-5
- Hawaii For Dummies
  0-7645-7402-7

- Italy For Dummies
  0-7645-7386-1
- Las Vegas For Dummies
  0-7645-7382-9
- London For Dummies
  0-7645-4277-X
- Paris For Dummies
  0-7645-7630-5
- RV Vacations For Dummies
  0-7645-4442-X
- Walt Disney World & Orlando
  For Dummies
  0-7645-9660-8

GRAPHICS, DESIGN & WEB DEVELOPMENT

0-7645-8815-X

0-7645-9571-7

Also available:
- 3D Game Animation For Dummies
  0-7645-8789-7
- AutoCAD 2006 For Dummies
  0-7645-8925-3
- Building a Web Site For Dummies
  0-7645-7144-3
- Creating Web Pages For Dummies
  0-470-08030-2
- Creating Web Pages All-in-One Desk
  Reference For Dummies
  0-7645-4345-8
- Dreamweaver 8 For Dummies
  0-7645-9649-7

- InDesign CS2 For Dummies
  0-7645-9572-5
- Macromedia Flash 8 For Dummies
  0-7645-9691-8
- Photoshop CS2 and Digital
  Photography For Dummies
  0-7645-9580-6
- Photoshop Elements 4 For Dummies
  0-471-77483-9
- Syndicating Web Sites with RSS Feeds
  For Dummies
  0-7645-8848-6
- Yahoo! SiteBuilder For Dummies
  0-7645-9800-7

NETWORKING, SECURITY, PROGRAMMING & DATABASES

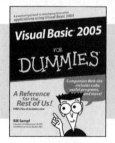
0-7645-7728-X

0-471-74940-0

Also available:
- Access 2007 For Dummies
  0-470-04612-0
- ASP.NET 2 For Dummies
  0-7645-7907-X
- C# 2005 For Dummies
  0-7645-9704-3
- Hacking For Dummies
  0-470-05235-X
- Hacking Wireless Networks
  For Dummies
  0-7645-9730-2
- Java For Dummies
  0-470-08716-1

- Microsoft SQL Server 2005 For Dummies
  0-7645-7755-7
- Networking All-in-One Desk Reference
  For Dummies
  0-7645-9939-9
- Preventing Identity Theft For Dummies
  0-7645-7336-5
- Telecom For Dummies
  0-471-77085-X
- Visual Studio 2005 All-in-One Desk
  Reference For Dummies
  0-7645-9775-2
- XML For Dummies
  0-7645-8845-1

HEALTH & SELF-HELP

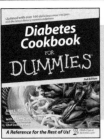

0-7645-8450-2

0-7645-4149-8

Also available:

- Bipolar Disorder For Dummies
0-7645-8451-0
- Chemotherapy and Radiation For Dummies
0-7645-7832-4
- Controlling Cholesterol For Dummies
0-7645-5440-9
- Diabetes For Dummies
0-7645-6820-5* †
- Divorce For Dummies
0-7645-8417-0 †

- Fibromyalgia For Dummies
0-7645-5441-7
- Low-Calorie Dieting For Dummies
0-7645-9905-4
- Meditation For Dummies
0-471-77774-9
- Osteoporosis For Dummies
0-7645-7621-6
- Overcoming Anxiety For Dummies
0-7645-5447-6
- Reiki For Dummies
0-7645-9907-0
- Stress Management For Dummies
0-7645-5144-2

EDUCATION, HISTORY, REFERENCE & TEST PREPARATION

0-7645-8381-6

0-7645-9554-7

Also available:

- The ACT For Dummies
0-7645-9652-7
- Algebra For Dummies
0-7645-5325-9
- Algebra Workbook For Dummies
0-7645-8467-7
- Astronomy For Dummies
0-7645-8465-0
- Calculus For Dummies
0-7645-2498-4
- Chemistry For Dummies
0-7645-5430-1
- Forensics For Dummies
0-7645-5580-4

- Freemasons For Dummies
0-7645-9796-5
- French For Dummies
0-7645-5193-0
- Geometry For Dummies
0-7645-5324-0
- Organic Chemistry I For Dummies
0-7645-6902-3
- The SAT I For Dummies
0-7645-7193-1
- Spanish For Dummies
0-7645-5194-9
- Statistics For Dummies
0-7645-5423-9

Get smart @ dummies.com®

- **Find a full list of Dummies titles**
- **Look into loads of FREE on-site articles**
- **Sign up for FREE eTips e-mailed to you weekly**
- **See what other products carry the Dummies name**
- **Shop directly from the Dummies bookstore**
- **Enter to win new prizes every month!**